AQA Chemistry

AS

Exclusively endorsed

Ted Lister

Janet Renshaw

 Nelson Thornes

Text © Ted Lister and Janet Renshaw 2008
Original illustrations © Nelson Thornes Ltd 2008

Published in 2008 by:
Nelson Thornes Ltd
Delta Place
27 Bath Road
CHELTENHAM
GL53 7TH
United Kingdom

08 09 10 11 12 / 10 9 8 7 6 5 4 3 2 1

A catalogue record for this book is available from the British Library

ISBN 978 0 7487 8280 2

Cover photograph by Alamy / Jupiter Images / Brand X
Illustrations include artwork drawn by GreenGate Publishing
Page make-up by GreenGate Publishing, Kent

Printed and bound in Great Britain by Scotprint

Contents

■ Contents

Introduction

Nelson Thornes and AQA

Nelson Thornes has worked in collaboration with AQA to ensure that this book offers you the best support for your AS level course and helps you to prepare for your exams. The partnership means that you can be confident that the range of learning, teaching and assessment practice materials has been checked by the senior examining team at AQA before formal approval, and is closely matched to the requirements of your specification.

Blended learning

Printed and electronic resources are blended: this means that links between the topics in the book and activities in the electronic resources help you to work in the way that best suits you, and enable extra support to be provided online. For example, you can test yourself online and feedback from the test will direct you back to the relevant parts of the book.

Electronic resources are available in a simple-to-use online platform called Nelson Thornes *learning space*. If your school or college has a licence to use the service, you will be given a password through which you can access the materials through any internet connection.

Icons in this book indicate where there is material online related to that topic. The following icons are used:

Learning activity

These resources include a variety of interactive and non-interactive activities to support your learning:

- Animations
- Simulations
- Maths skills
- Key diagrams
- Glossary

Progress tracking

These resources include a variety of tests which you can use to check your knowledge on particular topics (Test yourself) and a range of resources that enable you to analyse and understand examination questions (On your marks...).

Research support

These resources include WebQuests, in which you are assigned a task and provided with a range of web links to use as source material for research.

These are designed as Extension resources to stretch you and broaden your learning, in order for you to attain the highest possible marks in your exams.

Web links

Our online resources feature a list of recommended weblinks, split by chapter. This will give you a head start, helping you to navigate to the best websites that will aid your learning and understanding of the topics in your course.

How science works

These resources are a mixtures of interactive and non-interactive activities to help you learn the skills required for success in this new area of the specification.

Practical

This icon signals where there is a relevant practical activity to be undertaken, and support is provided online.

When you see an icon, go to Nelson Thornes *learning space* at www.nelsonthornes.com/aqagce, enter your access details and select your course. The materials are arranged in the same order as the topics in the book, so you can easily find the resources you need.

How to use this book

This book covers the specification for your course and is arranged in a sequence approved by AQA.

The textbook will cover all three of the Assessment Objectives required in your AQA A Level Chemistry course.

The main text of the book will cover AO1 – Knowledge and understanding. This consists of the main factual content of the specification. The other Assessment Objectives (AO2 – Application of knowledge and understanding and AO3 – How science works) make up around 50% of the assessment weighting of the specification, and as such will be covered in the textbook in the form of the features 'Applications and How science works' (see below).

The book content is divided into the two theory units of the AQA Chemistry AS specification: Unit 1 (Foundation Chemistry) and Unit 2 (Chemistry in Action). Units are then further divided into chapters, and then topics, making the content clear and easy to use.

Unit openers give you a summary of the content you will be covering, and a recap of ideas from GCSE that you will need.

The features in this book include:

Learning objectives

At the beginning of each section you will find a list of learning objectives that contain targets linked to the requirements of the specification. The relevant specification reference is also provided.

Key terms

Terms that you will need to be able to define and understand are highlighted in bold blue type within the text, e.g. **isomer**. You can look up these terms in the Glossary.

Hint

Hints to aid your understanding of the content.

Applications and How science works

This feature may cover either or both of the assessment objectives AO2 – Application of knowledge and understanding and AO3 – How science works, both key parts of the new specification.

As with the specification, these objectives are integrated throughout the content of the book. This feature highlights opportunities to apply your knowledge and understanding and draws out aspects of 'How science works' as they occur within topics, so that it is always relevant to what you are studying. The ideas provided in these features intend to teach you the skills you will need to tackle this part of the course, and give you experience that you can draw upon in the examination. You will **not be examined** on the exact information provided in this book with relation to Application and How science works.

For more information, see the 'How science works' spread on page 1 for more detail.

Summary questions

Short questions that test your understanding of the subject and allow you to apply the knowledge and skills you have acquired to different scenarios. Answers are supplied at the back of the book.

AQA Examiner's tip

Hints from AQA examiners to help you with your studies and to prepare you for your exam.

AQA Examination-style questions

Questions in the style that you can expect in your exam, including the new 'How science works' strand. These occur at the end of each chapter to give practice in examination-style questions for a particular topic. They also occur at the end of each unit; the questions here may cover any of the content of the unit.

AQA examination questions are reproduced by permission of the Assessment and Qualifications Alliance.

Nelson Thornes is responsible for the solution(s) given and they may not constitute the only possible solution(s).

Web links in the book

Because Nelson Thornes is not responsible for third party content online, there may be some changes to this material that are beyond our control. In order for us to ensure that the links referred to in the book are as up-to-date and stable as possible, the websites provided are usually homepages with supporting instructions on how to reach the relevant pages if necessary.

Please let us know at **webadmin@nelsonthornes.com** if you find a link that doesn't work and we will do our best to correct this at reprint, or to list an alternative site.

Studying AS Chemistry

The successful study of any subject at AS level requires commitment and determination to gain the knowledge and understanding of the subject matter. This is certainly true of chemistry. Students should commit their time and effort to gain a knowledge of the principles and theories to form the base on which understanding is built. The rewards for this effort will be repaid many times over, both for those who continue to study the subject at a higher level and those who decide to end their formal study of the subject at A level.

This AS course builds on a knowledge and understanding of chemistry gained during a study of the subject during a GCSE course. Each topic is revisited and further developed and new concepts are introduced. This textbook leads you through the new information and helps you to recognise the underlining patterns and to gain an understanding of the concepts involved. Questions are included at the end of each chapter to help you check that you have gained the required knowledge and understanding.

During this course you will perform many experiments which will help you develop your ability to make accurate observations and measurements. With guidance from your teachers you will be challenged to interpret the results and to suggest additional experiments. The results of some experiments will not fit an expected pattern and you will need to search for reasons why this is the case.

The assessment of practical and investigative skills form part of the AS course. Practical skills will be assessed by your teacher who will observe your work throughout the course checking it using guidelines provided by the Examination Board. Investigative skills will be assessed using exercises devised by the Examination Board which will be marked either by your teachers, the PSA + ISA route, or by an external board appointed examiner, the EMPA route. Both routes form 20% of the total AS assessment.

This textbook contains a wealth of information and guidance to help you to develop your understanding of chemistry. Delight in the subject can be achieved when you have gained both knowledge and understanding of the basic principles. The rewards are certainly worthy of the effort required.

How science works

This book also contains many sections headed 'How science works' which build on ideas introduced during your GCSE course. The issues considered here will help you recognise how the interpretation of experimental results obtained by research scientists lead to theories and predictions which can be tested by further experiments. In some cases the results obtained from one series of experiments conflict with those obtained from related experiments performed by other scientists. In these cases you will see that there is insufficient experimental evidence for a firm theory to be made.

Your study of chemistry and the 'How science works' issues included in this and the resources online will help you to choose and carry out experimental and investigative activities to answer scientific questions and solve scientific problems. They should further develop your ability to think as a chemist. You will develop the ability to analyse and to question the validity of information given to you. You will be able to appreciate the contribution that chemists have made, and continue to make to our society and understand why it is necessary for chemists to be involved in decisions which affect our society.

Your understanding of the concepts and principles included in these sections will be assessed in the AS examination. Some questions will build on topics included in the specification content but in other cases you may be given information from which you will be required to make deductions.

By the end of the course you should be able to use scientific logic to assess critically a wide range of ideas presented in newspapers, books and in television and radio programmes.

Foundation chemistry

Chapters in this unit

It is only around a century ago that scientists began to realise the nature of atoms, for example, that they were built up from smaller particles. Once this was understood it unlocked the understanding of how atoms were held together, how the arrangement of the periodic table made perfect sense and indeed how the properties of elements and compounds could be explained. This unit applies the idea of the atom to these different aspects of chemistry.

Atomic structure revises the idea of the atom, looking at some of the evidence for sub-atomic particles. It introduces the mass spectrometer, which is used for measuring the masses of atoms. The evidence for the arrangement of electrons is studied and you will see how a more sophisticated model using atomic orbitals rather than circular orbits was developed.

Amount of substance is about quantitative chemistry, that is, how much product we get from a given amount of reactants. The idea of the mole is used as the unit of quantity to compare equal numbers of atoms and molecules of different substances, including gases and solutions. Balanced equations are used to describe and measure the efficiency of chemical processes.

Bonding revisits the three types of strong bonds that hold atoms together: ionic, covalent and metallic. It introduces three weaker types of forces that act between molecules, the most significant of these being hydrogen bonding. It examines how the various types of forces are responsible for the solid, liquid and gaseous states, and explores how the electrons contribute to the shapes of molecules and ions.

Periodicity looks at the periodic table of elements and then concentrates on the trends in properties of the elements in Period 3.

Introduction to organic chemistry looks at the nature of carbon compounds and deals with the principles of the special naming system needed to keep track of them. It looks at isomers. These are compounds which have the same formula but a different arrangement of atoms.

Alkanes is about crude oil and its fractional distillation. It also looks at the different ways that large alkane molecules can be cracked into smaller, more useful molecules. It deals with the combustion of carbon compounds.

The concepts of how science works, including the applications of science, are found throughout the chapters, where they will provide you with an opportunity to apply your knowledge in a fresh context.

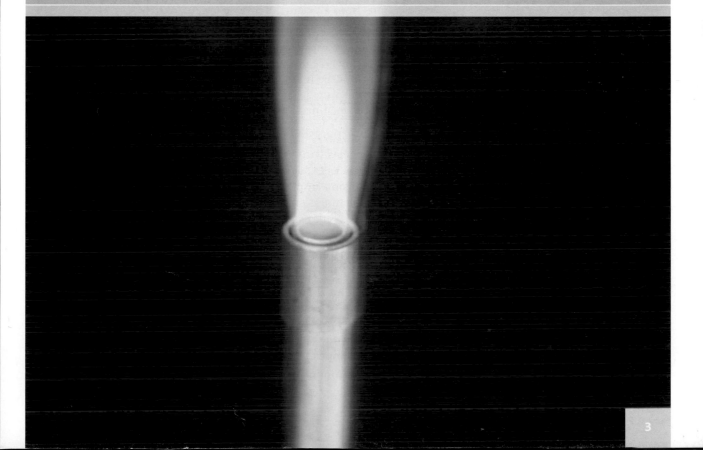

What you already know:

The material in this unit builds upon knowledge and understanding that you will have developed at GCSE, in particular the following:

- There are just over 100 elements all made up of atoms.

- The atoms of any element are essentially the same as each other but they are different from the atoms of any other element.

- Atoms are extremely tiny and cannot be weighed individually.

- Atoms are made of protons, neutrons and electrons.

- Atoms bond together to obtain full outer shells of electrons.

- Each element has its own symbol and is part of the periodic table of elements.

- Groups in the periodic table are vertical; periods are horizontal.

- Organic chemistry deals with carbon compounds.

1 Atomic structure

1.1 Fundamental particles

Learning objectives:

■ What are the relative masses of protons, neutrons and electrons?

■ What are the relative charges of protons, neutrons and electrons?

■ How are these particles arranged in an atom?

Specification reference: 3.1.1

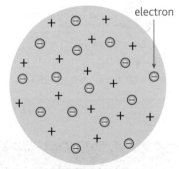

Figure 1 *The plum pudding model of the atom – electrons located in circular arrays within a sphere of positive charge*

electron

sphere of positive charge

Figure 2 *Atoms can only be seen indirectly. This photograph was taken by an instrument called a scanning tunnelling electron microscope.*

i Developing ideas of the atom

The Greek philosophers had a model that matter was made up of a single continuous substance that produced the four elements – earth, fire, water and air. The idea that matter was made of individual atoms was not taken seriously for another 2000 years. During this time alchemists built up a lot of evidence about how substances behave and combine. Their aim was to change other metals into gold. Here are a few of the steps that led to our present model.

1661 Robert Boyle proposed that there were some substances that could not be made simpler. These were the chemical elements, as we now know them.

1803 John Dalton suggested that elements were composed of indivisible atoms. All the atoms of a particular element had the same mass, and atoms of different elements had different masses. Atoms could not be broken down.

1896 Henri Becquerel discovered radioactivity. This showed that particles could come from inside the atom. Therefore the atom was not indivisible. The following year, J J Thomson discovered the electron. This was the first sub-atomic particle to be discovered. He showed that electrons were negatively charged and electrons from all elements were the same.

As electrons had a negative charge, there had to be some source of positive charge inside the atom, too. Also, as electrons were much lighter than whole atoms, there had to be something to account for the rest of the mass of the atom. Thompson suggested that the electrons were located within the atom in circular arrays, like plums in a pudding of positive charge, see Figure 1.

1911 Ernest Rutherford and his team found that most of the mass and all the positive charge of the atom was in a tiny central nucleus.

So, for many years, we have known that atoms themselves are made up of smaller particles, called sub-atomic particles. The complete picture is still being built up in 'atom smashers' such as the one at CERN, near Geneva.

The sub-atomic particles

Atoms are made of three fundamental particles – **protons**, **neutrons** and **electrons**.

The protons and neutrons form the **nucleus**, in the centre of the atom.

■ Protons and neutrons are sometimes called **nucleons** because they are found in the nucleus.

■ The electrons surround the nucleus.

The properties of the sub-atomic particles are shown in Table 1.

Table 1 *The properties of the sub-atomic particles*

Property	Proton, p	Neutron, n	Electron, e
Mass / kg	1.673×10^{-27}	1.675×10^{-27}	0.911×10^{-30} (very nearly 0)
Charge / C	$+1.602 \times 10^{-19}$	0	-1.602×10^{-19}
Position	in the nucleus	in the nucleus	around the nucleus

These numbers are extremely small. In practice, we use the **relative** masses and charges.

The relative charge on a proton is taken to be $+1$, so the charge on an electron is -1.

Neutrons have no charge, see Table 2.

Table 2 *The relative masses and charges of the sub-atomic particles*

	Proton, p	Neutron, n	Electron, e
Relative mass	1	1	1/1840
Relative charge	+1	0	−1

In a neutral atom, the number of electrons must be the same as the number of protons because their charge is equal in size and opposite in sign.

■ The arrangement of the sub-atomic particles

The sub-atomic particles (protons, neutrons and electrons) are arranged in the atom as shown in Figure 3.

The protons and neutrons are in the centre of the atom, held together by a force called the **strong nuclear force**. This is much stronger than the **electrostatic forces** that hold electrons and protons together in the atom, so it overcomes the repulsion between the protons in the nucleus. It acts only over very short distances, i.e. within the nucleus.

The nucleus is surrounded by electrons. Electrons are found in a series of levels, sometimes referred to as orbits or shells which get further and further away from the nucleus. This is a simplified picture which we will develop in Topic 1.5.

■ **Hint**

Remember that charge is measured in coulomb, C.

■ **Hint**

The diameter of the nucleus of a hydrogen atom is about 2×10^{-15} m, while the diameter of the atom itself is about 1×10^{-10} m, about 50 000 times larger. This means that if the nucleus were the size of a football, the whole atom would have the volume of a football stadium.

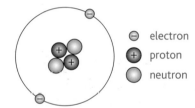

⊖ electron
⊕ proton
◯ neutron

Figure 3 *The sub-atomic particles in a helium atom (not to scale)*

AQA Examiner's tip

You must remember the relative masses and charges of a proton, neutron, and an electron.

■ Summary questions

1 Answer the following questions by using one or more of the following terms: proton, neutron, electron.

  a Which are nucleons?

  b Which have the same mass?

  c Which have opposite charges?

  d Which has/have no charge?

  e Which is/are found outside the nucleus?

2 a Why do we assume that there are the same number of protons and electrons in an atom?

  b What is the difference between J J Thompson's model of the atom and Rutherford's model?

3 Extension question. Find out what experimental evidence led Rutherford to develop his model of the atom.

1.2 The arrangement of the electrons

Learning objectives:

- How are electrons arranged in an atom?

- Is the electron a particle, a wave or a cloud of charge?

- How has the structure of an atom developed from Dalton to Schrödinger?

Specification reference: 3.1.1

The atom and electrons

During the early years of the twentieth century, physicists made great strides in understanding the structure of the atom. These are some of the landmarks:

1913 Niels Bohr put forward the idea that the atom consisted of a tiny positive nucleus orbited by negatively-charged electrons to form an atom like a tiny solar system. The electrons orbited in shells of fixed size, and the movement of electrons from one shell to the next explained how atoms absorbed and gave out light. This was the beginning of what is called quantum theory.

1926 Erwin Schrödinger, a mathematical physicist, worked out an equation that used the idea that electrons had some of the properties of waves as well as those of particles.

1932 James Chadwick discovered the neutron.

At the same time, chemists were developing their ideas about how electrons allowed atoms to bond together. One important contributor was the American, Gilbert Lewis. He put forward the ideas that:

- the inertness of the noble gases was related to their having full outer shells of eight electrons

- ions were formed by atoms losing or gaining electrons to attain full outer shells (and thus become stable)

- atoms could also bond by sharing electrons to form full outer shells.

Evolving ideas

Early theories model the electron as a minute solid particle. Later theories suggest we can also think of electrons as smeared out clouds of charge, so we can never say exactly where an electron is at any moment. We can merely state the probability that it can be found in a particular volume of space that has a particular shape. However, chemists still use different models of the atom for different purposes.

- Dalton's model can still be used to explain the geometries of crystals.

- Bohr's model can be used for a simple model of ionic and covalent bonding.

- The charge cloud idea is used for a more sophisticated explanation of bonding and the shapes of molecules.

- The simple model of electrons orbiting in shells is useful for many purposes, particularly for working out bonding between atoms.

Electron shells

The first shell, which is closest to the nucleus, fills first, then the second and so on. The number of electrons in each shell $= 2n^2$, where n is the number of the shell, so:

- the first shell holds up to 2 electrons
- the second shell holds up to 8 electrons
- the third shell holds up to 18 electrons.

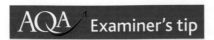

Examiner's tip

You must remember the number of electrons in each shell.

Electron diagrams

If we know the number of protons in an atom, we also know the number of electrons it has. This is because the atom is neutral. We can therefore draw an electron diagram for any element. For example, carbon has six electrons. The four electrons in the outer shell are usually drawn spaced out around the atom, as in Figure 1.

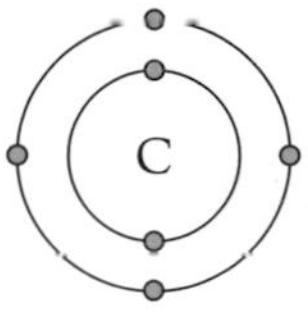

Sulfur has 16 electrons. It has six electrons in its outer shell. It helps when drawing bonding diagrams to space out the first four (as in carbon), and then add the next two electrons to form pairs, as shown in Figure 2.

We can also draw electron diagrams of ions, as long as we know the number of electrons. For example, a sodium *atom*, Na, has 11 electrons, but its *ion* has 10, so it has a positive charge, Na^+.

An oxygen *atom* has 8 electrons, but its *ion* has 10, so it has a negative charge, O^{2-}.

We can write electron diagrams in shorthand:

- Write the number of electrons in each shell, starting with the inner shell and working outwards.
- Separate each number by a comma.
- For carbon we write 2,4, for sulfur 2,8,6 and for Na^+ 2,8.

carbon (2,4)

Figure 1 *Electron diagram of carbon*

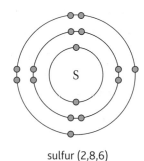

sulfur (2,8,6)

Figure 2 *Electron diagram of sulfur*

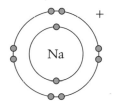

Na^+ sodium ion
11 protons, 10 electrons
(2,8)

Figure 3 *Electron diagram of a sodium ion*

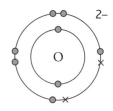

O^{2-} oxygen ion
8 protons,
10 electrons (2,8)

Figure 4 *Electron diagram of an oxygen ion*

Summary questions

1. Draw the electron arrangement diagrams of atoms which have the following numbers of electrons:

    a 3   b 9   c 14

2. Write in shorthand the electron arrangements of atoms with:

    a 4 electrons

    b 13 electrons

    c 18 electrons.

3. Which of the following are atoms, positive ions or negative ions? Give the size and charge on each ion.

	Number of protons	Number of electrons
A	12	10
B	2	2
C	17	18
D	10	10
E	3	2

Mass number, atomic number and isotopes

Learning objectives:

■ What are the definitions of the terms mass number, atomic number and isotope?

■ Why do isotopes of the same element have identical chemical properties?

Specification reference: 3.1.1

■ Mass number and atomic number

Atomic number, *Z*

As we have seen in Topics 1.1 and 1.2, atoms consist of a tiny nucleus made up of protons and neutrons that is surrounded by electrons. The number of protons in the nucleus is called the atomic number or the **proton number**, symbol *Z*.

The number of electrons in the atom is equal to the proton number, so atoms are electrically neutral. The number of electrons in the outer shell of an atom determines the chemical properties of an element, that is, how it reacts, what sort of elements it is. The atomic number defines the chemical identity of an element.

Atomic number (proton number), *Z* = number of protons

All atoms of the same element have the same atomic number. Atoms of different elements have different atomic numbers.

Mass number, *A*

The total number of protons plus neutrons in the nucleus (the total number of nucleons) is called the mass number, *A*. It is the nucleons that are responsible for almost all of the mass of an atom because electrons weigh virtually nothing.

Mass number, *A* = number of protons + number of neutrons

■ Isotopes

Every single atom of any particular element has the same number of protons in its nucleus and therefore the same number of electrons. But the number of neutrons may vary.

■ Atoms with the same number of protons but different numbers of neutrons are called isotopes.

■ Different isotopes of the same element react chemically in exactly the same way.

■ Atoms of different isotopes of the same element vary in mass number because of the different number of neutrons in their nuclei.

All atoms of the element carbon, for example, have atomic number 6. That is what makes them carbon rather than any other element. However, carbon has three isotopes with mass numbers 12, 13 and 14 respectively, see Table 1. All three isotopes will react in the same way, burning in oxygen to form carbon dioxide, for example.

Isotopes are often written like this $^{13}_{6}C$. The superscript 13 is the mass number of the isotope and the subscript 6 the atomic number.

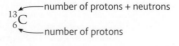

$$^{13}_{6}C \begin{matrix} \longleftarrow \text{number of protons + neutrons} \\ \longleftarrow \text{number of protons} \end{matrix}$$

■ Hint

The mass number of an isotope must always be bigger than the atomic number (except in $^{1}_{1}H$). Typically it is around twice as big.

Table 1 *Isotopes of carbon*

Name of isotope	carbon-12	carbon-13	carbon-14
Symbol	$^{12}_{6}C$	$^{13}_{6}C$	$^{14}_{6}C$
Number of protons	6	6	6
Number of neutrons	6	7	8
Abundance	98.89 %	1.11 %	Trace

Applications and How science works

Carbon dating

Isotopes of an element have different numbers of neutrons in their nuclei, and most elements have some isotopes. Sometimes these isotopes are unstable and the nucleus of the atom itself breaks down giving off either bits of the nucleus or energetic rays. This is the cause of radioactivity. Radioactive isotopes have many uses. Each radioactive isotope decays at a rate measured by its half-life. This is the time taken for half of its radioactivity to decay.

One well-known radioactive isotope is carbon-14. It has a half-life of 5730 years and is produced by cosmic-ray activity in the atmosphere. It is used to date organic matter. Radiocarbon dating can find the age of carbon-based material up to 60000 years old, though it is most accurate for materials up to 2000 years old.

There is always a tiny fixed proportion of carbon-14 in all living matter. All living matter takes in and gives out carbon in the form of food and carbon dioxide, respectively. As a result, the level of carbon-14 stays the same. Once the living material dies, this stops happening. The radioactive carbon breaks down and the level of radioactivity slowly falls. So, knowing the half-life of carbon-14, scientists work backwards. They work out how long it has taken for the level of radioactivity to fall from what it is in a living organism to what it is in the sample. So, a sample with half the level of radioactivity expected in a living organism would have been dead for 5730 years, while one with a quarter of the expected level would have been dead for twice as long.

Carbon dating has been used to estimate the age of the Turin shroud. Could it have been the burial cloth of Jesus Christ?

The radioactivity in a wooden bowl was found to be ⅛th of that found in a sample of living wood.

Questions

1 How old is the wood from the bowl?

2 Does this tell us the age of the bowl? Explain your answer.

Summary questions

1 Isotopes are usually identified by the name of the element and the mass number of the isotope as in carbon-13. Isotopes of hydrogen, however, have their own names: hydrogen-2 is often called deuterium and hydrogen-3 tritium. However, both these isotopes behave chemically just like the commonest isotope, hydrogen-1. How many protons, neutrons and electrons do atoms of the following have?

a Deuterium

b Tritium

2 $^{31}_{15}W$, $^{14}_{7}X$, $^{16}_{8}Y$, $^{15}_{7}Z$: which of these atoms (not their real symbols) is a pair of isotopes?

3 For each of the elements in question 2, give:

a the number of protons

b the mass number

c the number of neutrons.

1.4 The mass spectrometer

Learning objectives:

■ How does a mass spectrometer work and what does it measure?

Specification reference: 3.1.1

The mass spectrometer is the most useful instrument for the accurate determination of relative atomic masses. (We will see in Topic 17.1 that it can also measure relative molecular masses and much more.) Relative atomic masses are measured on a scale on which the mass of an atom of ^{12}C is defined as **exactly** 12 (Topic 2.1). No other isotope has a relative atomic mass which is exactly a whole number. This is because protons and neutrons do not have relative masses of exactly 1.

The mass spectrometer determines the mass of separate atoms (or molecules). Mass spectrometers are an essential part of a chemist's equipment. For example, they are used by forensic scientists to help identify substances, such as illegal drugs.

The layout of one type of mass spectrometer is shown in Figure 2.

Figure 1 *A mass spectrometer*

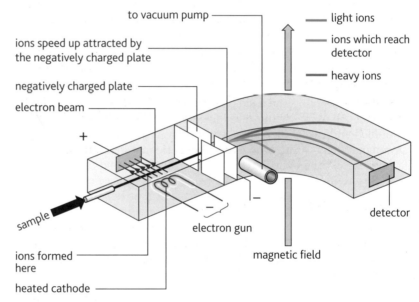

Figure 2 *The layout of a mass spectrometer*

What happens in a mass spectrometer?

In outline, atoms are converted into ions, accelerated and deflected according to their masses and their charges and then arrive at a detector. These steps are explained further below.

■ The instrument is kept under a high vacuum so that the ions do not collide with air molecules, which might stop them reaching the detector.

■ The sample is investigated in the gaseous state. If the sample is a gas or a volatile liquid it is injected into the instrument directly. If the sample is a solid it is vaporised first by heating.

- **Ionisation** – a beam of electrons from an 'electron gun' knocks out electrons from atoms or molecules of the sample so that they form positive ions. Nearly all the atoms or molecules lose just one electron and form ions with a 1^+ charge but a small number (typically around 5%) lose two electrons to form ions with a 2^+ charge.

- **Acceleration** – these positive ions are attracted towards negatively charged plates and are accelerated to a high speed. The speed they reach depends on their mass – the lighter the ions, the faster they go.

- Some ions pass through slits in the plates. This forms the ions into a beam.

- **Deflection** – the beam of ions then moves into a magnetic field at right angles to its direction of travel. The magnetic field deflects the beam of ions into an arc of a circle. The deflection of an ion depends on the ratio of its mass to charge (m/z), where z is the charge on the ion (usually 1^+). Heavier ions are deflected less than lighter ones and 2^+ ions are deflected twice as much as 1^+ ions with the same mass. The deflection also depends on the magnetic field strength – the stronger the field, the greater the deflection.

- **Detection** – the magnetic field is gradually increased so that ions of increasing mass enter the detector one after another. Ions strike the detector, accept electrons, lose their charge and create a current which is proportional to the **abundance** of each ion.

- From the strength of the magnetic field at which a particular ion hits the detector, a computer works out the value of the mass to charge ratio, usually called m/z, of the original ion. A read-out called a **mass spectrum** is produced. (Figure 3 shows the mass spectrum of neon.) This is normally presented as a graph of relative abundance of ions against the mass to charge ratio (m/z).

To summarise, the four key stages are: **ionisation**, **acceleration**, **deflection**, and **detection**.

Mass spectra of elements

The mass spectrometer can be used to identify the different isotopes that make up an element. It detects individual ions, so different isotopes are detected separately because they have different masses. This is how the data for the chlorine isotopes in Figure 5 was obtained.

Mass spectrometers can measure relative atomic masses to five decimal places of an atomic mass unit. This is called high resolution mass spectrometry. But most work is done to the nearest whole number – this is called low resolution mass spectrometry.

Low resolution mass spectrometry

The low resolution mass spectrum of neon is shown in Figure 3. This shows that neon has two isotopes, of mass numbers 20 and 22, with abundances to the nearest whole number of 90% and 10%, respectively. From this we can say that neon has an average relative atomic mass of:

$$\frac{(90 \times 20) + (10 \times 22)}{100} = 20.2$$

Another example is the mass spectrum of the element germanium which is shown in Figure 4. (The percentage abundance of each peak has been given to help you with summary question 5.)

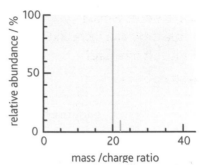

Figure 3 *The mass spectrum of neon*

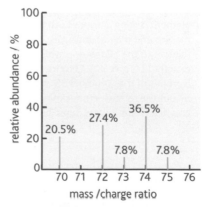

Figure 4 *The mass spectrum of germanium (the percentage abundance of each peak is given)*

> ### Hint
>
> - There is no peak at 20.2 because no neon atoms actually have this mass.
>
> - The peak height gives the **relative abundance** of each isotope and the horizontal scale gives the m/z which, for a singly charged ion is numerically the same as the mass number, M.
>
> - When calculating the relative atomic mass of an element, you must take account of the relative abundances of the isotopes. The relative atomic mass of neon is not 21 because there are far more atoms of the lighter isotope.

Isotopes of chlorine

Chlorine has two isotopes. They are $^{35}_{17}\text{Cl}$, with a mass number of 35, and $^{37}_{17}\text{Cl}$, with a mass number of 37. They occur in the ratio of almost exactly 3 : 1.

^{35}Cl ^{35}Cl ^{35}Cl ^{37}Cl

three of these   to every one of this

So we have 75% ^{35}Cl and 25% ^{37}Cl atoms in naturally occurring chlorine gas.

The average mass of these is 35.5, as shown below.

Mass of 100 atoms $= (35 \times 75) + (37 \times 25) = 3550$

Average mass $= \dfrac{3550}{100} = 35.5$

This explains why the **relative atomic mass** of chlorine is *approximately* 35.5. You will learn about relative atomic masses in Topic 2.1.

■ Applications and How science works

Doubly charged ions

During ionisation, a small number of ions with a 2^+ charge are formed. Because of their double charge, these are accelerated and deflected more than singly charged ions. In fact they behave like ions with half the mass of a singly charged ion. So a close look at the mass spectrum of neon would show peaks at mass/charge ratio 10 and 11. However, since double ionisation is rare, these peaks will have very small abundances.

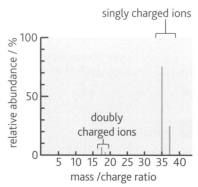

Figure 5 *The mass spectrum of chlorine up to m/z = 40 showing peaks due to 2+ ions as well as peaks at m/z = 35 and 37*

■ Identifying elements

All elements have a characteristic pattern that shows the relative abundances of their isotopes. This can be used to help identify any particular element. Chlorine, for example, shows two peaks, at mass 35 and mass 37. The one of mass 35 has three times the height of the one of mass 37 because there are three times as many of these. The spectrum also shows smaller peaks at *m/z* 17.5 and 18.5 caused by doubly charged ions, see Figure 5.

The spectrum will also show peaks caused by ionised Cl_2 molecules. These are called **molecular ions**. There will be three of these:

- ■ at *m/z* 70, due to $^{35}\text{Cl}^{35}\text{Cl}$
- ■ at *m/z* 72, due to $^{35}\text{Cl}^{37}\text{Cl}$
- ■ at *m/z* 74, due to $^{37}\text{Cl}^{37}\text{Cl}$

High resolution mass spectrometers can measure the masses of atoms to several decimal places. This allows us to identify elements by the exact masses of their atoms that, apart from carbon-12 whose relative atomic mass is exactly 12, are not exactly whole numbers.

Mass spectrometers in space

Space probes such as the Viking Martian lander carry mass spectrometers. They are used to identify the elements in rock samples. The Giotto space probe passed very close to Halley's Comet. The probe had two mass spectrometers. These enabled scientists to work out what the comet was composed of. Mass spectrometers have to be under a high vacuum, which is usually produced by a pump. A mass spectrometer in an interplanetary probe such as Giotto has no need for a pump as it is being used in the vacuum of space.

Hint

In the mass spectrum, the heaviest ion (the one with the greatest *m/z* value) is likely to be the molecular ion.

Figure 6 *The Giotto space probe carried two mass spectrometers*

Summary questions

1 Explain why the ions formed in a mass spectrometer have a positive charge.

2 Explain what causes the ions to accelerate through the mass spectrometer.

3 What forms the ions into a beam?

4 What bends the ions into a curved path?

5 Use the information about germanium in Figure 4, to work out its relative atomic mass.

6 Figure 7 shows the mass spectrum of copper. Work out the relative atomic mass of copper.

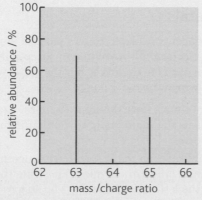

Figure 7 *The mass spectrum of copper*

1.5 More about electron arrangements in atoms

Learning objectives:

- How are the electron configurations of atoms and ions written in terms of s, p, and d electrons?

Specification reference 3.1.1

As we have seen in Topic 1.2, in a simple model of the atom we think of electrons as being arranged in shells around the nucleus. The shells can hold increasing numbers of electrons as they get further from the nucleus; the pattern is 2, 8, 18, etc.

💡 Energy levels

Electrons in different shells have differing amounts of energy. We can therefore represent them on an energy level diagram. We call the shells main energy levels, and they are labelled 1, 2, 3, etc., see Figure 1. Each main energy level can hold up to a maximum number of electrons given by the formula $2n^2$, where n is the number of the main level. So, we can have 2 electrons in the first main level, 8 in the next, 18 in the next, etc.

Apart from the first level, which has only an s sub-level, these main energy levels are divided into sub-levels, called s, p, d and f, which have slightly different energies, see Figure 2. Level 2 has an s sub-level and a p sub-level. Level 3 an s sub-level, a p sub-level and a d sub-level.

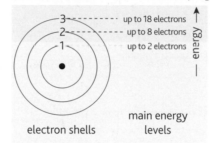

Figure 1 *Electron shells and energy levels*

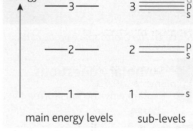

Figure 2 *Energy levels and sub-levels*

Quantum mechanics

For a more complete description of the electrons in atoms we use a theory called quantum mechanics, which was developed during the 1920s. This describes the atom mathematically with an equation (the Schrödinger equation). The solutions to this equation give the **probability** of finding an electron in a given **volume** of space called an atomic orbital.

Atomic orbitals

The electron is no longer considered to be a particle, but a cloud of negative charge. An electron fills a volume in space called its **atomic orbital**. The concept of the main levels and the sub-levels is then included in the following way:

- Different atomic orbitals have different energies. Each orbital has a number that tells us the main energy level that it corresponds to: 1, 2, 3, etc.
- The atomic orbitals of each main level have different shapes, which in turn have slightly different energies. These are the sub-levels. They are described by the letters s, p, d and f. The shapes of the s-, p- and d-orbitals are shown in Figure 3. (The shapes of f-orbitals are even more complicated.)

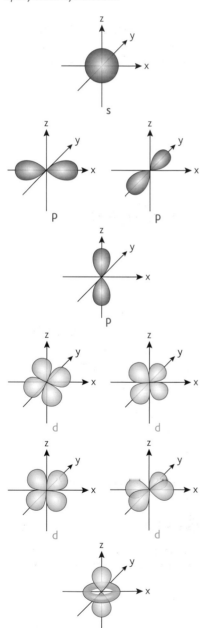

Figure 3 *The shapes of s-, p- and d-orbitals*

- These shapes represent a volume of space in which there is a 95% probability of finding an electron and they influence the shapes of molecules, see Topic 3.9.

- The first main energy level consists of a single s-orbital. The second main level has a single s-orbital and three p-orbitals of a slightly higher energy, the third main level has a single s-orbital, three p-orbitals of slightly higher energy and five d-orbitals of slightly higher energy still, and so on, see Figure 4.

- Any single atomic orbital can hold a maximum of two electrons.

- s-orbitals can hold up to two electrons.

- p-orbitals can hold up to two electrons each, but always come in groups of three of the same energy, to give a total of up to six electrons in the p sub-level.

- d-orbitals can hold up to two electrons each, but come in groups of five of the same energy to give a total of up to 10 electrons in the d sub-level.

Table 1 summarises the number of electrons in the different levels and sub-levels.

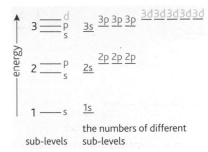

Figure 4 *The subdivisions of orbitals*

> **Hint**
>
> The terms s, p, d and f come from the history of spectroscopy. They come from descriptions of spectroscopic lines as **s**harp, **p**rincipal, **d**iffuse and **f**ine.

Table 1 *The number of electrons in the different levels and sub-levels*

Main energy level (shell)	1	2		3			4			
Sub-level(s)	s	s	p	s	p	d	s	p	d	f
Number of orbitals in sub-level	1 (2 electrons)	1 (2e)	3 (6e)	1 (2e)	3 (6e)	5 (10e)	1 (2e)	3 (6e)	5 (10e)	7 (14e)
Total number of electrons in main energy level	2	8		18			32			

The energy level diagram in Figure 5 shows the energies of the orbitals for the first few elements of the Periodic Table. Notice that the first main energy level has only an s-orbital. The second main level has an s and p sub-level and the p sub-level is composed of three p-orbitals of equal energy. The third main level has an s, a p and a d sub-level, and the d sub-level is composed of five atomic orbitals of equal energy.

- Each 'box' in Figure 5 represents an orbital of the appropriate shape that can hold up to two electrons.

- Notice that 4s is actually of slightly lower energy than 3d for neutral atoms, though this can change when ions are formed.

Spin

Electrons also have the property called spin.

- Two electrons in the same orbital must have opposite spins.

- The electrons are usually represented by arrows pointing up or down to show the different directions of spin.

■ Putting electrons into atomic orbitals

Remember that the label of an atomic orbital tells us about the energy (and shape) of an electron cloud. For example, the atomic orbital 3s means the main energy level is 3 and the sub-level (and therefore the shape) is spherical.

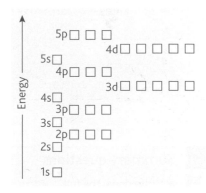

Figure 5 *The energy levels of the first few atomic orbitals*

> **Hint**
>
> Although we use the term 'spin', the electrons are not actually spinning.

There are three rules for allocating electrons to atomic orbitals.

■ Atomic orbitals of lower energy are filled first – so the lower main level is filled first, and within this level, sub-levels of lower energy are filled first.

■ Atomic orbitals of the same energy fill singly before pairing starts. This is because electrons repel each other.

■ No atomic orbital can hold more than two electrons.

The electron diagrams for the elements hydrogen to sodium are shown in Figure 6.

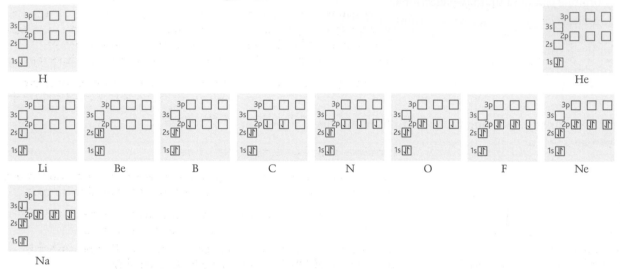

Figure 6 *The electron arrangements for the elements hydrogen to sodium*

Writing electronic structures

A shorthand way of writing electronic structures is as follows, for example for sodium, which has 11 electrons:

$$1s^2 \qquad 2s^2\ 2p^6 \qquad 3s^1$$
$$2 \qquad\quad 8 \qquad\quad 1$$

Note how this matches the simpler 2,8,1 you used at GCSE.

Calcium, with 20 electrons would be:

$$1s^2 \qquad 2s^2\ 2p^6 \qquad 3s^2\ 3p^6 \qquad 4s^2 \qquad \text{which matches 2,8,8,2}$$

Notice how the 4s orbital is filled before the 3d orbital because it is of lower energy.

After calcium, electrons begin to fill the 3d orbitals, so vanadium with 23 electrons is:

$$1s^2\ 2s^2\ 2p^6\ 3s^2\ 3p^6\ 3d^3\ 4s^2$$

and krypton, with 36 electrons is: $1s^2\ 2s^2\ 2p^6\ 3s^2\ 3p^6\ 3d^{10}\ 4s^2\ 4p^6$

Sometimes it simplifies things to use to the previous noble gas symbol. So the electron arrangement of calcium, Ca, could be written $[Ar]\ 4s^2$ as a shorthand for $[1s^2\ 2s^2\ 2p^6\ 3s^2\ 3p^6]\ 4s^2$ because $1s^2\ 2s^2\ 2p^6\ 3s^2\ 3p^6$ is the electron arrangement of argon.

We can use the same notation for ions. So a sodium ion, Na^+, would have the electron arrangement $1s^2\ 2s^2\ 2p^6$, one less than a sodium atom, $1s^2\ 2s^2\ 2p^6\ 3s^1$.

Summary questions

1 a Write down the full electron arrangement for phosphorus.

 b Write the electron arrangement for phosphorus using an inert gas symbol as a shorthand.

2 a Write down the full electron arrangement for **i** Ca^{2+} and **ii** F^-

 b Write their electron arrangement using an inert gas symbol as a shorthand.

Electron arrangements and ionisation energy

Learning objectives:

- What is the definition of ionisation energy?

- What is the trend in ionisation energies a) down a group b) across a period in terms of electron configurations?

- How do trends in ionisation energies provide evidence for the existence of electron energy levels and sub-levels?

Specification reference: 3.1.1

Hint

The energy change for the formation of a negative ion is called the electron affinity. The term ionisation energy is used **only** for the formation of **positive** ions.

The patterns in first ionisation energies across a period provide evidence for electron energy sub-levels.

💡 Ionisation energy

Electrons can be removed from atoms by hitting the atoms with a beam of electrons from an 'electron gun'. This allows us to measure the energy it takes to remove the electrons. This is called **ionisation energy** because as the electrons are removed, the atoms become positive ions.

- Ionisation energy is the energy required to remove a mole of electrons from a mole of atoms in the gaseous state and is measured in $kJ\,mol^{-1}$.

- Ionisation energy has the abbreviation IE.

Removing the electrons one by one

We can measure the energies required to remove the electrons one by one from an atom, starting from the outer electrons and working inwards.

- The first electron needs the least energy to remove it because it is being removed from a neutral atom. This is the first IE.

- The second electron needs more energy than the first because it is being removed from a 1^+ ion. This is the second IE.

- The third electron needs even more energy to remove it because it is being removed from a 2^+ ion. This is the third IE.

- The fourth needs yet more, and so on.

We call these **successive ionisation energies**.

For example, sodium:

$$Na(g) \longrightarrow Na^+(g) + e^- \quad \text{first IE} \quad = +496\,kJ\,mol^{-1}$$
$$Na^+(g) \longrightarrow Na^{2+}(g) + e^- \quad \text{second IE} = +4563\,kJ\,mol^{-1}$$
$$Na^{2+}(g) \longrightarrow Na^{3+}(g) + e^- \quad \text{third IE} \quad = +6913\,kJ\,mol^{-1}$$

and so on, see Table 1.

Notice that the second IE is *not* the energy change for

$$Na(g) \longrightarrow Na^{2+}(g) + 2e^-$$

The energy for this process would be (first IE + second IE).

If we plot a graph of the values shown in Table 1 we get Figure 1.

Notice that one electron is relatively easy to remove, then comes a group of eight that are more difficult to remove, and finally two that are very difficult to remove.

This suggests that sodium has:

- **one** electron furthest away from the positive nucleus (easy to remove)
- **eight** nearer in to the nucleus (harder to remove)
- **two** very close to the nucleus (very difficult to remove because they are nearest to the positive charge of the nucleus).

Table 1 *Successive ionisation energies of sodium*

Electron removed	Ionisation energy / kJ mol⁻¹
1st	496
2nd	4563
3rd	6913
4th	9544
5th	13352
6th	16611
7th	20115
8th	25491
9th	28934
10th	141367
11th	159079

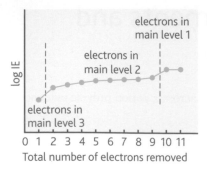

Figure 1 *The successive ionisation energies of sodium against number of electrons removed. Note that the log of the ionisation energy has been plotted in order to fit the large range of values on the scale.*

■ **Hint**

The shape of the graph in Figure 1 has to be looked at carefully. The first electron removed is in the outer main level and the tenth and eleventh electrons removed are in the innermost main level.

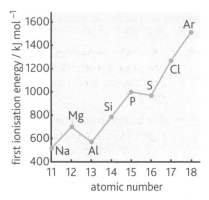

Figure 2 *Trends in first ionisation energies across Period 3*

This tells us about the number of electrons in each main level or orbit: 2,8,1. The eight electrons are in fact sub-divided into two further groups that correspond to the $2s^2$, $2p^6$ electrons in the second main level, but this is not visible on the scale of Figure 1.

We can find the number of electrons in each main level of *any* element by looking at the jumps in successive ionisation energies.

⚡ Trends in ionisation energies across a period in the periodic table

The trends in first ionisation energies as we go across a period in the periodic table can also tell us about the energies of electrons in main levels and sub-levels. Ionisation energies generally increase across a period because the nuclear charge is increasing and this makes it more difficult to remove an electron.

The data for Period 3 are shown in Table 2.

Table 2 *The first ionisation energies of the elements in Period 3 in kJ mol^{-1}*

Na	Mg	Al	Si	P	S	Cl	Ar
496	738	578	789	1012	1000	1251	1521

(nuclear charge increasing) $\longrightarrow$

Plotting a graph of these values shows that the increase is not regular, see Figure 2. Notice that as we go from magnesium ($1s^2$, $2s^2$, $2p^6$, $3s^2$) to aluminium ($1s^2$, $2s^2$, $2p^6$, $3s^2$, $3p^1$), the ionisation energy actually goes down, despite the increase in nuclear charge. This is because the outer electron in aluminium is in a 3p orbital which is of a slightly higher energy than the 3s orbital. It therefore needs less energy to remove it, see Figure 3.

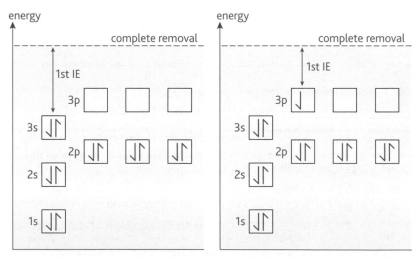

magnesium $1s^2\ 2s^2\ 2p^6\ 3s^2$ aluminium $1s^2\ 2s^2\ 2p^6\ 3s^2\ 3p^1$

💡 **Figure 3** *The first ionisation energy of aluminium is less than that of magnesium*

In Figure 2, notice the small drop between phosphorus ($1s^2$, $2s^2$, $2p^6$, $3s^2$, $3p^3$) and sulfur ($1s^2$, $2s^2$, $2p^6$, $3s^2$, $3p^4$). In phosphorus, each of the three 3p orbitals contains just one electrons, while in sulfur, one of the 3p orbitals must contain two electrons. The repulsion between these paired electrons makes it easier to remove one of them, despite the increase in nuclear charge, see Figure 4.

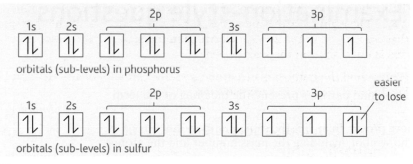

Figure 4 *Electron arrangements of phosphorus and sulfur*

Both these cases, which go against the expected trend, are evidence that confirms the existence of s and p as sub-levels. These were predicted by quantum theory and the Schrödinger equation.

Trends in ionisation energies down a group in the periodic table

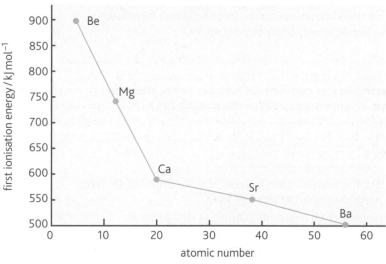

Figure 5 *The first ionisation energies of the elements of Group 2*

Figure 5 shows that there is a general decrease in first ionisation energy as we go down Group 2, and the same pattern is seen in other groups. This is because the outer electron is in a main level that gets further from the nucleus in each case.

As we go down a group, the nuclear charge increases. At first sight we might expect that this would make it *more* difficult to remove an electron. However, the actual positive charge 'felt' by an electron in the outer shell is less than the full nuclear charge. This is because of the effect of the inner electrons shielding the nuclear charge.

Summary questions

1 Why is the second ionisation energy of any atom larger than the first ionisation energy?

2 Sketch a graph similar to Figure 1 of the successive ionisation energies of aluminium (electron arrangement 2,8,3).

3 An element X has the following values (in $kJ\,mol^{-1}$) for successive ionisation energies: 1093, 2359, 4627, 6229, 37838, 47285.

   a What group in the periodic table is it in?

   b Explain your answer to a.

1 (a) State, in terms of the fundamental particles present, the meaning of the term *isotopes*. *(1 mark)*

(b) An atom contains one more proton than, but the same number of neutrons as, an atom of ^{36}S. Deduce the symbol, including the mass number and the atomic number, of this atom. *(2 marks)*

(c) The table below gives the relative abundance of each isotope in a mass spectrum of a sample of germanium, Ge.

m/z	70	72	74
Relative abundance (%)	24.4	32.4	43.2

(i) Copy and complete the electron arrangement of a Ge atom.
$1s^2$

(ii) Use the data above to calculate the relative atomic mass of this sample of germanium. Give your answer to one decimal place.

(iii) State what is adjusted in a mass spectrometer in order to direct ions with different *m/z* values onto the detector. Explain your answer. *(6 marks)*

AQA, 2006

2 A sample of element **Q** was extracted from a meteorite. The table below shows the relative abundance of each isotope in a mass spectrum of this sample of **Q**.

m/z	64	66	67	68
Relative abundance (%)	38.9	27.8	14.7	18.6

(a) Use the data above to calculate the relative atomic mass of this sample of **Q**. Give your answer to one decimal place. Suggest the identity of **Q**. *(3 marks)*

(b) In order to obtain a mass spectrum of **Q**, a gaseous sample is first ionised. Describe how ionisation is achieved in a mass spectrometer. Give **three** reasons why ionisation is necessary. *(5 marks)*

AQA, 2006

3 (a) Give the relative charge and relative mass of an electron. *(2 marks)*

(b) Isotopes of chromium include ^{54}Cr and ^{52}Cr

(i) Give the number of protons present in an atom of ^{54}Cr

(ii) Deduce the number of neutrons present in an atom of ^{52}Cr

(iii) Apart from the relative mass of each isotope, what else would need to be known for the relative atomic mass of chromium to be calculated? *(3 marks)*

(c) In order to obtain a mass spectrum of a gaseous sample of chromium, the sample must first be ionised.

(i) Give **two** reasons why it is necessary to ionise the chromium atoms in the sample.

(ii) State what is adjusted so that each of the isotopes of chromium can be detected in turn.

(iii) Explain how the adjustment given in part (c)(ii) enables the isotopes of chromium to be separated. *(4 marks)*

AQA, 2003

4 (a) One isotope of sodium has a relative mass of 23.
   (i) Define, in terms of the fundamental particles present, the meaning of the term *isotopes*.
   (ii) Explain why isotopes of the same element have the same chemical properties. *(3 marks)*
   (b) Give the electronic configuration, showing all sub-levels, for a sodium atom. *(1 mark)*
   (c) Explain why chromium is placed in the d block in the periodic table. *(1 mark)*
   (d) An atom has half as many protons as an atom of ^{28}Si and also has six fewer neutrons than an atom of ^{28}Si. Give the symbol, including the mass number and the atomic number, of this atom. *(2 marks)*

AQA, 2004

5 The values of the first ionisation energies of neon, sodium and magnesium are 2080, 494 and 736 kJ mol^{-1}, respectively.
   (a) Explain the meaning of the term *first ionisation energy* of an atom. *(2 marks)*
   (b) Write an equation to illustrate the process occurring when the **second** ionisation energy of magnesium is measured. *(2 marks)*
   (c) Explain why the value of the first ionisation energy of magnesium is higher than that of sodium. *(2 marks)*
   (d) Explain why the value of the first ionisation energy of neon is higher than that of sodium. *(2 marks)*

AQA, 2004

6 A sample of iron from a meteorite was found to contain the isotopes ^{54}Fe, ^{56}Fe and ^{57}Fe.
   (a) The relative abundances of these isotopes can be determined using a mass spectrometer. In the mass spectrometer, the sample is first vaporised and then ionised.
      (i) State what is meant by the term *isotopes*.
      (ii) Explain how, in a mass spectrometer, ions are detected and how their abundance is measured. *(5 marks)*
   (b) (i) Define the term *relative atomic mass* of an element.
      (ii) The relative abundances of the isotopes in this sample of iron were found to be as follows.

m/z	54	56	57
Relative abundance (%)	5.8	91.6	2.6

Use the data above to calculate the relative atomic mass of iron in this sample. Give your answer to one decimal place. *(2 marks)*
   (c) (i) Give the electron arrangement of an Fe^{2+} ion.
      (ii) State why iron is placed in the d block of the periodic table.
      (iii) State the difference, if any, in the chemical properties of isotopes of the same element. Explain your answer. *(4 marks)*

AQA, 2005

2 Amount of substance

2.1 Relative atomic and molecular masses, the Avogadro constant and the mole

Learning objectives:

■ What is the definition of relative atomic mass?

■ What is the definition of relative molecular mass?

■ What does the Avogadro constant mean?

■ What do the same numbers of moles of different substances have in common?

■ How is the number of moles present in a given mass of an element or compound calculated?

Specification reference 3.1.2

■ Relative atomic mass, A_r

The actual mass in grams of any atom or molecule is too tiny to find by weighing. Instead, we compare the masses of atoms, and use *relative* masses.

This was done in the past by defining the relative atomic mass of hydrogen, the lightest element, as 1. The average mass of an atom of oxygen (for example) is sixteen times heavier, so oxygen has a relative atomic mass of 16. Scientists now use carbon-12 as the baseline for **relative atomic mass** because the mass spectrometer has allowed us to measure the masses of individual isotopes extremely accurately. One twelfth of the relative atomic mass of carbon-12 is given a value of *exactly* 1. The carbon-12 standard (defined below) is now accepted by all chemists throughout the world.

The relative atomic mass, A_r, is the weighted average mass of an atom of an element, taking into account its naturally occurring isotopes, relative to $\frac{1}{12}$th the relative atomic mass of an atom of carbon-12.

$$A_r = \frac{\text{average mass of one atom of an element}}{\frac{1}{12}\text{th mass of an atom of }^{12}C}$$

$$= \frac{\text{average mass of one atom of an element} \times 12}{\text{mass of an atom of }^{12}C}$$

💡 Relative molecular mass, M_r

We can handle molecules in the same way, by comparing the mass of a molecule with that of an atom of carbon-12.

The relative molecular mass, M_r, of a molecule is the mass of that molecule compared to $\frac{1}{12}$th the relative atomic mass of an atom of carbon-12.

$$M_r = \frac{\text{average mass of one molecule}}{\frac{1}{12}\text{th mass of an atom of }^{12}C}$$

$$= \frac{\text{average mass of one molecule} \times 12}{\text{mass of an atom of }^{12}C}$$

We find the **relative molecular mass** by adding up the relative atomic masses of all the atoms present in the molecule and we find this from the formula.

Table 1 shows some examples.

■ Hint

The weighted average mass must be used to allow for the presence of isotopes, using their percentage abundances in calculations.

AQA Examiner's tip

You need to learn the exact definitions of A_r and M_r.

Table 1 *Examples of relative molecular mass*

Molecule	Formula	A_r of atoms	M
water	H_2O	$(2 \times 1.0) + 16.0$	18.0
carbon dioxide	CO_2	$12.0 + (2 \times 16.0)$	44.0
methane	CH_4	$12.0 + (4 \times 1.0)$	16.0

Relative formula mass

We use the term **relative formula mass** for ionic compounds because they don't exist as molecules. However, we use the same symbol, M_r.

Here are some examples.

Ionic compound	Formula	A_r of atoms	M_r
calcium chloride	CaF_2	$40.1 + (2 \times 19.0)$	78.1
sodium sulfate	Na_2SO_4	$(2 \times 23.0) + 32.1 + (4 \times 16.0)$	142.1
magnesium nitrate	$Mg(NO_3)_2$	$24.3 + (2 \times (14.0 + (16.0 \times 3)))$	148.3

The Avogadro constant and the mole

One atom of any element is too small to see with an optical microscope and impossible to weigh individually. So, to count atoms, chemists must weigh large numbers of them. This is how cashiers count money in a bank.

Working to the nearest whole number, a helium atom $(A_r = 4)$ is four times heavier than an atom of hydrogen. A lithium atom $(A_r = 7)$ is seven times heavier than an atom of hydrogen. To get the same number of atoms in a sample of helium or lithium, as the number of atoms in 1 gram of hydrogen, we must take 4 grams of helium or 7 grams of lithium.

In fact if we weigh out the relative atomic mass of *any* element, this amount will also contain this same number of atoms.

The same logic applies to molecules. Water, H_2O, has a relative molecular mass, M_r, of 18. So, one molecule of water is 18 times heavier than one atom of hydrogen. Therefore, 18 g of water contains the same number of *molecules* as there are *atoms* in 1 g of hydrogen. A molecule of carbon dioxide is 44 times heavier than an atom of hydrogen, so 44 g of carbon dioxide contains this same number of molecules.

If we weigh out the relative or formula mass M_r of a compound in grams we have *this same number* of entities.

The Avogadro constant

The actual number of atoms in 1 g of hydrogen atoms is unimaginably huge:

602 200 000 000 000 000 000 000 usually written 6.022×10^{23}.

The difference between this scale, based on H = 1 and the scale used today based on ^{12}C, is negligible.

> **The definition of the Avogadro constant or Avogadro number is the number of atoms in 12 g of carbon-12.**

The mole

The amount of substance that contains 6.022×10^{23} particles is called a **mole**.

Hint

The word entity is a general word for a particle. It can refer to an atom, molecule, ion and even an electron. It also refers to the simplest formula unit of a giant ionic structure, such as sodium chloride, NaCl, or magnesium oxide, MgO.

Hint

Note that this is the same as the number of **atoms** in 1 g of hydrogen, H_2, not the number of hydrogen **molecules**.

350 g   700 g

Figure 1 *Large numbers of coins or bank notes are counted by weighing them*

■ Hint

We can also use the term **molar mass**, which is the mass per mole of substance. It has units $kg\,mol^{-1}$ or $g\,mol^{-1}$. The molar mass in $g\,mol^{-1}$ is the same numerically as M_r.

The relative atomic mass of any element in grams contains one mole of atoms.

The relative molecular mass (or relative formula mass) of a substance in grams contains one mole of **entities**.

We can also have a mole of ions or electrons.

It is easy to confuse moles of *atoms* and moles of *molecules*, so always give the formula when working out the mass of a mole of entities. For example, 10 moles of hydrogen could mean 10 moles of hydrogen atoms, H, or 10 moles of hydrogen molecules, H_2, which contains twice the number of atoms.

Using the mole, we can compare the *numbers* of different particles that take part in chemical reactions.

Table 2 *Examples of moles*

Entities	Formula	Relative mass to nearest whole number	Mass of a mole / g = molar mass
oxygen atoms	O	16.0	16.0
oxygen molecules	O_2	32.0	32.0
sodium ions	Na^+	23.0	23.0
sodium fluoride	NaF	42.0	42.0

🔋 Number of moles

If we want to find out how many moles are present in a particular mass of a substance we need to know the substance's formula. From the formula we can then work out the mass of one mole of the substance.

We use:

$$\text{Number of moles} = \frac{\text{mass in g}}{\text{mass of 1 mole in g}}$$

Worked example:

How many moles of atoms are there in 64.2 g of sulfur, S? (A_r S = 32.1, so 1 mole of sulfur has a mass of 32.1 g)

$$\text{Number of moles} = \frac{64.2}{32.1} = 2.00\,mol$$

Worked example:

How many moles are there in 0.53 g of sodium carbonate, Na_2CO_3? (A_r Na = 23.0, A_r C = 12.0, A_r O = 16.0, so M_r of Na_2CO_3 = $(23.0 \times 2) + 12.0 + (16.0 \times 3) = 106.0$, so 1 mole of calcium carbonate has a mass of 106.0 g)

$$\text{Number of moles} = \frac{0.53}{106.0} = 0.0050\,mol$$

Worked example:

You have 3.94 g of gold, Au, and 2.70 g of aluminium, Al. Which contains the greater number of atoms? (A_r Au = 197.0, A_r Al = 27.0)

$$\text{Number of moles of gold} = \frac{3.94}{197.0} = 0.0200\,mol$$

$$\text{Number of moles of aluminium} = \frac{2.70}{27.0} = 0.100\,mol$$

There are more atoms of aluminium.

■ Summary questions

1. Work out the M_r for each of the following compounds.

   a CH_4 b Na_2CO_3

   c $Mg(OH)_2$ d $(NH_4)_2SO_4$

   Use these values for the relative atomic masses (A_r): C = 12.0, H = 1.0, Na = 23.0, O = 16.0, Mg = 24.3, N = 14.0, S = 32.0

2. Imagine an 'atomic seesaw' with an oxygen atom on one side. Find six combinations of other atoms that would make the seesaw balance. For example, one sodium atom and one hydrogen atom would balance the seesaw.

3. Use the periodic table to find the element for which the mass of a mole is

   a 79.0 g

   b 9.0 g

   c 45.0 g.

4. How many moles of the specified entities are there in each of the following?

   a 32.0 g CH_4

   b 5.30 g Na_2CO_3

   c 5.83 g $Mg(OH)_2$

5. Which contains the fewest molecules? 0.5 g of hydrogen, H_2, 4.0 g of oxygen, O_2, or 11.0 g of carbon dioxide, CO_2

6. Which of the quantities in question 5 contains the greatest number of atoms?

2.2 The ideal gas equation

- What is the ideal gas equation?
- How is it used to calculate the number of moles of a gas at a given volume, temperature and pressure?

Specification reference 3.1.2

Figure 1 *The German airship Hindenburg held about 210 000 m³ of hydrogen gas*

How science works

Robert Boyle

Robert Boyle, an Irish-born scientist, put forward the relationship between pressure and volume in 1660. He is often considered to be the father of modern chemistry. He was noted for keeping accurate experimental logs.

How science works

Jacques Charles

Jacques Charles, 1746–1823, a French scientist, discovered how the temperature and volume of gases are related. He was also the first to make an ascent in a hydrogen balloon.

How science works

Joseph Gay-Lussac

Joseph Gay-Lussac, 1788–1850, another Frenchman, recognised the relationship between the pressure and temperature of gases. He also did important work on combining volumes of gases.

The Hindenburg airship was originally designed in the 1930s to use helium as its lifting gas, rather than hydrogen, but the only source of large volumes of helium was the USA and they refused to sell it to Germany because of Hitler's aggressive policies. It held about 210 000 m³ of hydrogen gas but this volume varied with temperature and pressure.

The volume of a given mass of any gas is not fixed. It changes with pressure and temperature. However, there are a number of simple relationships that connect the pressure, temperature and volume of a gas.

For any given mass of gas:

Boyle's law

The product of pressure and volume is a constant as long as the temperature remains constant.

$$PV = \text{constant}$$

Charles' law

The volume is proportional to the temperature as long as the pressure remains constant.

$$V \propto T \quad \text{and} \quad \frac{V}{T} = \text{constant}$$

Gay-Lussac's law (also called the constant volume law)

The pressure is proportional to the temperature as long as the volume remains constant.

$$P \propto T \quad \text{and} \quad \frac{P}{T} = \text{constant}$$

Combining these relationships gives us the equation:

$$\frac{PV}{T} = \text{constant for a fixed mass of gas}$$

💡 The ideal gas equation

If we take one mole of gas, the constant is given the symbol R and is called the gas constant. For n moles of gas we have:

$$PV = nRT$$

The value of R is $8.31\,\mathrm{J\,K^{-1}\,mol^{-1}}$.

This is called the ideal gas equation. No gases obey it exactly, but at room temperature and pressure it holds quite well for many gases. It is often useful to imagine a gas which obeys the equation perfectly – an ideal gas.

Notes on units

When using the ideal gas equation, consistent units must be used. If you want to calculate n, the number of moles:

P must be in Pa $(\mathrm{N\,m^{-2}})$

How science works

SI units

The units used here are part of the Système Internationale (SI) of units. This is a system of units for measurements used by scientists throughout the world. The basic units used by chemists are: metre, second, Kelvin and kilogram.

Hint

To convert °C to K add 273.

V must be in m^3

T must be in K

R must be in J K^{-1} mol^{-1}

💡 Using the ideal gas equation

Using the ideal gas equation, we can calculate the volume of one mole of gas at any temperature and pressure. Since none of the terms of the equation refers to a particular gas, this volume will be the same for any gas.

This may seem very unlikely at first sight, but it is the space between the gas molecules that accounts for the volume of a gas. Even the largest gas particle is extremely small compared with the space in between the particles.

Rearranging the ideal gas equation to find a volume gives:

$$V = \frac{nRT}{P}$$

Worked example:

If the temperature = 20.0 °C (293.0 K), pressure = 100 000 Pa, and $n = 1$ for one mole of gas,

$$V = \frac{8.31\,J\,K^{-1}\,mol^{-1} \times 293\,K}{100\,000\,Pa}$$

$$= 0.0243\,m^{-3} = 0.0243 \times 10^6\,cm^3 = 24\,300\,cm^3$$

This tells us that the volume of a mole of *any* gas at room temperature and pressure is approximately $24\,000\,cm^3$ ($24\,dm^3$). For example, one mole of sulfur dioxide gas, SO_2 (mass 64.1 g) has the same volume as one mole of hydrogen gas, H_2 (mass 2.0 g).

In a similar way, pressure can be found using $P = \dfrac{nRT}{V}$

Finding the number of moles, n, of a gas

If we rearrange the equation

$PV = nRT$ so that n is on the left-hand side, we get:

$$n = \frac{PV}{RT}$$

If we know T, P and V then we can find n, the number of moles.

 Examiner's tip

Using 24 000 cm^3 as the volume of a mole of any gas is not precise and it is always necessary to apply the ideal gas equation in calculations in the exam.

Worked example:

How many moles of hydrogen are present in a volume of 100 cm^3 at a temperature of 20.0 °C and a pressure of 100 kPa? $R = 8.31\,J\,K^{-1}\,mol^{-1}$

First, convert to the base units:

P must be in Pa , and 100 kPa = 100 000 Pa

V must be in m^3, and 100 cm^3 = 100 × 10^{-6} m^3

T must be in K, and 20 °C = 293 K (add 273 to the temperature in °C)

Substituting into the ideal gas equation:

$$n = \frac{PV}{RT}$$

$$= \frac{100\,000 \times 100 \times 10^{-6}}{8.31 \times 293}$$

$$= 0.00411 \text{ moles}$$

Finding the relative molecular mass of a gas.

If we know the number of moles present in a given mass of gas, we can find the mass of one mole of gas, and this tells us the relative molecular mass.

Applications and How science works

Finding the relative molecular mass of lighter fuel.

The apparatus used to find the relative molecular mass of lighter fuel is shown in Figure 2.

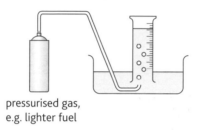

pressurised gas,
e.g. lighter fuel

Figure 2 *Measuring the relative molecular mass for lighter fuel*

The lighter fuel canister was weighed.

$1000\,\text{cm}^3$ of gas was dispensed into the measuring cylinder, keeping the levels of the water inside and outside the measuring cylinder the same, so that the pressure of the collected gas was the same as atmospheric pressure.

The canister was reweighed.

Atmospheric pressure and temperature were noted.

These were the results:

Loss of mass of the can $= 2.29\,\text{g}$

Temperature $= 14\,°C = 287\,K$

Atmospheric pressure $= 100\,000\,\text{Pa}$

Volume of gas $= 1000\,\text{cm}^3 = 1000 \times 10^{-6}\,\text{m}^3$

$$n = \frac{PV}{RT}$$

$$n = \frac{100\,000 \times 1000 \times 10^{-6}}{8.31 \times 287}$$

$$n = 0.042\,\text{mol}$$

0.042 mol has a mass of 2.29 g

So, 1 mol has a mass of $\frac{2.29}{0.042\,\text{g}} = 54.5\,\text{g}$

So, $M_r = 55$ (to 2 s.f.)

Summary questions

1 a How many moles of H_2 molecules were contained in the Hindenburg airship at 298 K?

b The original design proposed using helium, He. How many moles of helium atoms would it have contained?

2 Use the ideal gas equation to find the following.

a The volume of 2 moles of a gas if the temperature is 30 °C, and the pressure is 100 000 Pa

b The pressure of 0.5 moles of a gas if the volume is 11 000 cm³, and the temperature is 25 °C

3 How many moles of hydrogen are present in a volume of 48 000 cm³, at 100 000 Pa and 25 °C?

4 How many moles of carbon dioxide would be present in question **3**? Explain your answer.

2.3 Empirical and molecular formulae

Learning objectives:

- What are the definitions of empirical formula and molecular formula?

- How is an empirical formula worked out from the masses or percentage masses of the elements present in a compound?

- What additional information is needed to work out a molecular formula from an empirical formula?

Specification reference 3.1.2

Hint

If we work in grams, the mass of 1 mole in grams is the same as the relative atomic mass of the element.

The empirical formula

The **empirical formula** is the formula that represents the simplest ratio of the atoms of each element present in a compound. For example, the empirical formula of carbon dioxide, CO_2, tells us that for every carbon atom there two oxygen atoms.

To find an empirical formula:

1 Find the masses of each of the elements present in a compound (by experiment).

2 Work out the number of moles of atoms of each element.

Use: number of moles $= \dfrac{\text{mass of element}}{\text{mass of 1 mol of element}}$

3 Convert the number of moles of each element into a whole number ratio.

Worked example:

> 10.01 g of a white solid contains 4.01 g of calcium, 1.20 g of carbon and 4.80 g of oxygen. What is its empirical formula?
>
> (A_r Ca = 40.1, A_r C = 12.0, A_r O = 16.0)
>
> 1 Find the masses of each element.
>
> Mass of calcium = 4.01 g
> Mass of carbon = 1.20 g
> Mass of oxygen = 4.80 g
>
> 2 Find the number of moles of atoms of each element.
>
> A_r Ca = 40.1
>
> Number of moles of calcium $= \dfrac{4.01}{40.1} = 0.10$ mol
>
> A_r C = 12.0
>
> Number of moles of carbon $= \dfrac{12.0}{12.0} = 0.10$ mol
>
> A_r O = 16
>
> Number of moles of oxygen $= \dfrac{4.8}{16.0} = 0.30$ mol
>
> 3 Find the simplest ratio.
>
> | Ratio in moles of | calcium : carbon : oxygen |
> |---|---|
> | | 0.10 : 0.10 : 0.30 |
> | So the simplest whole number ratio is: | 1 : 1 : 3 |
>
> The formula is therefore $CaCO_3$. (This is calcium carbonate.)

Applications and How science works

Finding the empirical formula of copper oxide

0.795 g of black copper oxide is reduced to 0.635 g of copper when heated in a stream of hydrogen. What is the formula of copper oxide? A_r Cu = 63.5, A_r O = 16.0

1 Find the masses of each element.

    Mass of copper = 0.635 g

We started with 0.795 g of copper oxide and 0.635 g of copper were left, so:

    Mass of oxygen = 0.795 − 0.635 = 0.160 g

2 Find the number of moles of atoms of each element.

    A_r Cu = 63.5

    Number of moles of copper $= \dfrac{0.635}{63.5} = 0.01$

    A_r O = 16.0

    Number of moles of oxygen $= \dfrac{0.16}{16.0} = 0.01$

3 Find the simplest ratio.

    The ratio of moles of copper to moles of oxygen is:

        copper : oxygen

        0.01 : 0.01

    So the simplest whole number ratio is 1 : 1

The simplest formula of copper oxide is therefore one Cu to one O, CuO.

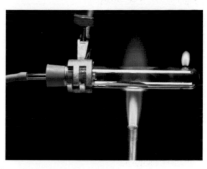

Figure 1 *Finding the empirical formula of copper oxide*

	Copper, Cu	Oxygen, O
Mass of element	0.635 g	0.160 g
A_r of element	63.5	16.0
Number of moles $= \dfrac{\text{mass of element}}{A_r}$	$\dfrac{0.635}{63.5} = 0.01$	$\dfrac{0.160}{16.0} = 0.01$
Ratio of elements	1	1

Hint

You may find it easier to make a table like this one:

Finding the simplest ratio of elements

Sometimes you will end up with ratios of moles of atoms of elements that are not easy to convert to whole numbers. If you divide each number by the smallest number you will end up with whole numbers (or ratios you can recognise easily). Here is an example.

Worked example:

Compound X contains 50.2 g sulfur and 50.0 g oxygen. What is its empirical formula? A_r S = 32.1, A_r O = 16.0

1 Find the mass of each element.

    Mass of sulfur = 50.2 g
    Mass of oxygen = 50.0 g

2 Find the number of moles of atoms of each element.

    A_r S = 32.1

    Number of moles of sulfur $= \dfrac{50.2}{32.1} = 1.564$

    A_r O = 16

    Number of moles of oxygen $= \dfrac{50.0}{16.0} = 3.125$

3 Find the simplest ratio.

Ratio of sulfur : oxygen

1.564 : 3.125

Now divide each of the numbers by the smaller number.

Ratio of sulfur : oxygen

$$\frac{1.564}{1.564} : \frac{3.125}{1.564}$$

1 : 2

= 1 : 2

The empirical formula is therefore SO_2. (This is sulfur dioxide.)

💡 Finding the molecular formula

The **molecular formula** gives the actual number of atoms of each element in one molecule of the compound. (It applies only to substances that exist as molecules.)

The empirical formula is not always the same as the molecular formula. There may be several units of the empirical formula in the molecular formula.

For example, ethane (molecular formula C_2H_6) would have an empirical formula of CH_3.

> To find the number of units of the empirical formula in the molecular formula, divide the relative molecular mass by the relative mass of the empirical formula.

For example, ethene is found to have a relative molecular mass of 28.0 but its empirical formula, CH_2, has a relative mass of 14.0.

$$\frac{\text{Relative molecular mass of ethene}}{\text{Relative mass of empirical formula of ethene}} = \frac{28.0}{14.0} = 2$$

So there must be two units of the empirical formula in the molecule of ethene. So ethene is $(CH_2)_2$ or C_2H_4.

Worked example:

An organic compound containing only carbon, hydrogen and oxygen was found to have 52.17% carbon and 13.04% hydrogen. What is its molecular formula if $M_r = 46.0$?

100 g of this compound would contain 52.17 g carbon, 13.04 g hydrogen and (the rest) 34.79 g oxygen

Step 1: Find the empirical formula:

	Carbon	Hydrogen	Oxygen
Mass of element/g	52.17	13.04	34.79 g
A_r of element	12.0	1.0	16.0
Number of moles = $\dfrac{\text{mass of element}}{A_r}$	$\dfrac{52.17}{12.0} = 4.348$	$\dfrac{13.04}{10.0} = 13.04$	$\dfrac{34.79}{16.0} = 2.174$
Divide through by the smallest (2.174)	$\dfrac{4.348}{2.174} = 2$	$\dfrac{13.04}{2.174} = 6$	$\dfrac{2.174}{2.174} = 1$
Ratio of elements	2	6	1

AQA Examiner's tip

■ When calculating empirical formulae from percentages, check that all the percentages of the compositions by mass add up to 100%. (Don't forget any oxygen that may be present.)

■ Remember to use relative atomic masses from the periodic table, not the atomic number.

So the empirical formula is C_2H_6O.

Step 2: Find M_r of the empirical formula.

$(2 \times 12.0) + (6 \times 1.0) + (1 \times 16.0) = 46.0$

     C   H   O

So, the molecular formula is the same as the empirical formula, C_2H_6O.

💡 Combustion analysis

Organic compounds are based on carbon and hydrogen. The basic method for finding empirical formulae of new compounds is called combustion analysis. It is used routinely in the pharmaceutical industry. It involves burning the unknown compound in excess oxygen and measuring the amounts of water, carbon dioxide and other oxides that are produced.

The basic method measures carbon, hydrogen, sulfur and nitrogen. We assume oxygen makes up the difference after the other four elements have been measured. Once the sample has been weighed and placed in the instrument, the process is automatic and controlled by computer.

The sample is burned completely in a stream of oxygen. The final combustion products are water, carbon dioxide, sulfur dioxide. The instrument measures the amounts of these by infra-red absorption. They are removed from the gas stream to leave the unreacted nitrogen which is measured by thermal conductivity. The measurements are used to calculate the masses of each gas present and hence the masses of hydrogen, sulfur, carbon and nitrogen in the original sample. Oxygen is found by difference.

Traditionally, the amounts of water and carbon dioxide were measured by absorbing them in suitable chemicals and measuring the increase in mass of the absorbents.

From the masses of the combustion products the empirical formula can be found as shown in the example below. The molecular formula can then be found, if the relative molecular mass has been found using a mass spectrometer.

Worked example:

0.23 g of a compound X containing only carbon, hydrogen and oxygen, gave 0.44 g of carbon dioxide and 0.27 g of water on complete combustion in oxygen. What is its empirical formula? What is its molecular formula if its relative molecular mass is 46?

To calculate the empirical formula:

Carbon   0.44 g of CO_2 ($M_r = 44.0$) is $\dfrac{0.44}{44.0} = 0.01\,mol\ CO_2$

As each mole of CO_2 has 1 mole of C, the sample contained 0.01 mol of C atoms.

Hydrogen   0.27 g of H_2O ($M_r = 18.0$) is $\dfrac{0.27}{18.0} = 0.015\,mol\ H_2O$

As each mole of H_2O has 2 moles of H, the sample contained 0.03 mol of H atoms.

Oxygen   0.01 mol of carbon atoms ($A_r = 12.0$) has a mass of 0.12 g

0.03 mol of hydrogen atoms ($A_r = 1.0$) has a mass of 0.03 g

Total mass of carbon and hydrogen is 0.15 g

The rest (0.23 – 0.15) must be oxygen, so the sample contained 0.08 g of oxygen.

0.08 g of oxygen ($A_r = 16.0$) is $\dfrac{0.08}{16.0} = 0.005$ mol oxygen atoms

Formula

So the sample contains   0.01 mol C

0.03 mol H

0.005 mol O

Dividing through by the smallest number (0.005) gives the ratio:

C	H	O
2	6	1

so the **empirical formula** is C_2H_6O.

M_r of this unit is 46, so the molecular formula is also C_2H_6O.

Summary questions

1 What is the empirical formula of each of the following compounds? (You could try to name them too.)

  a A liquid containing 2.0 g of hydrogen, 32.1 g sulfur, and 64.0 g oxygen

  b A white solid containing 4.0 g calcium, 3.2 g oxygen, 0.2 g hydrogen

  c A white solid containing 0.243 g magnesium and 0.710 g chlorine.

2 3.888 g magnesium ribbon was burnt completely in air and 6.448 g of magnesium oxide were produced.

  a How many moles of magnesium and oxygen are present in 6.488 g of magnesium oxide?

  b What is the empirical formula of magnesium oxide?

3 What is the empirical formula of each of the following molecules?

  a Cyclohexane C_6H_{12}

  b Dichloroethene $C_2H_2Cl_2$

  c Benzene C_6H_6

4 M_r for ethane-1,2-diol is 62.0. It is composed of carbon, hydrogen and oxygen in the ratio by moles of 1 : 3 : 1.

  What is its molecular formula?

5 An organic compound containing only carbon, hydrogen and oxygen was found to have 62.07% carbon and 10.33% hydrogen. What is its molecular formula if $M_r = 58.0$?

6 A sample of benzene of mass 7.8 g contains 7.2 g of carbon and 0.6 g of hydrogen. If M_r is 78.0, work out:

  a the empirical formula

  b the molecular formula.

2.4 Moles in solutions

Learning objectives:

■ How is the number of moles of substance calculated from the volume of a solution and its concentration?

Specification reference 3.1.2

A solution consists of a solvent with a solute dissolved in it, see Figure 1.

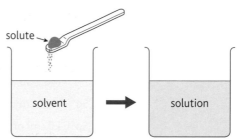

Figure 1 *A solution contains a solute and a solvent*

■ **How science works**

Making a 1 mol dm⁻³ solution

To get a solution with a concentration of 1 mol dm⁻³ you have to add the solvent to the solute until you have 1 dm³ of solution. You **do not** add 1 mol of solute to 1 dm³ of solvent. This would give more than 1 dm³ of solution.

■ **Hint**

1 decimetre = 10 cm, so one cubic decimetre, 1 dm³, is 10 cm × 10 cm × 10 cm = 1000 cm³. This is the same as 1 litre (1 l or 1 L).

The small negative in mol dm⁻³ means 'per' and is sometimes written as a slash, mol/dm³.

The units of concentration

The concentration of a solution tells us how much solute is present in a known volume of solution.

■ Concentrations of solutions are measured in the unit moles per cubic decimetre, mol dm⁻³.
■ 1 mol dm⁻³ means there is 1 mole of solute per cubic decimetre of solution; 2 mol dm⁻³ means there are 2 moles of solute per cubic decimetre of solution and so on.

Finding the concentration in mol dm⁻³

For example, 1.17 g of sodium chloride was dissolved in water to make 500 cm³ of solution.

What is the concentration in mol dm⁻³? A_r Na = 23.0, A_r Cl = 35.5

The mass of 1 mole of sodium chloride, NaCl, is 23.0 + 35.5 = 58.5 g.

$$\text{Number of moles} = \frac{\text{mass in g}}{\text{mass of 1 mol in g}}$$

So 1.17 g of NaCl contains $\frac{1.17}{58.5}$ mol = 0.0200 mol

This is dissolved in 500 cm³, so 1000 cm³ (1 dm³) would contain 0.0400 mol of NaCl. This means that the concentration is 0.0400 mol dm⁻³.

A more general way of finding a concentration is to remember the relationship:

$$\text{Concentration} = \frac{\text{number of moles}}{\text{volume in dm}^3}$$

Substituting into this gives:

$$\text{Concentration} = \frac{0.0200}{0.500} = 0.0400 \text{ mol dm}^{-3}$$

💡 The number of moles in a given volume of solution

You often have to work out how many moles are present in a particular volume of a solution of known concentration. The general formula for the number of moles in a solution of concentration M mol dm⁻³ and volume V cm³ is:

$$\text{Number of moles in solution, } n = \frac{M \times V}{1000}$$

Here is an example of how we reach this formula in steps.

Worked example:

How many moles are present in 25.0 cm^3 of a solution of concentration 0.10 mol dm^{-3}?

From the definition,

1000 cm^3 of a solution of 1.00 mol dm^{-3} contains 1 mol

So 1000 cm^3 of a solution of 0.100 mol dm^{-3} contains 0.100 mol

So 1.0 cm^3 of a solution of 0.100 mol dm^{-3} contains $\frac{0.10}{1000}$ mol = 0.00010 mol

So 25.0 cm^3 of a solution of 0.10 mol dm^{-3} contains 25.0 × 0.00010 = 0.0025 mol

Using the formula gives the same answer:

$$\text{Number of moles in solution } = \frac{M \times V}{1000}$$

$$= \frac{0.10 \times 250}{1000} = 0.0025$$

How science works

Error in measurements

Every measurement has an inherent uncertainty (also known as error). In general, the uncertainty in a single measurement from an instrument is *half the value of the smallest division*. Find out more about errors in measurements online.

Summary questions

1 What is the concentration in mol dm^{-3} of the following?

a 0.500 mol acid in 500 cm^3 of solution

b 0.250 mol acid in 2000 cm^3 of solution

c 0.200 mol solute in 20 cm^3 of solution

2 How many moles of solute are there in the following?

a 20.0 cm^3 of a 0.100 mol dm^{-3} solution

b 50.0 cm^3 of a 0.500 mol dm^{-3} solution

c 25.0 cm^3 of a 2.00 mol dm^{-3} solution

3 0.234 g of sodium chloride was dissolved in water to make 250 cm^3 of solution.

a What is M_r for NaCl? A_r Na = 23.0, A_r Cl = 35.5

b How many moles of NaCl is 0.234 g?

c What is the concentration in mol dm^{-3}?

2.5 Balanced equations and related calculations

Learning objectives:

■ How can an equation be balanced if the reactants and products are known?

■ How can the amount of a product be calculated using experimental data and a balanced equation?

Specification reference 3.1.2

Equations represent what happens when chemical reactions take place. They are based on experimental evidence. The starting materials are reactants. After these have reacted we end up with products.

$$\text{reactants} \longrightarrow \text{products}$$

Word equations only give the names of the reactants and products, for example:

$$\text{hydrogen} + \text{oxygen} \longrightarrow \text{water}$$

Once the idea of atoms had been established, chemists realised that atoms react together in simple whole number ratios. For example, two hydrogen molecules react with one oxygen molecule to give two water molecules.

$$\text{2 hydrogen molecules} + \text{1 oxygen molecule} \longrightarrow \text{2 water molecules}$$
$$2 \quad : \quad 1 \quad : \quad 2$$

The ratio in which the reactants react and the products are produced, in simple whole numbers, is called the **stoichiometry** of the reaction.

We can build up a stoichiometric relationship from experimental data by working out the number of moles that react together. This leads us to a balanced symbol equation.

Balanced symbol equations

Balanced symbol equations use the formulae of reactants and products. There are the same number of atoms of each element on both sides of the arrow. (This is because atoms are never created or destroyed in chemical reactions.) Balanced equations tell us about the **amounts** of substances that react together and are produced.

State symbols can also be added. These are letters, in brackets, which can be added to the formulae in equations to say what state the reactants and products are in: (s) means solid; (l) means liquid; (g) means gas; (aq) means aqueous solution (dissolved in water).

Writing balanced equations

When aluminium burns in oxygen it forms solid aluminium oxide. We can build up a balanced symbol equation from this and the formulae of the reactants and product: Al, O_2 and Al_2O_3.

1 Write the word equation

$$\text{aluminium} + \text{oxygen} \longrightarrow \text{aluminium oxide}$$

2 Write in the correct formulae

$$Al + O_2 \longrightarrow Al_2O_3$$

This is not balanced because:

■ there is one aluminium atom on the reactants side (left-hand side) but two on the products side (right-hand side)

■ there are two oxygen atoms on the reactants side (left-hand side) but three on the products side (right-hand side).

3 To get two aluminium atoms on the left-hand side put a 2 in front of the Al:

$$2Al \quad + \quad O_2 \quad \longrightarrow \quad Al_2O_3$$

Now the aluminium is correct but not the oxygen.

4 If we multiply the oxygen on the left-hand side by 3, and the aluminium oxide by 2, we have six Os on each side:

$$2Al \quad + \quad 3O_2 \quad \longrightarrow \quad 2Al_2O_3$$

5 Now we return to the aluminium. We need four Al on the left-hand side:

$$4Al \quad + \quad 3O_2 \quad \longrightarrow \quad 2Al_2O_3$$

The equation is balanced because there are the same numbers of atoms of each element on both sides of the equation.

The numbers in front of the formulae (4, 3 and 2) are called coefficients.

6 We can add state symbols.

The equation tells us the numbers of moles of each of the substances that are involved. From this we can work out the masses that will react together: (using Al = 27.0, O = 16.0)

$$4Al(s) \quad + \quad 3O_2(g) \quad \longrightarrow \quad 2Al_2O_3(s)$$

| 4 moles | 3 moles | 2 moles |
| 108.0 g | 96.0 g | 204.0 g |

The total mass is the same on both sides of the equation. This is another good way of checking whether the equation is balanced.

Ionic equations

In some reactions we can simplify the equation by considering the ions present. Sometimes there are ions that do not take part in the overall reaction. For example, when any acid reacts with an alkali in solution, we end up with a salt (also in solution) and water. Look at the reaction between hydrochloric acid and sodium hydroxide:

$$HCl(aq) \quad + \quad NaOH(aq) \quad \longrightarrow \quad NaCl(aq) \quad + \; H_2O(l)$$

hydrochloric acid $\quad$ + $\quad$ sodium hydroxide $\quad \longrightarrow \quad$ sodium chloride $\quad$ + $\quad$ water

The ions present are:

$HCl(aq)$: $\qquad$ $H^+(aq)$ and $Cl^-(aq)$

$NaOH(aq)$: $\qquad$ $Na^+(aq)$ and $OH^-(aq)$

$NaCl(aq)$: $\qquad$ $Na^+(aq)$ and $Cl^-(aq)$

If we write the equation using these ions and then strike out the ions that appear on each side we have:

$H^+(aq) + \cancel{Cl^-(aq)} + \cancel{Na^+(aq)} + OH^-(aq) \longrightarrow \cancel{Na^+(aq)} + \cancel{Cl^-(aq)} + H_2O(l)$

Overall, the equation is

$$H^+(aq) + OH^-(aq) \longrightarrow H_2O(l)$$

$Na^+(aq)$ and $Cl^-(aq)$ are called spectator ions; they do not take part in the reaction.

Whenever an acid reacts with an alkali, the overall reaction will be the same as the one above.

Useful tips for balancing equations

■ You **must** use the correct formulae; you cannot change them to make the equation balance.

■ You can only change the numbers of atoms by putting a number, called a coefficient, in front of formulae.

■ The coefficient in front of the symbol tells you how many moles of that substance are reacting.

■ It often takes more than one step to balance an equation, but too many steps suggests that you may have an incorrect formula.

■ When dealing with ionic equations the total of the charges on each side must be the same.

■ Working out amounts

We can use a balanced symbol equation to work out how much product is produced from a reaction. For example, the reaction between magnesium and hydrochloric acid produces hydrogen gas, see Figure 1.

Worked example:

How much gas is produced by 0.12 g of magnesium ribbon and excess hydrochloric acid at 298 K (25 °C) and 100 kPa pressure? A_r Mg = 24.3, A_r H = 1.0, A_r Cl = 35.5

(The word **excess** means there is more than enough acid to react with all the magnesium.)

First write the balanced symbol equation.

1 Write the correct formulae.

$$Mg(s) \quad + \quad HCl(aq) \quad \longrightarrow \quad MgCl_2(aq) \quad + \quad H_2(g)$$

magnesium + hydrochloric acid ⟶ magnesium chloride + hydrogen

2 Balance the equation. The number of Mg atoms is correct. There are two Cl atoms and two H atoms on the right-hand side so we need to add a 2 in front of the HCl.

$$Mg(s) \quad + \quad 2HCl(aq) \quad \longrightarrow \quad MgCl_2(aq) \quad + \quad H_2(g)$$

Now find the numbers of moles that react:

$$Mg(s) \quad + \quad 2HCl(aq) \quad \longrightarrow \quad MgCl_2(aq) \quad + \quad H_2(g)$$

1 mol   2 mol   1 mol   1 mol

1 mol of Mg has a mass of 24.3 g because its A_r = 24.3.

So, 0.12 g of Mg is $\dfrac{0.12}{24.3}$ = 0.0050 mol.

From the equation, we can see that 1 mol of magnesium reacts to give 1 mol of hydrogen gas.

Therefore, 0.0050 mol of Mg produces 0.0050 mol H_2.

Next find the volume of 0.0050 mol of gas from the ideal gas equation, using R = 8.31 J K^{-1} mol^{-1} and T = 298 K:

$$V = \frac{nRT}{P} = 0.0050 \times 8.31 \times \frac{298}{100\,000}$$

$$= 0.000124 \, m^3$$

$$= 124 \, cm^3$$

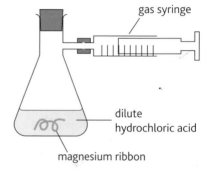

gas syringe

dilute hydrochloric acid

magnesium ribbon

■ **Figure 1** *Apparatus for collecting hydrogen gas*

■ **Hint**

To convert m³ to cm³, multiply by 10⁶

AQA **Examiner's tip**

Remember to use the correct units, see Topic 2.3.

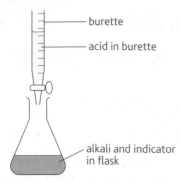

burette

acid in burette

alkali and indicator in flask

Figure 2 *Apparatus for a titration*

Summary questions

1 **a** Balance the following equations:

   i $Mg + O_2 \longrightarrow MgO$

   ii $Ca(OH)_2 + HCl \longrightarrow CaCl_2 + H_2O$

   iii $Na_2O + HNO_3 \longrightarrow NaNO_3 + H_2O$

   b Under each of the balanced equations, write down the number of moles of each reactant and product that take part in the reaction.

2 Deduce the concentration of hydrochloric acid if 20.0 cm³ is neutralised by 25.0 cm³ of sodium hydroxide of concentration 0.200 mol dm⁻³.

3 In the reaction
   $Mg(s) + 2HCl(aq) \longrightarrow MgCl_2(aq) + H_2$

   2.60 g of magnesium was added to 100 cm³ of 1.00 mol dm⁻³ hydrochloric acid.

   a Would there be any magnesium left when the reaction finished? Explain your answer.

   b Calculate the volume of hydrogen produced at 25 °C and 100 kPa.

4 **a** Write the balanced symbol equation for the reaction between sulfuric acid and sodium hydroxide

   i   in full

   ii in terms of ions.

   b What are the spectator ions in this reaction?

   c What is the overall reaction?

🛈 💡 🔬 Finding concentrations using titrations

We often carry out a titration to find the concentration of a solution, for example an alkali. We react the acid with an alkali using a suitable indicator.

We need to know:

- the concentration of the acid
- the equation for the reaction between the acid and alkali.

The apparatus is shown in Figure 2.

The steps in a titration:

- Fill a burette with the acid of unknown concentration.
- Accurately measure an amount of the alkali using a calibrated pipette and pipette filler.
- Add the alkali to a conical flask with a few drops of a suitable indicator.
- Run in acid from the burette until the colour just changes, showing that the solution in the conical flask is now neutral.
- Repeat the procedure until two values for the volume of acid used at neutralisation are the same, within experimental error.

Worked example:

25.0 cm³ of a solution of sodium hydroxide, NaOH, of unknown concentration was neutralised by 20.0 cm³ of a 0.100 mol dm⁻³ solution of hydrochloric acid, HCl. What is the concentration of the alkali?

First write a balanced symbol equation and then the numbers of moles that react:

$NaOH(aq)$ + $HCl(aq)$ $\longrightarrow$ $NaCl(aq)$ + $H_2O(l)$

sodium hydroxide   hydrochloric acid   sodium chloride   water

1 mol   1 mol   1 mol   1 mol

So 1 mol of sodium hydroxide reacts with 1 mol of hydrochloric acid.

Number of moles in a solution $= \dfrac{M \times V}{1000}$

So   Number of moles of HCl $= \dfrac{20.0 \times 0.100}{1000}$

Since we know from the equation that there must be an equal number of moles of sodium hydroxide and hydrochloric acid for neutralisation, we can say:

Number of moles of NaOH = number of moles of HCl

So we must have $\dfrac{20.0 \times 0.100}{1000}$ mol of NaOH in the 25.0 cm³ of sodium hydroxide solution.

The concentration of a solution is the number of moles in 1000 cm³.

Therefore the concentration of the alkali $= \dfrac{20.0 \times 0.100}{1000} \times \dfrac{1000}{25.0}$ mol dm⁻³

$= 0.080$ mol dm⁻³

Balanced equations, atom economies and percentage yields

Learning objectives:

■ What is the atom economy of a chemical reaction?

■ How is an equation used to calculate an atom economy?

■ What is the percentage yield of a chemical reaction?

■ How are percentage yields calculated?

Specification reference 3.1.2

Once we know the balanced equation for a chemical reaction, we can calculate the theoretical amount that we should be able to make of any of the products. Most chemical reactions produce two (or more) products but often only one of them is required. This means that some of the products will be wasted. In a world of scarce resources, this is obviously not a good idea. One technique that chemists use to assess a given process is to determine the percentage atom economy.

Atom economy

The atom economy of a reaction is found directly from the balanced equation. It is theoretical rather than practical. It is defined as follows:

$$\% \text{ Atom economy} = \frac{\text{mass of desired product}}{\text{total mass of reactants}} \times 100$$

We can see what atom economy means by considering the following real reaction.

Chlorine (Cl_2) reacts with sodium hydroxide (NaOH) to form sodium chloride (NaCl), water (H_2O) and sodium chlorate (NaOCl). Sodium chlorate is used as household bleach; this is the product we want.

From the equation we can work out the mass of each reactant and product involved.

$$2NaOH \quad + \quad Cl_2 \quad \longrightarrow \quad NaCl \quad + \quad H_2O \quad + \quad NaOCl$$

2 mol	1 mol	→	1 mol	1 mol	1 mol
80 g	71 g	→	58.5 g	18 g	74.5 g
Total	151 g	→	Total	151 g	

$$\% \text{ Atom economy} = \frac{\text{mass of desired product}}{\text{total mass of reactants}} \times 100$$

$$= \frac{74.5}{151} \times 100$$

$$= 49.3$$

So only 49.3% of the starting materials are included in the desired product, the rest is wasted.

It may be easier to see what has happened if we colour the atoms involved. Those coloured in green are included in the final product and those in red are wasted: one atom of sodium, one of chlorine, two of hydrogen and one of oxygen.

$$NaOH + NaOH + ClCl \longrightarrow NaCl + H_2O + NaOCl$$

Another example is the reaction where ethanol breaks down to ethene, the product we want, and water, which is wasted.

$$C_2H_5OH \quad \longrightarrow \quad CH_2{=}CH_2 \quad + \quad H_2O$$

46 g	→	28 g	18 g

$$\% \text{ Atom economy} = \frac{28}{46} \times 100 = 60.9$$

Some reactions, in theory at least, have no wasted atoms.

For, example, ethene reacts with bromine to form 1,2-dibromoethane

$$CH_2\!\!=\!\!CH_2 \quad + \quad Br_2 \quad \longrightarrow \quad CH_2BrCH_2Br$$
$$\underset{28\,g}{} \qquad\qquad \underset{160\,g}{} \qquad\qquad \underset{188\,g}{}$$

Total 188 g   Total 188 g

$$\% \text{ Atom economy} = \frac{188}{(28+160)} \times 100 = 100$$

🔬 The yield of a chemical reaction

The yield of a reaction is different from the atom economy.

■ The atom economy tells us *in theory* how many atoms *must* be wasted in a reaction.

■ The yield tells us about the practical efficiency of the process, how much is lost by:

   a   the *practical* process of obtaining a product and

   b   as a result of reactions that do not go to completion.

As we have seen, once we know the balanced symbol equation for a chemical reaction, we can calculate the amount of any product that we should be able to get from given amounts of starting materials if the reaction goes to completion. For example:

$$2KI(aq) \quad + \quad Pb(NO_3)_2(aq) \quad \longrightarrow \quad PbI_2(s) \quad + \quad 2KNO_3(aq)$$

potassium iodide   lead nitrate   lead iodide   potassium nitrate

2 mol	1 mol	1 mol	2 mol
332 g	331 g	461 g	202 g

So starting from 3.32 g ($^2/_{100}$ mol) of potassium iodide in solution and adding 3.31 g ($^1/_{100}$ mol) of lead nitrate in aqueous solution should produce 4.61 g ($^1/_{100}$ mol) of a precipitate of lead iodide which can be filtered off and dried.

However, this is in theory only. When we pour one solution into another, some droplets will be left in the beaker. When we remove the precipitate from the filter paper, some will be left on the paper. This sort of problem means that in practice we never get as much product as the equation predicts. Much of the skill of the chemist, both in the laboratory and in industry, lies in minimising these sorts of losses.

$$\text{The yield of a chemical reaction} = \frac{\text{the number of moles of a specified product}}{\text{theoretical maximum number of moles of the product}} \times 100\%$$

It can equally well be defined as:

$$\frac{\text{the number of grams of a specified product obtained in a reaction}}{\text{theoretical maximum number of grams of the product}} \times 100\%$$

If we had obtained 4.00 g of lead iodide in the above reaction, the yield would have been:

$$\frac{4.00}{4.61} \times 100\% = 86.8\%$$

A further problem arises with reactions that are reversible and do not go to completion. This is not uncommon. One example is the Haber process in which ammonia is made from hydrogen and nitrogen. Here is it impossible to get a yield of 100% even with the best practical skills. However, chemists can improve the yield by changing the conditions – see Topic 9.2.

Applications and How science works

The syntheses of ibuprofen – old and new

Ibuprofen is a mild painkiller and anti-inflammatory drug. It was patented by the Boots company in the 1960s and became available without prescription in the UK in the mid-1980s. It is sold under a number of brand names including Nurofen and Cuprofen. Its structural formula is shown in Figure 1.

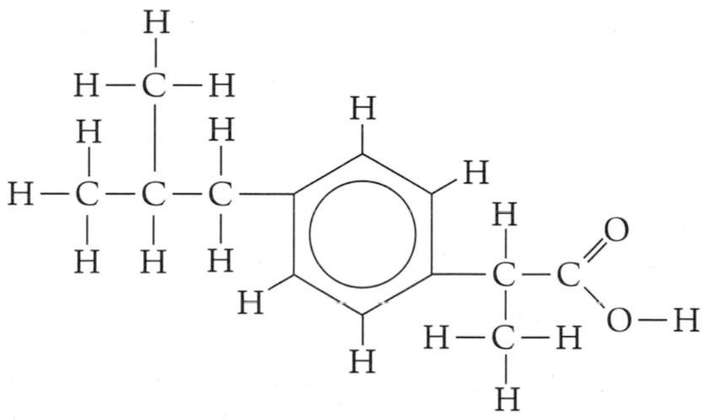

Figure 1 *Structural formula of ibuprofen*

Ibuprofen was originally made by a seven-step process with an atom economy of only 40%, which meant that more material used in its manufacture was being discarded than was being incorporated into the final product, ibuprofen.

Once the patent on ibuprofen ran out in the 1980s, anyone could manufacture and sell ibuprofen, not just Boots. A new company called BHC developed a new method of manufacture that used just three steps and had an overall atom economy of 77%.

Both methods of synthesis use the same starting material, 2-methypropylbenzene (Figure 2), which is obtained from crude oil.

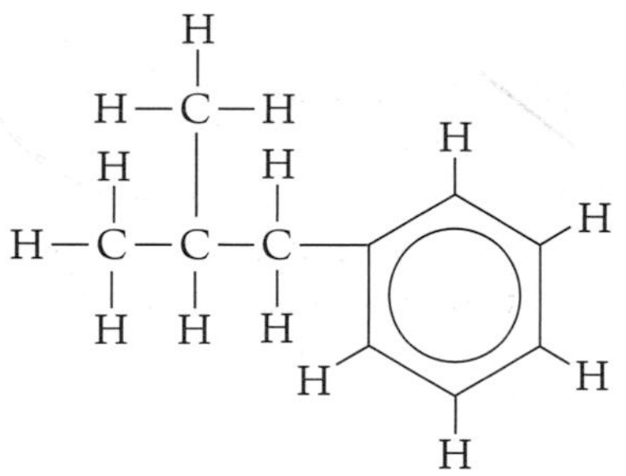

Figure 2 *Structural formula of 2-methypropylbenzene*

The relative molecular mass of 2-methypropylbenzene is 134 and that of ibuprofen is 206.

Questions

1 What is the maximum mass of ibuprofen that could theoretically be made starting from 26.8 kg of 2-methylpropylbenzene?

2 If the overall yield of the process were 40%, what mass would actually be produced?

Summary questions

1 Lime (calcium oxide, CaO), used for treating acidic soil, is made by heating limestone (calcium carbonate, $CaCO_3$) to drive off carbon dioxide gas (CO_2).

$$CaCO_3 \longrightarrow CaO + CO_2$$

Calculate the atom economy of the reaction.

2 Sodium sulfate can be made from sulfuric acid and sodium hydroxide.

$$H_2SO_4 + 2NaOH \longrightarrow Na_2SO_4 + H_2O$$

If sodium sulfate is the required product, calculate the atom economy of the reaction.

3 Ethanol (C_2H_6O) can be made by reacting ethene (C_2H_4) with water (H_2O).

$$C_2H_4 + H_2O \longrightarrow C_2H_6O$$

Without doing a calculation, what is the atom economy of the reaction? Explain your answer.

4 Consider the reaction $CaCO_3 \longrightarrow CO_2 + CaO$, then answer the following questions.

a What is the theoretical maximum number of moles of calcium oxide (CaO) that can be obtained from 1 mole of calcium carbonate ($CaCO_3$)?

b Starting from 10 g calcium carbonate, what is the theoretical maximum number of grams of calcium oxide that can be obtained?

c If we actually obtain 3.6 g of calcium oxide, what is the yield of the reaction?

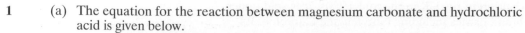

AQA Examination-style questions

1 (a) The equation for the reaction between magnesium carbonate and hydrochloric acid is given below.

$$MgCO_3 + 2HCl \longrightarrow MgCl_2 + H_2O + CO_2$$

When $75.0\,cm^3$ of $0.500\,mol\,dm^{-3}$ hydrochloric acid were added to $1.25\,g$ of impure $MgCO_3$ some acid was left unreacted. This unreacted acid required $21.6\,cm^3$ of a $0.500\,mol\,dm^{-3}$ solution of sodium hydroxide for complete reaction.

   (i) Calculate the number of moles of HCl in $75.0\,cm^3$ of $0.500\,mol\,dm^{-3}$ hydrochloric acid.

   (ii) Calculate the number of moles of NaOH used to neutralise the unreacted HCl.

   (iii) Show that the number of moles of HCl which reacted with the $MgCO_3$ in the sample was 0.0267

   (iv) Calculate the number of moles and the mass of $MgCO_3$ in the sample, and hence deduce the percentage by mass of $MgCO_3$ in the sample.   *(8 marks)*

(b) A compound contains 36.5% of sodium and 25.5% of sulfur by mass, the rest being oxygen.

   (i) Use this information to show that the empirical formula of the compound is Na_2SO_3

   (ii) When Na_2SO_3 is treated with an excess of hydrochloric acid, aqueous sodium chloride is formed and sulfur dioxide gas is evolved. Write an equation to represent this reaction.   *(4 marks)*

AQA, 2004

2 (a) Ammonium sulfate reacts with aqueous sodium hydroxide as shown by the equation below.

$$(NH_4)_2SO_4 + 2NaOH \longrightarrow 2NH_3 + Na_2SO_4 + 2H_2O$$

A sample of ammonium sulfate was heated with $100\,cm^3$ of $0.500\,mol\,dm^{-3}$ aqueous sodium hydroxide. To ensure that all the ammonium sulfate reacted, an excess of sodium hydroxide was used.

Heating was continued until all of the ammonia had been driven off as a gas.

The unreacted sodium hydroxide remaining in the solution required $27.3\,cm^3$ of $0.600\,mol\,dm^{-3}$ hydrochloric acid for neutralisation.

   (i) Calculate the original number of moles of NaOH in $100\,cm^3$ of $0.500\,mol\,dm^{-3}$ aqueous sodium hydroxide.

   (ii) Calculate the number of moles of HCl in $27.3\,cm^3$ of $0.600\,mol\,dm^{-3}$ hydrochloric acid.

   (iii) Deduce the number of moles of the unreacted NaOH neutralised by the hydrochloric acid.

   (iv) Use your answers from parts (a)(i) and (a)(iii) to calculate the number of moles of NaOH which reacted with the ammonium sulfate.

   (v) Use your answer in part (a)(iv) to calculate the number of moles and the mass of ammonium sulfate in the sample.

   (If you have been unable to obtain an answer to part (a)(iv), you may assume that the number of moles of NaOH which reacted with ammonium sulfate equals $2.78 \times 10^{-2}\,mol$. This is not the correct answer.)   *(7 marks)*

(b) A $0.143\,g$ gaseous sample of ammonia occupied a volume of $2.86 \times 10^{-4}\,m^3$ at a temperature T and a pressure of $100\,kPa$.

State the ideal gas equation, calculate the number of moles of ammonia present and deduce the value of the temperature T.

(The gas constant $R = 8.31\,J\,K^{-1}\,mol^{-1}$)   *(4 marks)*

AQA, 2005

3 (a) Lead(II) nitrate may be produced by the reaction between nitric acid and lead(II) oxide as shown by the equation below.

$$PbO + 2HNO_3 \longrightarrow Pb(NO_3)_2 + H_2O$$

An excess of lead(II) oxide was allowed to react with $175\,cm^3$ of $1.50\,mol\,dm^{-3}$ nitric acid. Calculate the maximum mass of lead(II) nitrate which could be obtained from this reaction. *(4 marks)*

   (b) An equation representing the thermal decomposition of lead(II) nitrate is shown below.

$$2Pb(NO_3)_2(s) \longrightarrow 2PbO(s) + 4NO_2(g) + O_2(g)$$

A sample of lead(II) nitrate was heated until the decomposition was complete. At a temperature of $500\,K$ and a pressure of $100\,kPa$, the total volume of the gaseous mixture produced was found to be $1.50 \times 10^{-4}\,m^3$.

   (i) State the ideal gas equation and use it to calculate the total number of moles of gas produced in this decomposition.

(The gas constant $R = 8.31\,J\,K^{-1}\,mol^{-1}$)

   (ii) Deduce the number of moles, and the mass of NO_2 present in this gaseous mixture. (If you have been unable to calculate the total number of moles of gas in part (b)(i), you should assume this to be $2.23 \times 10^{-3}\,mol$. This is not the correct answer.) *(7 marks)*

AQA, 2005

4 Nitroglycerine, $C_3H_5N_3O_9$, is an explosive which, on detonation, decomposes rapidly to form a large number of gaseous molecules. The equation for this decomposition is given below.

$$4C_3H_5N_3O_9(l) \longrightarrow 12CO_2(g) + 10H_2O(g) + 6N_2(g) + O_2(g)$$

   (a) A sample of nitroglycerine was detonated and produced $0.350\,g$ of oxygen gas.

   (i) State what is meant by the term *one mole* of molecules.

   (ii) Calculate the number of moles of oxygen gas produced in this reaction, and hence deduce the total number of moles of gas formed.

   (iii) Calculate the number of moles, and the mass, of nitroglycerine detonated. *(7 marks)*

   (b) A second sample of nitroglycerine was placed in a strong sealed container and detonated. The volume of this container was $1.00 \times 10^{-3}\,m^3$. The resulting decomposition produced a total of $0.873\,mol$ of gaseous products at a temperature of $1100\,K$.

State the ideal gas equation and use it to calculate the pressure in the container after detonation.

(The gas constant $R = 8.31\,J\,K^{-1}\,mol^{-1}$) *(4 marks)*

AQA, 2006

5 Potassium nitrate, KNO_3, decomposes on strong heating, forming oxygen and solid **Y** as the only products.

   (a) A $1.00\,g$ sample of KNO_3 ($M_r = 101.1$) was heated strongly until fully decomposed into **Y**.

   (i) Calculate the number of moles of KNO_3 in the $1.00\,g$ sample.

   (ii) At $298\,K$ and $100\,kPa$, the oxygen gas produced in this decomposition occupied a volume of $1.22 \times 10^{-4}\,m^3$.

State the ideal gas equation and use it to calculate the number of moles of oxygen produced in this decomposition.

(The gas constant $R = 8.31\,J\,K^{-1}\,mol^{-1}$) *(5 marks)*

   (b) Compound **Y** contains 45.9% of potassium and 16.5% of nitrogen by mass, the remainder being oxygen.

   (i) State what is meant by the term *empirical formula*.

   (ii) Use the data above to calculate the empirical formula of **Y**. *(4 marks)*

   (c) Deduce an equation for the decomposition of KNO_3 into **Y** and oxygen. *(1 mark)*

AQA, 2006

3 Bonding

3.1 The nature of ionic bonding

Learning objectives:

- How are ions formed and why do they attract each other?

- What are the properties of ionically bonded compounds?

- What kind of structure do ionically bonded compounds have?

Specification reference 3.1.3

Why do chemical bonds form?

The bonds between atoms always involve their outer electrons.

- Noble gases have full outer main levels of electrons (see Figure 1) and are very unreactive.
- When atoms bond together they share or transfer electrons to achieve a more stable electron arrangement, often a full outer main level of electrons, like the noble gases.
- There are three types of strong chemical bonds: **ionic**, **covalent** and **metallic**

Ionic bonding

Metals have one, two or three electrons in their outer main levels, so the easiest way for them to attain the electron structure of a noble gas is to lose their outer electrons. Non-metals have spaces in their outer main levels, so that the easiest way for them to attain the electron structure of a noble gas is to gain electrons.

- Ionic bonding occurs between metals and non-metals.
- Electrons are transferred from metal atoms to non-metal atoms.
- Positive and negative ions are formed.

Sodium chloride, shown in Figure 2, has ionic bonding.

Sodium, $_{11}$Na, has 11 electrons (and 11 protons). The electron arrangement is 2,8,1

Chlorine, $_{17}$Cl, has 17 electrons (and 17 protons). The electron arrangement is 2,8,7

- An electron is transferred. The single outer electron of the sodium atom moves into the outer main level of the chlorine atom.
- Each outer main level is now full.
- Both sodium and chlorine now have a noble gas electron arrangement. Sodium has the neon noble gas arrangement whereas chlorine the argon noble gas arrangement (compare the ions in Figure 3 with the noble gas atoms in Figure 1).

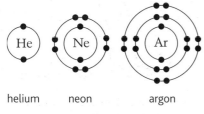

helium   neon   argon

Figure 1 *Noble gases*

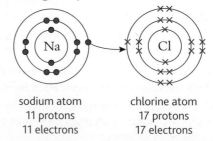

sodium atom
11 protons
11 electrons

chlorine atom
17 protons
17 electrons

Figure 2 *A 'dot-and-cross' diagram to show the transfer of an electron from a sodium atom to a chlorine atom. Remember that electrons are all identical whether shown by a dot or a cross.*

Na⁺ sodium ion
11 protons, 10 electrons (2,8)

Cl⁺ chlorine ion (called chloride)
17 protons, 18 electrons (2,8,8)

Figure 3 *The ions that result from electron transfer*

The two charged particles that result from the transfer of an electron are called ions.

- The sodium ion is positively charged because it has lost a negative electron.
- The chloride ion is negatively charged because it has gained a negative electron.
- The two ions are attracted to each other and to other oppositely charged ions in the sodium chloride compound by **electrostatic forces**.

Therefore ionic bonding is the result of electrostatic attraction between oppositely charged ions. The attraction extends throughout the compound. Every positive ion attracts every negative ion and *vice versa*. There is also a repulsive force between all the ions of the same charge. So, ionic compounds always exist in a structure called a **lattice** in which the attractive forces and the repulsive forces are balanced. Figure 4 shows the three-dimensional lattice for sodium chloride with its singly charged ions.

The formula of sodium chloride is NaCl because we know that for every one sodium ion there is one chloride ion.

Example: magnesium oxide

Magnesium, Mg, has 12 electrons. The electron arrangement is 2,8,2.

Oxygen, O, has 8 electrons. The electron arrangement is 2,6.

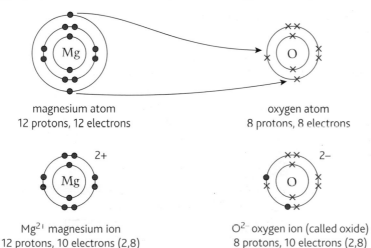

magnesium atom
12 protons, 12 electrons

oxygen atom
8 protons, 8 electrons

Mg^{2+} magnesium ion
12 protons, 10 electrons (2,8)

O^{2-} oxygen ion (called oxide)
8 protons, 10 electrons (2,8)

This time, two electrons are transferred from each magnesium atom. Each oxygen atom receives two electrons.

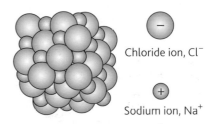

Chloride ion, Cl^-

Sodium ion, Na^+

Figure 4 *The sodium chloride structure. This is an example of a giant ionic structure. The strong bonding extends throughout the compound, and because of this it will be difficult to melt.*

AQA Examiner's tip

You will not be asked to draw dot-and-cross diagrams in an exam but they will help you to understand the principles of bonding and to predict the shapes of molecules.

■ The magnesium ion, Mg^{2+}, is positively charged because it has lost two negative electrons.

■ The oxide ion, O^{2-}, is negatively charged because it has gained two negative electrons.

■ The formula of magnesium oxide is MgO.

Properties of ionically bonded compounds

Ionic compounds are always solids at room temperature. They have **giant structures** and therefore high melting temperatures. This is because in order to melt an ionic compound, energy must be supplied to break up the lattice of ions.

Ionic compounds conduct electricity when molten or dissolved in water (aqueous) but not when solid. This is because the ions that carry the current are free to move in the liquid state but are not free in the solid state, see Figure 5.

①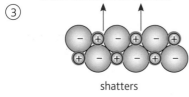

a small displacement causes contact between ions with the same charge...

②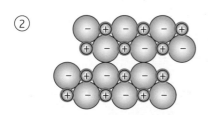

...and the structure shatters

③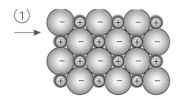

shatters

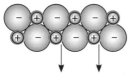

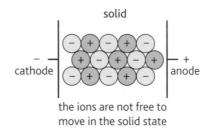

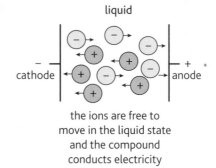

💡 **Figure 5** *Ionic liquids conduct electricity, ionic solids do not*

💡 **Figure 6** *The brittleness of ionic compounds*

Ionic compounds are **brittle** and shatter easily when given a sharp blow. This is because they form a lattice of alternating positive and negative ions, see Figure 6. A blow in the direction shown may move the ions and produce contact between ions with like charges.

Summary questions

1 Which of the following are ionic compounds and why?

    a CO   **b** KF   **c** CaO   **d** HF

2 Why do ionic compounds have high melting temperatures?

3 Under what conditions do ionic compounds conduct electricity?

4 Draw 'dot-and-cross' diagrams to show the following:

    a The ions being formed when magnesium and fluorine react

    b The ions being formed when sodium and oxygen react

5 What are the formulae of the compounds formed in question 4?

6 Look at the electron arrangements of the Mg^{2+} and O^{2-} ions. What noble gas do they correspond to?

3.2 Covalent bonding

Learning objectives:

- What is a covalent bond?
- What is a co-ordinate bond?
- What are the properties of covalently bonded molecules?

Specification reference 3.1.3

Non-metal atoms need to *receive* electrons to fill the spaces in their outer shells.

- A covalent bond forms between a pair of non-metal atoms.
- The atoms *share* some of their outer electrons so that each atom has a stable noble gas arrangement.
- A covalent bond is a shared pair of electrons.

Forming molecules by covalent bonding

A small group of covalently bonded atoms is called a molecule.

For example, chlorine, Cl, exists as a gas that is made of molecules, Cl_2, see Figure 1.

Chlorine has 17 electrons and an electron arrangement 2,8,7. Two chlorine atoms make a chlorine molecule, Cl_2:

- The two atoms share one pair of electrons.
- Each atom now has a stable noble gas arrangement.
- The formula is Cl_2.
- Molecules are neutral because no electrons have been transferred from one atom to another.

We can represent one pair of shared electrons in a covalent bond by a line, Cl—Cl.

Example: methane

Methane gas is a covalently bonded compound of carbon and hydrogen. Carbon, C, has six electrons with electron arrangement 2,4 and hydrogen, H, has just one electron.

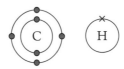

carbon (2,4)   hydrogen

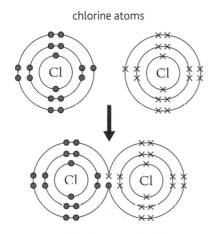

chlorine atoms

a chlorine molecule, Cl_2

Figure 1 *Forming a chlorine molecule*

In order for carbon to attain a stable noble gas arrangement, there are four hydrogen atoms to every carbon atom.

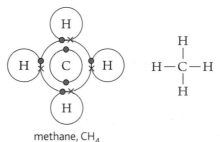

methane, CH_4

The formula of methane is CH_4.

Hint

Notice that hydrogen has a filled outer main level with only two electrons. (It is filling the first shell to get the structure of the noble gas helium.)

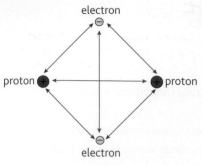

Figure 2 *The electrostatic forces within a hydrogen molecule*

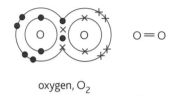

oxygen, O_2

Figure 3 *An oxygen molecule has a double bond*

How does sharing electrons hold atoms together?

Atoms with covalent bonds are held together by the electrostatic attraction between the nuclei and the shared electrons. This takes place within the molecule. The simplest example is hydrogen. The hydrogen molecule consists of two protons held together by a pair of electrons. The electrostatic forces are shown in Figure 2. The attractive forces are in black and the repulsive forces in red. These forces just balance when the nuclei are a particular distance apart.

Double covalent bonds

In a double bond, four electrons are shared. The two atoms in an oxygen molecule share two pairs of electrons so that the oxygen atoms have a double bond between them, see Figure 3. We can represent the two pairs of shared electrons in a covalent bond by a double line, $O=O$.

When you are drawing covalent bonding diagrams you may leave out the inner main levels because the inner shells are not involved at all. Other examples of molecules with covalent bonds are shown in Table 1.

All the examples in Table 1 are neutral molecules. The atoms within the molecules are strongly bonded together with covalent bonds within the molecule. However, the molecules are *not* strongly attracted to each other.

Table 1 *Examples of covalent molecules. Only the outer shells are shown.*

Formula	Name	Formula	Name
H_2	Hydrogen. Each hydrogen atom has a full outer main level with just two electrons	NH_3	Ammonia
HCl	Hydrogen chloride	C_2H_4	Ethene. There is a carbon–carbon double bond in this molecule
H_2O	Water	CO_2	Carbon dioxide. There are two carbon–oxygen double bonds in this molecule

Properties of substances with molecular structures

■ Substances composed of molecules are gases, liquids or solids with low melting temperatures. This is because the strong covalent bonds are only *between the atoms* within the molecules. There is only weak attraction between the molecules so the molecules do not need much energy to move apart from each other.

- They are poor conductors of electricity because the molecules are neutral overall. This means that there are no charged particles to carry the current.
- If they dissolve in water, and remain as molecules, the solutions do not conduct electricity. Again, this is because there are no charged particles.

Co-ordinate bonding

A single covalent bond consists of a pair of electrons shared between two atoms. In most covalent bonds, each atom provides one of the electrons. But, in some bonds, one atom provides both the electrons. This is called **co-ordinate bonding**. It is also called **dative covalent bonding**.

In a co-ordinate or dative covalent bond:

- the atom that accepts the electron pair is an atom that does not have a filled outer main level of electrons; we say the atom is electron-deficient
- the atom that is *donating* the electrons has a pair of electrons that is not being used in a bond, called a **lone pair**.

Example: the ammonium ion

For example, ammonia, NH_3, has a lone pair of electrons. In the ammonium ion, NH_4^+, the nitrogen uses its lone pair of electrons to form a co-ordinate bond with an H^+ ion (a 'bare' proton with no electrons at all and therefore electron-deficient).

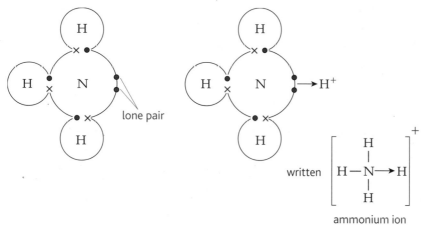

lone pair

written

ammonium ion

Co-ordinate covalent bonds are represented by an arrow →. The arrow points towards the atom that is accepting the electron pair. However, this is only to show how the bond was made. The ammonium ion is completely symmetrical and all the bonds have exactly the same strength and length.

- Co-ordinate bonds have exactly the same strength and length as ordinary covalent bonds between the same pair of atoms.

The ammonium ion has *covalently* bonded atoms but is a charged particle.

Electronegativity – bond polarity in covalent bonds

Learning objectives:

■ What is meant by the term electronegativity?

■ What is it that makes one atom more electronegative than another?

■ What do the symbols δ+ and δ– mean when placed above atoms in a covalent bond?

Specification reference 3.1.3

The forces that hold atoms together are all about the attraction of positive charges to negative charges. In ionic bonding we have complete transfer of electrons from one atom to another. But, even in covalent bonds, the electrons shared by the atoms will not be evenly spread if one of the atoms is better at attracting electrons than the other. We say this atom is more **electronegative** than the other.

■ Electronegativity

Electronegativity is the power of an atom to attract the electron density in a covalent bond towards itself. For example, fluorine is better at attracting electrons than hydrogen. We say that fluorine is more electronegative than hydrogen.

When we consider the electrons as charge clouds, the term **electron density** is often used to describe the way the negative charge is distributed in a molecule.

The Pauling scale is used as a measure of electronegativity. It runs from 0 to 4. The greater the number, the more electronegative the atom, see Table 1. The noble gases have no number because they do not, in general, form covalent bonds.

Table 1 *Some values for Pauling electronegativity*

H							He
2.1							
Li	Be	B	C	N	O	F	Ne
1.0	1.5	2.0	2.5	3.0	3.5	4.0	
Na	Mg	Al	Si	P	S	Cl	Ar
0.9	1.2	1.5	1.8	2.1	2.5	3.0	
						Br	Kr
						2.8	

Electronegativity depends on:

1. the nuclear charge
2. the distance between the nucleus and the outer shell electrons
3. the shielding of the nuclear charge by electrons in inner shells.

Note the following:

■ The smaller the atom, the closer the nucleus is to the shared outer main level electrons and the greater its electronegativity.

■ The larger the nuclear charge (for a given shielding effect), the greater the electronegativity.

Trends in electronegativity

■ As we go up a group in the periodic table, electronegativity increases (the atoms get smaller) and there is less shielding by electrons in inner shells.

AQA Examiner's tip

Learn the definition of electronegativity.

Hint

Think of electronegative atoms as having more 'electron-pulling power'.

- As we go across a period in the periodic table, the electronegativity increases. The nuclear charge increases, the number of inner main levels remain the same and the atoms become smaller.

- So, the most electronegative atoms are found at the top right-hand corner of the periodic table (ignoring the noble gases which form few compounds). The most electronegative atoms are fluorine, oxygen and nitrogen followed by chlorine.

Table 2 *Trends in electronegativity*

Increasing electronegativity →

Li	Be	B	C	N	O	F
1.0	1.5	2.0	2.5	3.0	3.5	4.0
						Cl
						3.0
						Br
						2.8

Increasing electronegativity ↑

🧪 Polarity of covalent bonds

Polarity is about the unequal sharing of the electrons between atoms that are bonded together covalently. It is a property of the *bond*.

Covalent bonds between two atoms that are the same

When both atoms are the same, for example in fluorine, F_2, the electrons in the bond *must* be shared equally between the atoms (Figure 1); both atoms have exactly the same electronegativity and the bond is completely non-polar.

If we think of the electrons as being in a cloud of charge, then the cloud is uniformly spread between the two atoms, as shown in Figure 2.

Covalent bonds between two atoms that are different

In a covalent bond between two atoms of *different* electronegativity, the electrons in the bond will not be shared equally between the atoms. For example, the molecule hydrogen fluoride, HF, shown in Figure 3.

Hydrogen has an electronegativity of 2.1 and fluorine of 4.0. This means that the electrons in the covalent bond will be attracted more by the fluorine than the hydrogen. The electron cloud is distorted towards the fluorine, as shown in Figure 4.

The fluorine end of the molecule is therefore relatively negative and the hydrogen end relatively positive. We show this by adding partial charges to the formula:

$$^{\delta+}H{-}F^{\delta-}$$

Covalent bonds like this are said to be **polar**. The greater the difference in electronegativity, the more polar is the covalent bond.

You could say that although the H—F bond is covalent, it has some ionic character. It is going some way towards the separation of the atoms into charged ions. It is also possible to have ionic bonds with some covalent character.

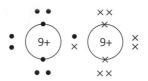

Figure 1 *Electron diagram of fluorine molecule*

Figure 2 *Electron cloud around fluorine molecule*

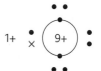

Figure 3 *Electron diagram of hydrogen fluoride molecule*

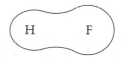

Figure 4 *Electron cloud around hydrogen fluoride molecule*

Hint

$\delta+$ and $\delta-$ are pronounced 'delta plus' and 'delta minus'.

The + and − signs represent one 'electron's worth' of charge.

$\delta+$ and $\delta-$ represent a small charge of less than one 'electron's worth'.

Summary questions

1 Explain why fluorine is more electronegative than chlorine.

2 Write $\delta+$ and $\delta-$ signs to show the polarity of the bonds in a hydrogen chloride molecule.

3 a Which of these covalent bonds is non-polar?

  b Explain your answer.

   i   H—H

   ii F—F

   iii H—F

4 a Arrange the following covalent bonds in order of increasing polarity:
H—O, H—F, H—N

  b Explain your answer.

3.4 Metallic bonding

Learning objectives:

- What is the nature of bonding in a metal?

- What are the properties of metals?

Specification reference 3.1.3

Metals are shiny elements made up of atoms that can easily lose up to three outer electrons, leaving positive metal ions. For example, sodium, Na, 2,8,1 loses its one outer electron; aluminium, Al, 2,8,3 loses its three outer electrons.

Metallic bonding

The atoms in a metal element cannot transfer electrons (as happens in ionic bonding) unless there is a non-metal atom present to receive them. In a metal element, the outer main levels of the atoms merge. The outer electrons are no longer associated with any one particular atom. A simple picture of metallic bonding is that metals consist of a lattice of positive ions existing in a 'sea' of outer electrons. These electrons are **delocalised**. This means that they are not tied to a particular atom. Magnesium metal is shown in Figure 1. The positive ions tend to repel one another and this is balanced by the electrostatic attraction of these positive ions for the negatively charged 'sea' of delocalised electrons.

Hint

In Figure 1 the metal ions are shown spaced apart for clarity. In fact metal atoms are more closely packed, and so metals tend to have high densities.

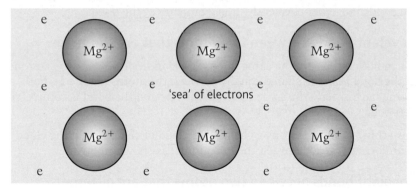

Figure 1 *The delocalised 'sea' of electrons in magnesium*

Hint

The word **delocalised** is often used to describe electron clouds that are spread over more than two atoms.

- The number of delocalised electrons depends on how many electrons have been lost by each metal atom.
- The metallic bonding spreads throughout so metals have giant structures.

Properties of metals

Metals are good conductors of electricity and heat

The delocalised electrons that can move throughout the structure explain why metals are such good conductors of electricity. An electron from the negative terminal of the supply joins the electron sea at one end of a metal wire while *at the same time* a different electron leaves the wire at the positive terminal, as shown in Figure 2.

Metals are also good conductors of heat. We say they have high thermal conductivities. The sea of electrons is partly responsible for this property, with energy also spread by increasingly vigorous vibrations of the closely-packed ions.

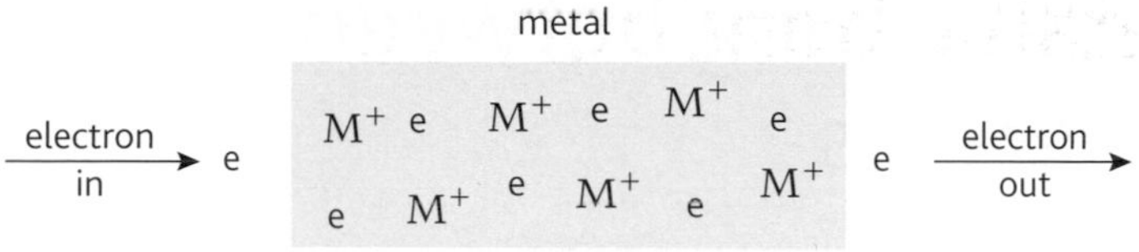

metal

$\xrightarrow[\text{in}]{\text{electron}}$ e | M⁺ e   M⁺ e   M⁺   e | e $\xrightarrow{\text{electron out}}$
e   M⁺   e   M⁺   e   M⁺

Figure 2 *The conduction of electricity by a metal*

The strength of metals

In general, the strength of any metallic bond depends on the following.

- The charge on the ion: the greater the charge on the ion, the greater the number of delocalised electrons and the stronger the attraction between the positive ions and the electrons.
- The size of ion: the smaller the ion, the closer the electrons are to the positive nucleus and the stronger the bond.

Metals tend to be strong. The delocalised electrons also explain this. These extend throughout the solid so there are no individual bonds to break.

Metals are malleable and ductile

Metals are malleable (they can be beaten into shape) and ductile (they can be pulled into thin wires). After a small distortion, each metal ion is still in exactly the same environment as before so the new shape is retained, see Figure 3.

Contrast this with the brittleness of ionic compounds in Topic 3.1.

Metals have high melting points

Metals generally have high melting and boiling points because they have giant structures. There is strong attraction between metal ions and the delocalised sea of electrons. This makes the atoms difficult to separate.

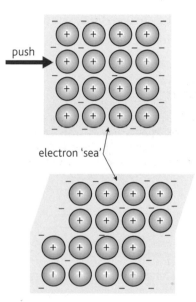

push

electron 'sea'

Figure 3 *The malleability and ductility of metals*

Summary questions

1. Give three differences in physical properties between metals and non-metals.

2. Write the electron arrangement of a calcium atom, Ca, which has 20 electrons.

3. How many electrons will a calcium atom lose to gain a stable noble gas configuration?

4. How many electrons will each calcium atom contribute to the delocalised sea of electrons that holds the metal atoms together?

5. Sodium forms 1+ ions with a metallic radius of 0.191 nm. Magnesium forms 2+ ions with a metallic radius of 0.160 nm. How would you expect the following properties of the two metals to compare? Explain your answers.

   a The melting point

   b The strength of the metals

3.5 Forces acting between molecules

Learning objectives:

- What are the three types of intermolecular force?

- How do dipole–dipole and van der Waals forces arise?

- How do van der Waals forces affect boiling temperatures?

Specification reference 3.1.3

> **Hint**
>
> van der Waals really is spelt with a small v, even at the beginning of a sentence.

Atoms in molecules and in giant structures are held together by strong covalent, ionic or metallic bonds. Molecules and separate atoms are attracted to one another by other, weaker forces called intermolecular forces. 'Inter' means between. If the intermolecular forces are strong enough, then molecules are held closely enough together to be liquids or even solids.

Intermolecular forces

There are three types of intermolecular forces:

- **van der Waals forces**
  act between *all* atoms and molecules.   weakest

- **Dipole–dipole forces**
  act only between certain types of molecules.

- **Hydrogen bonding**
  acts only between certain types of molecules.   strongest

Dipole–dipole forces

Dipole moments

Polarity is the property of a particular bond, see Topic 3.3, but molecules with polar bonds may have a **dipole moment**. This sums up the effect of the polarity of *all* the bonds in the molecule.

In molecules with more than one polar bond, the effects of each bond may cancel, to leave a molecule with no dipole moment. The effects may also add up and so reinforce each other. It depends on the shape of the molecule.

For example, carbon dioxide is a linear molecule and the dipoles cancel.

$$^{\delta-}O = C^{\delta+} = O^{\delta-}$$

Tetrachloromethane is tetrahedral and here too the dipoles cancel.

$$
\begin{array}{c}
^{\delta-}Cl \\
^{\delta-}Cl \cdots C^{\delta+} — Cl^{\delta-} \quad \text{tetrachloromethane} \\
^{\delta-}Cl
\end{array}
$$

But in dichloromethane the dipoles do not cancel because of the shape of the molecule.

$$
\begin{array}{c}
H \\
^{\delta-}Cl \cdots C^{\delta+} — H \quad \text{dichloromethane} \\
^{\delta-}Cl
\end{array}
$$

Dipole–dipole forces act between molecules that have permanent dipoles. For example, in the hydrogen chloride molecule, chlorine is more electronegative than hydrogen. So the electrons are pulled towards the chlorine atom rather than the hydrogen atom. The molecule therefore has a dipole and is written $H^{\delta+}–Cl^{\delta-}$.

Two molecules which both have dipoles will attract one another, see Figure 1.

Whatever their starting positions, the molecules with dipoles will 'flip' to give an arrangement where the two molecules attract.

Examiner's tip

Do not confuse intermolecular forces with covalent bonds. These are at least 10 times stronger.

💡 van der Waals forces

All atoms and molecules are made up of positive and negative charges even though they are neutral overall. These charges produce very weak electrostatic attractions between all atoms and molecules. We call these **van der Waals forces**.

How do van de Waals forces work?

Imagine a helium atom. It has two positive charges on its nucleus and two negatively charged electrons. The atom as a whole is neutral but at any moment in time the electrons could be anywhere, see Figure 2. This means the distribution of charge is changing *at every instant*.

Any of the arrangements in Figure 2 mean the atom has a dipole at that moment. An instant later, the dipole may be in a different direction. But, almost certainly the atom *will* have a dipole at any point in time, even though any particular dipole will be just for an instant – a temporary dipole. This dipole then affects the electron distribution in nearby atoms, so that they are attracted to the original helium atom for that instant. The original atom has induced dipoles in the nearby atoms, as shown Figure 3 in which the electron distribution is shown as a cloud.

As the electron distribution of the original atom changes, it will induce new dipoles in the atoms around it, which will be attracted to the original one. These forces are sometimes called instantaneous dipole-induced

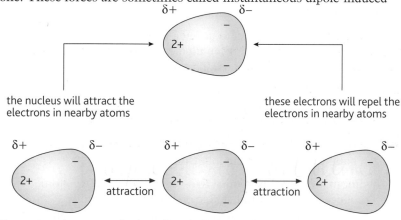

Figure 3 *Instantaneous dipoles induce dipoles in nearby atoms*

dipole forces, but this is rather a mouthful. The more usual name is van der Waals forces after the Dutch scientist, Johannes van der Waals.

- van der Waals forces act between *all* atoms or molecules at all times.
- They are in addition to any other intermolecular forces.
- The dipole is caused by the changing position of the electron cloud, so the more electrons there are, the larger the instantaneous dipole will be.

Therefore the size of the van der Waals forces increases with the number of electrons present. This means that atoms or molecules with large atomic or molecular masses produce stronger van der Waals forces than atoms or molecules with small atomic or molecular masses.

This explains why:

- the boiling points of the noble gases increase as the atomic numbers of the noble gases increase
- the boiling points of hydrocarbons increase with increased chain length.

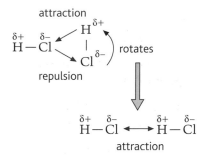

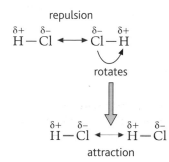

Figure 1 *Two polar molecules, such as hydrogen chloride, will always attract one another*

Figure 2 *Possible arrangements of the electrons in helium*

Summary questions

1. Place the following elements in order of the strength of the van der Waals forces between the atoms (weakest first): Ar, He, Kr, Ne. Explain your answer.

2. Which one of the following molecules **cannot** have dipole–dipole forces acting between them? H_2O, HCl, H_2

3. Explain why hexane is a liquid at room temperature whereas butane is a gas.

4. Draw two hydrogen bromide molecules to show how they would be attracted together by dipole–dipole forces.

3.6 Hydrogen bonding

Learning objectives:

- What is needed for hydrogen bonding to occur?

- Why do NH_3, H_2O and HF have higher boiling temperatures than might be expected?

Specification reference 3.1.3

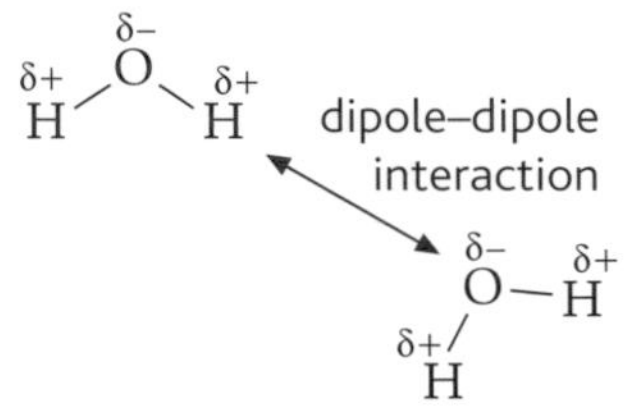

Figure 1 *Dipole attraction between water molecules*

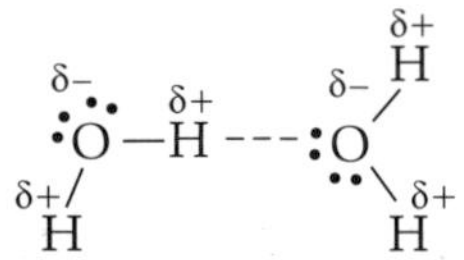

Figure 2 *Hydrogen bond between water molecules*

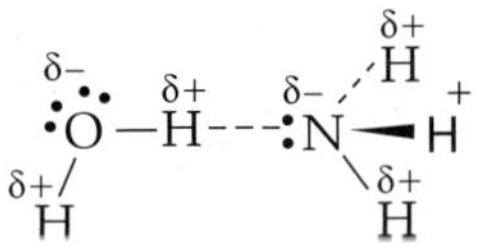

Figure 3 *Hydrogen bond between a water molecule and an ammonia molecule*

Hydrogen bonding is a special type of intermolecular force with some characteristics of dipole–dipole attraction and some of a covalent bond. It consists of a hydrogen atom 'sandwiched' between two very electronegative atoms. There are conditions that have to be present for hydrogen bonding to occur. We need a very electronegative atom with a lone pair of electrons covalently-bonded to a hydrogen atom. Water molecules fulfil these conditions. Oxygen is much more electronegative than hydrogen so water is polar, see Figure 1.

We would expect to find weak dipole–dipole attractions as shown in Figure 1, but in this case the intermolecular bonding is much stronger for two reasons:

1 The oxygen atoms in water have lone pairs of electrons.

2 In water the hydrogen atoms are highly electron deficient. This is because the oxygen is very electronegative and attracts the shared electrons in the bond towards it. The hydrogen atoms in water are positively charged and very small. These exposed protons have a very strong electric field because of their small size.

The lone pair of electrons on the oxygen atom of another water molecule is strongly attracted to the electron deficient hydrogen atom.

This strong intermolecular force is called a hydrogen bond. Hydrogen bonds are considerably stronger than dipole–dipole attractions, though much weaker than a covalent bond. They are usually represented by dashes – – –, as in Figure 2.

When do hydrogen bonds form?

Water is not the only example of hydrogen bonding. In order to form a hydrogen bond we must have the following:

- A hydrogen atom that is bonded to a very electronegative atom. This will produce a strong partial charge on the hydrogen atom.

- A very electronegative atom with a lone pair of electrons. These will be attracted to the partially charged hydrogen atom in another molecule and form the bond.

The only atoms that are electronegative enough to form hydrogen bonds are oxygen, O, nitrogen, N, and fluorine, F. For example, ammonia molecules, NH_3, form hydrogen bonds with water molecules, see Figure 3.

Notice that the nitrogen–hydrogen–oxygen system is linear. This is because the pair of electrons in the O—H covalent bond repels those in the H to N hydrogen bond, see Topic 3.9. This linearity is always the case with hydrogen bonds.

The boiling points of the hydrides

The effect of hydrogen bonding between molecules can be seen if we look at the boiling points of hydrides of elements of Group 4, 5, 6 and 7 plotted against the period number, see Figure 4.

The noble gases show a gradual increase in boiling point because the only forces acting between the atoms are van der Waals forces and these increase with the number of electrons present.

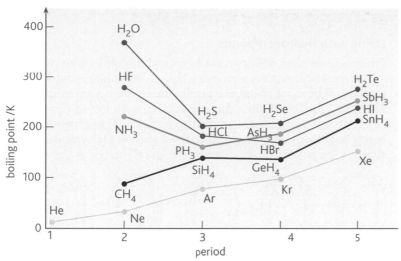

Figure 4 *Boiling points of the hydrides of Group 4, 5, 6 and 7 elements with the noble gases for comparison*

The boiling points of water, H_2O, hydrogen fluoride, HF, and ammonia, NH_3, are all higher than those of the hydrides of the other elements in their group, whereas we would expect them to be lower if only van der Waals forces were operating. This is because hydrogen bonding is present between the molecules in each of these compounds, and these stronger intermolecular forces of attraction make the molecules more difficult to separate. Oxygen, nitrogen and fluorine are the three elements that are electronegative enough to make hydrogen bonding possible.

The importance of hydrogen bonding

Although hydrogen bonds are only about 10% of the strength of covalent bonds, their effect can be significant – especially when there are a lot of them. The very fact that they are weaker than covalent bonds, and can break or make under conditions where covalent bonds are unaffected is very significant.

The structure and density of ice

In water in its liquid state, the hydrogen bonds break and reform easily as the molecules are moving about. When water freezes, the water molecules are no longer free to move about and the hydrogen bonds hold the molecules in fixed positions. The resulting three-dimensional structure, shown in Figure 5, resembles the structure of diamond, see Topic 3.7.

In order to fit into this structure, the molecules are slightly less closely packed than in liquid water. This means that ice is less dense than water and forms on top of ponds rather than at the bottom. This insulates the ponds and enables fish to survive through the winter. This must have helped life to continue, in the relative warmth of the water under the ice, during the Ice Ages.

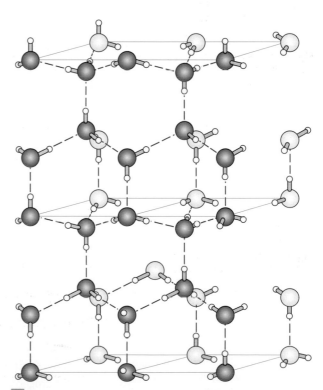

Figure 5 *The three-dimensional network of covalent bonds (grey) and hydrogen bonds (red) in ice. The blue lines are only construction lines.*

Figure 6 *The protein in an egg is denatured by heat*

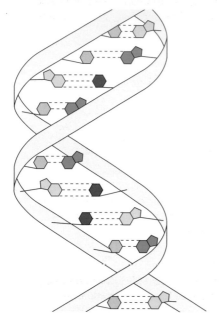

Figure 7 *The DNA double helix is held together by hydrogen bonds*

Summary questions

1 In which of the following does hydrogen bonding **not** occur between molecules: H_2O, NH_3, HBr, HF

2 Explain why hydrogen bonds do not form between:

a methane molecules, CH_4

b tetrachloromethane molecules, CCl_4.

3 Draw a dot-and-cross diagram for a molecule of water.

a How many lone pairs does it have?

b How many hydrogen atoms does it have?

c Explain why water molecules form on average two hydrogen bonds per molecule, whereas the ammonia molecule, NH_3, forms only one.

Living with hydrogen bonds

Proteins are a class of important biological molecules that fulfil a wide variety of functions in living things, including enzyme catalysts. The exact shape of a protein molecule is vital to its function. Proteins are long chain molecules with lots of $C=O$ and N—H groups which can form hydrogen bonds. These hydrogen bonds hold the protein chains into fixed shapes. One common shape is the protein chain that forms a spiral (helix), as shown here.

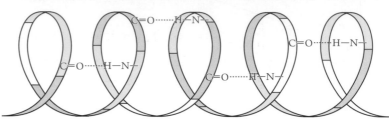

Another example is the beta-pleated sheet. Here protein chains line up side by side, held in position by hydrogen bonds to form a two-dimensional sheet. The protein that forms silk has this structure.

The relative weakness of hydrogen bonds means that the shapes of proteins can easily be altered. Heating proteins much above body temperature starts to break hydrogen bonds and causes the protein to lose its shape and thus its function. This is why enzymes lose their effect as catalysts when heated. We say the protein is denatured. We can see this when frying an egg. The clear liquid protein albumen is transformed into an opaque white solid.

Ironing

When we iron clothes, the iron provides heat to break hydrogen bonds in the crumpled material and pressure to force the molecules into new positions so that the material is flat. When we remove the iron, the hydrogen bonds reform and hold the molecules in these new positions, keeping the fabric flat.

DNA

Another vital biological molecule is DNA (deoxyribonucleic acid). It is the molecule that stores and copies genetic information that makes offspring resemble their parents. This molecule exists as a double-stranded helix. The two strands of the spiral are held together by hydrogen bonds. When cells divide or replicate, the hydrogen bonds break (but the covalently bonded main chains stay unchanged). The two separate helixes then act as templates for a new helix to form on each, so we end up a copy of the original helix.

3.7 States of matter: gases, liquids and solids

Learning objectives:

- What energy changes occur when solids melt and liquids vaporise?

- How are the values of enthalpies of fusion (melting) and vaporisation explained?

- What are the physical properties of ionic solids, metals, macromolecular solids and molecular solids in terms of their detailed structures and bonding?

Specification reference 3.1.3

One of the key ideas of science is that matter, which is anything with mass, is made of tiny particles; it is particulate. These particles are in motion, which means they have kinetic energy. To understand the differences between the three states of matter – gas, liquid and solid, we need to be able to explain the energy changes associated with these physical states.

The three states of matter

Table 1 sets out the simple model we use for the three states of matter.

Table 1 *The three states of matter*

	Solid	Liquid	Gas
Arrangement of particles	Regular	Random	Random
Evidence	Crystal shapes have straight edges. Solids have definite shapes.	None direct but a liquid changes shape to fill the bottom of its container.	None direct but a gas will fill its container.
Spacing	Close	Close	Far apart
Evidence	Solids are not easily compressed	Liquids are not easily compressed	Gases are easily compressed
Movement	Vibrating about a point	Rapid 'jostling'	Rapid
Evidence	*Diffusion is very slow. Solids expand on heating.	*Diffusion is slow. Liquids evaporate.	*Diffusion is rapid. Gases exert pressure
Models	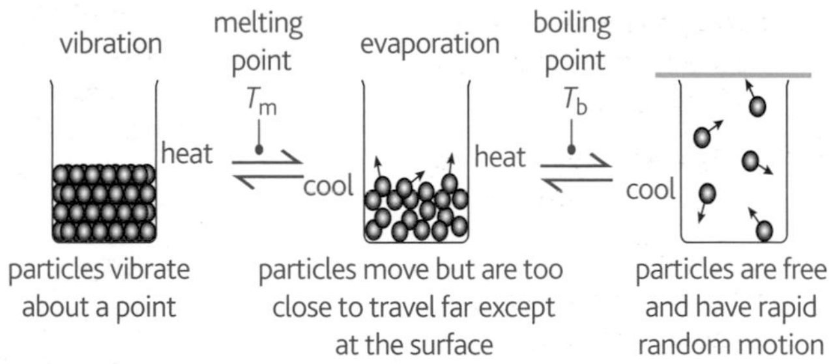		
	particles vibrate about a point	particles move but are too close to travel far except at the surface	particles are free and have rapid random motion

*Brownian motion

Energy changes on heating

Heating a solid

When we first heat a solid and supply energy to the particles, it makes them vibrate more about a fixed position. This slightly increases the average distance between the particles and so the solid expands.

Turning a solid to liquid (melting – also called fusion)

In order to turn a solid, with its ordered, closely packed, vibrating particles into a liquid, where the particles are moving independently but still closely together, we have to supply more energy. This energy is needed to weaken the forces that act between the particles, holding them together in the solid state. The energy needed is called the latent heat of fusion, or more correctly the **enthalpy change of fusion**. While a solid is melting, the temperature does not change because the heat energy provided is absorbed as the forces between particles are weakened.

Enthalpy is the heat measured under constant pressure, see Topic 7.2. The temperature depends on the average kinetic energy of the particles and is therefore related to their speed; the greater the energy, the faster they go.

Heating a liquid

When we heat a liquid, we supply energy to the particles, which makes them move more quickly; we say they have more kinetic energy. On average, the particles move a little further apart so liquids also expand on heating.

Turning a liquid to gas (boiling – also called vaporisation)

In order to turn a liquid into a gas, we need to supply enough energy to break all the intermolecular forces between the particles. A gas consists of particles that are far apart and moving independently. The energy needed is called the latent heat of vaporisation or more correctly the **enthalpy change of vaporisation**. As with melting, there is no temperature change during the process of boiling.

Heating a gas

As we heat a gas, the particles gain kinetic energy and move faster. They get much further apart and so gases expand a great deal on heating.

■ Crystals

Crystals are solids. The particles have a regular arrangement and are held together by forces of attraction. These could be strong bonds – covalent, ionic or metallic, or weaker intermolecular forces – van der Waals, dipole–dipole or hydrogen bonds. The strength of the forces of attraction between the particles in the crystal affects the physical properties of the crystals. For example the stronger the force, the higher the melting temperature and the greater the enthalpy of fusion (the more difficult they are to melt). There are four basic crystal types: ionic, metallic, molecular and macromolecular.

Ionic crystals

Ionic compounds have strong electrostatic attractions between oppositely charged ions. Sodium chloride is a typical ionic crystal, see Topic 3.1. Ionic compounds have high melting points. This is a result of the strong electrostatic attractions which extend throughout the structure. These require a lot of energy to break in order for the ions to move apart from each other.

Metallic crystals

Metals exist as a lattice of positive ions embedded in a delocalised sea of electrons, see magnesium, Figure 1 in Topic 3.4. Again the attraction of positive to negative extends throughout the crystal. The high melting temperature is a result of these strong metallic bonds.

Molecular crystals

Molecular crystals consist of molecules held in a regular array by one or more of the three types of intermolecular forces: van der Waals forces, dipole–dipole

distance between a pair of covalently-bonded iodine atoms = 0.267 nm

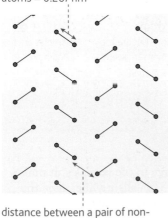

distance between a pair of non-bonded iodine atoms (held by van der Waals forces) = 0.354 nm

Figure 1 *The arrangement of an iodine crystal*

forces and hydrogen bonding. Covalent bonds *within* the molecules hold the atoms together but they do not act *between* the molecules. Intermolecular forces are much weaker than covalent, ionic or metallic bonds, so molecular crystals have low melting temperatures and low enthalpies of fusion.

Iodine (Figure 1) is an example of a molecular crystal. A strong covalent bond holds pairs of iodine atoms together to form I_2 molecules. Since iodine molecules have a large number of electrons, the van der Waals forces are strong enough to hold the molecules together as a solid. But van der Waals forces are much weaker than covalent bonds, giving iodine the following properties:

- Its crystals are soft and break easily.
- It has a low melting temperature and sublimes readily to form gaseous iodine molecules.
- It does not conduct electricity because there are no charged particles to carry charge.

Macromolecular crystals

Covalent compounds are not always made up of small molecules. In some substances the covalent bonds extend throughout the compound and we have the typical property of a giant structure held together with strong bonds: a high melting temperature.

Diamond and graphite

Diamond and graphite are both made of the element carbon only. They are called polymorphs or allotropes of carbon. They are very different materials because their atoms are differently bonded and arranged. They are examples of macromolecular structures.

Diamond

Diamond consists of pure carbon with covalent bonding between every carbon atom. The bonds spread throughout the structure, which is why it is a giant structure.

A carbon atom has four electrons in its outer shell. In diamond, each carbon atom forms four single covalent bonds with other carbon atoms, as shown in Figure 2. These four electron pairs repel each other, following the rules of the electron pair repulsion theory (see Topic 3.9). In three dimensions the bonds actually point to the corners of a tetrahedron (with bond angles of 109.5°).

Each carbon atom is in an identical position in the structure, surrounded by four other carbon atoms. Figure 4 shows this three-dimensional arrangement.

The atoms form a giant three-dimensional lattice of strong covalent bonds, which is why diamond has the following properties:

- It is a very hard material (one of the hardest known).
- It has a very high melting point, over 3700 K.
- It does not conduct electricity because there are no free charged particles to carry charge.

Graphite

Graphite also consists of pure carbon but the atoms are bonded and arranged differently than in diamond. Graphite has two sorts of bonding: strong covalent, and the weaker van der Waals forces.

In graphite, each carbon atom forms three single covalent bonds to other carbon atoms. As predicted by bonding electron pair repulsion theory (see Topic 3.9), these form a flat trigonal arrangement, sometimes called

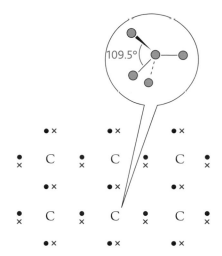

Figure 2 *A 'dot-and-cross' diagram showing the bonding in diamond*

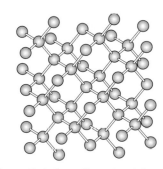

Figure 3 *A three-dimensional diagram of diamond*

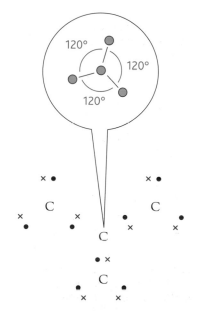

Figure 4 *A 'dot-and-cross' diagram showing the three covalent bonds in graphite*

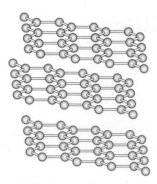

Figure 5 *The layers of hexagons in graphite*

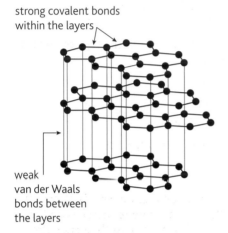

strong covalent bonds
within the layers

weak
van der Waals
bonds between
the layers

Figure 6 *van der Waals forces between the layers of carbon atoms in graphite*

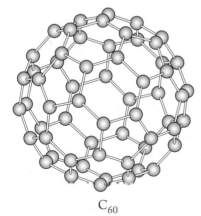

C_{60}

Figure 7 *Buckminsterfullerene*

How science works

Sliding layers of carbon

It is now believed that molecules such as oxygen can slide in between the layers of carbon and it is this that allows them to slide.

---

trigonal planar, with a bond angle of 120° (Figure 4). This leaves each carbon atom with a 'spare' electron in a p orbital that is not part of the three single covalent bonds.

This arrangement produces a two-dimensional layer of linked hexagons of carbon atoms, rather like a chicken-wire fence (Figure 5).

The p orbitals with the 'spare' electron merge above and below the plane of the carbon atoms in each layer. These electrons can move anywhere within the layer. They are delocalised. This adds to the strength of the bonding and is rather like the delocalised sea of electrons in a metal, but in two dimensions only.

These delocalised electrons are what make graphite conduct electricity (very rare for a non-metal). They can travel freely through the material, though graphite will only conduct along the hexagonal planes, not at right angles to them.

There is no covalent bonding *between* the layers of carbon atoms. They are held together by the much weaker van der Waals forces, see Figure 6. This weak intermolecular force of attraction means that the layers can slide across one another and so graphite is soft and flaky. It is the 'lead' in pencils. The flakiness allows the graphite to transfer from the pencil to the paper.

■ Graphite is a soft material.

■ It has a very high melting temperature and in fact it breaks down before it melts. This is because of the strong network of covalent bonds, which make it a giant structure.

■ It conducts electricity along the planes of the hexagons.

How science works

Giant footballs

More recently a number of other forms of pure carbon have been discovered. Chemists found the first one whilst they were looking for molecules in outer space. The structures of these new forms of carbon include closed cages of carbon atoms and also tubes called nanotubes. The most famous is buckminsterfullerene, C_{60} in which atoms are arranged in a football-like shape (Figure 7). Harry Kroto and colleagues received the Nobel Prize for the discovery. Now, scientists are investigating many uses for these new materials.

Summary questions

1 What is the difference between a macromolecular crystal and a molecular crystal in terms of the following?

a bonding

b properties

2 Phosphorus consists of P_4 molecules and has a melting point of 317 K while sulfur, S_8, has a melting point of 386 K. Explain this difference in terms of bonding.

3 Explain why graphite can be used as a lubricant.

4 Explain how graphite conducts electricity. How does it conduct differently from metals?

5 Why do both diamond and graphite have high melting points?

3.8 Bonding and structure – summary

Learning objectives:

■ What are the three types of strong bonds?

■ What are the three types of intermolecular forces?

■ How are melting temperatures and structure related?

■ How is electrical conductivity related to bonding?

Specification reference: 3.1.3

Bonding

There are three types of **strong** bonding that hold atoms together: ionic, covalent and metallic. All three involve the outer electrons of the atoms concerned:

■ In covalent bonding, the electrons are shared between atoms.

■ In ionic bonding, electrons are transferred from metal atoms to non-metal atoms.

■ In metallic bonding, electrons are spread between metal atoms to form a lattice of ions held together by delocalised electrons.

If we know what the compound is, we can usually tell the type of bonding from the types of atoms that it contains:

■ Metal atoms only – metallic bonding

■ Metal and non-metal – ionic bonding

■ Non-metal atoms only – covalent bonding

The three types of bonding give rise to different properties.

Electrical conductivity

The property that best tells us what sort of bonding we have is electrical conductivity. Metals and alloys (an alloy is a mixture of metals) conduct electricity well, in both the solid and liquid states due to their **metallic bonding**. The current is carried by the delocalised electrons that hold the metal ions together, see Figure 1.

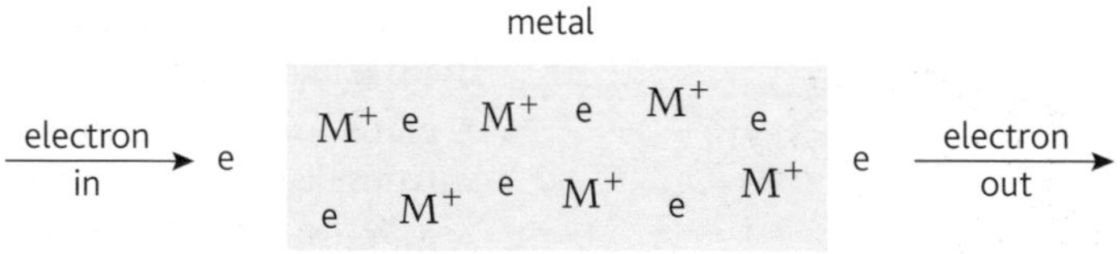

$$\text{metal}$$

$$\xrightarrow[\text{in}]{\text{electron}} \quad e \quad \boxed{\begin{array}{cccccc} M^+ & e & M^+ & e & M^+ & e \\ e & M^+ & e & M^+ & e & M^+ \end{array}} \quad e \quad \xrightarrow[\text{out}]{\text{electron}}$$

Figure 1 *The conduction of electricity by a metal*

Ionic compounds only conduct electricity in the liquid state (or when dissolved in water). They do *not* conduct when they are solid. The current is carried by the movement of ions towards the electrode of opposite charge. The ions are free to move when the ionic compound is liquid or dissolved in water. In the solid state they are fixed rigidly in position in the ionic lattice, Figure 2.

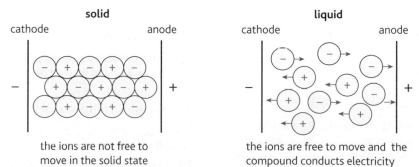

Figure 2 *Ionic liquids conduct electricity, ionic solids do not*

■ Link

Note there are some covalently bonded substances that do conduct electricity, for example graphite, see Topic 3.7.

Covalently bonded substances do not conduct electricity in either the solid or liquid state. This is because there are no charged particles to carry the current. Covalent compounds are often insoluble in water but some react to form ions e.g. ethanoic acid (present in vinegar). The solutions can then conduct electricity.

We can therefore decide what type of bonding a substance has by looking at how it conducts electricity. This is summarised in Table 1.

Table 1 *The pattern of electrical conductivity tells us about the type of bonding*

Type of bonding	Electrical conductivity		
	Solid	Liquid	Aqueous solution
Metallic	✓	✓	Does not dissolve but may react
Ionic	✗	✓	✓
Covalent	✗	✗	✗ (but may react)

■ Structure

Structure describes the arrangement in which atoms, ions or molecules are held together in space. There are four main types: simple molecular, macromolecular (giant covalent), giant ionic and metallic.

- A **simple molecular** structure is composed of small molecules; small groups of atoms strongly held together by covalent bonding. The forces of attraction *between* molecules are much weaker (often over 50 times weaker than a covalent bond) and are called intermolecular forces. Examples of molecules include Cl_2, H_2O, H_2SO_4 and NH_3.

- A **macromolecular** structure is one in which large numbers of atoms are linked in a regular three-dimensional arrangement by covalent bonds. Examples include diamond and silicon dioxide (silica), the main constituent of sand.

- A **giant ionic** structure consists of a lattice of positive ions each surrounded in a regular arrangement by negative ions and *vice versa*.

- A **metallic** structure consists of a regular lattice of positively charged metal ions held together by a cloud of delocalised electrons.

Macromolecular, giant ionic and metallic structures are often called giant structures because they have regular three-dimensional arrangements of atoms in contrast with simple molecular structures.

Melting and boiling points

The property that best tells us if a structure is giant or simple molecular is the melting (or boiling) point

- Simple molecular compounds have low melting (and boiling) points.
- Giant structures generally have high melting (and boiling) points.

We know that if a compound has a low melting (and boiling) point, it has a simple molecular structure. We know that all molecular compounds are covalently bonded. So all compounds with low melting (and boiling) points must have covalent bonding.

But take care: a compound with covalent bonding may have either a giant structure or a simple molecular structure and therefore may have either a high or low melting (and boiling) point.

■ Hint

Generally any substance with a high melting point also has a high boiling point. However, there are some substances, such as iodine, that sublime; they turn directly from solid to vapour.

Intermolecular forces

When we melt and boil simple molecular compounds, we are breaking the intermolecular forces *between* the molecules, not the covalent bonds *within* them. So, the strength of the intermolecular forces determines the melting (and boiling) points.

There are three types of intermolecular force. In order of increasing strength, these are:

■ van der Waals, which act between all atoms

■ dipole–dipole forces, which act between molecules with permanent dipoles: $X^{\delta+}–Y^{\delta-}$

■ hydrogen bonds, which act between the molecules formed when highly electronegative atoms (O, N or F) and hydrogen atoms are covalently bonded.

Table 2 is a summary of the different properties of substances with covalent, ionic and metallic bonding.

Table 2 *Summary of properties of substances with covalent, ionic and metallic bonding*

	Melting point, T_m	Structure	Bond	Electrical conductivity		
				Solid	Liquid	Aqueous solution
	high	giant	Ionic	No	Yes	Yes
	high	giant (macromolecular)	covalent	No	No	No
	low	simple molecular	covalent	No	No	No (but may react)
	high	giant	metallic	Yes	Yes	– (does not dissolve) (may react)

Summary questions

The table at the right gives some information about four substances.

1 Which substances have giant structures?

2 Which substance is a gas at room temperature?

3 Which substance is a metal?

4 Which substances are covalently bonded?

5 Which substance has ionic bonding?

6 Which substance is a macromolecule?

Substance	Melting point / K (°C)	Boiling point / K (°C)	Electrical conductivity	
			As solid	As liquid
A	1356 (1083)	2840 (2567)	good	good
B	91 (–182)	109 (–164)	poor	poor
C	1996 (1723)	2503 (2230)	poor	good
D	1266 (993)	1968 (1695)	poor	poor

The shapes of molecules and ions

Learning objectives:

- What rules govern the shapes of simple molecules?

- How does the number of electron pairs around an atom affect the shape of the molecule?

- What happens to the shape of a molecule when a bonding pair of electrons is replaced with a non-bonding pair?

Specification reference: 3.1.3

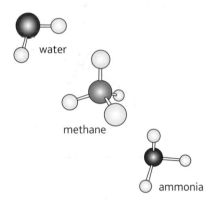

Figure 1 *The shapes of water, methane and ammonia molecules*

Molecules are three-dimensional and they come in many different shapes, see Figure 1.

💡 ⓘ Electron pair repulsion theory

We have seen that electrons in molecules exist in pairs in volumes of space called orbitals. We can predict the shape of a simple covalent molecule, for example, one consisting of a central atom surrounded by a number of other atoms, by using the ideas that:

- each pair of electrons around an atom will repel all other electron pairs

- the pairs of electrons will therefore take up positions as far apart as possible to minimise repulsion.

This is called the **electron pair repulsion theory**.

Electron pairs may be:

- a shared pair

- a lone pair.

The shape of a simple molecule depends on the number of pairs of electrons that surround the central atom. To work out the shape of any molecule you first need to draw a 'dot-and-cross' diagram to find the number of pairs of electrons.

Two pairs of electrons

If there are two pairs of electrons around the atom, the molecule will be **linear**. The furthest away from each other the two pairs can get is 180° apart. Beryllium chloride, which is a covalently bonded molecule in the gas phase, despite being a metal–non-metal compound, is an example of this:

two groups of electrons

$$\ :Cl \overset{\bullet}{\underset{\times}{\bullet}} Be \overset{\bullet}{\underset{\times}{\bullet}} Cl: \qquad Cl - \overset{180°}{Be} - Cl$$

Three pairs of electrons

If there are three pairs of electrons around the central atom, they will be 120° apart. The molecule is flat and the shape is called **trigonal planar**. Boron trifluoride is an example of this:

$$F, \overset{120°}{\underset{F}{B}} - F$$

Hint

It is acceptable to draw electron diagrams that show electrons in the outer shells only.

AQA Examiner's tip

Draw structures ahowing bonds and lone electron pairs.

Four pairs of electrons

If there are four pairs of electrons, they are furthest apart when they are arranged so that they point to the four corners of a tetrahedron. This shape, with one atom positioned at the centre, is called **tetrahedral**, see Figure 2.

Methane, CH_4, is an example. The carbon atom is situated at the centre of the tetrahedron with the hydrogen atoms at the vertices. The angles here are 109.5°. This is a three-dimensional, not a flat, arrangement so the sum of the angles can be more than 360°:

The ammonium **ion** is also tetrahedral. It has four groups of electrons surrounding the nitrogen atom. The fact that the ion has an overall charge does not affect the shape:

Five pairs of electrons

If there are five pairs of electrons, the shape usually adopted is that of a trigonal bipyramid. Phosphorus pentachloride is an example:

Six pairs of electrons

If there are six pairs of electrons, the shape adopted is octahedral, with bond angles of 90°. The sulfur hexafluoride, SF_6, molecule is an example of this:

Molecules with lone pairs of electrons

Some molecules have unshared (lone) pairs of electrons. These are electrons that are not part of a covalent bond. The lone pairs affect the shape of the molecule. Always watch out for the lone pairs in your 'dot-and-cross' diagram because otherwise you might overlook their effect. Ammonia and water are good examples of molecules where lone pairs affect the shape.

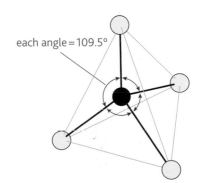

each angle = 109.5°

Figure 2 *A tetrahedron has four points and four faces*

Ammonia, NH_3

Ammonia has four pairs of electrons and one of the groups is a lone pair:

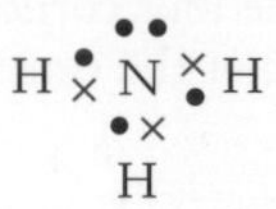

$$H \overset{\bullet}{\underset{\bullet}{\times}} \overset{\bullet\bullet}{\underset{\bullet\times}{N}} \overset{\times}{} H$$

$$H$$

With its four pairs of electrons around the nitrogen atom, the ammonia molecule has a shape based on a tetrahedron. However, there are only three 'arms' so the shape is that of a triangular pyramid:

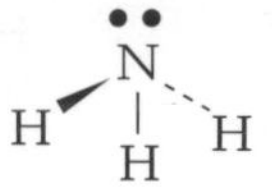

Another way of looking at this is that the *electron pairs* form a tetrahedron but the *bonds* form a triangular pyramid. (There is an atom at each vertex but, unlike the tetrahedral arrangement, no atom in the centre.)

Bonding pair–lone pair repulsion

The angles of a regular tetrahedron, see Figure 2, are all 109.5° but lone pairs affect these angles. In ammonia, for example, the *shared* pairs of electrons are attracted towards the nitrogen nucleus and also the hydrogen nucleus. However, the *lone* pair is attracted only by the nitrogen nucleus and is therefore pulled closer to it than the shared pairs. So repulsion between a lone pair of electrons and a bonding pair of electrons is greater than that between two bonding pairs. This effect 'squeezes' the hydrogen atoms together, reducing all the H–N–H angles. The approximate rule of thumb is 2° per lone pair, so the bond angles in ammonia are approximately 107°:

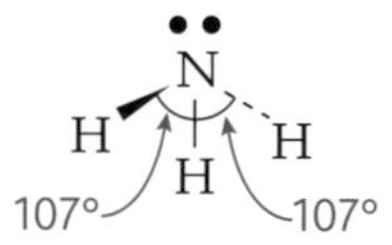

Water, H_2O

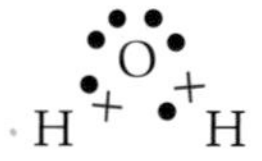

Look at the 'dot-and-cross' diagram for water. There are four pairs of electrons around the oxygen atom so, as with ammonia, the shape is based on a tetrahedron. However, two of the 'arms' of the tetrahedron are lone pairs that are not part of a bond. This results in a **V-shaped** or angular molecule. As in ammonia (above) the electron pairs form a tetrahedron but the bonds form a V-shape. With two lone pairs, the H–O–H angle is reduced to 104.5°:

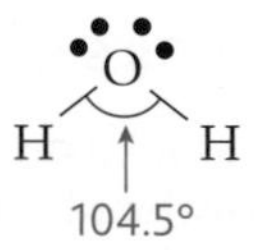

104.5°

Chlorine tetrafluoride ion, ClF_4

The 'dot-and-cross' diagram for this ion is as shown:

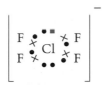

There are four bonding pairs of electrons and two lone pairs. One of the lone pairs contains an electron that has been donated to it, so the charge on the ion is negative (-1). This electron is shown as a square in the dot-and-cross diagram. This means that there are six pairs of electrons around the Cl atom: four bonds and two lone pairs. The shape is therefore based on an octahedron in which two arms are not part of a bond.

As lone pairs repel the most, they adopt a position furthest apart. This leaves a flat square-shaped ion described as square planar. The lone pairs are above and below the plane, as in Figure 3.

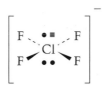

A summary of the repulsion between electron pairs

bonding pair–bonding pair $\downarrow$

lone pair–bonding pair   repulsion increases

lone pair–lone pair $\downarrow$

Summary questions

1. Draw a 'dot-and-cross' diagram for NF_3 and predict its shape.

2. Explain why NF_3 has a different shape to BF_3.

3. Draw a 'dot-and-cross' diagram for the molecule silane, SiH_4, and describe its shape.

4. What is the H—Si—H angle in the silane molecule?

5. Predict the shape of the H_2S molecule *without* drawing a dot-and-cross diagram.

1   The equation below shows the reaction between boron trifluoride and a fluoride ion.

$$BF_3 + F^- \longrightarrow BF_4^-$$

(a) Draw diagrams to show the shape of the BF_3 molecule and the shape of the BF_4^- ion. In each case, name the shape. Account for the shape of the BF_4^- ion and state the bond angle present.

(b) In terms of the electrons involved, explain how the bond between the BF_3 molecule and the F^- ion is formed. Name the type of bond formed in this reaction.   *(9 marks)*

AQA, 2006

2   Phosphorus exists in several different forms, two of which are white phosphorus and red phosphorus. White phosphorus consists of P_4 molecules, and melts at 44 °C.

Red phosphorus is macromolecular, and has a melting point above 550 °C.

Explain what is meant by the term *macromolecular*. By considering the structure and bonding present in these two forms of phosphorus, explain why their melting points are so different.   *(5 marks)*

AQA, 2006

3   The table below shows the electronegativity values of some elements.

	Fluorine	Chlorine	Bromine	Iodine	Carbon	Hydrogen
Electronegativity	4.0	3.0	2.8	2.5	2.5	2.1

(a) Define the term *electronegativity*.   *(2 marks)*

(b) The table below shows the boiling points of fluorine, fluoromethane (CH_3F) and hydrogen fluoride.

	Fluorine	Fluoromethane	Hydrogen fluoride
	F—F		H—F
Boiling point /K	85	194	293

(i)   Name the strongest type of intermolecular force present in:

Liquid F_2 Liquid CH_3F Liquid HF

(ii) Explain how the strongest type of intermolecular force in liquid HF arises.   *(6 marks)*

(c) The table below shows the boiling points of some other hydrogen halides.

	HCl	HBr	HI
Boiling point /K	188	206	238

(i)   Explain the trend in the boiling points of the hydrogen halides from HCl to HI.

(ii) Give **one** reason why the boiling point of HF is higher than that of all the other hydrogen halides.   *(3 marks)*

AQA, 2006

4   (a) Methanol has the structure

$$H-\overset{\overset{\displaystyle H}{|}}{\underset{\underset{\displaystyle H}{|}}{C}}-O-H$$

Explain why the O—H bond in a methanol molecule is polar.   *(2 marks)*

(b) The boiling point of methanol is +65 °C; the boiling point of oxygen is −183 °C. Methanol and oxygen each have an M_r value of 32. Explain, in terms of the intermolecular forces present in each case, why the boiling point of methanol is much higher than that of oxygen.

(3 marks)

AQA, 2005

5 (a) Both HF and HCl are molecules having a polar covalent bond. Their boiling points are 293 K and 188 K respectively.

    (i) State which property of the atoms involved causes a bond to be polar.

    (ii) Explain, in terms of the intermolecular forces present in each compound, why HF has a higher boiling point than HCl.

(4 marks)

(b) When aluminium chloride reacts with chloride ions, as shown by the equation below, a co-ordinate bond is formed.

$$AlCl_3 + Cl^- \longrightarrow AlCl_4^-$$

Explain how this co-ordinate bond is formed.

(2 marks)

(c) Draw the shape of the PCl_5 molecule and of the PCl_4^+ ion. State the value(s) of the bond angles.

(4 marks)

AQA, 2003

6 (a) Predict the shapes of the SF_6 molecule and the $AlCl_4^-$ ion. Draw diagrams of these species to show their three-dimensional shapes. Name the shapes and suggest values for the bond angles. Explain your reasoning.

(8 marks)

(b) Perfume is a mixture of fragrant compounds dissolved in a volatile solvent.

When applied to the skin the solvent evaporates, causing the skin to cool for a short time. After a while, the fragrance may be detected some distance away. Explain these observations.

(4 marks)

AQA, 2003

7 (a) The shape of the molecule BCl_3 and that of the unstable molecule CCl_2 are shown below.

    (i) Why is each bond angle exactly 120° in BCl_3?

    (ii) Predict the bond angle in CCl_2 and explain why this angle is different from that in BCl_3.

(5 marks)

(b) Give the name which describes the shape of molecules having bond angles of 109° 28'. Give an example of one such molecule.

(2 marks)

(c) The shape of the XeF_4 molecule is shown below.

$$F \cdots \overset{\cdot\cdot}{\underset{\underset{F}{\cdot\cdot}}{Xe}} \cdots F$$

    (i) State the bond angle in XeF_4.

    (ii) Suggest why the lone pairs of electrons are opposite each other in this molecule.

    (iii) Name the shape of this molecule, given that the shape describes the positions of the Xe and F atoms only.

(4 marks)

(d) Draw a sketch of the NF_3 molecule. Indicate in your sketch any lone pairs of electrons on nitrogen.

(2 marks)

AQA, 2002

8 (a) (i) Describe the bonding in a metal.

    (ii) Explain why magnesium has higher melting point than sodium.

(4 marks)

(b) Why do diamond and graphite both have high melting points?

(3 marks)

(c) Why is graphite a good conductor of electricity?

(1 mark)

(d) Why is graphite soft?

(2 marks)

AQA, 2002

4 Periodicity

4.1 The periodic table

Learning objectives:

■ Where are the s-, p- and d-blocks of elements in the periodic table?

Specification reference 3.1.4

The periodic table is a list of all the elements in order of increasing atomic number. We can predict the properties of an element from its position in the table. We can use it to explain the similarities of certain elements and the trends in their properties, in terms of their electronic arrangements.

The structure of the periodic table

The periodic table has been written in many forms including pyramids and spirals. The one shown at the end of the book is one common layout. Some areas of the periodic table are given names. These are shown in Figure 1.

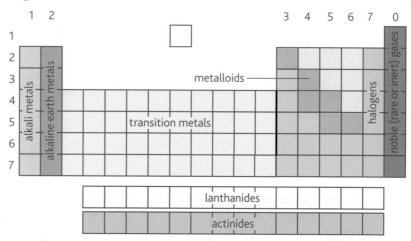

■ **Figure 1** *Named areas of the periodic table*

Metals and non-metals

The black stepped line in Figure 1 divides metals (on its left) from non-metals (on its right). Elements that touch this line, such as silicon, have a combination of metallic and non-metallic properties. They are called metalloids or semi-metals. Silicon, for example, is a non-metal but it looks quite shiny and conducts electricity, although not as well as a metal.

A common form of the periodic table

The version of the periodic table used in AQA examinations is shown in Figure 2. The lanthanides and actinides are omitted and two alternative numbering schemes for groups are shown.

■ **How science works**

The modern periodic table

The development of the periodic table is one of the greatest achievements in chemistry. A number of chemists contributed but the credit for the final version goes firmly to a Russian, Dmitri Mendeleev, in 1869.

He realised that there were undiscovered elements. He left spaces for some unknown elements, and arranged the known elements so that similar elements lined up in columns. Since then, new elements have been discovered that fit into the gaps he left. Mendeleev even accurately predicted the properties of the missing elements, confirming the success of his periodic table.

1	2		key									3	4	5	6	7	0
																	(18)

key:
relative atomic mass
atomic symbol
name
atomic (proton) number

1.0
H
hydrogen
1

(1)	(2)											(13)	(14)	(15)	(16)	(17)	4.0 **He** helium 2
6.9 **Li** lithium 3	9.0 **Be** beryllium 4											10.8 **B** boron 5	12.0 **C** carbon 6	14.0 **N** nitrogen 7	16.0 **O** oxygen 8	19.0 **F** fluorine 9	20.2 **Ne** neon 10
23.0 **Na** sodium 11	24.3 **Mg** magnesium 12	(3)	(4)	(5)	(6)	(7)	(8)	(9)	(10)	(11)	(12)	27.0 **Al** aluminium 13	28.1 **Si** silicon 14	31.0 **P** phosphorus 15	32.1 **S** sulfur 16	35.5 **Cl** chlorine 17	39.9 **Ar** argon 18
39.1 **K** potassium 19	40.1 **Ca** calcium 20	45.0 **Sc** scandium 21	47.9 **Ti** titanium 22	50.9 **V** vanadium 23	52.0 **Cr** chromium 24	54.9 **Mn** manganese 25	55.8 **Fe** iron 26	58.9 **Co** cobalt 27	58.7 **Ni** nickel 28	63.5 **Cu** copper 29	65.4 **Zn** zinc 30	69.7 **Ga** gallium 31	72.6 **Ge** germanium 32	74.9 **As** arsenic 33	79.0 **Se** selenium 34	79.9 **Br** bromine 35	83.8 **Kr** krypton 36
85.5 **Rb** rubidium 37	87.6 **Sr** strontium 38	88.9 **Y** yttrium 39	91.2 **Zr** zirconium 40	92.9 **Nb** niobium 41	95.9 **Mo** molybdenum 42	[98] **Tc** technetium 43	101.1 **Ru** ruthenium 44	102.9 **Rh** rhodium 45	106.4 **Pa** palladium 46	107.9 **Ag** silver 47	112.4 **Cd** cadmium 48	114.8 **In** indium 49	118.7 **Sn** tin 50	121.8 **Sb** antimony 51	127.6 **Te** tellurium 52	126.9 **I** iodine 53	131.3 **Xe** xenon 54
132.9 **Cs** caesium 55	137.3 **Ba** barium 56	138.9 **La*** lanthanum 57	178.5 **Hf** hafnium 72	180.9 **Ta** tantalum 73	183.8 **W** tungsten 74	186.2 **Re** rhenium 75	190.2 **Os** osmium 76	192.2 **Ir** iridium 77	195.1 **Pt** platinum 78	197.0 **Au** gold 79	200.6 **Hg** mercury 80	204.4 **Tl** thallium 81	207.2 **Pb** lead 82	209.0 **Bi** bismuth 83	[209] **Po** polonium 84	[210] **At** astatine 85	[222] **Rn** radon 86
[223] **Fr** francium 87	[226] **Ra** radium 88	[227] **Ac*** actinium 89	[261] **Rf** rutherfordium 104	[262] **Db** dubnium 105	[266] **Sg** seaborgium 106	[264] **Bh** bohrium 107	[277] **Hs** hassium 108	[268] **Mt** meitnerium 109	[271] **Ds** darmstadtium 110	[272] **Rg** roentgenium 111		elements with atomic numbers 112–116 have been reported but are not fully authenticated					

*the lanthanides (atomic numbers 58–71) and the actinides (atomic numbers 90–103) have been omitted

Figure 2 *The full form of the periodic table*

The s-, p-, d- and f-blocks of the periodic table

Figure 3 shows the elements described in terms of their electronic arrangement.

Areas of the table are labelled s-block, p-block, d-block and f-block.

■ All the elements that have their highest energy electrons in s-orbitals are in the s-block, e.g. sodium, Na $(1s^2\ 2s^2\ 2p^6\ 3s^1)$.

■ All the elements that have their highest energy electrons in p-orbitals, e.g. carbon, C $(1s^2\ 2s^2\ 2p^2)$ are called p-block.

■ All the elements that have their highest energy electrons in d-orbitals, e.g. iron, Fe $(1s^2\ 2s^2\ 2p^6\ 3s^2\ 3p^6\ 4s^2\ 3d^6)$ are called d-block and so on.

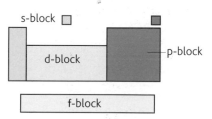

Figure 3 *The s-, p-, d- and f-block areas of the periodic table*

Strictly speaking the transition metals and the d-block elements are not exactly the same. Scandium and zinc are not transition elements because they do not form any compounds in which they have partly filled d-orbitals, which is the characteristic of transition metals.

The origin of the terms s, p, d and f is historical. When elements are heated they give out light energy at certain wavelengths, as excited electrons fall back from one energy level to a lower one. This causes lines to appear in the spectrum of light they give out. The letters s, p, d and f stand for words that were used first to describe the lines: s for sharp, p for principal, d for diffuse and f for fine.

■ Groups

A **group** is a vertical column of elements. The elements in the same group form a chemical 'family'; they have similar properties. Elements in the same group have the same number of electrons in the outer main level. The groups were traditionally numbered I–VII in Roman numerals plus zero for the noble gases, missing out the transition elements. It is now common to number them in ordinary numbers as 1–7 and 0 (or 1–8) and sometimes as 1–18 including the transition metals.

Reactivity

In the s-block, elements (metals) get more reactive as we down a group. To the right (non-metals), elements tend to get more reactive as we go up a group.

Transition elements are a block of rather unreactive metals. This is where most of the useful metals are found.

Lanthanides are metals which are not often encountered. They all tend to form 3+ ions in their compounds and have broadly similar reactivity.

Actinides are radioactive metals. Only thorium and uranium occur naturally in the Earth's crust in anything more than trace quantities.

■ Periods

Horizontal rows of elements in the periodic table are called **periods**. The periods are numbered starting from Period 1, which contains only hydrogen and helium. Period 2 contains the elements lithium to neon, and so on. There are trends in physical properties and chemical behaviour as we go across a period, see Topic 4.2.

The placing of hydrogen and helium

The positions of hydrogen and helium vary in different versions of the table. Helium is usually placed above the noble gases (Group 0) because of its properties. But, it is not a p-block element; its electronic arrangement is $1s^2$.

Hydrogen is sometimes placed above Group 1 but is often placed on its own. It usually forms singly charged 1+ (H^+) ions like the Group 1 elements but otherwise is not similar to them since they are all reactive metals and hydrogen is a gas. It is sometimes placed above the halogens because it can form H^- ions and also bond covalently.

■ Summary questions

1 From the elements, Br, Cl, Fe, K, Cs and Sb, pick out:

a two elements

  i in the same period **ii** in the same group **iii** that are non-metals

b one element

  i that is in the d-block **ii** that is in the s-block.

2 From the elements Tl, Ge, Xe, Sr and W, pick out:

a a noble gas

b the element described by Group 4, Period 4

c an s-block element

d a p-block element

e a d-block element.

4.2 Trends in the properties of elements of Period 3

Learning objectives:

■ What are the trends in melting and boiling temperatures of the elements in Period 3?

■ How can these trends be explained in terms of bonding and structure?

Specification reference 3.1.4

The periodic table reveals patterns in the properties of elements. For example, every time we go across a period we go from metals on the left to non-metals on the right. This is an example of **periodicity**. The word 'periodic' means recurring regularly.

💡 Periodicity and properties of elements in Period 3

Periodicity is explained by the electron arrangements of the elements.

■ The elements in Groups 1, 2 and 3, sodium, magnesium and aluminium, are metals. They have giant structures. They lose their outer electrons to form ionic compounds.

■ Silicon in Group 4 has four electrons in its outer shell with which it forms four covalent bonds. The element has some metallic properties and is classed as a semi-metal.

■ The elements in Groups 5, 6 and 7, phosphorus, sulfur and chlorine, are non-metals. They either accept electrons to form ionic compounds, or share their outer electrons to form covalent compounds.

■ Argon in Group 0 is a noble gas; it has a full outer shell and is unreactive.

Table 1 shows some trends across Period 3. Similar trends are found in other periods.

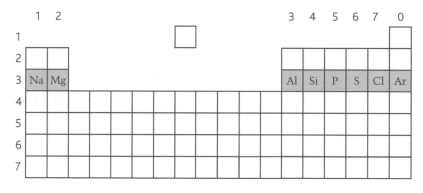

Figure 1 *The periodic table with Period 3 highlighted*

🔁 Trends in melting and boiling points

The trends in melting and boiling points are shown in Figure 2.

There is a clear break in the middle of the table between elements with high melting points (on the left, with sodium in Group 1 as the exception) and those with low melting points (on the right). These trends are due to their structures.

Table 1 *Some trends across Period 3*

Group	1	2	3	4	5	6	7	0
Element	Sodium	Magnesium	Aluminium	Silicon	Phosphorus	Sulfur	Chlorine	Argon
Electron arrangement	[Ne] $3s^1$	[Ne] $3s^2$	[Ne] $3s^2\,3p^1$	[Ne] $3s^2\,3p^2$	[Ne] $3s^2\,3p^3$	[Ne] $3s^2\,3p^4$	[Ne] $3s^2\,3p^5$	[Ne] $3s^2\,3p^6$
	s-block			p-block				
	Metals			Semi-metal	Non-metals			Noble gas
Structure of element	Giant metallic			Macro-molecular (giant covalent)	Molecular			Atomic
					P_4	S_8	Cl_2	Ar
Melting point, T_m / K	371	922	933	1683	317 (white)	392 (monoclinic)	172	84
Boiling point, T_b / K	1156	1380	2740	2628	553 (white)	718	238	87

■ Giant structures (found on the left) tend to have high melting points and boiling points.

■ Molecular or atomic structures (found on the right) tend to have low melting points and boiling points.

The melting points and boiling points of the metals increase from sodium to aluminium because of the strength of metallic bonding, see Topic 3.4. As we go from left to right the charge on the ion increases so more electrons join the delocalised electron 'sea' that holds the giant metallic lattice together.

The melting points of the non-metals with molecular structures depend on the sizes of the van der Waals forces between the molecules. This in turn depends on the number of electrons in the molecule and how closely the molecules can pack together. As a result the melting points of these non-metals are ordered: $S_8 > P_4 > Cl_2$. Silicon with its giant structure has a much higher melting point.

Summary questions

1 Whereabouts in a period do we find the following? Choose from 'left', 'right', 'middle'

   a Elements that lose electrons when forming compounds

   b Elements that accept electrons when forming compounds

2 In what group do we find an element that exists as the following?

   a Separate atoms

   b A macromolecule

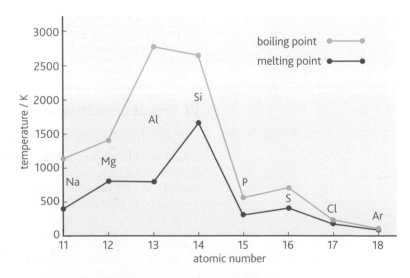

Figure 2 *Melting and boiling points of elements in Period 3*

4.3 More trends in the properties of the elements of Period 3

Learning objectives:

- What are the trends in atomic radius and first ionisation energy of the elements in Period 3?

- How can these trends be explained?

Specification reference 3.1.4

Some key properties of atoms, such as size and ionisation energy, are periodic, that is, there are similar trends as we go across each period in the periodic table.

Atomic radii

These tell us about the sizes of atoms. We cannot measure the radius of an isolated atom because there is no clear point at which the electron cloud density around it drops to zero. Instead we use half the distance between the centres of a pair of atoms, see Figure 1.

The atomic radius of an element can differ as it is a general term. It depends on the type of bond that it is forming: covalent, ionic, metallic, van der Waals, etc. The covalent radius is most commonly used as a measure of the size of the atom. Figure 2 shows a plot of covalent radius against atomic number.

(Even metals can form covalent molecules in the gas phase. Since noble gases do not bond covalently with one another, they do not have covalent radii, and so they are often left out of comparisons of atomic sizes.)

The graph shows that:

- atomic radius is a periodic property because it decreases across each period and there is a jump when we start the next period
- atoms get larger as we go down any group.

Why the radii of atoms decrease across a period

We can explain this trend by looking at the electronic structures of the elements in a period, for example, sodium to chlorine, Period 3, as shown in Figure 3.

As we move from sodium to chlorine we are adding protons to the nucleus and electrons to the outer main level, the third shell. The charge on the nucleus increases from 11+ to 17+. This increased charge pulls the electrons in closer to the nucleus. There are no additional electron shells to provide more shielding. So the size of the atom *decreases* as we go across the period.

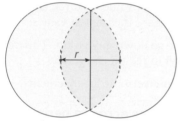

Figure 1 *Atomic radii are taken to be half the distance between the centres of a pair of atoms*

> **Hint**
>
> 1 nm is 1×10^{-9} m

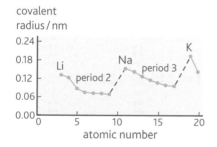

covalent radius / nm

Figure 2 *The periodicity of covalent radii. The noble gases are not included because they do not form covalent bonds with one another.*

atom	Na	Mg	Al	Si	P	S	Cl
size of atom	2,8,1	2,8,2	2,8,3	2,8,4	2,8,5	2,8,6	2,8,7
atomic (covalent) radius /nm	0.156	0.136	0.125	0.117	0.110	0.104	0.099
nuclear charge	11+	12+	13+	14+	15+	16+	17+

Figure 3 *The sizes and electronic structures of the elements sodium to chlorine*

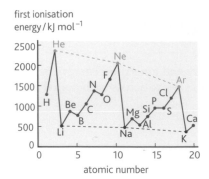

first ionisation
energy / kJ mol⁻¹

Figure 4 *The periodicity of first ionisation energies*

Why the radii of atoms increase down a group

As we go down a group in the periodic table, the atoms of each element have one extra complete main level of electrons compared with the one before. So, for example, in Group 1 the outer electron in potassium is in main level 4, whereas in sodium it is in main level 3. So as we go down the group, the outer electron main level is further from the nucleus and the atomic radii increase.

💡 First ionisation energy

The first ionisation energy is the energy required to convert a mole of isolated gaseous atoms into a mole of singly positively charged gaseous ions, i.e. to remove one electron from each atom, see Topic 1.6.

$$E(g) \longrightarrow E^+(g) + e^-(g) \qquad \text{where E stands for any element}$$

The first ionisation energies also have periodic patterns. These are shown in Figure 4.

The first ionisation energy generally increases across a period; alkali metals like sodium, Na, and lithium, Li, have the lowest values and the noble gases (helium, He, neon, Ne, and argon, Ar) have the highest values.

The first ionisation energy decreases as we go down any group. The trend for Group 1 and Group 0 are shown dotted in red on the graph.

We can explain these patterns by looking at electronic arrangements.

Why the first ionisation energy increases across a period

As we go across a period from left to right, the number of protons in the nucleus increases but the electrons enter the same main level, see Figure 5. The increased charge on the nucleus means that it gets increasingly difficult to remove an electron.

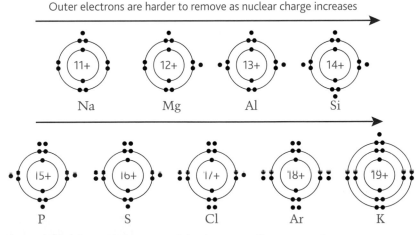

Figure 5 *The electronic structures of the elements sodium to potassium*

Why the first ionisation energy decreases going down a group

The number of filled inner levels increases down the group. This results in an increase in shielding. Also, the electron to be removed is at an increasing distance from the nucleus and is therefore held less strongly. Thus the outer electrons get easier to remove as we go down a group because they are further away from the nucleus.

Why there is a drop in ionisation energy from one period to the next

When we move from neon in Period 0 (far right) with electron arrangement 2,8 to sodium, 2,8,1 (Period 1, far left) there is a sharp drop in the first ionisation energy. This is because at sodium we start a new main level and so there is an increase in atomic radius, the outer electron is further from the nucleus, less strongly attracted and easier to remove.

Summary questions

1 What happens to the size of atoms as we go from left to right across a period? Choose from 'increase', 'decrease', 'no change'.

2 What happens to the first ionisation energy as we go from left to right across a period? Choose from 'increase', 'decrease', 'no change'.

3 What happens to the nuclear charge of the atoms as we go left to right across a period?

4 Why do the noble gases have the highest first ionisation energy of all the elements in their period?

4.4 A closer look at ionisation energies

Hint

Ionisation energies are sometimes called ionisation enthalpies.

This chapter revisits the trends in ionisation energies first dealt with in Topic 1.6, in the context of periodicity. The graph of first ionisation energy against atomic number across a period (Figure 4, Topic 4.3) is not smooth. Figure 1 below shows the same plot for Period 3 on a larger scale.

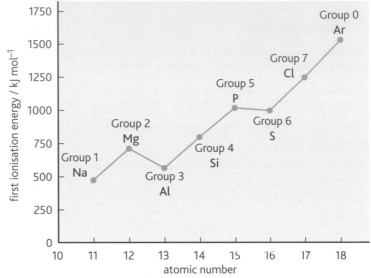

Figure 1 *Graph of first ionisation energy against atomic number for the elements of Period 3*

It shows that :

■ the first ionisation energy actually drops between Group 2 and Group 3, so that aluminium has a lower ionisation energy than magnesium

■ the ionisation energy drops again slightly between Group 5 (phosphorus) and Group 6 (sulfur).

Similar patterns occur in other periods. We can explain this if we look at the electron arrangements of these elements, see Topic 1.6.

The drop in first ionisation energy between Groups 2 and 3

This is to do with the sub-level from which the first electron is removed. For the first ionisation energy:

■ magnesium, $1s^2\,2s^2\,2p^6\,3s^2$, loses a 3s electron

■ aluminium, $1s^2\,2s^2\,2p^6\,3s^2\,3p^1$, loses the 3p electron.

The electron in the p sub-shell is already in a higher energy level than the s-electron, so it takes less energy to remove it, see Figure 2.

The drop in first ionisation energy between Groups 5 and 6

This is about the pairing of electrons. An electron in a pair will be easier to remove that one in an orbital on its own because it is already being repelled by the other electron. As shown in Figure 3:

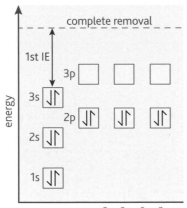

magnesium $1s^2\,2s^2\,2p^6\,3s^2$

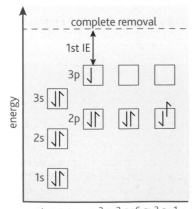

aluminium $1s^2\,2s^2\,2p^6\,3s^2\,3p^1$

Figure 2 *The first ionisation energies of magnesium and aluminium (not to scale)*

- phosphorus, $1s^2\,2s^2\,2p^6\,3s^2\,3p^3$, has no paired electrons because each p-electron is in a different orbital
- sulfur, $1s^2\,2s^2\,2p^6\,3s^2\,3p^4$, has two of its p-electrons paired so one of these will be easier to remove than an unpaired one.

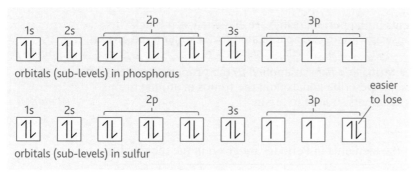

orbitals (sub-levels) in phosphorus

orbitals (sub-levels) in sulfur

Figure 3 *Electron arrangements of phosphorus and sulfur*

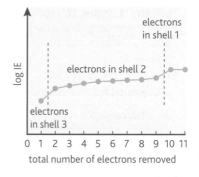

Figure 4 *Graph of successive ionisation energies against number of electrons removed for sodium. Note that the log of the ionisation energies is plotted in order to fit the large range of values onto the scale.*

Successive ionisation energies

If we remove the electrons from an atom one at a time, each one is harder to remove than the one before. Figure 4 is a graph of ionisation energy against number of electrons removed for sodium, electron arrangement 2,8,1.

We can see that there is a sharp increase in ionisation energy between the first and second electrons. This is followed by a gradual increase over the next eight electrons and then another jump before the final two electrons. Sodium, in Group 1 of the periodic table, has one electron in its outer main level (the easiest one to remove), eight in the next main level and two (very hard to remove) in the innermost main level.

Figure 5 is a graph of successive ionisation energies against number of electrons removed for aluminium, electron arrangement 2,8,3.

It shows three electrons that are relatively easy to remove – those in the outer main level, and then a similar pattern to that for sodium.

If we plotted a graph for chlorine, the first seven electrons would be relatively easier to remove than the next eight.

This means that the number of electrons that are relatively easy to remove tells us the group number in the periodic table. For example, the values of 906, 1763, 14 855 and 21 013 kJ mol⁻¹ for the first five ionisation energies of an element, tell us that the element is in Group 2. This is because the big jump occurs after two electrons have been removed.

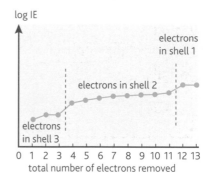

Figure 5 *Graph of successive ionisation energy against number of electrons removed for aluminium*

Summary questions

1 Write the electron arrangement in the form $1s^2$... for:
   a beryllium
   b boron.

2 If one electron is lost from for the following atoms, from what main level does it come?
   a beryllium
   b boron.

3 Why is the first ionisation energy of boron less than that of beryllium?

4 An element X has the following values for successive ionisation enthalpies (in kJ mol⁻¹): 1042, 2856, 4578, 7475, 8445, 53 268, 64 362.
   a What group in the periodic table is it in?
   b Explain your answer to a.

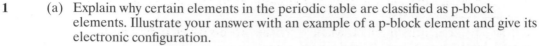

1 (a) Explain why certain elements in the periodic table are classified as p-block elements. Illustrate your answer with an example of a p-block element and give its electronic configuration. *(3 marks)*

(b) Explain the meaning of the term *periodicity* as applied to the properties of rows of elements in the periodic table. Describe and explain the trends in atomic radius and in conductivity for the elements sodium to argon. *(9 marks)*

AQA, 2002

2 Values for the covalent radii of the elements in Period 3 are given in the table below.

Elements	Na	Mg	Al	Si	P	S	Cl	Ar
Covalent radius/nm	0.157	0.136	0.125	0.117	0.110	0.104	0.099	–

Explain the decrease in the values shown in the table. *(3 marks)*

AQA, 2000

3 The diagram below shows the trend in the first ionisation energies of the elements from neon to aluminium.

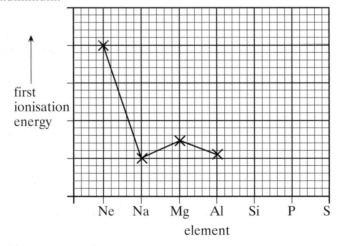

(a) Draw crosses on the graph to show the first ionisation energies of silicon, phosphorus and sulfur. *(3 marks)*

(b) Write an equation to illustrate the process which occurs during the first ionisation of neon. *(1 mark)*

(c) Explain why the first ionisation energy of neon and that of magnesium are both higher than that of sodium. *(4 marks)*

(d) Explain why the first ionisation energy of aluminium is lower than that of magnesium. *(2 marks)*

(e) State which one of the elements neon, sodium, magnesium, aluminium and silicon has the lowest melting point and explain your answer in terms of the structure and bonding present in that element. *(3 marks)*

(f) State which one of the elements neon, sodium, magnesium, aluminium and silicon has the highest melting point and explain your answer in terms of the structure and bonding present in that element. *(3 marks)*

AQA, 2001

4 (a) When aluminium is added to an aqueous solution of copper(II) chloride, $CuCl_2$, copper metal and aluminium chloride, $AlCl_3$, are formed. Write an equation to represent this reaction. *(1 mark)*

(b) (i) State the general trend in the first ionisation energy of the Period 3 elements from Na to Ar.

(ii) State how, and explain why, the first ionisation energy of aluminium does not follow this general trend. *(4 marks)*

(c) Give the equation, including state symbols, for the process which represents the second ionisation energy of aluminium. *(1 mark)*

(d) State and explain the trend in the melting points of the Period 3 metals Na, Mg and Al. *(3 marks)*

AQA, 2005

5 (a) The diagram below shows the melting points of some of the elements in Period 3.

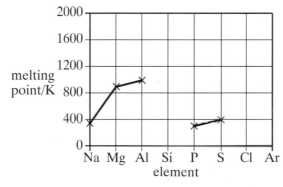

(i) On a copy of the diagram, use crosses to mark the approximate positions of the melting points for the elements silicon, chlorine and argon. Complete the diagram by joining the crosses.

(ii) By referring to its structure and bonding, explain your choice of position for the melting point of silicon.

(iii) Explain why the melting point of sulfur, S_8, is higher than that of phosphorus, P_4. *(8 marks)*

(b) State and explain the trend in melting point of the Group 2 elements Ca–Ba. *(3 marks)*

AQA, 2006

6 The table below gives the melting point for each of the Period 3 elements Na–Ar.

Element	Na	Mg	Al	Si	P	S	Cl	Ar
Melting point / K	371	923	933	1680	317	392	172	84

In terms of structure and bonding, explain why silicon has a high melting point, and why the melting point of sulfur is higher than that of phosphorus. *(7 marks)*

AQA, 2003

7 (a) State the meaning of the term *first ionisation energy* of an atom. *(2 marks)*

(b) Copy and complete the electron arrangement for the Mg^{2+} ion.
$1s^2$ *(1 mark)*

(c) Identify the block in the periodic table to which magnesium belongs. *(1 mark)*

(d) Write an equation to illustrate the process occurring when the **second** ionisation energy of magnesium is measured. *(1 mark)*

(e) The Ne atom and the Mg^{2+} ion have the same number of electrons. Give **two** reasons why the first ionisation energy of neon is lower than the third ionisation energy of magnesium. *(2 marks)*

(f) There is a general trend in the first ionisation energies of the Period 3 elements, Na–Ar

(i) State and explain this general trend.

(ii) Explain why the first ionisation energy of sulfur is lower than would be predicted from the general trend. *(5 marks)*

AQA, 2006

5 Introduction to organic chemistry
5.1 Carbon compounds

Learning objectives:

- What is meant by the terms empirical formula, molecular formula and structural formula?

Specification reference 3.1.5

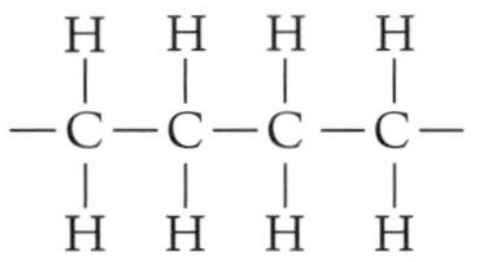

Figure 1 *Part of a hydrocarbon chain*

How science works

From inorganic to organic

Organic compounds were originally thought to be produced by living things only. This was disproved by Friedrich Wöhler in 1828. He made urea (an organic compound found in urine) from ammonium cyanate (an inorganic compound).

Organic chemistry is the chemistry of carbon compounds. Life on our planet is based on carbon and organic means 'to do with living beings'. Nowadays, we make our own carbon-based materials, like plastics and drugs, and there are large industries based on synthetic materials. There are far more compounds of carbon known than those of all the other elements put together, well over 10 million.

What is special about carbon?

Carbon can form rings and very long chains, which may be branched. This is because:

- a carbon atom has four electrons in its outer shell, so it forms four covalent bonds
- carbon–carbon bonds are relatively strong ($347\,kJ\,mol^{-1}$) and non-polar.

The carbon–hydrogen bond is also strong ($413\,kJ\,mol^{-1}$), and hydrocarbon chains form the skeleton of most organic compounds, see Figures 1, 2 and 3.

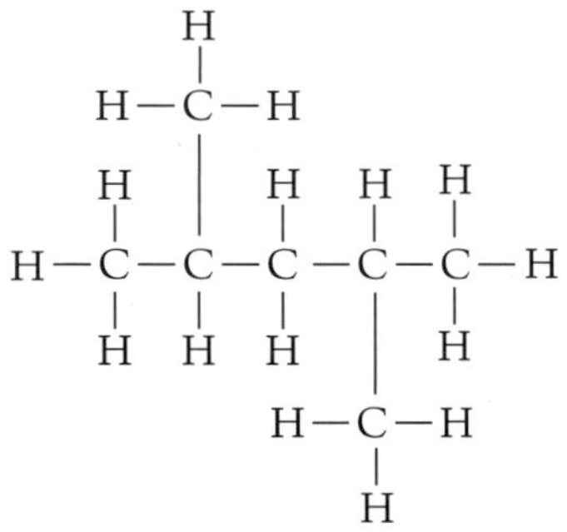

Figure 2 *A branched hydrocarbon chain*

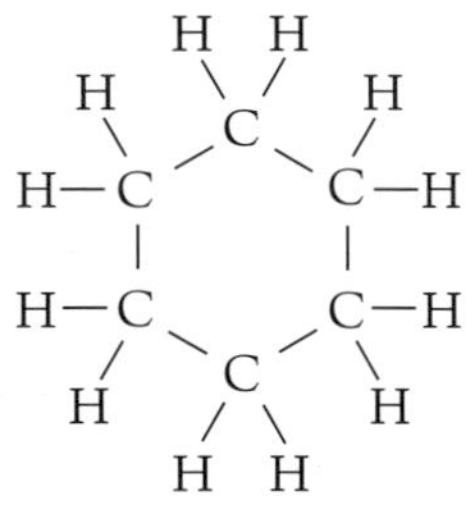

Figure 3 *A hydrocarbon ring*

Bonding in carbon compounds

In *all* stable carbon compounds, carbon forms four covalent bonds and has eight electrons in its outer shell. It can do this by forming bonds in different ways.

- By forming four single bonds as in methane:

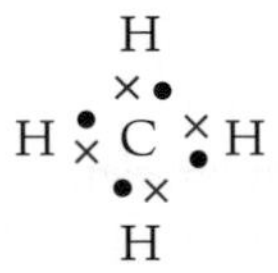

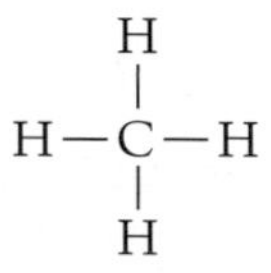

- By forming two single bonds and one double bond as in ethane:

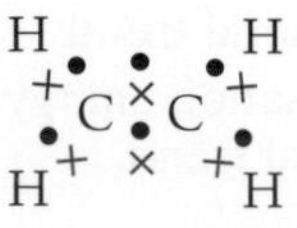

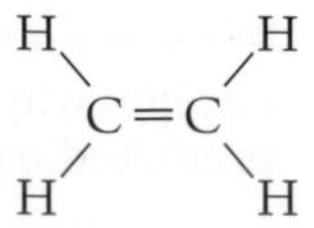

■ By forming one single bond and one triple bond as in ethyne:

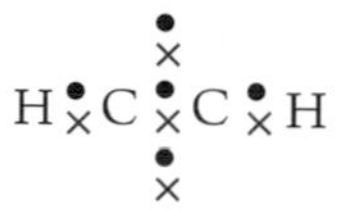

$$H \overset{\bullet}{\underset{\times}{\bullet}} C \overset{\times}{\underset{\bullet}{\times}} C \overset{\bullet}{\underset{\times}{\bullet}} H \qquad\qquad H-C \equiv C-H$$

■ Formulae of carbon compounds

The empirical formula

The empirical formula is a formula that shows the simplest ratio of the atoms of each element present in a compound. For example, ethane:

3.00 g of ethane contains 2.40 g of carbon, $A_r = 12.0$, and 0.600 g of hydrogen, $A_r = 1.0$. What is its empirical formula?

number of moles of carbon = 2.40/12.0 = 0.200 mol of carbon

number of moles of hydrogen = 0.600/1 = 0.600 mol of hydrogen

Dividing through by the smallest number (0.200) gives C : H as 1 : 3

So the empirical formula of ethane is CH_3.

The molecular formula

The molecular formula is the formula that shows the actual number of atoms of each element in the molecule. It is found from:

■ the empirical formula

■ the relative molecular mass of the empirical formula

■ the relative molecular mass of the molecule.

For example:

The empirical formula of ethane is CH_3 and this group of atoms has a relative molecular mass of 15.0.

The relative molecular mass of ethane is 30.0, which is 2×15.0. So, there must be two units of the empirical formula in every molecule of ethane.

The molecular formula is therefore $(CH_3)_2$ or C_2H_6.

Look back at Topic 2.4 if you are not sure about this calculation.

■ Other formulae

We use other, different types of formulae in organic chemistry because, compared with inorganic compounds, organic molecules are more varied. The type of formula required depends on the information that you are dealing with. We may want to know about the way the atoms are arranged within the molecule, as well as just the number of each atom present. There are different ways of doing this.

The displayed formula

This shows every atom and every bond in the molecule:

— is a single bond

= is a double bond

≡ is a triple bond

For ethene, C_2H_4, the displayed formula is:

$$H\diagdown \quad \diagup H$$
$$C=C$$
$$H\diagup \quad \diagdown H$$

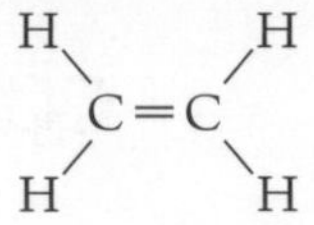

For ethanol, C_2H_6O, the displayed formula is:

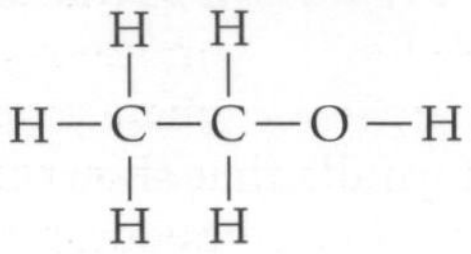

$$\begin{array}{cc} H & H \\ | & | \\ H-C-C-O-H \\ | & | \\ H & H \end{array}$$

The structural formula

This shows the unique arrangement of atoms in a molecule in a simplified form, without showing all the bonds.

Each carbon is written separately, with the atoms or groups that are attached to it.

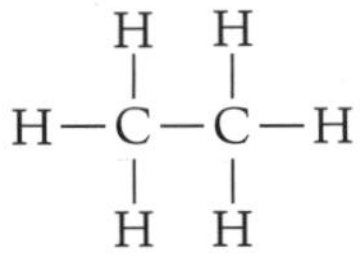

$$\begin{array}{cc} H & H \\ | & | \\ H-C-C-H \\ | & | \\ H & H \end{array} \qquad \text{is written } CH_3CH_3$$

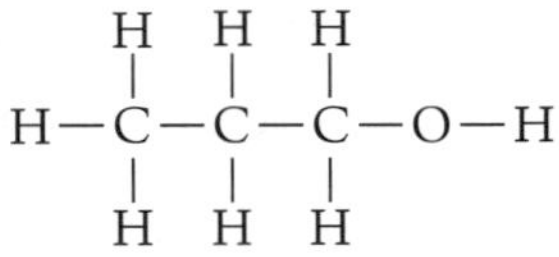

$$\begin{array}{ccc} H & H & H \\ | & | & | \\ H-C-C-C-O-H \\ | & | & | \\ H & H & H \end{array} \quad \text{is written } CH_3CH_2CH_2OH$$

Branches in the carbon chains are shown in brackets:

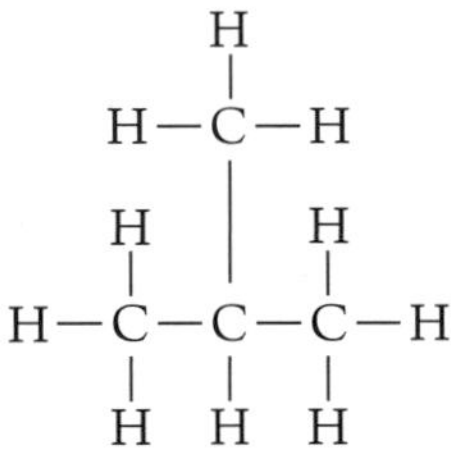

$$\begin{array}{c} H \\ | \\ H-C-H \\ | \end{array}$$
$$\begin{array}{ccc} H & | & H \\ | & | & | \\ H-C-C-C-H \\ | & | & | \\ H & H & H \end{array} \quad \text{is written } CH_3CH(CH_3)CH_3$$

Summary questions

1   A compound comprising only carbon and hydrogen, in which 4.8 g of carbon combine with 1.0 g of hydrogen, has a relative molecular mass of 58.

   a How many moles of carbon are there in 4.8 g?

   b How many moles of hydrogen are there in 1.0 g?

   c What is the empirical formula of this compound?

   d What is the molecular formula of this compound?

   e Draw the structural formula of the compound that has a straight chain.

   f Draw the displayed formula of the compound that has a straight chain.

5.2 Nomenclature – naming organic compounds

Learning objectives:

- What are the IUPAC rules for naming alkanes and alkenes?
- What is a functional group?
- What is an homologous series?

Specification reference 3.5.2

Table 1 *The first six roots used in naming organic compounds*

Number of carbons	Root
1	meth
2	eth
3	prop
4	but
5	pent
6	hex

The system we use for naming compounds was developed by the International Union of Pure and Applied Chemistry or **IUPAC**. This is an international organisation of chemists that draws up standards so that chemists throughout the world use the same conventions, rather like a universal language of chemistry. Systematic names tell us about the structures of the compounds rather than just the formula. Only the basic principles are covered here.

Roots

A systematic name has a **root** that tells us the longest unbranched hydrocarbon chain or ring, see Table 1.

The syllable after the root tells us whether there are any double bonds.

-ane means no double bonds. For example, ethane

$$\begin{array}{c} \text{H} \quad \text{H} \\ | \quad | \\ \text{H}-\text{C}-\text{C}-\text{H} \\ | \quad | \\ \text{H} \quad \text{H} \end{array}$$

has two carbon atoms and no double bond.

-ene means there is a double bond. For example, ethene

$$\begin{array}{c} \text{H} \quad\quad \text{H} \\ \diagdown \quad\quad \diagup \\ \text{C}=\text{C} \\ \diagup \quad\quad \diagdown \\ \text{H} \quad\quad \text{H} \end{array}$$

has two carbon atoms and one double bond.

Prefixes and suffixes

Prefixes and suffixes describe the changes that have been made to the root molecule.

- Prefixes are added to the beginning of the root.

For example, side chains are shown by a prefix, whose name tells us the number of carbons:

methyl	CH_3-	ethyl	C_2H_5-
propyl	C_3H_7-	butyl	C_4H_9-

For example,

$$\begin{array}{c} \text{H} \\ | \\ \text{H}-\text{C}-\text{H} \\ \text{H} \quad \text{H} \quad | \quad \text{H} \\ | \quad | \quad | \quad | \\ \text{H}-\text{C}-\text{C}-\text{C}-\text{C}-\text{H} \\ | \quad | \quad | \quad | \\ \text{H} \quad \text{H} \quad \text{H} \quad \text{H} \end{array}$$

is called **methyl**butane. The longest unbranched chain is four carbons long, which gives us butane (as there are no double bonds) and there is a side chain of one carbon, a methyl group.

- Suffixes are added to the end of the root.

For example alcohols (—OH) have the suffix -ol, as in methan**ol**, CH_3OH (see Topic 16.1).

■ Functional groups

Most organic compounds are made up of a hydrocarbon chain that has one or more reactive groups attached to it. We call these reactive groups **functional groups**. The functional group reacts in the same way, whatever the length of the hydrocarbon chain. So, for example, if you learn the reactions of one alkene, such as ethene, you can apply this knowledge to any alkene.

Functional groups are named by using a suffix or prefix as shown in Table 2.

Table 2 *The suffixes and prefixes of some functional groups*

Family	Formula	Suffix	Example
alkanes	$CH_3(CH_2)_nCH_3$ R—H	-ane	ethane
alkenes	$CH_3(CH_2)_nCH=CH_2$ R–CH$=$CH$_2$	-ene	propene
haloalkanes	$CH_3(CH_2)_nCH_2X$ (X = F, Cl, Br or I) R—X	none	chloromethane CH_3Cl
alcohols	$CH_3(CH_2)_nCH_2OH$ R—OH	-ol	ethanol C_2H_5OH
aldehydes	$CH_3(CH_2)_nCHO$ R—CHO	-al	ethanal CH_3CHO
ketones	$CH_3(CH_2)_nCO(CH_2)_nCH_3$ R—COR'	-one	propanone CH_3COCH_3
carboxylic acids	$CH_3(CH_2)_nCOOH$ R—COOH	-oic acid	ethanoic acid CH_3COOH

Note that the haloalkanes are named using the 'halo- prefix' (fluoro-, chloro-, bromo-, iodo-) rather than a suffix. R is often used to represent a hydrocarbon chain (of any length). Think of it as representing the **r**est of the molecule.

Examples

bromoethane

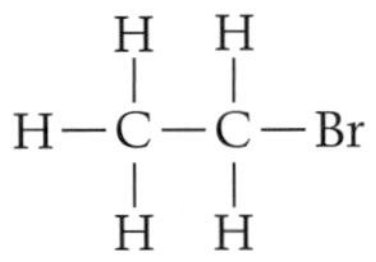

$$H-\overset{\overset{\displaystyle H}{|}}{C}-\overset{\overset{\displaystyle H}{|}}{\underset{\underset{\displaystyle H}{|}}{C}}-Br$$

eth indicates that the molecule has a chain of two carbon atoms, **ane** that it is has no double or triple bonds and **bromo** that one of the hydrogen atoms of ethane is replaced by a bromine atom.

propene

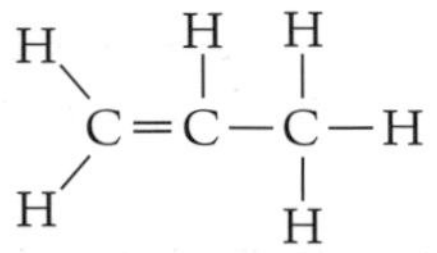

$$\overset{H}{\underset{H}{>}}C=\overset{\overset{\displaystyle H}{|}}{C}-\overset{\overset{\displaystyle H}{|}}{\underset{\underset{\displaystyle H}{|}}{C}}-H$$

Prop indicates a chain of three carbon atoms and **ene** that there is one C$=$C (double bond).

$$\text{methanol} \quad H-\overset{\displaystyle H}{\underset{\displaystyle H}{\overset{\displaystyle |}{\underset{\displaystyle |}{C}}}}-O-H$$

Meth indicates a single carbon, **an** that there are no double bonds and **ol** that there is an OH group (an alcohol).

Chain and position isomers

With longer chains, we need to say where a side chain or a functional group is located on the main chain. For example, methylpentane could refer to:

2–methylpentane   or   3–methylpentane

We use a number (sometimes called a locant) to tell us the position of any branching in a chain and the position of any functional group. The examples above are structural isomers. Structural isomers have the same molecular formula but different structural formulae, see Topic 5.3.

are both 1-bromopropane. The right-hand one is not 3-bromopropane because we always use the smallest possible number.

1-bromopropane may also be represented by either of the structural formulae below because all the hydrogens on carbon 1 are equivalent.

Molecules with more than one functional group or side chain

We may have more than one functional group:

2-bromo-1-iodopropane

bromo is written before **iodo** because we put the substituting groups in **alphabetical order**, rather than in the numerical order of the functional groups.

We can show that we have more than one of the same substituting group by adding prefixes as well as functional groups. di-, tri- and tetra- mean two, three and four respectively.

> **Hint**
>
> Take care. Don't get confused by the way the way the formula is drawn.

> **Hint**
>
> In chemical names, strings of numbers are separated by commas. A hyphen is placed between words and numbers.

So,

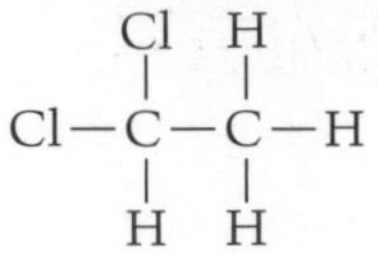

Cl—C—C—H is called 1,1-dichloroethane

(with Cl, H at top and H, H at bottom)

and H—C—C—H is called 1,2-dichloroethane.

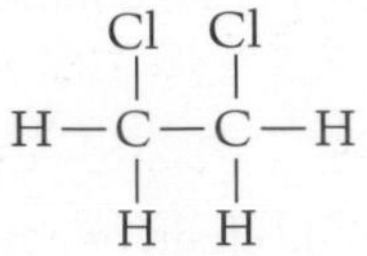

(with Cl, Cl at top and H, H at bottom)

Table 3 *Examples of systematic naming of organic compounds. Try covering up the name or structure to test yourself.*

Structural formula	Name
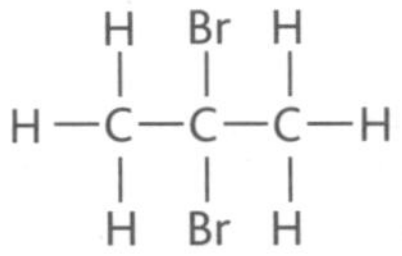 H—C—C—C—H (with H, Br, H at top and H, Br, H at bottom)	2,2-dibromopropane
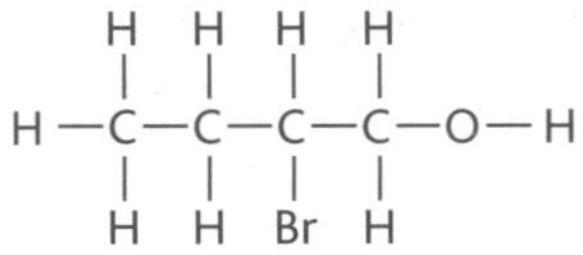 H—C—C—C—C—O—H (with H, H, H, H at top and H, H, Br, H at bottom)	2-bromobutan-1-ol **Note** The suffix -ol defines the end of the chain we count from
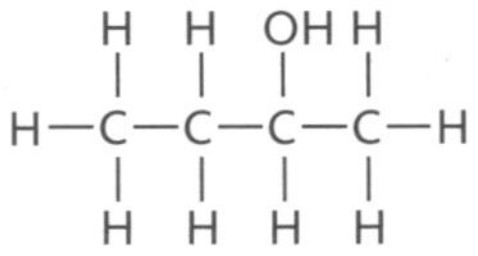 H—C—C—C—C—H (with H, H, OH, H at top and H, H, H, H at bottom)	butan-2-ol
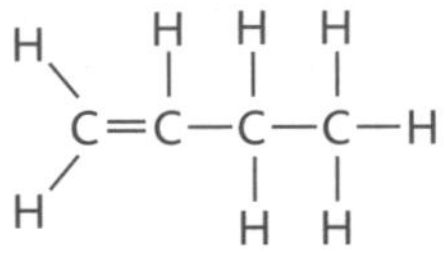 C=C—C—C—H (with H, H at left and H, H, H at top and H, H at bottom)	but-1-ene **Note** *Not* but-2-ene, but-3-ene or but-4-ene as we use the smallest locant possible

Learn the formal definition:

■ An homologous series is a series of chemically similar compounds which conform to a general formula. Each member of the series differs from the next by CH_2 and the members of the series show a gradation in physical properties.

Summary questions

1. What is the name of each of the following?
   a $CH_3CH_2CH_2Cl$
   b $CH_3CH_2CH_2CH_2CH_3$
   c $CH_3CH_2CH=CHCH_3$
   d $CH_3CH_2CH_2CH(CH_3)CH_3$

2. Draw the displayed formulae for:
   a methylbutanone
   b but-2-ene
   c 2-chlorohexane
   d but-1-ene.

💡 Homologous series

An **homologous series** is a family of organic compounds, with the same functional group, but different carbon chain length.

■ Members of an homologous series have a general formula. For example, the alkanes are C_nH_{2n+2} and alkenes, with one double bond, are C_nH_{2n}.

■ Each member of the series differs from the next by CH_2.

■ The length of the carbon chain has little effect on the *chemical* reactivity of the functional group.

■ The length of the carbon chain affects physical properties, like melting point, boiling point and solubility. Melting points and boiling points increase by a small amount as the number of carbon atoms in the chain increases. This is because the intermolecular forces increase. In general, small molecules are gases; larger ones liquids or solids.

■ Chain branching generally reduces melting points because the molecules pack together less well.

5.3 Isomerism

Learning objectives:

■ What are structural isomers?

■ What are the three ways in which structural isomerism can occur?

Specification reference 3.1.5

Link

Stereoisomerism is covered in A2.

💡 ⚠ Isomers

Isomers are molecules that have the same molecular formula but whose atoms are arranged differently. There are two basic types of isomerism in organic chemistry, structural isomerism and stereoisomerism.

Structural isomerism

Structural isomers are defined as having the same molecular formula but different structural formulae, see Topic 5.1. There are three sub-divisions. Structural isomers can have:

1 the same functional groups attached to the main chain at different points; this is called positional isomerism
2 functional groups that are different; this is called functional group isomerism
3 a different arrangement of the hydrocarbon chain (such as branching); this is called chain isomerism.

Positional isomerism

The functional group is attached to the main chain at different points. For example, the molecular formula C_3H_7Cl could represent:

$CH_3CH_2CH_2Cl$ or $CH_3CHClCH_3$
1-chloropropane   2-chloropropane

Functional group isomerism

There are different functional groups. For example, the molecular formula C_2H_6O could represent:

$$H-\overset{\overset{\displaystyle H}{|}}{\underset{\underset{\displaystyle H}{|}}{C}}-\overset{\overset{\displaystyle H}{|}}{\underset{\underset{\displaystyle H}{|}}{C}}-OH \qquad \text{or} \qquad H-\overset{\overset{\displaystyle H}{|}}{\underset{\underset{\displaystyle H}{|}}{C}}-O-\overset{\overset{\displaystyle H}{|}}{\underset{\underset{\displaystyle H}{|}}{C}}-H$$

ethanol (an alcohol)   methoxymethane (an ether)

Chain isomerism

The hydrocarbon chain is arranged differently. For example, the molecular formula C_4H_9OH could represent:

butan-1-ol   or   2-methylpropan-1-ol

These isomers are called chain-branching isomers.

The existence of isomers makes the task of identifying an unknown organic compound more difficult. This is because there may be a number of compounds with different structures that all have the same molecular formula. So, we have to use analytical methods that tell us about the structure.

Summary questions

1 What type of structural isomerism is shown by the following pairs of molecules? Choose from: A = functional groups at different points, B = different functional groups, C = chain branching.

  a $CH_3CH_2OCH_3$ and $CH_3CH_2CH_2OH$

  b $CH_3CH_2CH_2OH$ and $CH_3CH(OH)CH_3$

  c $CH_3CH_2CH_2CH_2CH_3$ and $CH_3CH(CH_3)CH_2CH_3$

2 a Write the displayed and structural formulae for all the five isomers of hexane, C_6H_{14}.

  b Name these isomers.

1   The fractions obtained from petroleum contain saturated hydrocarbons that belong to
     the homologous series of alkanes.
     (a) Any homologous series can be represented by a general formula.
          (i)   State **two** other characteristics of homologous series.   *(2 marks)*
     (b) Decane has the molecular formula $C_{10}H_{22}$
          (i)   State what is meant by the term *molecular formula*.
          (ii) Give the molecular formula of the alkane which contains 14 carbon atoms.   *(2 marks)*

AQA, 2006

2   The alkanes form an homologous series of hydrocarbons. The first four straight-chain
     alkanes are shown below.

           methane CH_4
           ethane CH_3CH_3
           propane $CH_3CH_2CH_3$
           butane $CH_3CH_2CH_2CH_3$

     (a) (i)   State what is meant by the term *hydrocarbon*.
          (ii) Give the general formula for the alkanes.
          (iii) Give the molecular formula for hexane, the sixth member of the series.   *(3 marks)*
     (b) Each homologous series has its own general formula. State **two** other
          characteristics of an homologous series.   *(2 marks)*
     (c) Branched-chain structural isomers are possible for alkanes which have more than
          three carbon atoms.
          (i)   State what is meant by the term *structural isomers*.
          (ii) Name the **two** isomers of hexane shown below.

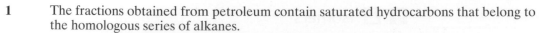

                       CH_3 CH_3
                        | |
           $H_3C-CH-CH_2CH_2CH_3$ $H_3C-CH-CH_2CH_3$
                                                         |
                                                       CH_3

                isomer 1   *isomer 2*

          (iii) Give the structures of **two** other branched-chain isomers of hexane.   *(6 marks)*
     (d) A hydrocarbon, **W,** contains 92.3% carbon by mass. The relative molecular mass
          of **W** is 78.0
          (i)   Calculate the empirical formula of **W**.
          (ii) Calculate the molecular formula of **W**.   *(4 marks)*

AQA, 2003

3   (a) Give the systematic chemical name of CCl_2F_2.   *(1 mark)*
     (b) Give the systematic chemical name of CCl_4.   *(1 mark)*
     (c) Give the systematic chemical name of $CHCl_2CHCl_2$.   *(1 mark)*

AQA, 2001

4 There are five structural isomers of the molecular formula C_5H_{10} which are alkenes. The displayed formulae of two of these isomers are given.

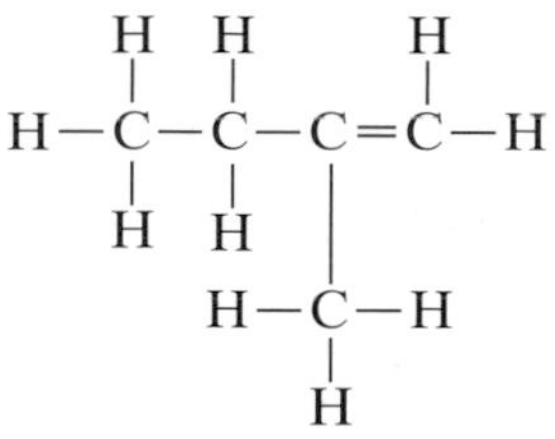

isomer 1

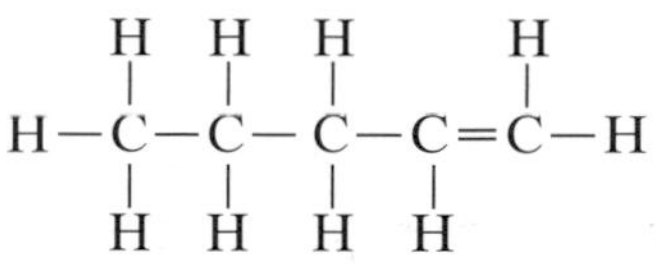

isomer 2

(a) Draw the displayed formulae of **two** of the remaining alkene structural isomers. *(2 marks)*

(b) Consider the reaction scheme shown below and answer the questions that follow.

$$\textbf{Isomer 1} \xrightarrow{HBr} CH_3CH_2CBr(CH_3)_2$$

Y

Give the name of compound **Y**. *(1 mark)*

AQA, 2000

5 There are four structural isomers of molecular formula C_4H_9Br. The structural formulae of two of these isomers are given below.

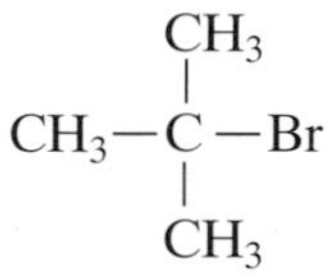

isomer 1

$CH_3CH_2CH_2CH_2Br$

isomer 2

(i) Draw the structural formulae of the remaining two isomers. *(3 marks)*

(ii) Name isomer 1.

AQA, 2001

6 Alkanes

6.1 Alkanes

Learning objectives:

- What is an alkane?
- How are alkanes named?
- What are their properties?

Specification reference 3.1.6

Alkanes are **saturated hydrocarbons**; they contain only carbon–carbon and carbon–hydrogen *single* bonds. They are among the least reactive organic compounds. They are used as fuels and lubricants and as starting materials for a range of other compounds. This means that they are very important to industry. The main source of alkanes is crude oil.

The general formula

The general formula for all chain alkanes is C_nH_{2n+2}. Hydrocarbons may be unbranched chains, branched chains or rings.

Unbranched chains

For example, pentane, C_5H_{12}:

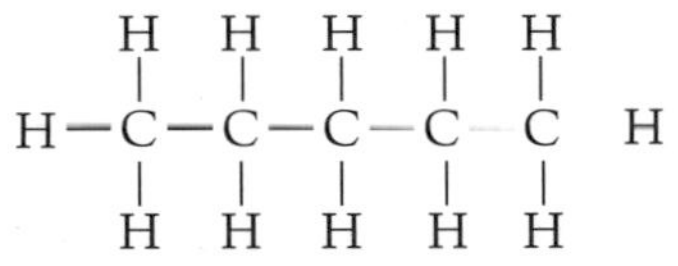

$CH_3CH_2CH_2CH_2CH_3$

(displayed

(structural)

Unbranched chains are often called 'straight' chains but the C–C–C angle is 109.5° (Topic 3.9). This means that the chains are not actually straight. In an unbranched alkane, each carbon atom has two hydrogen atoms except the end carbons which have one extra.

Branched chains

For example, methylbutane, C_5H_{12}, which is an isomer of pentane:

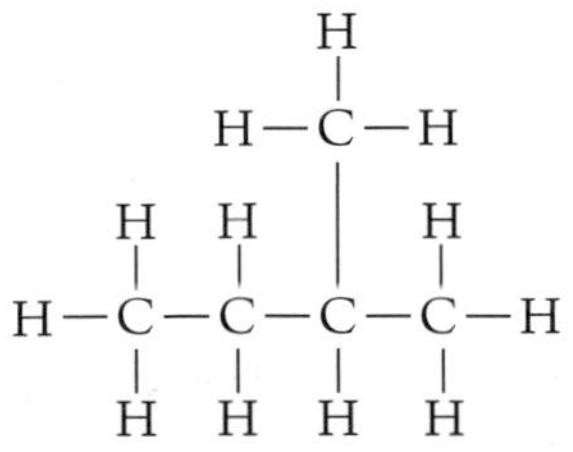

$CH_3CH_2CH(CH_3)CH_3$

(displayed)

(structural)

Ring alkanes

Ring alkanes have the general molecular formula C_nH_{2n} because the 'end' hydrogens are not required.

How to name alkanes

Straight chains

Alkanes are named from the root, which tells us the number of carbon atoms, and the suffix -ane, denoting an alkane, see Table 1.

Branched chains

When you are naming a hydrocarbon with a branched chain, you must first find the longest unbranched chain – sometimes a bit tricky, see the example below. This gives the root name. Then name the branches or **side chains** as prefixes: methyl-, ethyl-, propyl-, etc. Finally, add numbers to say which carbon atoms the side chains are attached to.

Example

Both the hydrocarbons below are the same, though they seem different at first sight.

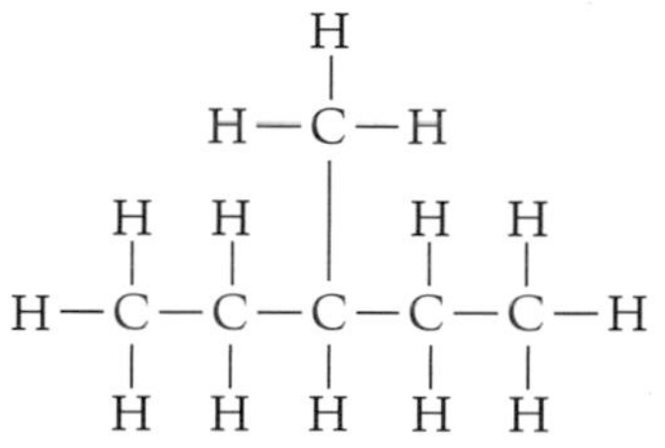

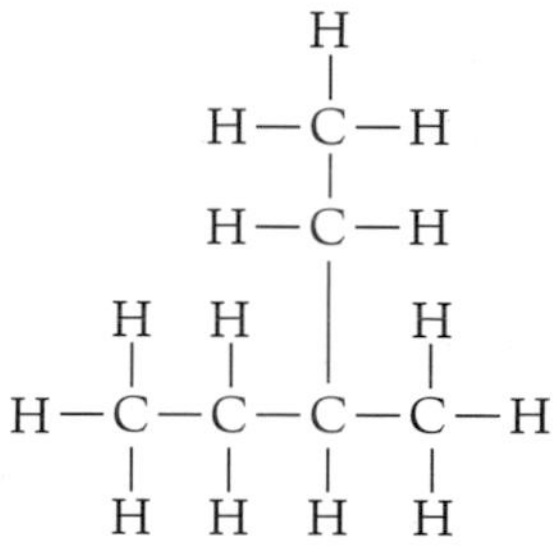

Table 1 *Names of the first six alkanes*

methane	CH_4
ethane	C_2H_6
propane	C_3H_8
butane	C_4H_{10}
pentane	C_5H_{12}
hexane	C_6H_{14}

In both representations, the longest unbranched chain (in red) is five carbons, so the root is pentane. The only side chain has one carbon so it is methyl-. It is attached at carbon number 3 so the full name is 3-methylpentane.

Structure

Isomerism

Methane, ethane and propane have no isomers but, after that, the number of possible isomers increases with the number of carbons in the alkane. For example, butane, with four carbons, has two isomers while pentane has three:

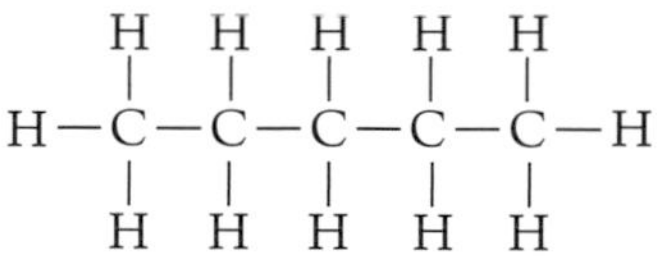

pentane

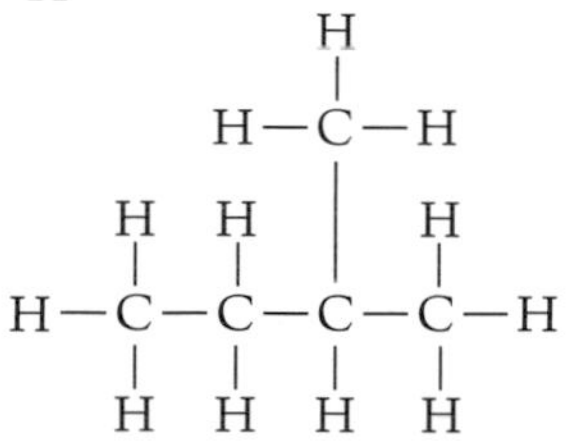

methylbutane

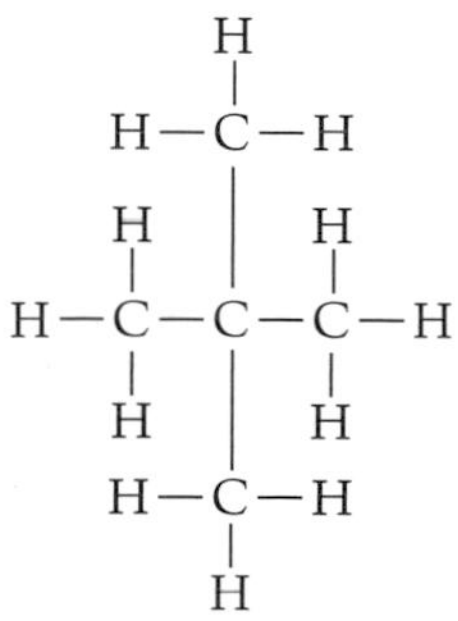

2,2-dimethylpropane

The number of isomers rises rapidly with chain length. Decane $(C_{10}H_{22})$ has 75 and $C_{30}H_{62}$ has over 4 billion.

Figure 1 *Camping Gaz is a mixture of propane and butane. Polar expeditions use special gas mixtures with a higher proportion of propane, because butane is liquid below 272 K.*

Figure 2 *The effect of increasing chain length on the physical properties of alkanes*

■ Physical properties

Polarity

Alkanes are almost non-polar because the electronegativities of carbon (2.5) and hydrogen (2.1) are so similar, see Topic 3.3. As a result, the only intermolecular forces between their molecules are weak van der Waals forces; and the larger the molecule, the stronger the van der Waals forces.

▦ Boiling points

This increasing intermolecular force is why the boiling points of alkanes increase as the chain length increases. The shorter chains are gases at room temperature. Pentane, with five carbons, is a liquid with a low boiling point of 309 K (36 °C). Then when we reach a chain length of about 18 carbons, the alkanes become solids at room temperature. The solids have a waxy feel.

Alkanes with branched chains have lower melting points than straight chain alkanes with the same number of carbon atoms. This is because they cannot pack together as closely as unbranched chains and so the van der Waals forces are not so effective.

Solubility

Alkanes are insoluble in water. This is because water molecules are held together by hydrogen bonds which are much stronger than the van der Waal's forces that act between alkane molecules. However, alkanes do mix with other relatively non-polar liquids.

■ How alkanes react

Alkanes are relatively unreactive. They have strong carbon–carbon and carbon–hydrogen bonds. They do not react with acids, bases, oxidising and reducing agents. However, they do burn and they will react with halogens under suitable conditions. They burn in a plentiful supply of oxygen to form carbon dioxide and water (or, in a restricted supply of oxygen, to form carbon monoxide or carbon).

Summary questions

1. Name the alkane $CH_3CH_2CH(CH_3)CH_3$ and draw its displayed formula.

2. Draw the displayed formula and structural formula of 2-methylhexane.

3. Name an isomer of 2-methylhexane that has a straight chain.

4. Which of the two isomers in question 3 will have the higher melting point? Explain your answer.

6.2 Fractional distillation of crude oil

Learning objectives:

■ What is the origin of crude oil?

■ How is crude oil separated into useful fractions on an industrial scale?

Specification reference 3.1.6

Hint

Crude oil is being produced now but accumulation of a deposit is a very slow process.

Crude oil is at present the world's main source of organic chemicals. It is called a fossil fuel because it was formed millions of years ago by the breakdown of plant and animal remains at the high pressures and temperatures deep below the Earth's surface. Because it originated so long ago it is not renewable.

Crude oil is a mixture mostly of alkanes, both unbranched and branched. Crude oils from different sources have different compositions. The composition of a typical North Sea oil is given in Table 1.

Crude oil contains small amounts of other compounds dissolved in it. These come from other elements in the original plants and animals the oil was formed from, for example, some contain sulfur. These produce sulfur dioxide, SO_2, when they are burned. This is one of the causes of acid rain; sulfur dioxide reacts with oxygen high in the atmosphere to form sulfur trioxide. This reacts with water in the atmosphere to form sulfuric acid.

Table 1 *The composition of a typical North Sea oil*

Product	Gases	Petrol	Naptha	Kerosene	Gas oil	Fuel oil and wax
Approximate boiling temperature / K	310	310–450	400–490	430–523	590–620	above 620
Chain length	1–5	5–10	8–12	11–16	16–24	25+
Percentage present	2	8	10	14	21	45

⚠ Fractional distillation of crude oil

To convert crude oil into useful products we have to separate the mixture. We do this by heating it and collecting the **fractions** that boil over different ranges of temperatures. Each fraction is a mixture of hydrocarbons of similar chain length and therefore similar properties, see Figure 1. The process is called **fractional distillation** and it is done in a **fractionating tower**.

■ The crude oil is first heated in a furnace.

■ A mixture of liquid and vapour passes into a tower that is cooler at the top than at the bottom.

■ The vapours pass up the tower via a series of trays containing bubble caps until they arrive at a tray that is sufficiently cool (at a lower temperature than their boiling point). Then they condense to liquid.

■ The mixture of liquids that condenses on each tray is piped off.

■ The shorter chain hydrocarbons condense in the trays nearer to the top of the tower, where it is cooler, because they have lower boiling points.

■ The thick residue that collects at the base of the tower is called tar or bitumen. It can be used for road surfacing but, as supply often exceeds demand, this fraction is often further processed to give more valuable products.

AQA Examiner's tip

You do not need to memorise the various fractions and their boiling temperatures but you should understand the principle of fractional distillation.

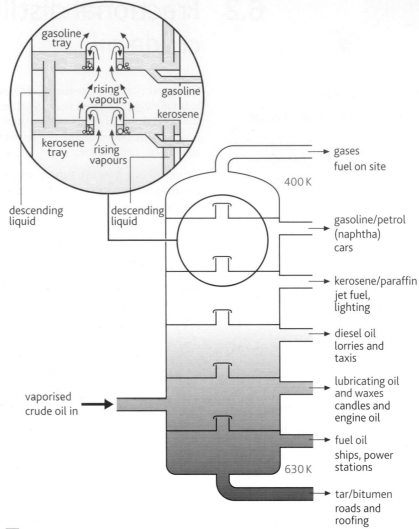

Figure 1 *The fractional distillation of crude oil*

Figure 2 *Crude oil is separated into fractions by distillation in cylindrical towers typically 8 m in diameter and 40 m high. Oil refineries vary but a typical one might process 3.5 million tonnes of crude oil per year.*

Hint

Fractional distillation is a physical process so no covalent bonds within the molecules are broken. It is the van der Waals forces between the molecules that are broken during vaporisation and reform on condensing.

Summary questions

1 Draw the displayed formula and structural formula of hexane.

2 In which of the crude oil fractions named in Table 1 is hexane most likely to be found?

3 What is fractional distillation and how is it different from distillation?

6.3 Industrial cracking

Learning objectives:

■ What is cracking?

■ What are the conditions for, and the products of, thermal cracking?

■ What are the conditions for, and products of, catalytic cracking?

■ What are the economic reasons for cracking?

Specification reference 3.1.6

AQA Examiner's tip

You should understand the commercial benefits of cracking.

Figure 1 The range of products obtained from crude oil

The naphtha fraction from the fractional distillation of crude oil is in huge demand, for petrol and by the chemical industry. The longer chain fractions are not as useful and therefore of lower value economically. Most crude oil has more of the longer chain fractions than is wanted and not enough of the naphtha fraction.

The shorter chain products are economically more valuable than the longer chain material. To meet the demand for the shorter chain hydrocarbons, many of the longer chain fractions are broken into shorter lengths (cracked). This has two useful results:

1 Shorter, more useful, chains are produced, especially petrol.

2 Some of the products are alkenes, which are more reactive than alkanes.

Note that petrol is a mixture of mainly alkanes containing between four and twelve carbon atoms.

Alkenes are used as chemical feedstock (which means they supply industries with the starting materials to make different materials) and are converted into a huge range of other compounds including polymers and a variety of products from paints to drugs. Perhaps the most important alkene is ethene, which is the starting material for poly(ethene) (polythene) and a wide range of other everyday materials.

■ Alkanes are very unreactive, and harsh conditions are required to break them down. There are a number of different ways of carrying out cracking.

■ Thermal cracking

This reaction involves heating alkanes to a high temperature, 700–1200 K, under high pressure, up to 7000 kPa. Carbon–carbon bonds break in such a way that one electron from the pair in the covalent bond goes to each carbon atom. So, initially two shorter chains are produced each ending in a carbon atom with an unpaired electron. These fragments are called free radicals. Free radicals are highly reactive intermediates and react in a number of ways to form a variety of shorter chain molecules.

As there are not enough hydrogen atoms to produce two alkanes, one of the new chains must have a carbon–carbon double bond, and is therefore an alkene:

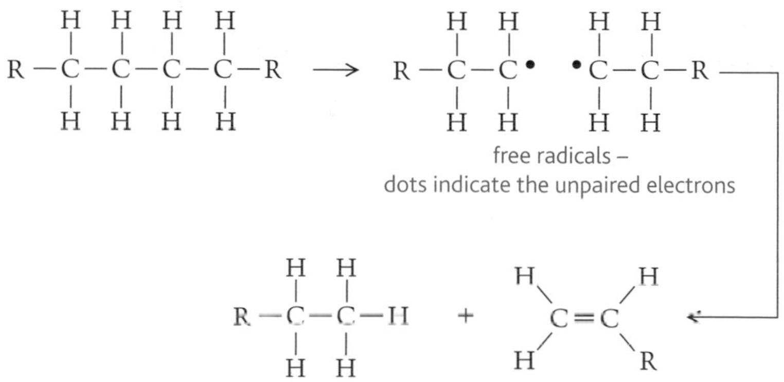

free radicals – dots indicate the unpaired electrons

Figure 2 Thermal cracking

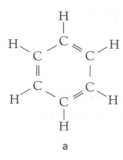

a

b

Figure 3 *Aromatic compounds are based on the benzene ring C_6H_6. Although it appears to have three double bonds as in* **a**, *the electrons are spread around the ring, making it more stable than expected. It is usually represented as in* **b**.

Any number of carbon–carbon bonds may break and the chain does not necessarily break in the middle. Hydrogen may also be produced. Thermal cracking tends to produce a high proportion of alkenes. To avoid too much decomposition (ultimately to carbon and hydrogen) the alkanes are kept in these conditions for a very short time, typically one second. The equation above (Figure 2) shows cracking of a long chain alkane to give a shorter chain alkene and an alkane. The chain could break at any point.

⚠ Catalytic cracking

Catalytic cracking takes place at a lower temperature (approximately 720 K) and lower pressure (but more than atmospheric), using a zeolite catalyst, consisting of silicon dioxide and aluminium oxide. Zeolites have a honeycomb structure with an enormous surface area. They are also acidic. This form of cracking is used mainly to produce motor fuels. The products are mostly branched alkanes, cycloalkanes (rings) and aromatic compounds, see Figure 3.

The products obtained from cracking are separated by fractional distillation.

In the laboratory, catalytic cracking may be carried out in the apparatus shown in Figure 4, using lumps of aluminium oxide as a catalyst.

The products are mostly gases, showing that they have chain lengths of less than C_5 and the mixture decolourises bromine solution. This is a test for a carbon–carbon double bond showing that the product contains alkenes.

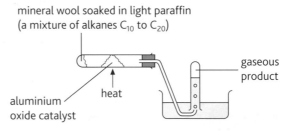

Figure 4 *Laboratory cracking of alkanes*

Summary questions

1 Complete the word equation for one possibility for the thermal cracking of decane.

decane ⟶ octane + ?

2 In the laboratory cracking of alkanes, how can you tell that the products have shorter chains than the starting materials?

3 Why would we not crack octane industrially?

4 How can the temperature required for cracking be reduced?

5 Give two economic reasons for cracking long chain alkanes.

6.4 Combustion of alkanes

Learning objectives:

■ What is a fuel?

■ Why are alkanes good fuels?

■ What are the environmental problems associated with the use of alkanes as fuels?

■ What are we doing about these problems now?

■ How might these problems be solved in the future?

Specification reference 3.1.6

Alkanes are quite unreactive. They do not react with acids, bases, oxidising and reducing agents. However, they do burn and they will react with halogens under suitable conditions.

Combustion

The shorter chain alkanes burn completely in a plentiful supply of oxygen to give carbon dioxide and water.

For example, methane:

$$CH_4(g) + 2O_2(g) \longrightarrow CO_2(g) + 2H_2O(l) \qquad \Delta H = -890 \, kJ \, mol^{-1}$$

Or ethane:

$$C_2H_6(g) + 3\tfrac{1}{2}O_2(g) \longrightarrow 2CO_2(g) + 3H_2O(l) \qquad \Delta H = -1559.7 \, kJ \, mol^{-1}$$

These combustion reactions give out heat. They have a large negative enthalpy of combustion (see Topic 7.2) and the more carbons present, the greater the heat output. For this reason they are important to us as fuels. Fuels are substances that release heat energy when they undergo combustion. They also store a large amount of energy for a small amount of weight. For example, octane produces approximately 48 kJ of energy per gram when burnt, which is about twice the energy output per gram of coal. Examples of alkane fuels include:

■ methane (the main component of natural or 'North Sea' gas)

■ propane ('camping' gas)

■ butane ('Calor' gas)

■ petrol (a mixture of hydrocarbons of approximate chain length C_8)

■ paraffin (a mixture of hydrocarbons of chain lengths C_{10} to C_{18}).

Incomplete combustion

In a limited supply of oxygen, the poisonous gas carbon monoxide, CO, is formed. For example, with propane:

$$C_3H_8(g) + 3\tfrac{1}{2}O_2(g) \longrightarrow 3CO(g) + 4H_2O(l)$$

This is called incomplete combustion.

With even less oxygen, carbon (soot) is produced. For example, when a Bunsen burner is used with a closed air hole, the flame is yellow, and a black sooty deposit appears on the apparatus. Incomplete combustion often happens with longer chain hydrocarbons, which need more oxygen to burn compared with shorter chains.

🛈 Polluting the atmosphere

All hydrocarbon-based fuels derived from crude oil may produce polluting products when they burn. They include the following:

■ Carbon monoxide, CO, a poisonous gas produced by incomplete combustion

AQA Examiner's tip

You must be able to balance combustion equations.

Figure 1 *Incomplete combustion is potentially dangerous because of carbon monoxide formation. Carbon monoxide detectors in kitchens can warn of dangerous levels of this gas.*

AQA Examiner's tip

Make sure you know the problems with using carbon-based fuels.

■ Nitrogen oxides, NO, NO_2 and N_2O_4 often abbreviated to NO_x, produced when there is enough energy for N_2 and O_2 in the air to combine, for example:

$$N_2(g) + O_2(g) \longrightarrow 2NO(g)$$

This happens in a petrol engine, at the high temperatures present, when the sparks ignite the fuel. These oxides may react with water vapour and oxygen in the air to form nitric acid. They are therefore contributors to acid rain and photochemical smog.

■ Sulfur dioxide is another contributor to acid rain. It is produced from sulfur-containing impurities present in crude oil. This oxide combines with water vapour and oxygen in the air to form sulfuric acid.

$$SO_2 + H_2O \longrightarrow H_2SO_3 + \tfrac{1}{2}O_2 \longrightarrow H_2SO_4$$

■ Carbon particles, called particulates, which can exacerbate asthma and cause cancer

■ Unburnt hydrocarbons may also enter the atmosphere and these are significant greenhouse gases. They contribute to photochemical smog which can cause a variety of health problems.

■ Carbon dioxide, CO_2 is a greenhouse gas. It is always produced when hydrocarbons burn. Although carbon dioxide is necessary in the atmosphere, its level is rising, and this is a possible cause of the increase in the Earth's temperature and consequent climate change, see below.

■ Water vapour which is also a greenhouse gas

Figure 2 *Photochemical smog is the chemical reaction of sunlight, nitrogen oxides (NO$_x$) and volatile organic compounds in the atmosphere, which leaves airborne particles (called particulate matter) and ground-level ozone.*

Removing sulfur

Power stations burn either coal, or more usually in the UK, natural gas, to produce electricity. Some chimneys (flues) now use calcium oxide, CaO, or limestone, $CaCO_3$, to absorb the sulfur dioxide. This produces gypsum, $CaSO_4$, which is used as plaster. This process is called flue gas desulfurisation.

Catalytic converters

Figure 3 *A catalytic converter*

The internal combustion engine produces most of the pollutants listed above, though sulfur is now removed from petrol so that sulfur dioxide has become less of a problem.

All new cars with petrol engines are now equipped with catalytic converters in their exhaust systems. These reduce the output of carbon monoxide, nitrogen oxides and unburnt hydrocarbons in the exhaust gas mixture.

The catalytic converter is a honeycomb made of a ceramic material coated with platinum and rhodium metals. These are the catalysts. The honeycomb shape provides an enormous surface area, so a little of these expensive metals goes a long way.

As the polluting gases pass over the catalyst, they react with each other to form less-harmful products by the following reactions:

1
$$\underset{\text{carbon monoxide}}{2CO(g)} + \underset{\text{nitrogen oxide}}{2NO(g)} \longrightarrow \underset{\text{nitrogen}}{N_2(g)} + \underset{\text{carbon dioxide}}{2CO_2(g)}$$

2
hydrocarbons + nitrogen oxide $\longrightarrow$ nitrogen + carbon dioxide + water

For example, $C_8H_{18} + 25NO \longrightarrow 12\tfrac{1}{2}N_2 + 8CO_2 + 9H_2O$

The reactions take place on the surface of the catalyst, on the layer of platinum and rhodium metals.

Global warming and the greenhouse effect

Greenhouses become very warm inside. This is because the visible rays from the sun pass through the glass. Rather than escaping, their energy is absorbed by everything inside the greenhouse and re-radiated as infra-red energy, which is heat. Infra-red energy has a longer wavelength so cannot pass back out through the glass.

Carbon dioxide behaves rather like glass. It traps infra-red radiation so that the Earth's atmosphere heats up. This is important for life because without carbon dioxide and other greenhouse gases, the Earth would be too cold to sustain life. Other greenhouse gases are water vapour and methane. These are even more effective than carbon dioxide, but there has not been as much change in the level of these gases in the atmosphere in recent years. However, since the industrial revolution fossil fuels have been used to fuel industrial plants, and the level of carbon dioxide has been rising. Gradually, the Earth's temperature has been rising too, and the majority of scientists believe that the increasing level of carbon dioxide is the cause of global warming.

The concentration of water vapour, the most abundant greenhouse gas, in the atmosphere tends to stay roughly the same (except locally – by waterfalls, for example) because of the equilibrium that exists between water vapour and water (liquid). However, if the temperature of the atmosphere rises, there will be more water vapour in the air, and therefore more greenhouse warming. This may be offset by greater cloud formation, and clouds reflect solar radiation, though. The role of water is therefore recognised as very important but as yet not fully understood.

The current global warming should, however, be seen in the context of the fact that the Earth's average temperature in the past has been both significantly higher and significantly lower than it is now.

How science works

Sun spots or global warming?

Sun spots are magnetic zones that appear on the sun as dark spots and appear to increase the Sun's energy output. However, there is still some debate about whether the increasing number of sun spots, rather than increasing levels of carbon dioxide, is driving the change in our climate, in which case, there is nothing we can do. One theory is that the increasing temperatures, which are a result of sunspot activity, could be causing an increase in the level of carbon dioxide by driving out dissolved carbon dioxide from the sea.

However, until we know whether it is sun spots or our increasing output of carbon dioxide that is causing global warming, it is essential to devise ways of reducing our carbon dioxide output – by finding alternative fuels such as hydrogen, or using wind, wave, solar or nuclear power to provide electricity.

Carbon neutral activities

Many people are concerned about activities, such as airline flights, that produce large amounts of carbon dioxide. A flight from London to Paris produces about 350 kg of carbon dioxide per passenger (from burning hydrocarbon fuels). Activities that produce no carbon dioxide emissions overall are referred to as carbon neutral.

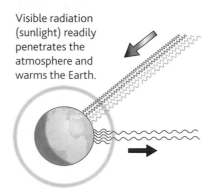

Visible radiation (sunlight) readily penetrates the atmosphere and warms the Earth.

Invisible infra-red radiation is emitted by the Earth and cools it down. But some of this infra-red is trapped by greenhouse gases in the atmosphere which act as a blanket, keeping the heat in.

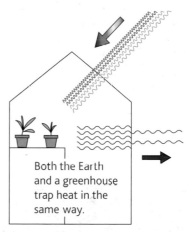

Both the Earth and a greenhouse trap heat in the same way.

Figure 4 *The greenhouse effect*

Summary questions

1 Write word and balanced symbol equations for:

a the complete combustion of propane

b the incomplete combustion of butane to produce carbon monoxide and water.

2 a What are the problems with using carbon-based fuels?

b What steps are taken to reduce these problems?

3 Pick two alternative sources of power which do not use carbon-based fuels and discuss the pros and cons for each.

1   The fractions obtained from petroleum contain saturated hydrocarbons that belong to the homologous series of alkanes.

   (a) (i)   Name the process which is used to obtain the fractions from petroleum.

        (ii) State what is meant by the term *saturated*, as applied to hydrocarbons.   *(2 marks)*

   (b) Write an equation for the incomplete combustion of decane, $C_{10}H_{22}$, to produce carbon and water only.   *(1 mark)*

   (c) When petrol is burned in an internal combustion engine, some nitrogen monoxide, NO, is formed. This pollutant is removed from the exhaust gases by means of a reaction in a catalytic converter.

        (i)   Write an equation for the reaction between nitrogen and oxygen to form nitrogen monoxide.

        (ii) Identify a catalyst used in a catalytic converter.

        (iii) Write an equation to show how nitrogen monoxide is removed from the exhaust gases as they pass through a catalytic converter.   *(3 marks)*

AQA, 2006

2   The burning of fossil fuels can produce atmospheric pollutants.

   (a) The combustion of petrol in an internal combustion engine can lead to the formation of carbon monoxide, CO, and nitrogen monoxide, NO.

        (i)   Write an equation for the incomplete combustion of octane, C_8H_{18}, to produce CO and water only.

        (ii) State **one** essential condition for the formation of NO in an engine. Write an equation for the reaction in which NO is formed.   *(3 marks)*

   (b) All new petrol-engined cars must be fitted with a catalytic converter.

        (i)   Name **one** of the metals used as a catalyst in a catalytic converter.

        (ii) Write an equation to show how CO and NO react with each other in a catalytic converter.   *(2 marks)*

   (c) State why sulfur dioxide gas is sometimes found in the exhaust gases of petrol-engined cars. Give **one** adverse effect of sulfur dioxide on the environment.   *(2 marks)*

AQA, 2004

3   (a) (i)   Name the process used to separate petroleum into fractions.

        (ii) Give the molecular formula for an alkane with nine carbon atoms.

        (iii) Write an equation for the complete combustion of the alkane $C_{11}H_{24}$

        (iv) Write an equation for the incomplete combustion of $C_{11}H_{24}$ to produce carbon and water only.   *(4 marks)*

   (b) Alkenes can be produced by cracking the naphtha fraction obtained from petroleum.

        (i)   Write an equation for the thermal cracking of one molecule of $C_{10}H_{22}$ to give one molecule of propene and one molecule of an alkane only.   *(1 mark)*

AQA, 2005

4 Petroleum is separated into fractions by fractional distillation.

The petrol fraction (C_4 to C_{12}) is burned in internal combustion engines and the naphtha fraction (C_7 to C_{14}) is cracked.

(a) Petroleum is separated into fractions when it is heated and the vapour mixture is passed into a fractionating column.

   (i) Explain what is meant by the term *fraction* as applied to fractional distillation.

   (ii) State a property of the molecules in petroleum which allows the mixture to be separated into fractions.

   (iii) Describe the temperature gradient in the column. *(3 marks)*

(b) The fractions from petroleum contain alkane hydrocarbons.

Write an equation for the incomplete combustion of the alkane C_8H_{18} to produce carbon monoxide and water only. *(1 mark)*

(c) State **one** economic reason for the cracking of petroleum fractions. *(1 mark)*

(d) (i) Give the type of reactive intermediate formed during catalytic cracking.

   (ii) Identify a catalyst used in catalytic cracking. *(2 marks)*

(e) (i) Give the type of reactive intermediate formed during thermal cracking.
State how this reactive intermediate is formed.

   (ii) Identify the different type of hydrocarbon produced in a high percentage by the thermal cracking of alkanes. *(3 marks)*

AQA, 2005

5 (a) Butane, C_4H_{10}, is a hydrocarbon which is used as a fuel.

   (i) Explain what is meant by the term *hydrocarbon*.

   (ii) Explain what is meant by the term *fuel*.

   (iii) Write an equation for the complete combustion of butane.

   (iv) Write an equation for the incomplete combustion of butane to produce carbon monoxide and water.

   (v) Under what conditions would you expect incomplete combustion to occur? *(5 marks)*

(b) Three different carbocations are formed by breaking C—C bonds in separate molecules of butane during catalytic cracking. One of these structures is shown below. Give the structures of the other two carbocations.

$CH_3CH_2\overset{+}{C}H_2$ *(2 marks)*

(c) Ethane can be cracked in the presence of a catalyst to produce ethene and hydrogen.

   (i) Write an equation for this reaction.

   (ii) Give a suitable catalyst for this reaction.

   (iii) State **one** reason why cracking is important. *(3 marks)*

AQA, 2003

6 (a) Crude oil is composed mainly of alkanes, which are saturated hydrocarbons.

   (i) State what is meant by the term *hydrocarbon*.

   (ii) State what is meant by the term *saturated*, as applied to a hydrocarbon. *(2 marks)*

(b) Some of the naphtha fraction is thermally cracked to produce more useful products.

   (i) Give the molecular formula of an alkane with ten carbon atoms.

   (ii) Write an equation to illustrate the thermal cracking of one molecule of tetradecane, $C_{14}H_{30}$, in which the products are ethene and propene, in the ratio of 2 : 1, and one other product.

   (iii) Name the mechanism involved in thermal cracking. *(4 marks)*

AQA, 2004

7   (a) Crude oil is separated into fractions by fractional distillation. Outline how
         different fractions are obtained by this process.   *(3 marks)*
     (b) The table below gives details of the supply of, and demand for, some crude oil fractions.

Fractions	Approximate %	
	Typical supply from crude oil	Global demand
Gases	2	4
Petrol and naphtha	16	27
Kerosine	13	8
Gas oil	19	23
Fuel oil and bitumen	50	38

         (i) Use the data given above to explain why catalytic cracking of crude oil
              fractions is commercially important.
         (ii) Give the two main types of product obtained by catalytic cracking.   *(4 marks)*
     (c) Name a catalyst used in catalytic cracking. State the type of mechanism involved
         and outline the industrial conditions used in the process.   *(4 marks)*

AQA, 2002

8   (a) Thermal cracking of large hydrocarbon molecules is used to produce alkenes.
         State the type of mechanism involved in this process. Write an equation for the
         thermal cracking of $C_{21}H_{44}$ in which ethene and propene are produced in a 3 : 2
         molar ratio together with one other product.   *(3 marks)*
     (b) Write equations, where appropriate, to illustrate your answers to the questions below.
         (i) Explain why it is desirable that none of the sulfur-containing impurities
              naturally found in crude oil are present in petroleum fractions.
         (ii) The pollutant gas NO is found in the exhaust gases from petrol engines.
              Explain why NO is formed in petrol engines but is not readily formed when
              petrol burns in the open air.
         (iii) The pollutant gas CO is also found in the exhaust gases from petrol engines.
              Explain how CO and NO are removed from the exhaust gases and why the
              removal of each of them is desirable.   *(12 marks)*

AQA, 2002

Unit 1 questions: Foundation chemistry

1 (a) Complete the following table.

	Relative mass	Relative charge
Proton		
Electron		

(2 marks)

(b) An atom has twice as many protons and twice as many neutrons as an atom of ^{19}F

Deduce the symbol, including the mass number, of this atom. *(2 marks)*

(c) The Al^{3+} ion and the Na^+ ion have the same electron arrangement.

(i) Give the electron arrangement of these ions.

(ii) Explain why more energy is needed to remove an electron from the Al^{3+} ion than from the Na^+ ion. *(3 marks)*

AQA, 2007

2 (a) An acid, H_2X, reacts with sodium hydroxide as shown in the equation below.

$$H_2X\,(aq) + 2NaOH(aq) \longrightarrow 2Na^+(aq) + X^{2-}(aq) + 2H_2O(l)$$

A solution of this acid was prepared by dissolving 1.92 g of H_2X in water and making the volume up to $250\,cm^3$ in a volumetric flask.

A $25.0\,cm^3$ sample of this solution required $21.70\,cm^3$ of $0.150\,mol\,dm^{-3}$ aqueous NaOH for complete reaction.

(i) State a precaution you should take when using the unknown acid H_2X

(ii) Calculate the number of moles of NaOH in $21.70\,cm^3$ of $0.150\,mol\,dm^{-3}$ aqueous NaOH

(iii) Calculate the number of moles of H_2X which reacted with this amount of NaOH. Hence deduce the number of moles of H_2X in the original sample.

(iv) Calculate the relative molecular mass, M_r, of H_2X *(6 marks)*

(b) Analysis of a compound **Y** showed that it contained 49.31% of carbon, 6.85% of hydrogen and 43.84% of oxygen by mass. The M_r of **Y** is 146.0

(i) State what is meant by the term *empirical formula*.

(ii) Use the above data to calculate the empirical formula and the molecular formula of **Y**. *(4 marks)*

(c) Sodium hydrogencarbonate decomposes on heating as shown in the equation below.

$$2NaHCO_3(s) \longrightarrow Na_2CO_3(s) + CO_2(g) + H_2O(g)$$

A sample of $NaHCO_3$ was heated until completely decomposed. The CO_2 formed in the reaction occupied a volume of $352\,cm^3$ at $1.00 \times 10^5\,Pa$ and 298 K.

(i) State the ideal gas equation and use it to calculate the number of moles of CO_2 formed in this decomposition.

(The gas constant $R = 8.31\,J\,K^{-1}\,mol^{-1}$)

(ii) Suggest a way that the CO_2 produced in this reaction could be removed to stop it being released into the air .

(iii) Use your answer from part (c)(i) to calculate the mass of the $NaHCO_3$ that has decomposed.

(If you have been unable to calculate the number of moles of CO_2 in part (c)(i), you should assume this to be 0.0230 mol. This is not the correct value.) *(8 marks)*

AQA, 2007

3   Molecules of NH_3, H_2O and HF contain covalent bonds. The bonds in these molecules are polar.

(a) (i)   Explain why the H–F bond is polar.

(ii) State which of the molecules NH_3, H_2O or HF contains the least polar bond.

(iii) Explain why the bond in your chosen molecule from part (b)(ii) is less polar than the bonds found in the other two molecules.   *(4 marks)*

(b) The boiling points of NH_3, H_2O and HF are all high for molecules of their size. This is due to the type of intermolecular force present in each case.

(i)   Identify the type of intermolecular force responsible.

(ii) Draw a diagram to show how two molecules of ammonia are attracted to each other by this type of intermolecular force. Include partial charges and all lone pairs of electrons in your diagram.   *(4 marks)*

(c) When an H^+ ion reacts with an NH_3 molecule, an NH_4^+ ion is formed.

(i)   Give the name of the type of bond formed when an H^+ ion reacts with an NH_3 molecule.

(ii) Draw the shape, including any lone pairs of electrons, of an NH_3 molecule and of an NH_4^+ ion.

(iii) Name the shape produced by the arrangement of atoms in the NH_3 molecule.

(iv) Give the bond angle in the NH_4^+ ion.   *(7 marks)*

AQA, 2007

4   The cracking of alkanes gives useful products such as motor fuels and alkenes.

(a) Identify a catalyst used in catalytic cracking.   *(1 mark)*

(b) Write an equation for the thermal cracking of one molecule of the alkane $C_{10}H_{22}$ to produce a different alkane and propene only.   *(1 mark)*

(c) Suggest why propene is commercially more useful than the alkane you have formed in the equation in (b).   *(1 mark)*

(d) Motor fuels contain cyclohexane, C_6H_{12}

(i)   State which of the two types of cracking is more likely to produce cyclohexane as one of the products.

(ii) State the conditions for cyclohexane to undergo complete combustion.

(iii) State the problem caused to the atmosphere by combustion of alkanes such as cyclohexane and suggest how this pollution could be reduced.

(iv) Draw the structure of cyclohexane.

(v)   Write an equation for the incomplete combustion of C_6H_{12} to form carbon and water only   *(6 marks)*

(e) The burning of fuels in a petrol engine produces some carbon monoxide and some nitrogen monoxide.

These two gases are atmospheric pollutants which can be removed by the use of a catalytic converter.

(i)   Write an equation for the reaction in which nitrogen monoxide is formed in a petrol engine. State **one** essential condition for this reaction to occur.

(ii) Identify **one** of the metals used as a catalyst in a catalytic converter.

(iii) Write an equation to show how carbon monoxide and nitrogen monoxide react together in a catalytic converter.   *(4 marks)*

AQA, 2007

5 Sodium is an element in period 3 of the periodic table.

(a) Explain why sodium has a larger atomic radius than magnesium *(2 marks)*

(a) Write an equation to show the process occurring in the first ionisation of sodium. Explain why the first ionisation energy of sodium is less than its second ionisation energy. *(4 marks)*

(b) Sodium ions are found in crystals of sodium chloride. Under certain conditions sodium chloride conducts electricity. Draw a diagram to show how the particles are arranged in sodium chloride and explain in terms of bonding why it has a high melting point. State and explain a condition needed for sodium chloride to conduct electricity. *(6 marks)*

AQA, 2007

6 (a) Acceleration and detection are two processes involved in obtaining the mass spectrum of a vaporised sample of a metal.

Name the other two main processes involved. In each case, identify the part of the mass spectrometer responsible for that process. *(4 marks)*

(b) The diagram below shows the mass spectrum of a gaseous sample of a metal **Z**.

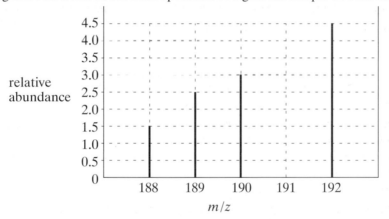

Use the spectrum to calculate the relative atomic mass of **Z** Give your answer to one decimal place.

Deduce the identity of **Z** *(4 marks)*

AQA, 2007

Chapters in this unit

This unit looks at the basics of how and why chemical reactions happen, and briefly covers some of the elements and compounds that have an important role in our modern civilisation.

Energetics revisits exothermic and endothermic reactions and introduces the concept of enthalpy, the heat energy measured under specific conditions. It looks at different ways of measuring enthalpy changes and then uses Hess's law to predict the energy changes of reactions. The idea of bond energies is explored to work out theoretical enthalpy changes by measuring the energy needed to make and break bonds.

Kinetics deals with the rate at which reactions take place, reinforcing the idea that reactions only happen when molecules of the reactants collide with enough energy to break bonds. The Maxwell–Boltzmann distribution shows us mathematically what fraction of the reactant molecules have enough collision energy at a given temperature. The role of catalysts is then explored.

Equilibria is about reactions that do not go to completion so that the end result is a mixture of reactants and products. It examines how to get the greatest proportion of desired products in the mixture by changing the conditions, and some important industrial applications of equilibrium reactions.

Redox reactions expands the definition of oxidation as addition of oxygen to include reactions which involve electron transfers. It explains the idea of an oxidation state for elements and ions, and uses this to help balance complex redox equations.

Group 7, the halogens deals with a reactive group of non-metal elements. It explains the reactivity trend in terms of electronic structures and looks at some of the reactions of the elements and their compounds using the idea of redox reactions and oxidation states. It explores the uses of chlorine and some of its compounds.

Group 2, the alkaline earth metals uses the ideas of electron arrangements to understand the bonding in compounds of these elements and the trend in reactivity in the elements.

The extraction of metals relates the method used to the reactivity of the metal. It examines the extraction of iron and other metals in more detail, and whether the metal can be economically recycled.

Haloalkanes, **Alkenes** and **Alcohols** introduce three significant organic families. They look at the important reactions of each family and develop an understanding of how necessary they are to our everyday lives.

Analytical techniques revisits the mass spectrometer and describes its use in determining the relative molecular masses of compounds and also their molecular formulae. Infra-red spectrometry is introduced as a vital tool for identifying the functional groups in organic compounds.

What you already know:

The material in this unit builds upon knowledge and understanding that you will have developed at GCSE, in particular the following:

- Matter is made of particles that are in motion.

- Reactions take place when particles collide.

- Some reactions are reversible.

- The rate of a reaction can depend on temperature, pressure, concentration and catalysts.

- When a reaction takes place, heat may be given out or taken in.

- Oxidation is the addition of oxygen and reduction is loss of oxygen.

- The relative molecular mass of a compound is found by adding the relative atomic masses of the elements in the compound.

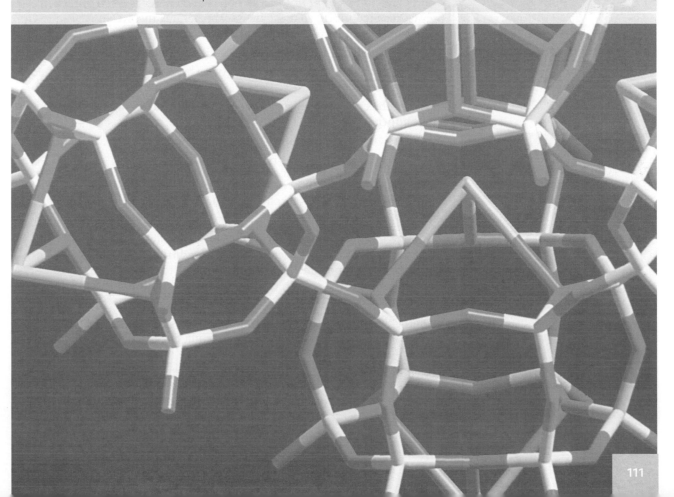

7.1 Endothermic and exothermic reactions

Learning objectives:

■ What do the terms endothermic and exothermic mean?

Specification reference 3.2.1

Most chemical reactions give out or take in energy as they proceed. The amount of energy involved when a chemical reaction takes place is important for many reasons. For example:

■ We can measure the energy values of fuels.

■ We can calculate the energy requirements for industrial processes.

■ We can work out the theoretical amount of energy to break bonds and the amount of energy released when bonds are made.

■ It helps us to predict whether or not a reaction will take place.

The energy involved may be in different forms: light, electrical or, most usually, heat.

■ Thermochemistry

Thermochemistry is the study of heat changes during chemical reactions.

■ When a chemical reaction takes place, chemical bonds break and new ones are formed.

■ Energy must be *put in* to break bonds and energy is *given out* when bonds are formed, so most chemical reactions involve an energy change.

■ The overall change may result in energy being given out or taken in.

■ If at the end of the reaction, energy has been given out, the reaction is **exothermic**.

■ If at the end of the reaction, energy has been taken in, the reaction is **endothermic**.

> **■ Hint**
>
> The unit of energy is the joule, J. One joule represents quite a small amount of heat. For example, in order to boil water for a cup of tea you would need about 80 000 J which is 80 kJ.

■ Exothermic and endothermic reactions

Some reactions give out heat as they proceed. These are called **exothermic** reactions. Neutralising an acid with an alkali is an example of an exothermic reaction.

Some reactions take in heat from their surroundings for the reaction to keep going. These are called **endothermic** reactions. The breakdown of limestone (calcium carbonate) to lime (calcium oxide) and carbon dioxide it is an example of an endothermic reaction; it needs heat to proceed.

Another example of an endothermic reaction is heating copper sulfate. Blue copper sulfate crystals have the formula $CuSO_4.5H_2O$. The water molecules are bonded to the copper sulfate. In order to break these bonds and make white, anhydrous, copper sulfate, heat energy must be supplied. This reaction takes in heat so it is endothermic:

$$CuSO_4.5H_2O \longrightarrow CuSO_4 + 5H_2O$$

blue copper sulfate   anhydrous copper sulfate   water

Figure 1 *Heating copper sulfate*

When you add water to anhydrous copper sulfate, the reaction gives out heat.

$$CuSO_4 \quad + \quad 5H_2O \quad \longrightarrow \quad CuSO_4.5H_2O$$

anhydrous copper sulfate   water   blue copper sulfate

In this direction the reaction is exothermic.

It is **always** the case that a reaction that is endothermic in one direction is exothermic in the reverse direction.

Quantities

The amount of heat given out or taken in during a chemical reaction depends on the quantity of reactants. This energy is usually measured in kilojoules per mole, $kJ\,mol^{-1}$. To avoid any confusion about quantities we need to give an equation. For example, in the combustion of methane, shown in the equation below, one mole of methane reacts with two moles of oxygen:

$$CH_4(g) + 2O_2(g) \longrightarrow CO_2(g) + 2H_2O(l)$$

890 kJ are given out when one mole of methane burns in two of oxygen.

Burning fuels

When fuels are burnt there is a large heat output. These are very exothermic reactions.

For example, coal is mostly carbon. Carbon gives out 393.5 kJ when one mole, 12 g, is burnt completely so that the most highly oxidised product is formed. This is carbon dioxide and not carbon monoxide. Carbon dioxide is the only product.

$$C(s) + O_2(g) \longrightarrow CO_2(g)$$

As we saw above, natural gas, methane, CH_4, gives out 890 kJ when one mole is burnt completely to carbon dioxide and water.

Hydrogen, which may well be the fuel of the future, burns in oxygen as follows:

$$2H_2(g) + O_2(g) \longrightarrow 2H_2O(l)$$

For this reaction 517.6 kJ are given out but notice that we are burning two moles of hydrogen.

■ **Hint**

The expression mol^{-1} is a shorthand for 'per mole' and could also be written /mol. So kJ/mol has the same meaning as $kJ\,mol^{-1}$. Also note that the state symbols such as (g), meaning the gaseous state, are used. These are also important here.

■ Applications and How science works

The energy values of fuels

One important practical application of the study of thermochemistry is that it enables us to compare the efficiency of different fuels. Most of the fuels used today for transport (petrol for cars, diesel for cars and lorries, kerosene for aviation fuel, etc.) are derived from crude oil. This is a resource that will eventually run out so chemists are actively studying alternatives. Possible replacements include ethanol and methanol, both of which can be made from plant material, and hydrogen, which can be made by the electrolysis of water.

Theoretical chemists refer to the energy given out when a fuel burns completely as its heat (or enthalpy) of combustion. They measure this energy in kilojoules per mole $(kJ\,mol^{-1})$ because this compares the same number of *molecules* of each fuel. For use as fuels, the energy given out per *gram* of fuel burned, or the **energy density** of a fuel, is more important.

Some approximate values are given in the Table 1.

Table 1 *Enthalpy of combustion for various fuels*

Fuel	Enthalpy of combustion / $kJ\,mol^{-1}$	Mass of 1 mole / g	Energy density / $kJ\,g^{-1}$
petrol (pure octane)	−5500	114	48.2
ethanol	−1370	46	29.8
methanol	−730	32	22.8
hydrogen	−242	2	121

Notice that petrol stores significantly more energy per gram that either ethanol or methanol. This is a factor that will be significant for vehicles fuelled by either of these alcohols.

At first sight, hydrogen's energy density seems amazing. However, there is a catch. The other three fuels are liquids whereas hydrogen is a gas. Although hydrogen stores lots of energy per gram, a gram of gaseous hydrogen takes up a lot of space because of the low density of gases. How to store hydrogen efficiently is a challenge for designers!

1 Write a balanced symbol equation for the combustion of hydrogen.

2 How do the product(s) of combustion vary between hydrogen and the other fuels?

3 What environmental significance does this have?

Summary questions

1 $CH_4(g) + 2O_2(g) \longrightarrow CO_2(g) + 2H_2O(l)$

Natural gas, methane, CH_4, gives out 890 kJ when one mole is burnt completely.

How much heat would be given out when 8 g of methane is burnt completely?

2 This reaction does not take place under normal conditions:

$CO_2(g) + 2H_2O(l) \longrightarrow CH_4(g) + 2O_2(g)$

If it did, would you expect it to be exothermic or endothermic?

3 Explain your answer to question **2**.

4 Approximately how much methane would have to be burnt to provide enough heat to boil a cup of tea? Choose from a, b or c.

a 16 g

b 1.6 g

c 160 g

7.2 Enthalpy

Learning objectives:

- What is enthalpy change?

- What is an enthalpy level diagram?

Specification reference 3.2.1

Hint

Don't be confused by the different terms. Heat is a form of energy so a heat change can also be described as an energy change. An enthalpy change is still an energy change but it is **measured under stated conditions of temperature and pressure**.

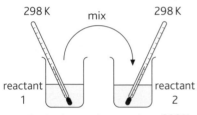

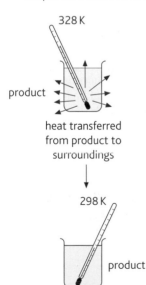

Figure 1 *A reaction giving out heat at 298 K*

The amount of heat given out or taken in by a reaction varies with the conditions: temperature, pressure, concentration of solutions, etc. This means that we must state the conditions under which measurements are made. For example, we normally measure heat changes at constant atmospheric pressure.

How science works

Constant pressure?

Chemists often use flasks open to the atmosphere to measure heat changes. The reaction is then carried out at atmospheric pressure. This varies slightly from day to day. Because these slight daily variations are small, this is only a small source of systematic error.

Enthalpy change, ΔH

When we measure a heat change at constant pressure, we call it an **enthalpy change**.

Enthalpy has the symbol H so enthalpy changes are given the symbol ΔH. The Greek letter Δ (delta) is used to indicate a *change* in any quantity.

There are standard conditions for measuring enthalpy changes:

- Pressure of 100 kPa (approximately normal atmospheric pressure)

- Temperature of 298 K (around normal room temperature, 25 °C)

(The standard state of an element is the state in which it exists at 298 K and 100 kPa.)

We write an enthalpy change measured under standard conditions as $\Delta H^{\ominus}_{298}$ although we usually leave out the 298. $\Delta H^{\ominus}$ is pronounced 'delta H standard'.

It may seem strange to talk about measuring heat changes at a constant temperature because heat changes normally *cause* temperature changes. The way to think about this is to imagine the reactants at 298 K, see Figure 1. Mix the reactants and heat is produced (this is an exothermic reaction). This heat is given out to the surroundings.

We don't think of the reaction as being over *until the products have cooled back to 298 K*. The heat given out to the surroundings while the reaction mixture cools is the enthalpy change for the reaction, $\Delta H^{\ominus}$.

- In an exothermic reaction the products end up with less heat energy than the starting materials because they have lost heat energy when they heated up their surroundings. This means that ΔH is negative. It is therefore given a negative sign.

Some endothermic reactions that take place in aqueous solution absorb heat from the water and cool it down, for example, dissolving ammonium nitrate in water. Again we don't think of the reaction as being *over until the products have warmed up* to the temperature at which they started.

In this case the solution has to take in heat from the surroundings to do this. Unless you remember this, it can seem strange that a reaction that is absorbing heat, initially gets cold.

■ In an endothermic reaction the products end up with more energy than the starting materials, so ΔH is positive. It is therefore given a positive sign.

Pressure affects the amount of heat energy given out by reactions that involve gases. If a gas is given out, then some energy is required to push away the atmosphere. The greater the atmospheric pressure, the more energy is used for this. This means that less energy remains to be given out as heat by the reaction. This is why it is important to have a standard of pressure for measuring energy changes.

The physical states of the reactants and products

The physical states (gas, liquid or solid) of the reactants and products also affect the enthalpy change of a reaction. For example, heat must be put in to change liquid to gas, and is given out when a gas is changed to a liquid. This means that we must always include state symbols in our equations.

For example, hydrogen burns in oxygen to form water but there are two possibilities:

1 Forming liquid water

$$H_2(g) + \tfrac{1}{2}O_2(g) \longrightarrow H_2O(l) \qquad \Delta H\ -285.8\,\text{kJ}\,\text{mol}^{-1}$$

2 Forming steam

$$H_2(g) + \tfrac{1}{2}O_2(g) \longrightarrow H_2O(g) \qquad \Delta H\ -241.8\,\text{kJ}\,\text{mol}^{-1}$$

The difference in ΔH represents the amount of heat needed to turn one mole of water into steam.

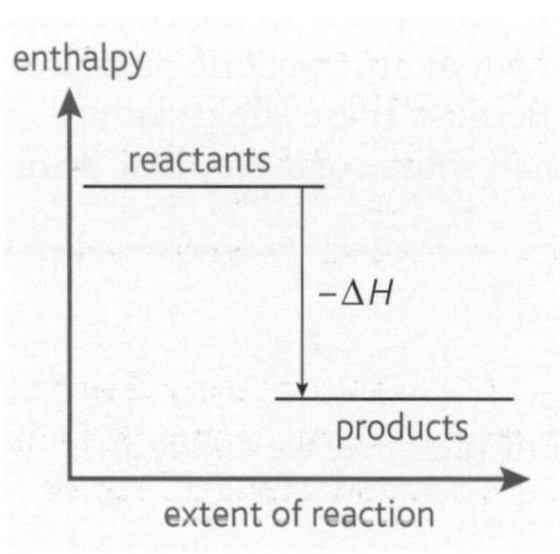

■ Enthalpy level diagrams

We use enthalpy level diagrams, sometimes called energy level diagrams, to represent enthalpy changes. They show the relative enthalpy levels of the reactants (starting materials) and the products. The vertical axis represents enthalpy, and the horizontal axis, the extent of the reaction. We are usually only interested in the beginning of the reaction, 100% reactants, and the end of the reaction, 0% reactants (and 100% products), so the horizontal axis is usually left without units.

Figure 2 shows a general enthalpy diagram for an exothermic reaction (the products have less enthalpy than the reactants) and Figure 3 an endothermic reaction (the products have more enthalpy than the reactants).

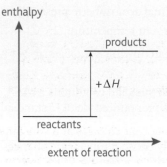

Figure 2 *Enthalpy diagram for an exothermic reaction*

Figure 3 *Enthalpy diagram for an endothermic reaction*

Summary questions

1 Consider this reaction:

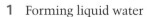

$$CH_4(s) + 2O_2(g) \longrightarrow CO_2(g) + 2H_2O(l) \qquad \Delta H^{\ominus}_{298} = -890\,\text{kJ}\,\text{mol}^{-1}$$

a What does the symbol Δ mean?

b What does the symbol H mean?

c What does the 298 indicate?

d What does the minus sign indicate?

e Is the reaction exothermic or endothermic?

f Draw an enthalpy diagram to show the reaction.

7.3 Measuring enthalpy changes

Learning objectives:

■ How is enthalpy change measured in a reaction?

■ How do we measure enthalpy changes more accurately?

■ How do we measure enthalpy changes in solution?

Specification reference 3.2.1

The general name for the enthalpy change for any reaction is the standard molar enthalpy change of reaction, $\Delta H^\ominus$. It is measured in kilojoules per mole, $kJ\,mol^{-1}$ (molar means 'per mole'). We write a balanced symbol equation for the reaction and then find the heat change for the quantities in moles given by this equation.

For example, ΔH for: $2NaOH + H_2SO_4 \longrightarrow Na_2SO_4 + 2H_2O$ is the enthalpy change when 2 moles of NaOH react with 1 mole of H_2SO_4.

■ Standard enthalpies

Some commonly used enthalpy changes are given names: for example, the enthalpy change of formation $\Delta H_f^\ominus$ and the enthalpy change of combustion $\Delta H_c^\ominus$. Both of these quantities are useful when calculating enthalpy changes for reactions. In addition, $\Delta H_c^\ominus$s are relatively easy to measure for compounds that burn readily in oxygen. Their formal definitions are as follows:

> The **standard molar enthalpy of formation**, $\Delta H_f^\ominus$, is the enthalpy change when one mole of compound is formed from its constituent elements under standard conditions, all reactants and products in their standard states.

> The **standard molar enthalpy of combustion**, $\Delta H_c^\ominus$, is the enthalpy change when one mole of compound is completely burned in oxygen under standard conditions, all reactants and products in their standard states.

Heat and temperature

Temperature is related to the *average* kinetic energy of the particles in a system. As the particles move faster, their average kinetic energy increases and the temperature goes up. But it doesn't matter how many particles there are; temperature is independent of the *number* present. We measure temperature with a thermometer.

Heat is a measure of the *total* energy of all the particles present in a given amount of substance. It *does* depend on how much of the substance is present. The energy of every particle is included. So a bath of lukewarm water has much more heat than a red hot nail because there are so many more particles in it. Heat always flows from high to low temperature, so heat will flow from the nail into the bath water, even though the water has much more heat than the nail.

💡 ⚠ Measuring the enthalpy change of a reaction

The enthalpy change of a reaction is the heat given out or taken in as the reaction proceeds. There is no instrument that measures heat directly. To measure the enthalpy *change* we arrange for the heat to be transferred into a particular mass of a substance, often water. Then we need to know three things:

1 The mass of the substance that is being heated up or cooled down

2 The temperature change

3 The specific heat capacity of the substance

Hint

The words 'heat' and 'temperature' are often used to mean the same thing in daily conversation but in science they are quite distinct and you must be clear about the difference.

Hint

The size of a kelvin is the same as the size of a degree Celsius. Only the starting point of the scale is different. A temperature *change* is numerically the same whether it is measured in Celsius or kelvin. To convert °C to K add 273.

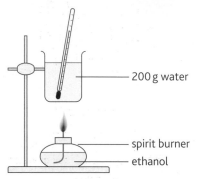

Figure 1 *A simple calorimeter*

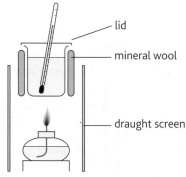

Figure 2 *An improved calorimeter*

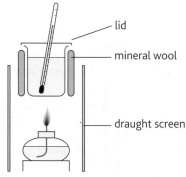 **Figure 3** *A flame calorimeter*

The **specific heat capacity**, *c*, is the amount of heat needed to raise the temperature of 1 g of substance by 1 K. Its units are joules per gram per kelvin, or $J g^{-1} K^{-1}$. For example, the specific heat capacity of water is $4.18 J g^{-1} K^{-1}$. This means that it takes 4.18 joules to raise the temperature of 1 gram of water by 1 kelvin. This is often rounded up to $4.2 J g^{-1} K^{-1}$.

Then:

$$\text{enthalpy change} = \frac{\text{mass of}}{\text{substance}} \times \frac{\text{specific heat}}{\text{capacity}} \times \frac{\text{temperature}}{\text{change}}$$

$$q = m \times c \times \Delta T \quad \text{or} \quad mc\Delta T$$

where *q* is the measured enthalpy change.

The simple calorimeter

We can use the apparatus in Figure 1 to find the enthalpy change when a fuel burns.

We burn the fuel to heat a known mass of water and then measure the temperature rise of the water. We assume that all the heat from the fuel goes into the water.

The apparatus used is called a **calorimeter** (from the Latin *calor* meaning heat).

⚙ Applications and How science works

Working out the enthalpy change – an example

The calorimeter in Figure 1 was used to measure the enthalpy change of combustion of methanol:

$$CH_3OH(l) + 1\tfrac{1}{2}O_2(g) \longrightarrow CO_2(g) + 2H_2O(l)$$

0.32 g (0.010 mol) of methanol was burned, and the temperature of the 200 g of water rose by 4.0 K.

Heat change = q = $m \times c \times \Delta T$

$= 200 \times 4.2 \times 4.0 = 3360 J$

0.01 mol gives 3360 J

So 1 mol would give 336 000 J or 336 kJ

$$\Delta H_c = -336 \text{ kJ mol}^{-1} \text{ (negative because heat is given out)}$$

1 This value is less than half the accepted value since not all the heat reaches the water. Give four reasons why you think this may be.

The simple calorimeter can be used to compare the ΔH_c values of a series of similar compounds because the errors will be similar for every experiment. However, we can improve the results by cutting down the heat loss as shown in Figure 2.

2 Think about how the calorimeter in Figure 2 reduces heat loss.

The flame calorimeter
The flame calorimeter, shown in Figure 3, is an improved version of the simple calorimeters used for measuring enthalpy changes of combustion. It incorporates the following features that are designed to reduce heat loss even further:

■ The spiral chimney is made of copper.

■ The flame is enclosed.

■ The fuel burns in pure oxygen, rather than air.

3 How do you think these features reduce heat loss?

How science works

The bomb calorimeter

This is the most accurate method for measuring enthalpies of combustion and is how accurate average bond enthalpies or 'Data Book' values are determined.

The actual 'bomb' is a thick stainless steel pressure vessel into which the sample is placed in a crucible. A 'wick' leads from the sample to an electrical ignition coil. The bomb is filled with oxygen at a pressure of several atmospheres. It is then sealed and placed in a calorimeter full of water which itself sits in a water-filled tank. The sample is ignited electrically and as the heat passes into the calorimeter, a thermostat and heater ensure that the water in the outer tank is kept at the same temperature as the water in the calorimeter. This eliminates heat loss from the calorimeter as its surroundings are always at its own temperature. The heat capacity of the calorimeter is calibrated by the combustion of benzoic acid as in the flame calorimeter. The mass of the sample is determined to 0.0001 g and the temperature measured to three decimal places using a platinum resistance thermometer.

Since the reaction takes place in a sealed container, the energy change measured is not in fact the enthalpy change. However, there is a simple relationship between the measured energy change and the enthalpy change.

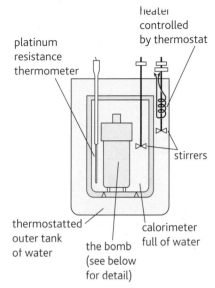

Figure 4 *A bomb calorimeter*

Measuring enthalpy changes of reactions in solution

It is relatively easy to measure heat changes for reactions that take place in solution. The heat is generated in the solutions themselves and only has to be kept in the calorimeter. We often use expanded polystyrene beakers for the calorimeters. These are good insulators (this reduces heat loss through their sides) and they have a low heat capacity so they absorb very little heat. We usually take the specific heat capacity of dilute solutions to be the same as that of water, $4.2 \, J \, g^{-1} \, K^{-1}$ (or more precisely $4.18 \, J \, g^{-1} \, K^{-1}$).

Neutralisation reactions

Neutralisation reactions in solution are exothermic; they give out heat.

When an acid is neutralised by an alkali the equation is:

$$\text{acid + alkali} \longrightarrow \text{salt + water}$$

When we find an enthalpy change for a reaction, we use the quantities in moles given by the balanced equation. For example, to find the molar enthalpy change of reaction for the neutralisation of hydrochloric acid by sodium hydroxide, we need to find the heat given out by the quantities in the equation:

$$\underset{\substack{\text{hydrochloric acid} \\ \text{1 mol}}}{\text{HCl(aq)}} + \underset{\substack{\text{sodium hydroxide} \\ \text{1 mol}}}{\text{NaOH(aq)}} \longrightarrow \underset{\substack{\text{sodium chloride} \\ \text{1 mol}}}{\text{NaCl(aq)}} + \underset{\substack{\text{water} \\ \text{1 mol}}}{\text{H}_2\text{O(l)}}$$

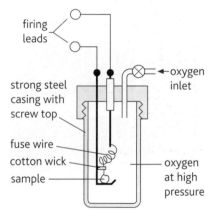

Figure 5 *The bomb calorimeter enlarged*

Worked example:

$50\,cm^3$ of $1.0\,mol\,dm^{-3}$ hydrochloric acid and $50\,cm^3$ of $1.0\,mol\,dm^{-3}$ sodium hydroxide solution were mixed in an expanded polystyrene beaker. The temperature rose by $6.6\,K$.

The total volume of the mixture is $100\,cm^3$. This has a mass of approximately $100\,g$ because the density of water and of dilute aqueous solutions is approximately $1\,g\,cm^{-3}$.

$$\text{Enthalpy change} = \underset{\text{water}}{\text{mass of}} \times \underset{\text{of solution}}{\text{specific heat capacity}} \times \underset{\text{change}}{\text{temperature}}$$

$$q = m \times c \times \Delta T$$

$$= 100 \times 4.2 \times 6.6 = 2772\,J$$

$$\text{Number of moles of acid (and also of alkali)} = \frac{M \times V}{1000}$$

where M is concentration in $mol\,dm^{-3}$ and V is volume in cm^3

$$= 1.0 \times \frac{50}{1000} = 0.05\,mol$$

so 1 mol would give $\frac{2772}{0.05}J$

$$= 55\,440\,J = 55.44\,kJ$$

$$\Delta H = -55.44\,kJ\,mol^{-1}$$

(negative because heat is given out)

$$\Delta H = -55\,kJ\,mol^{-1}\,(\text{to 2 s.f.})$$

Displacement reactions

A metal that is more reactive than another will displace the less reactive one from a compound. If the compound will dissolve in water, then this reaction can be investigated using a polystyrene beaker as before.

For example, zinc will displace copper from a solution of copper sulfate. The reaction is exothermic.

$$\underset{\text{1 mol}}{Zn(s)} + \underset{\text{1 mol}}{CuSO_4(aq)} \longrightarrow \underset{\text{1 mol}}{ZnSO_4(aq)} + \underset{\text{1 mol}}{Cu(s)}$$

We know from the equation that 1 mole of zinc reacts with 1 mole of copper sulfate.

Worked example:

$0.50\,g$ of zinc was added to $25.0\,cm^3$ of $0.20\,mol\,dm^{-3}$ copper sulfate solution. The temperature rose by $10\,K$.

$$\text{Enthalpy change, } q = m \times c \times \Delta T$$

$$= 25 \times 4.2 \times 10$$

$$= 1050\,J$$

A_r for zinc = 65.4, so $0.50\,g$ of zinc is $\frac{0.50}{65.4}$ moles

$$= 0.0076\,moles$$

Number of moles of
copper sulfate in solution $= \frac{M \times V}{1000}$

where M is concentration in $mol\,dm^{-3}$ and V is volume in cm^3

$$= 0.20 \times \frac{25.0}{1000} = 0.005\,mol$$

> **■ Hint**
>
> Remember to use the *total* volume of the mixture, $100\,cm^3$. A common mistake is to use $50\,cm^3$.

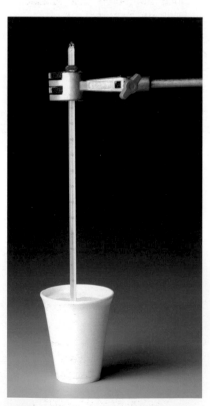

Figure 6 *Polystyrene beakers make good calorimeters because they are good insulators and have low heat capacities*

This means that the zinc was in excess; 0.005 mol of each reactant has taken part in the reaction, leaving some unreacted zinc behind.

Therefore, 1 mole of zinc would produce $\dfrac{1050}{0.005}$ J

$$= 210\,000\,\text{J}.$$

So, ΔH for this reaction is $-210\,\text{kJ}\,\text{mol}^{-1}$ (to two s.f.).

The sign of ΔH is negative because heat is given out.

Allowing for heat loss

Although expanded polystyrene cups are good insulators, some heat will still be lost from the sides and top leading to low values for enthalpy changes measured by this method. This can be allowed for by plotting a cooling curve. As an example, we will repeat the measurement of the heat of neutralisation of hydrochloric acid and sodium hydroxide using a cooling curve.

Before the experiment, all the apparatus and both solutions are left to stand in the laboratory for some time. This ensures that they all reach the same temperature, that of the laboratory itself.

Then proceed as follows:

- Place 50 cm³ of 1.0 mol dm⁻³ hydrochloric acid in one polystyrene cup and 50 cm³ of 1.0 mol dm⁻³ sodium hydroxide solution in another.

- Using a thermometer that reads to 0.1 °C, take the temperature of each solution every 30 seconds for four minutes to confirm that both solutions remain at the same temperature, that of the laboratory. A line of 'best fit' is drawn through these points. It is likely there will be very small variations around the line of best fit, indicating systematic errors.

- Now pour one solution into the other and stir, continuing to record the temperature every 30 seconds for a further six minutes.

The results are shown on the graph in Figure 7. The experiment can also be done using an electronic temperature sensor and data logging software to plot the graph directly.

On mixing, the temperature rises rapidly as the reaction gives out heat, and then drops slowly and regularly as heat is lost from the polystyrene cup. To find the best estimate of the temperature immediately after mixing, we draw the best straight line through the graph points after mixing and extrapolate back to the time of mixing. This gives a temperature rise of 6.9 °C.

The calculation is as before.

Enthalpy change, $q = m \times c \times \Delta T$

$$= 100 \times 4.2 \times 6.9$$

$$= 2898\,\text{J}$$

The number of moles of acid (and alkali) was 0.05 mol (as before).

So 1 mol would give $\dfrac{2898}{0.05}$ J

$$= 57\,960\,\text{J}$$

$$= 57.96\,\text{kJ}$$

$$\Delta H_{\text{neutralisation}} = 58\,\text{kJ}\,\text{mol}^{-1}\ (\text{to 2 s.f.})$$

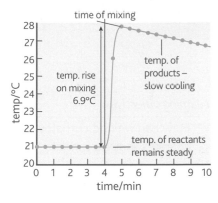

Figure 7 *Graph to show temperature as a neutralisation reaction proceeds*

Summary questions

1. 0.74 g (0.010 mol) of propanoic acid was burned in the simple calorimeter like that described above for the combustion of methanol. The temperature rose by 8.0 K. What value does this give for the enthalpy change of combustion of propanoic acid?

2. 50.0 cm³ of 2.00 mol dm⁻³ sodium hydroxide and 50.0 cm³ of 2.00 mol dm⁻³ hydrochloric acid were mixed in an expanded polystyrene beaker. The temperature rose by 11.0 K.
   a Calculate ΔH for the reaction.
   b How will this value compare with the accepted value for this reaction?
   c Explain your answer to **b**.

3. Consider the expression $\Delta H = mc\Delta T$
   a What does the term ΔH represent?
   b What does the term m represent?
   c What does the term c represent?
   d What does the term ΔT represent?

4. 0.46 g (0.010 mol) of ethanol was burnt in a simple calorimeter containing 100 g water. The temperature went up by 24.0 K. What is the enthalpy change of combustion of ethanol?

Learning objectives:

■ How can we find enthalpy changes that we cannot measure directly?

Specification reference 3.2.1

The enthalpy changes for some reactions cannot be measured directly. To find these we use an indirect approach. We use enthalpy changes that we can measure to work out enthalpy changes that we cannot. In particular, it is often easy to measure enthalpies of combustion. To do this we use Hess's law, first stated by Germain Hess, a Swiss-born Russian chemist, born in 1802.

💡 Hess's law

Hess's law states that the enthalpy change for a chemical reaction is the same, whatever route is taken from reactants to products.

It is a consequence of a more general scientific law, the Law of Conservation of Energy, which states that energy can never be created or destroyed. So, provided the starting and finishing points of a process are the same, the energy change must be the same. If not, energy would have been created or destroyed.

Using Hess's law

To see what Hess's law means, look at the following example where ethyne, C_2H_2, is converted to ethane, C_2H_6, by two different routes. How can we find the enthalpy of reaction?

Route 1: The reaction takes place directly; ethyne reacts with two moles of hydrogen to give ethane:

$$C_2H_2(g) + 2H_2(g) \longrightarrow C_2H_6(g) \quad \Delta H_1 = ?$$
$$\text{ethyne} \qquad\qquad\qquad \text{ethane}$$

Route 2: The reaction takes place in two stages.

a Ethyne, C_2H_2, reacts with one mole of hydrogen molecules to give ethene, C_2H_4.

b Ethene, C_2H_4, then reacts with a second mole of hydrogen to give ethane, C_2H_6.

a $C_2H_2(g) + H_2(g) \longrightarrow C_2H_4(g) \quad \Delta H_2 = -176\,\text{kJ mol}^{-1}$
　　ethyne　　　　　　　ethene

b $C_2H_4(g) + H_2(g) \longrightarrow C_2H_6(g) \quad \Delta H_3 = -137\,\text{kJ mol}^{-1}$
　　ethene　　　　　　　ethane

Hess's law tells us that the total energy change is the same whichever route we take, direct or via ethene (or, in fact, by any other route). We can show this on a diagram called a **thermochemical cycle**.

$$H-C\equiv C-H\,(g) + 2H_2\,(g) \xrightarrow[\text{1.}]{\Delta H_1\,(?)} \begin{array}{c} H\ \ H \\ |\ \ \ | \\ H-C-C-H\,(g) \\ |\ \ \ | \\ H\ \ H \end{array}$$

2. ΔH_2 ($-176\,\text{kJ}\,\text{mol}^{-1}$)

3. ΔH_3 ($-137\,\text{kJ}\,\text{mol}^{-1}$)

$$\begin{array}{cc} H & \quad H \\ \ \diagdown & \diagup \\ & C=C \quad (g) \\ \diagup & \diagdown \\ H & \quad H \end{array}$$

$+ H_2\,(g)$

Hess's law means that: $\Delta H_1 = \Delta H_2 + \Delta H_3$

The actual figures are: $\Delta H_2 = -176\,\text{kJ}\,\text{mol}^{-1}$

$\Delta H_3 = -137\,\text{kJ}\,\text{mol}^{-1}$

So $\Delta H_1 = -176 + -137 = -313\,\text{kJ}\,\text{mol}^{-1}$

This method of calculating ΔH_1 is fine if we know the enthalpy changes for the other two reactions. There are certain enthalpy changes that can be looked up for a large range of compounds. These include the enthalpy change of formation, $\Delta H_f^{\ominus}$, and enthalpy change of combustion, $\Delta H_c^{\ominus}$. In practice, many $\Delta H_f^{\ominus}$s are calculated from $\Delta H_c^{\ominus}$s via Hess's law cycles.

■ Using the enthalpy changes of formation $\Delta H_f^{\ominus}$

The enthalpy of formation, $\Delta H_f^{\ominus}$, is the enthalpy change when one mole of compound is formed from its constituent elements under standard conditions.

Another theoretical way to convert ethyne to ethane could be via the elements carbon and hydrogen.

■ Ethyne is first converted to its elements, carbon and hydrogen. This is the reverse of formation and the enthalpy change is the *negative* of the enthalpy of formation. This is a general rule. The reverse of a reaction has the negative of its ΔH value. It is in fact a consequence of Hess's law.

■ Then the carbon and hydrogen react to form ethane. This is the enthalpy of formation for ethane.

Hess's law tells us that $\Delta H_1 = \Delta H_4 + \Delta H_5$

$$H-C\equiv C-H\,(g) + 2H_2\,(g) \xrightarrow[\text{1.}]{\Delta H_1\,(?)} \begin{array}{c} H\ \ H \\ |\ \ \ | \\ H-C-C-H\,(g) \\ |\ \ \ | \\ H\ \ H \end{array}$$

4. ΔH_4

5. ΔH_5

$\boxed{2C\,(s,\ graphite) + 3H_2\,(g)}$

■ Hint

Graphite is the most stable form of carbon (another form is diamond). It has a special state symbol: s, graphite.

ΔH_5 is the enthalpy of formation, $\Delta H_f^{\ominus}$ of ethane while reaction 4 is the *reverse* of the formation of ethyne.

The values we need are: $\Delta H_f^{\ominus}(C_2H_2) = +228\,kJ\,mol^{-1}$

and $\Delta H_f^{\ominus}(C_2H_6) = -85\,kJ\,mol^{-1}$

So $\Delta H_4 = -228\,kJ\,mol^{-1}$
(Remember to change the sign)

$\Delta H_5 = -85\,kJ\,mol^{-1}$

Thus $\Delta H_1 = -228 + -85 = -313\,kJ\,mol^{-1}$

This was the result we got from the previous method, as we should expect from Hess's law.

Notice that in reaction 4 there are two moles of hydrogen 'spare' as only one of the three moles of hydrogen is involved.

$C_2H_2(g) \longrightarrow 2C(s, graphite) + H_2(g)$ is the reaction we are considering, but we have:

$C_2H_2(g) + 2H_2(g) \longrightarrow 2C(s, graphite) + 3H_2(g)$

However, this makes no difference. The 'extra' hydrogen *is not involved in the reaction* and it does not affect ΔH.

Hint

For an element, $\Delta H_f^{\ominus}$ is zero by definition.

Summary questions

1 Use the values of $\Delta H_f^{\ominus}$ in the table to calculate $\Delta H^{\ominus}$ for each of the reactions below using a thermochemical cycle.

a $CH_3COCH_3(l) + H_2(g) \longrightarrow CH_3CH(OH)CH_3(l)$

b $C_2H_4(g) + Cl_2(g) \longrightarrow C_2H_4Cl_2(l)$

c $C_2H_4(g) + HCl(g) \longrightarrow C_2H_5Cl(l)$

d $Zn(s) + CuO(s) \longrightarrow ZnO(s) + Cu(s)$

e $Pb(NO_3)_2(s) \longrightarrow PbO(s) + 2NO_2(g) + \frac{1}{2}O_2(g)$

Table 1

Compound	$\Delta H_f^{\ominus}/kJ\,mol^{-1}$
$CH_3COCH_3(l)$	−248
$CH_3CH(OH)CH_3(l)$	−318
$C_2H_4(g)$	+52
$C_2H_4Cl_2(l)$	−165
$C_2H_5Cl(l)$	−137
$HCl(g)$	−92
$CuO(s)$	−157
$ZnO(s)$	−348
$Pb(NO_3)_2(s)$	−452
$PbO(s)$	−217
$NO_2(g)$	+33

7.5 Enthalpy changes of combustion, $\Delta H_c^{\ominus}$

Learning objectives:

■ How can the enthalpy change of combustion be used to find the enthalpy change of a reaction?

Specification reference 3.2.1

The enthalpy change of combustion, $\Delta H_c^{\ominus}$, is the enthalpy change when one mole of substance is completely burned in oxygen under standard conditions.

💡 Thermochemical cycles using enthalpy changes of combustion

We can look again at the thermochemical cycle that we used to find $\Delta H^{\ominus}$ for the reaction between ethyne and hydrogen to form ethane:

$$C_2H_2(g) + 2H_2(g) \longrightarrow C_2H_6(g)$$

This time we will use enthalpy changes of combustion. In this case we can go via the combustion products of the three substances: carbon dioxide and water.

All three substances, ethyne, hydrogen and ethane, burn readily. This means their enthalpy changes of combustion can be easily measured. The thermochemical cycle is:

Putting in the values:

To get the enthalpy change for reaction 1 we must go round the cycle in the direction of the red arrows. This means reversing reaction 8 so we must change its sign.

So $\Delta H_1 = -1873 + 1560\,\text{kJ}\,\text{mol}^{-1}$

$\Delta H_1 = -313\,\text{kJ}\,\text{mol}^{-1}$ once again, the same answer as before

Notice that in reaction 1 there are $3\frac{1}{2}$ moles of oxygen on either side of the equation. They take no part in the reaction and do not affect the value of ΔH.

AQA Examiner's tip

Remember to multiply by the number of moles of reagents involved in each step.

Hint

■ Both reactions 6 and 7 have to occur to get from the starting materials to the combustion products. Do not forget the hydrogen.

■ In this case there are two moles of hydrogen so we need *twice* the value of $\Delta H_c^{\ominus}$ which refers to one mole of hydrogen.

$\Delta H_c^{\ominus}(C_2H_2) = -1301\,\text{kJ}\,\text{mol}^{-1}$

$\Delta H_c^{\ominus}(H_2) = -285\,\text{kJ}\,\text{mol}^{-1}$

$\Delta H_c^{\ominus}(C_2H_6) = -1560\,\text{kJ}\,\text{mol}^{-1}$

💡 Finding $\Delta H_f^\ominus$ from $\Delta H_c^\ominus$

Enthalpy changes of formation of compounds are often difficult or impossible to measure directly. This is because the reactants often do not react directly to form the compound that we are interested in.

For example, the following equation represents the formation of ethanol from its elements.

$$2C(s, \text{graphite}) + 3H_2(g) + \tfrac{1}{2}O_2 \longrightarrow C_2H_5OH(l)$$

This does not take place. However, all the species concerned will readily burn in oxygen so their enthalpy changes of combustion can be measured. The thermochemical cycle we need is:

$$3O_2(g) + 2C(s,\text{graphite}) + 3H_2(g) + \tfrac{1}{2}O_2 \xrightarrow[\quad 9. \quad]{\Delta H_f^\ominus \text{(ethanol)}} C_2H_5OH(l) + 3O_2(g)$$

11. $\;3 \times \Delta H_c^\ominus (H_2(g))$

$2 \times \Delta H_c^\ominus (C (s, \text{graphite}))$ 10.

12. $\;\Delta H_c^\ominus (C_2H_5OH(l))$

$$\boxed{2CO_2(g) + 3H_2O(l)}$$

Hint

The values we need are:

$\Delta H_c^\ominus(C(s, \text{graphite})) = -393.5\,\text{kJ}\,\text{mol}^{-1}$

$\Delta H_c^\ominus(H_2(g)) = -285.8\,\text{kJ}\,\text{mol}^{-1}$

$\Delta H_c^\ominus(C_2H_5OH(l)) = -1367.3\,\text{kJ}\,\text{mol}^{-1}$

Putting in the values:

$$3O_2(g) + 2C(s,\text{graphite}) + 3H_2(g) + \tfrac{1}{2}O_2 \xrightarrow[\quad 9. \quad]{\Delta H_f^\ominus \text{(ethanol)}} C_2H_5OH(l) + 3O_2(g)$$

11.
$3 \times -285.8\,\text{kJ}\,\text{mol}^{-1}$
$= -857.4\,\text{kJ}\,\text{mol}^{-1}$

10.
$2 \times -393.5\,\text{kJ}\,\text{mol}^{-1}$
$= -787\,\text{kJ}\,\text{mol}^{-1}$

12.
$-1367.3\,\text{kJ}\,\text{mol}^{-1}$

$$\boxed{2CO_2(g) + 3H_2O(l)}$$

$-1644.4\,\text{kJ}\,\text{mol}^{-1}$ $\qquad$ $+1367.3\,\text{kJ}\,\text{mol}^{-1}$

Note that in reaction 9 there are three moles of oxygen on either side of the equation that take no part in the reaction. This means that they do not affect the value of ΔH.

Note also that $\Delta H_c^\ominus(C(s, \text{graphite}))$ is the same as $\Delta H_f^\ominus(CO_2(g))$; and $\Delta H_c^\ominus(H_2(g))$ is the same as $\Delta H_f^\ominus(H_2O(l))$.

To get the enthalpy change for reaction 9, we must go round the cycle in the direction of the red arrows. This means reversing reaction 12 so we must change its sign.

So, $\Delta H_9 = -1664.4 + 1367.3\,\text{kJ}\,\text{mol}^{-1} = -277.1\,\text{kJ}\,\text{mol}^{-1}$

So, $\Delta H_f^\ominus(C_2H_5OH(l)) = -277.1\,\text{kJ}\,\text{mol}^{-1}$

Summary questions

1

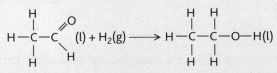

Calculate $\Delta H^\ominus$ for the reaction by thermochemical cycles:

a via $\Delta H_f^\ominus$ values

b via $\Delta H_c^\ominus$ values

Compound	$\Delta H_f^\ominus / \text{kJ}\,\text{mol}^{-1}$	$\Delta H_c^\ominus / \text{kJ}\,\text{mol}^{-1}$
CH_3CHO	−192	−1167
H_2	–	−286
CH_3CH_2OH	−277	−1367

We can use **enthalpy diagrams** rather than thermochemical cycles to represent the enthalpy changes in chemical reactions. These show the energy (enthalpy) levels of the reactants and products of a chemical reaction on a vertical scale, so we can compare their energies. If a substance is of lower energy than another, we say it is energetically more stable.

The enthalpy of elements

So far we have considered enthalpy *changes*, not absolute values. When drawing enthalpy diagrams we need a zero to work from. We can then give absolute numbers to the enthalpies of different substances.

> The enthalpies of all elements in their standard states (i.e. the states in which they exist at 298 K and 100 kPa) are taken as zero. (298 K and 100 kPa are approximately normal room conditions.)

This convention means that the standard state of hydrogen, for example, is H_2 and not H, because hydrogen exists as H_2 at room temperature and pressure.

Pure carbon can exist in a number of forms at room temperature including graphite, diamond and buckminsterfullerene ('buckyballs'). These are called **allotropes**. Graphite is the most stable of these and is taken as the standard state of carbon. It is given the special state symbol s, graphite, so C(s, graphite) represents graphite.

Thermochemical cycles and enthalpy diagrams

Here are two examples of reactions, with their enthalpy changes presented both as thermochemical cycles and as enthalpy diagrams.

Example 1

What is $\Delta H^{\ominus}$ for the change from methoxymethane to ethanol? (The compounds are a pair of isomers; they have the same formula but different structures, see Figure 1.)

The standard molar enthalpy changes of formation of the two compounds are:

$$CH_3OCH_3 \quad \Delta H_f^{\ominus} = -184 \,\text{kJ}\,\text{mol}^{-1}$$
$$C_2H_5OH \quad \Delta H_f^{\ominus} = -277 \,\text{kJ}\,\text{mol}^{-1}$$

💡 *Using a thermochemical cycle*

The following steps are shown in red on the thermochemical cycle.

1 Write an equation for the reaction.
2 Write down the elements in the two compounds with the correct quantities of each.
3 Put in the $\Delta H_f^{\ominus}$ values with arrows showing the direction, i.e. **from** elements **to** compounds.
4 Put in the arrows to go from starting materials to products via the elements (the red arrows).

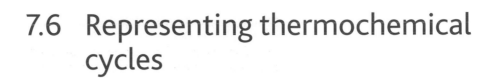

Learning objectives:

- What is an enthalpy diagram?
- What is used as the zero for enthalpy changes?

Specification reference 3.2.1

H—C—O—C—H (methoxymethane)

methoxymethane

H—C—C—OH (ethanol)

ethanol

Figure 1 *Isomers of C_2H_6O*

5 Reverse the sign of $\Delta H_f^{\ominus}$ if the red arrow is in the opposite direction to the black arrow.

6 Go round the cycle in the direction of the red arrows and add up the $\Delta H^{\ominus}$ values as you go.

Hess's law tells us that this is the same as $\Delta H^{\ominus}$ for the direct reaction.

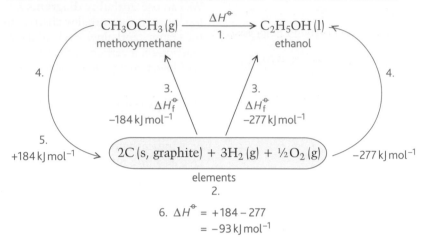

6. $\Delta H^{\ominus} = +184 - 277$
$= -93\,kJ\,mol^{-1}$

💡 *Using an enthalpy diagram*

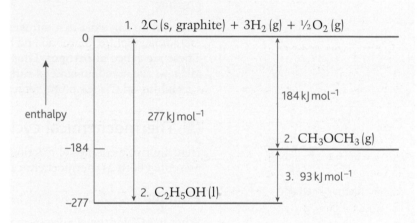

> **AQA** Examiner's tip
>
> Examiners do not expect candidates to draw these diagrams to scale.

The following steps are shown in red on the enthalpy diagram.

1 Draw a line at level 0 to represent the elements.

2 Look up the values of $\Delta H_f^{\ominus}$ for each compound and enter these on the enthalpy diagrams, taking account of the signs: negative values are below 0, positive values are above.

3 Find the difference in levels between the two compounds. This represents the difference in their enthalpies.

4 $\Delta H^{\ominus}$ is the difference in levels *taking account of the direction of change*. Up is positive and down is negative. From methoxymethane to ethanol is *down* so the sign is negative. From ethanol to methoxymethane the sign of $\Delta H^{\ominus}$ would be positive.

Notice how the enthalpy level diagram makes it much clearer than the thermochemical cycle does, that ethanol has less energy than methoxymethane. This means that it is the more energetically stable compound. The values of $\Delta H^{\ominus}$ for the reaction are the same whichever method we use.

💡 Example 2

To find $\Delta H^{\ominus}$ for the reaction: $NH_3(g) + HCl(g) \longrightarrow NH_4Cl(s)$

The standard molar enthalpy changes of formation of the compounds are:

NH_3	$\Delta H_f^{\ominus} = -46\,kJ\,mol^{-1}$
HCl	$\Delta H_f^{\ominus} = -92\,kJ\,mol^{-1}$
NH_4Cl	$\Delta H_f^{\ominus} = -314\,kJ\,mol^{-1}$

Using a thermochemical cycle

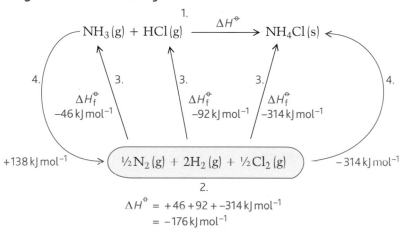

$$\Delta H^{\ominus} = +46 + 92 + -314\,kJ\,mol^{-1}$$
$$= -176\,kJ\,mol^{-1}$$

The following steps are shown in red on the thermochemical cycle.

1 Write an equation for the reaction.

2 Write down the elements that make up the two compounds with the correct quantities of each.

3 Put in the $\Delta H_f^{\ominus}$ values with arrows showing the direction i.e. from elements to compounds.

4 Put in the arrows to go from the starting materials to products via the elements (the red arrows).

5 Reverse the sign of $\Delta H_f^{\ominus}$ if the red arrow is in the opposite direction to the black arrow(s).

6 Go round the cycle in the direction of the red arrows and add up the values of $\Delta H^{\ominus}$ as you go.

💡 Using an enthalpy diagram

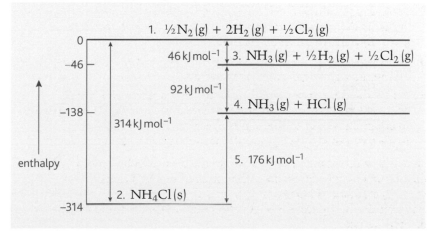

The following steps are shown in red on the enthalpy diagram.

1 Draw a line at level 0 to represent the elements.

2 Draw in NH_4Cl $314\,kJ\,mol^{-1}$ below this.

3 Draw a line representing ammonia $46\,kJ\,mol^{-1}$ below the level of the elements. (There is still $\frac{1}{2}H_2$ and $\frac{1}{2}Cl_2$ left unused.)

4 Draw a line $92\,kJ\,mol^{-1}$ below ammonia. This represents hydrogen chloride.

5 Find the difference in levels between the $(NH_3 + HCl)$ line and the NH_4Cl one. This represents $\Delta H^\ominus$ for the reaction. As the change from $(NH_3 + HCl)$ to NH_4Cl is down, $\Delta H^\ominus$ must be negative.

Notice how the enthalpy level diagram makes it much clearer than the thermochemical cycle does, that ammonium chloride is more energetically stable than the gaseous mixture of ammonia and hydrogen chloride. This is part of the reason why ammonia and hydrogen chloride react readily to form ammonium chloride. The values of $\Delta H^\ominus$ for the reaction are the same whichever method we use.

Summary questions

1 Use the values of $\Delta H_f^\ominus$ in the table to calculate $\Delta H^\ominus$ for each of the reactions below using enthalpy diagrams.

a $CH_3COCH_3(l) + H_2(g) \longrightarrow CH_3CH(OH)CH_3(l)$

b $C_2H_4(g) + Cl_2(g) \longrightarrow C_2H_4Cl_2(l)$

c $C_2H_4(g) + HCl(g) \longrightarrow C_2H_5Cl(l)$

d $Zn(s) + CuO(s) \longrightarrow ZnO(s) + Cu(s)$

e $Pb(NO_3)_2(s) \longrightarrow PbO(s) + 2NO_2(g) + \frac{1}{2}O_2(g)$

Table 1

Compound	$\Delta H_f^\ominus$ / kJ mol⁻¹
$CH_3COCH_3(l)$	−248
$CH_3CH(OH)CH_3(l)$	−318
$C_2H_4(g)$	+52
$C_2H_4Cl_2(l)$	−165
$C_2H_5Cl(l)$	−137
$HCl(g)$	−92
$CuO(s)$	−157
$ZnO(s)$	−348
$Pb(NO_3)_2(s)$	−452
$PbO(s)$	−217
$NO_2(g)$	+33

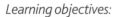

7.7 Bond enthalpies

Learning objectives:

■ What is a bond enthalpy?

■ How are mean bond enthalpies worked out from given data?

■ How are bond enthalpies used in calculations?

Specification reference 3.2.1

$\Delta H_c^{\ominus}$ is the enthalpy change of combustion. If we plot $\Delta H_c^{\ominus}$ against the number of carbon atoms in the molecule, for straight chain alkanes, we get a straight line graph, see Figure 1. For methane (with one carbon), $\Delta H_c^{\ominus}$ is the enthalpy change for:

$$CH_4(g) + 2O_2(g) \longrightarrow CO_2(g) + 2H_2O(l)$$

The straight line means that $\Delta H_c^{\ominus}$ changes by the same amount for each extra carbon atom in the chain.

Each alkane differs from the previous one by one CH_2 group, that is, there is one extra C—C bond in the molecule and two extra C—H bonds. This suggests that we can assign a definite amount of energy to a particular bond. This is called the bond enthalpy.

💡 Bond enthalpies

We have to put in energy to break a covalent bond; this is an endothermic change. The same amount of energy is given out when the bond is formed; this is an exothermic change. The same bond, for example C—H, may have slightly different bond enthalpies in different molecules, but we usually use the average value. The amount of energy involved is called the **mean bond enthalpy** (often called the bond energy). The fact that we get out the same amount of energy when we make a bond, as we put in to break it, is an example of Hess's law.

As mean bond enthalpies are averages, calculations using them for specific compounds will only give approximate answers. However, they are useful, and quick and easy to use. Mean bond enthalpies have been calculated from Hess's law cycles. They can be looked up in data books and databases.

The H—H bond energy is the energy required to separate the two atoms in a hydrogen molecule in the gas phase into separate gaseous atoms.

$$H_2(g) \longrightarrow 2H(g) \quad \Delta H^{\ominus} = +436\,kJ\,mol^{-1}$$

The C—H mean bond energy in methane is one quarter of the energy for the following process, in which four bonds are broken.

$$CH_4(g) \longrightarrow C(g) + 4H(g) \quad \Delta H^{\ominus} = +1664\,kJ\,mol^{-1}$$

So the mean (or average) C–H bond energy in methane $= \dfrac{1664}{4}$

$$= +416\,kJ\,mol^{-1}$$

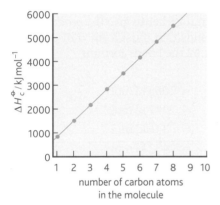

Figure 1 $\Delta H_c^{\ominus}$ against the number of carbon atoms in the alkane

Hint

■ If the bonds in the methane are broken one at a time, the energy required is not the same for each bond.

■ The value of $+416\,kJ\,mol^{-1}$ is the C–H bond energy in methane. The value in other compounds will vary slightly. The average over many compounds is $+413\,kJ\,mol^{-1}$.

■ All mean bond energies are positive because we have to put energy in to break bonds, i.e. it is an endothermic process.

💡 Using mean bond enthalpies to calculate enthalpy changes of reaction

We can use mean bond enthalpies to work out the enthalpy change of reactions, for example:

$$\underset{\text{ethane}}{C_2H_6(g)} + \underset{\text{chlorine}}{Cl_2(g)} \longrightarrow \underset{\text{chloroethane}}{C_2H_5Cl(g)} + \underset{\text{hydrogen chloride}}{HCl(g)}$$

The mean bond enthalpies you will need for this example are given in Table 1.

Table 1 *Mean bond enthalpies*

Bond	Bond enthalpy / kJ mol^{-1}
C—H	413
C—C	347
Cl—Cl	243
C—Cl	346
Cl—H	432
Br—Br	193
Br—H	366
C—Br	285

The steps are as follows:

1 First draw out the molecules and show all the bonds. (Formulae drawn showing all the bonds are called displayed formulae.)

$$
\begin{array}{c}
\text{H} \quad \text{H} \\
| \quad\; | \\
\text{H}-\text{C}-\text{C}-\text{H}\,(g) \;+\; \text{Cl}-\text{Cl}\,(g) \;\longrightarrow\; \text{H}-\text{C}-\text{C}-\text{Cl}\,(g) \;+\; \text{H}-\text{Cl}\,(g) \\
| \quad\; | \\
\text{H} \quad \text{H}
\end{array}
$$

2 Now imagine that all the bonds in the *reactants* break leaving separate atoms. Look up the bond enthalpy for each bond and add them all up. This will give you the total energy that must be *put in* to break the bonds and form separate atoms.

We need to *break* these bonds:

$6 \times$ C—H	6×413 kJ mol^{-1}	$= 2478$ kJ mol^{-1}
$1 \times$ C—C	1×347 kJ mol^{-1}	$= 347$ kJ mol^{-1}
$1 \times$ Cl—Cl	1×243 kJ mol^{-1}	$= 243$ kJ mol^{-1}
		$= 3068$ kJ mol^{-1}

So 3068 kJ mol^{-1} must be *put in* to convert ethane and chlorine to separate hydrogen, chlorine and carbon atoms.

3 Next imagine the separate atoms join together to give the *products*. Add up the bond enthalpies of the bonds that must form. This will give you the total enthalpy *given out* by the bonds forming.

We need to *make* these bonds:

$5 \times$ C—H	5×413 kJ mol^{-1}	$= 2065$ kJ mol^{-1}
$1 \times$ C—C	1×347 kJ mol^{-1}	$= 347$ kJ mol^{-1}
$1 \times$ C—Cl	1×346 kJ mol^{-1}	$= 346$ kJ mol^{-1}
$1 \times$ Cl—H	1×432 kJ mol^{-1}	$= 432$ kJ mol^{-1}
		$= 3190$ kJ mol^{-1}

So 3190 kJ mol^{-1} is *given out* when we convert the separate hydrogen, chlorine and carbon atoms to chloroethane and hydrogen chloride.

The difference between the energy put in to break the bonds and the energy given out to form bonds is the approximate enthalpy change of the reaction.

The difference is 3190 – 3068 = 122 kJ mol^{-1}.

4 Finally work out the sign of the enthalpy change. If more energy was put in than was given out, the enthalpy change is positive (the reaction is endothermic). If more energy was given out than was put in the enthalpy change is negative (the reaction is endothermic).

In this case, more enthalpy is given out than put in, so the reaction is exothermic and $\Delta H = -122$ kJ mol^{-1}

Note that in practice it would be impossible for the reaction to happen like this. However, Hess's law tells us that we will get the same answer whatever route we take, real or theoretical.

A shortcut

We can often shorten mean bond enthalpy calculations:

$$
\begin{array}{c}
\text{H} \quad \text{H} \\
| \quad\; | \\
\text{H}-\text{C}-\text{C}-\text{H}\,(g) \;+\; \text{Cl}-\text{Cl}\,(g) \;\longrightarrow\; \text{H}-\text{C}-\text{C}-\text{Cl}\,(g) \;+\; \text{H}-\text{Cl}\,(g) \\
| \quad\; | \\
\text{H} \quad \text{H}
\end{array}
$$

Only the bonds drawn in red make or break during the reaction so

we only need to break: $1 \times$ C—H $=$ 413 kJ mol^{-1}

$1 \times$ Cl—Cl $=$ 243 kJ mol^{-1}

Total energy put in $=$ 656 kJ mol^{-1}

We only need to make: $1 \times$ C—Cl $=$ 346 kJ mol^{-1}

$1 \times$ H—Cl $=$ 432 kJ mol^{-1}

Total energy given out $=$ 778 kJ mol^{-1}

The difference is 778 – 656 $=$ 122 kJ mol^{-1}

More energy is given out than taken in so

$$\Delta H = -122 \text{ kJ mol}^{-1} \text{ (as before)}$$

Comparing the result with that from a thermochemical cycle

This is only an approximate value. This is because the bond enthalpies are averages whereas in a compound any bond has a specific value for its enthalpy. We can find an accurate value for $\Delta H^{\ominus}$ by using a thermochemical cycle as shown here:

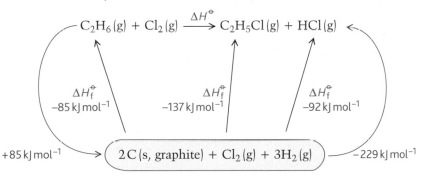

Remember $Cl_2(g)$ is an element so its $\Delta H_f^{\ominus}$ is zero.

$\Delta H^{\ominus} = 85 - 229 \text{ kJ mol}^{-1}$

$\Delta H^{\ominus} = -144 \text{ kJ mol}^{-1}$ (compared with -122 kJ mol^{-1} calculated from bond enthalpies)

This difference is typical of what might be expected using mean bond enthalpies. The answer obtained from the thermochemical cycle is the 'correct' one because all the $\Delta H_f^{\ominus}$ values have been obtained from the actual compounds involved.

Mean bond enthalpy calculations also allow us to calculate an approximate value for ΔH_f for a compound that has never been made.

Summary questions

These questions are about the reaction:

$$CH_3CH_3 + Br_2 \longrightarrow CH_3CH_2Br + HBr$$

1 Draw out the structural formulae of all the products and reactants so that all the bonds are shown.

2 a What bonds have to be broken to convert the reactants into separate atoms?

b How much energy does this take?

3 a What bonds have to be made to convert separate atoms into the products?

b How much energy does this take?

4 What is the difference between the energy put in to break bonds and the energy given out when the new bonds are formed?

5 a What is $\Delta H^{\ominus}$ for the reaction (this requires a sign)?

b Is the reaction in part **a** endothermic or exothermic?

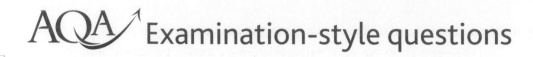

1 The table below contains some mean bond enthalpy data.

Bond	H—H	C—C	C=C	N≡N	N—H
Mean bond enthalpy / kJ mol^{-1}	436	348	612	944	388

(a) Explain the term *mean bond enthalpy*. *(2 marks)*

(b) (i) Write an equation for the formation of one mole of ammonia, NH_3, from its elements.

(ii) Use data from the table above to calculate a value for the enthalpy of formation of ammonia. *(4 marks)*

(c) Use the following equation and data from the table above to calculate a value for the C—H bond enthalpy in ethane.

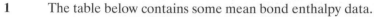

$\Delta H = -136 \, kJ \, mol^{-1}$

(3 marks)

AQA, 2003

2 (a) The table below contains some mean bond enthalpy data.

Bond	H—O	O—O	O=O
Mean bond enthalpy / kJ mol^{-1}	463	146	496

The bonding in hydrogen peroxide, H_2O_2, can be represented by H—O—O—H. Use these data to calculate the enthalpy change for the following reaction.

$$H_2O_2(g) \longrightarrow H_2O(g) + \tfrac{1}{2}O_2(g)$$ *(3 marks)*

(b) The standard enthalpy of formation, ΔH_f° for methane, is $-74.9 \, kJ \, mol^{-1}$. Write an equation, including state symbols, for the reaction to which this enthalpy change applies. *(2 marks)*

(c) The enthalpy changes for the formation of atomic hydrogen and atomic carbon from their respective elements in their standard states are as follows.

$$\tfrac{1}{2}H_2(g) \longrightarrow H(g) \qquad \Delta H^{\circ} = +218 \, kJ \, mol^{-1}$$
$$C(s) \longrightarrow C(g) \qquad \Delta H^{\circ} = +715 \, kJ \, mol^{-1}$$

(i) By reference to its structure, suggest why a large amount of heat energy is required to produce free carbon atoms from solid carbon.

(ii) Parts (b) and (c) give enthalpy data for the formation of $CH_4(g)$, $H(g)$ and $C(g)$.

Use these data and Hess's law to calculate the value of the enthalpy change for the following reaction.

$$CH_4(g) \longrightarrow C(g) + 4H(g)$$

(iii) Use your answer from part (c)(ii) to calculate a value for the mean bond enthalpy of a C—H bond in methane. *(5 marks)*

AQA, 2004

3 (a) Define the term *standard enthalpy of formation*, ΔH_f°. *(3 marks)*

(b) Use the data in the table to calculate the standard enthalpy of formation of liquid methylbenzene, C_7H_8

Substance	C(s)	$H_2(g)$	$C_7H_8(l)$
Standard enthalpy of combustion, ΔH_c° / kJ mol^{-1}	−394	−286	−3909

$$7C(s) + 4H_2(g) \longrightarrow C_7H_8(l)$$ *(3 marks)*

(c) An experiment was carried out to determine a value for the enthalpy of combustion of liquid methylbenzene using the apparatus shown in the diagram.

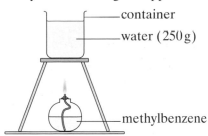

container
water (250 g)
methylbenzene

Burning 2.5 g of methylbenzene caused the temperature of 250 g of water to rise by 60 °C. Use this information to calculate a value for the enthalpy of combustion of methylbenzene, C_7H_8

(The specific heat capacity of water is $4.18\,J\,K^{-1}\,g^{-1}$. Ignore the heat capacity of the container.) *(4 marks)*

(d) A 25.0 cm³ sample of 2.00 mol dm⁻³ hydrochloric acid was mixed with 50.0 cm³ of a 1.00 mol dm⁻³ solution of sodium hydroxide. Both solutions were initially at 18.0 °C.

After mixing, the temperature of the final solution was 26.5 °C.

Use this information to calculate a value for the standard enthalpy change for the following reaction.

$$HCl(aq) + NaOH(aq) \longrightarrow NaCl(aq) + H_2O(l)$$

In your calculation, assume that the density of the final solution is 1.00 g cm⁻³ and that its specific heat capacity is the same as that of water. (Ignore the heat capacity of the container.) *(4 marks)*

(e) Give **one** reason why your answer to part (d) has a much smaller experimental error than your answer to part (c). *(1 mark)*

AQA, 2006

4 (a) Define the term *standard enthalpy of combustion, $\Delta H_c^\ominus$.* *(3 marks)*

(b) Use the mean bond enthalpy data from the table and the equation given below to calculate a value for the standard enthalpy of combustion of propene. All substances are in the gaseous state.

Bond	C=C	C—C	C—H	O=O	O=C	O—H
Mean bond enthalpy/kJ mol⁻¹	612	348	412	496	743	463

$$H-\underset{\underset{H}{|}}{\overset{\overset{H}{|}}{C}}-\underset{\underset{H}{|}}{\overset{\overset{H}{|}}{C}}=\overset{\overset{H}{|}}{C} \quad + \quad 4\tfrac{1}{2}\,O{=}O \quad \longrightarrow \quad 3\,O{=}C{=}O \quad + \quad 3\,H{-}O{-}H$$

(3 marks)

(c) State why the standard enthalpy of formation, $\Delta H_f^\ominus$, of oxygen is zero. *(1 mark)*

(d) Use the data from the table below to calculate a more accurate value for the standard enthalpy of combustion of propene.

Compound	$C_3H_6(g)$	$CO_2(g)$	$H_2O(g)$
Standard enthalpy of formation, $\Delta H_f^\ominus$/kJ mol⁻¹	+20	−394	−242

(3 marks)

(e) Explain why your answer to part (b) is a less accurate value than your answer to part (d). *(2 marks)*

AQA, 2006

8 Kinetics

8.1 Collision theory

Learning objectives:

■ What must happen before a reaction will take place?

■ Do all collisions result in a reaction?

Specification reference 3.2.2

Hint

A rough rule for many chemical reactions is that if the temperature goes up by 10 K (10 °C), the rate of reaction approximately doubles.

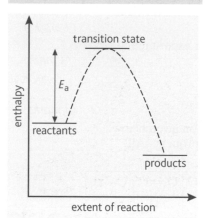

Figure 1 *An exothermic reaction with a large activation energy, E_a*

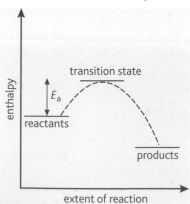

Figure 2 *An exothermic reaction with a small activation energy, E_a*

Kinetics is the study of the factors that affect rates of chemical reactions – how quickly they take place. There is a large variation in reaction rates. 'Popping' a test tube full of hydrogen is over in a fraction of a second, while the complete rusting away of an iron nail could take several years. Reactions can be speeded up or slowed down by changing the conditions.

Collision theory

For a reaction to take place between two particles, they must collide, and do so with enough energy to break bonds. The collision must also take place between the parts of the molecule that are going to react together, so orientation also has a part to play. To get a lot of collisions we need a lot of particles in a small volume. For the particles to have enough energy to break bonds they need to be moving fast. So, for a fast reaction rate we need plenty of rapidly moving particles in a small volume.

Most collisions between molecules do not lead to reaction. They either do not have enough energy, or they are in the wrong orientation.

Factors that affect the rate of chemical reactions

The following factors will increase the rate of a reaction:

■ **Increasing the temperature** This increases the speed of the molecules, which in turn increases both their energy and the number of collisions.

■ **Increasing the concentration of a solution** If there are more particles present in a given volume, collisions are more likely; therefore the reaction rate would be faster. However, as a reaction proceeds, the reactants are used up and their concentration falls. So, in most reactions the rate of reaction drops as the reaction goes on.

■ **Increasing the pressure of a gas reaction** This has the same effect as increasing the concentration of a solution; there are more molecules or atoms in a given volume so collisions are more likely.

■ **Increasing the surface area of solid reactants** The greater the *total* surface area of a solid, the more of its particles are available to collide with molecules in a gas or a liquid. This means that breaking a solid lump into smaller pieces increases the rate of its reaction because there are more sites for reaction.

■ **Using a catalyst** A catalyst is a substance that can change the rate of a chemical reaction without being chemically changed itself.

Activation energy

Only a very small proportion of collisions actually result in a reaction.

For a collision to result in a reaction, the molecules must have a certain minimum energy, enough to start breaking bonds. The minimum energy needed to start a reaction is called the **activation energy** and has the abbreviation E_a.

We can include the idea of activation energy on an enthalpy diagram that shows the course of a reaction.

Exothermic reactions

Figure 1 shows the reaction profile for an exothermic reaction with a large activation energy.

This reaction will take place extremely slowly at room temperature because very few collisions will have sufficient energy to bring about a reaction.

Figure 2 shows the reaction profile for an exothermic reaction with a small activation energy.

This reaction will take place rapidly at room temperature because many collisions will have enough energy to bring about a reaction.

The situation is a little like a ball on a hill, see Figure 3. A small amount of energy is needed in a), to set the ball rolling, while a large amount of energy is needed in b).

The species that exists at the top of the curve of an enthalpy diagram is called a **transition state** or **activated complex**. Some bonds are in the process of being made and some bonds are in the process of being broken. Like the ball at the very top of the hill, it has extra energy and is unstable.

Endothermic reactions

Endothermic reactions are those in which the products have more energy than the reactants. An endothermic reaction, with activation energy E_a, is shown in Figure 4. The transition state has been labelled.

Notice that the activation energy is measured from the reactants to the top of the curve.

> ### Hint
>
> Species is a term used by chemists to refer to an atom, molecule or ion.

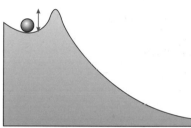

a With low 'activation energy'

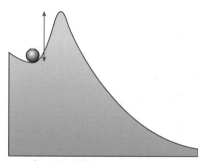

b With high 'activation energy'

Figure 3 *Ball on a mountainside models*

Summary questions

1 List five factors that affect the speed of a chemical reaction.

Use the reaction profile in the figure below to answer questions 2 and 3:

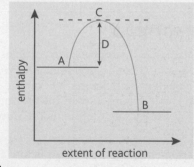

2 **a** What is A?

   b What is B?

   c What is C?

   d What is D?

3 **a** Does the enthalpy profile represent an endothermic or an exothermic reaction?

   b Explain your answer to part **a**.

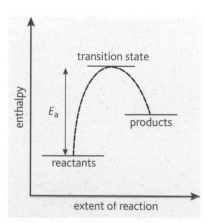

Figure 4 *An endothermic reaction with activation energy, E_a*

8.2 The Maxwell–Boltzmann distribution

Learning objectives:

- What is meant by activation energy?

- How does temperature affect the number of molecules with energy equal to or more than the activation energy?

- Why does a small increase in temperature have a large effect on the rate of a reaction?

Specification reference 3.2.2

The particles in any gas (or solution) are all moving at different speeds; a few are moving slowly, a few very fast but most are somewhere in the middle. The energy of a particle depends on its speed so the particles also have a range of energies. If we plot a graph of 'energy' against the 'fraction of particles that have that energy', we end up with the curve shown in Figure 1. This particular shape is called the **Maxwell–Boltzmann distribution**; it tells us about the distribution of energy amongst the particles.

- No particles have zero energy.
- Most particles have intermediate energies – around the peak of the curve.
- A few have very high energies indeed (the right-hand side of the curve). In fact there is no upper limit.
- Note also that the average energy is not the same as the most probable energy.

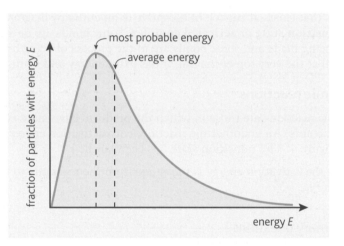

Figure 1 *The distribution of the energies of particles. The area under the graph represents the total number of particles.*

Activation energy, E_a

For a reaction to take place, a collision between particles must have enough energy to start breaking bonds, see Topic 8.1. We call this amount of energy the activation energy, E_a. If we mark E_a on the Maxwell–Boltzmann distribution graph, Figure 2, then the area under the graph to the right of the activation energy line represents the number of particles with enough energy to react.

The need for the activation energy to be present before a reaction takes place explains why not all reactions that are exothermic occur spontaneously at room temperature.

For example, fuels are mostly safe at room temperature, as in a petrol station. But, a small spark may provide enough energy to start the combustion reaction. The heat given out by the initial reaction is enough to supply the activation energy for further reactions. Similarly the chemicals in a match head are quite stable until the activation energy is provided by friction.

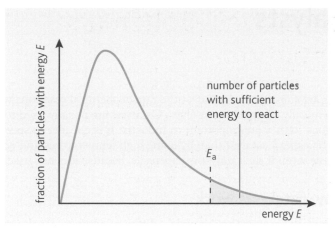

Figure 2 *Only particles with energy greater than E_a can react*

Even the high temperature of a single spark can set off a reaction. This is why if you smell gas, you must not even turn on a light. The electrical connection provided by the switch could produce enough energy to begin an explosion.

■ The effect of temperature on reaction rate

The shape of the Maxwell–Boltzmann graph changes with temperature, as shown in Figure 3.

At higher temperatures the peak of the curve is lower, and moves to the right. The number of particles with very high energy increases. The total area under the curve *is the same* for each temperature because it represents the total number of particles.

The shaded areas to the right of the E_a line represent the number of molecules that have greater energy than E_a at each temperature.

The graphs show that at higher temperatures more of the molecules have energy greater than E_a so a higher percentage of collisions will result in reaction. This is why reaction rates increase with temperature. In fact, a small increase in temperature produces a large increase in the number of particles with energy greater than E_a.

Also, the total *number* of collisions in a given time increases a little as the particles move faster. However, this is not as important to the rate of reaction as the increase in the number of *effective* collisions (those with energy greater than E_a).

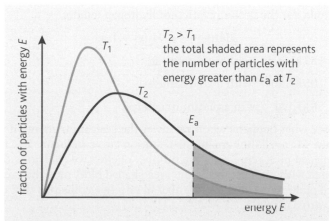

Figure 3 *The Maxwell–Boltzmann distribution of the energies of the same number of particles at two temperatures*

Summary questions

1 Use Figure 4 to answer the following questions:

   a What is the axis labelled A?

   b What is the axis labelled B?

   c What does area C represent?

   d If the temperature is increased, what happens to the peak of the curve?

   e If the temperature is increased, what happens to E_a?

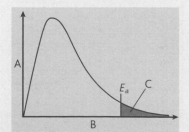

Figure 4 *The Maxwell–Boltzmann distribution of energies of particles at a particular temperature, with the activation energy, E_a marked*

8.3 Catalysts

Learning objectives:

- What is a catalyst?

- How does a catalyst affect activation energy?

- How does a catalyst affect enthalpy change?

Specification reference 3.2.2

Catalysts are substances that affect the rate of chemical reactions without being chemically changed themselves. Catalysts are usually used to *speed up* reactions so they are important in industry. It is cheaper to speed up a reaction by using a catalyst than by using high temperatures and pressures. This is true, even if the catalyst is expensive, because it is not used up.

⚗ How catalysts work

Catalysts work because they provide a different pathway for the reaction, one with a lower activation energy. Thus they reduce the activation energy of the reaction (the minimum amount of energy that is needed to start the reaction). We can see this on the enthalpy diagrams in Figure 1.

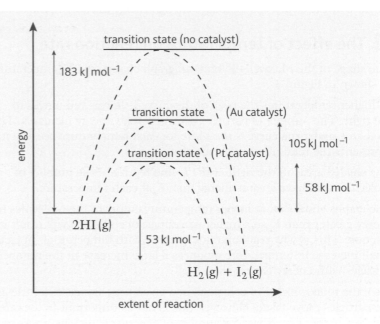

Figure 1 *The decomposition of hydrogen iodide with different catalysts*

For example, for the decomposition of hydrogen iodide:

$$2HI(g) \longrightarrow H_2(g) + I_2(g)$$

$E_a = 183 \, \text{kJ mol}^{-1}$ (without a catalyst)

$E_a = 105 \, \text{kJ mol}^{-1}$ (with a gold catalyst)

$E_a = 58 \, \text{kJ mol}^{-1}$ (with a platinum catalyst)

We can see what happens when we lower the activation energy if we look at the Maxwell–Boltzmann distribution curve in Figure 2. The area that is shaded pink represents the number of effective collisions that can happen without a catalyst. The area shaded blue, plus the area that is shaded pink, represents the number of effective collisions that can happen with a catalyst.

Catalysts do not affect the enthalpy change of the reactions, nor do they affect the position of equilibrium in a reversible reaction, see Topic 9.1.

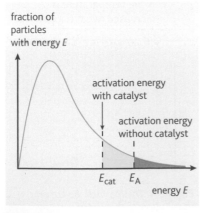

Figure 2 *With a catalyst the extra particles in the blue area react*

Table 1 *Examples of catalysts*

Reaction	Catalyst	Type	Use
$N_2(g) + 3H_2(g) \longrightarrow 2NH_3(g)$ Haber process	iron	heterogeneous	making fertilisers
$4NH_3 + 5O_2 \longrightarrow 4NO + 6H_2O$ Ostwald process for making nitric acid	platinum and rhodium	heterogeneous	making fertilisers and explosives
$H_2C=CH_2 + H_2 \longrightarrow CH_3CH_3$ Hardening of fats with hydrogen	nickel	heterogeneous	making margarine
Cracking hydrocarbon chains from crude oil	aluminium oxide and silicon dioxide zeolite (see 'How science works' on the next page)	heterogeneous	making petrol
Catalytic converter reactions in car exhausts	platinum and rhodium	heterogeneous	removing polluting gases
$H_2C=CH_2 + H_2O \longrightarrow CH_3CH_2OH$ Hydration of ethene to produce ethanol	H^+ absorbed on solid silica phosphoric acid (H_3PO_4)	heterogeneous	making ethanol – a fuel additive, solvent and chemical feedstock
$CH_3CO_2H(l) + CH_3OH(l) \longrightarrow CH_3CO_2CH_3(aq) + H_2O(l)$ Esterification	H^+	homogeneous	making solvents

Different catalysts work in different ways; most were discovered by trial and error.

We divide them into two categories:

■ **Heterogeneous catalysts**: where the catalyst is in a different phase to the reactants – usually a solid catalyst and liquid or gaseous reactants

■ **Homogeneous catalysts**: where catalyst and reactants are in the same phase

Different **phases** are separated by a distinct boundary, for example, oil and water form two separate liquid phases.

Some examples of catalysts are given in Table 1.

Catalytic converters

All new petrol-engine cars are now equipped with catalytic converters in their exhaust systems. These reduce the levels of a number of polluting gases, see Topic 6.4.

The catalytic converter is a honeycomb, made of a ceramic material coated with platinum and rhodium metals – the catalysts. The honeycomb shape provides an enormous surface area, on which the reactions take place, so a little of these expensive metals goes a long way.

As they pass over the catalyst, the polluting gases react with each other to form less harmful products by the following reactions:

carbon monoxide + nitrogen oxides $\longrightarrow$ nitrogen + carbon dioxide

hydrocarbons + nitrogen oxides $\longrightarrow$ nitrogen + carbon dioxide + water

The reactions take place on the surface of the catalyst in two steps:

1 The gases first form weak bonds with the metal atoms of the catalyst; this process is called **adsorption**. This holds the gases in just the right position for them to react together. The gases then react on the surface.

2 The products then break away from the metal atoms; this process is called **desorption**. This frees up room on the catalyst surface for more gases to take their place and react.

The strength of the weak bonds holding the gases onto the metal surface is critical. They must be strong enough to hold the gases for long enough to react, but weak enough to release the products easily.

How science works

Zeolites

Zeolites are *minerals* that have a very open pore structure that ions or molecules can fit into. Zeolites confine molecules in small spaces, which causes changes in their structure and reactivity. More than 150 zeolite types have been synthesized and 48 naturally occurring zeolites are known. Synthetic zeolites are widely used as catalysts in the petrochemical industry

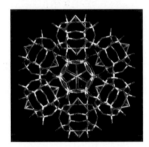

Figure 3 *Part of the structure of a synthetic zeolite*

Hardening fats

Unsaturated fats, used in margarines for example, are made more solid or 'hardened' when hydrogen is added across some of the double bonds. This is done by bubbling hydrogen into the liquid fat which has a nickel catalyst mixed with it. The nickel is filtered off after the reaction. This allows the manufacturer to tailor the 'spreadability' of the margarine.

Figure 4 *Margarine*

Catalysts and the ozone layer

Until recently, a group of apparently unreactive compounds called chlorofluorocarbons (CFCs) were used for a number of applications such as solvents, aerosol propellants and in expanded polystyrene foams. They escaped high into the atmosphere where they remain because they are so relatively unreactive. This is partly due to the strength of the carbon–halogen bonds.

CFCs do eventually decompose to produce separate chlorine atoms. These act as catalysts in reactions that bring about the destruction of ozone, O_3. Ozone is important because it forms a layer that acts as a shield. The layer prevents too much ultraviolet radiation from reaching the Earth's surface.

The overall reaction is shown below:

$$O_3(g) + O(g) \xrightarrow{\text{chlorine atom catalyst}} 2O_2(g)$$

Nitrogen monoxide acts as a catalyst in a similar way to chlorine atoms.

International agreements, such as the 1987 Montreal Protocol, have resulted in CFCs being phased out. Unfortunately there is still a reservoir of them remaining from before these agreements. Chemists have developed, and continue to work on, suitable substitutes for CFCs that do not result in damage to the upper atmosphere. These include hydrochlorofluorocarbons and hydrofluorocarbons. Former United Nations Secretary General, Kofi Annan, has referred to the Montreal Protocol as 'perhaps the single most successful international agreement to date'.

Summary questions

1 The following questions refer to Figure 3.

   a What are labels A, B, C, R and P?

   b What do the distances from D to R and from C to R represent?

   c Is the reaction exothermic or endothermic?

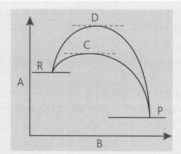

Figure 5 *A profile for a reaction with and without a catalyst*

1 Gas **G** decomposes as shown in the equation below.

$$G(g) \longrightarrow X(g) + Y(g)$$

(a) Draw, on a copy of the axes below, a Maxwell–Boltzmann distribution curve for a sample of **G** in which only a small proportion of molecules has energy greater than the activation energy, E_a.

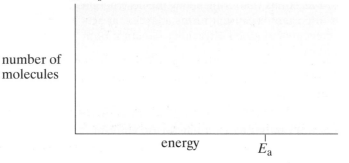

(3 marks)

(b) Define the term *activation energy*. *(2 marks)*

(c) At any time, most of the molecules of **G** have energy less than the activation energy. Suggest why, at a constant temperature, most of **G** eventually decomposes. *(2 marks)*

(d) State the effect, if any, of adding a catalyst on the time required for **G** to decompose, compared with a similar sample without a catalyst. Explain in general terms how the catalyst has this effect. *(3 marks)*

AQA, 2005

2 (a) Define the term *activation energy* for a chemical reaction. *(2 marks)*

(b) Draw, with labelled axes, a curve to represent the Maxwell–Boltzmann distribution of molecular energies in a gas. Label this curve T_1. On the same axes, draw a second curve to represent the same sample of gas at a lower temperature. Label this curve T_2.

Use these curves to explain why a small decrease in temperature can lead to a large decrease in the rate of a reaction. *(8 marks)*

(c) Give **one** reason why most collisions between gas-phase reactants do not lead to a reaction. State and explain **two** ways of speeding up a gas-phase reaction other than by changing the temperature. *(5 marks)*

AQA, 2006

3 The gas-phase reaction between hydrogen and chlorine is very slow at room temperature.

$$H_2(g) + Cl_2(g) \longrightarrow 2HCl(g)$$

(a) Define the term *activation energy*. *(2 marks)*

(b) Give **one** reason why the reaction between hydrogen and chlorine is very slow at room temperature. *(1 mark)*

(c) Explain why an increase in pressure, at constant temperature, increases the rate of reaction between hydrogen and chlorine. *(2 marks)*

(d) Explain why a small increase in temperature can lead to a large increase in the rate of reaction between hydrogen and chlorine. *(2 marks)*

(e) Give the meaning of the term *catalyst*. *(1 mark)*

(f) Suggest **one** reason why a solid catalyst for a gas-phase reaction is often in the form of a powder. *(1 mark)*

AQA, 2006

4   The diagram below shows the Maxwell–Boltzmann distribution of molecular energies in a sample of a gas.

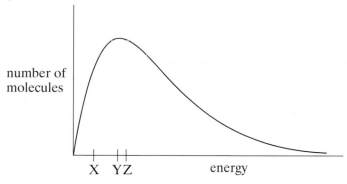

number of molecules

X YZ   energy

(a) (i)   State which one of **X**, **Y** or **Z** best represents the mean energy of the molecules.
    (ii) Explain the process that causes some molecules in this sample to have very low energies.   *(3 marks)*

(b) On the diagram above, sketch a curve to show the distribution of molecular energies in the same sample of gas at a higher temperature.   *(2 marks)*

(c) (i)   Explain why, even in a fast reaction, a very small percentage of collisions leads to a reaction.
    (ii) Other than by changing the temperature, state how the proportion of successful collisions between molecules can be increased. Explain why this method causes an increase in the proportion of successful collisions.   *(4 marks)*

AQA, 2006

5   The diagram below represents a Maxwell–Boltzmann distribution curve for the particles in a sample of a gas at a given temperature. The questions below refer to this sample of particles.

(a) Label the axes on a copy of the diagram.   *(2 marks)*

(b) On the diagram draw a curve to show the distribution for this sample at a **lower** temperature.   *(2 marks)*

(c) In order for two particles to react they must collide. Explain why most collisions do not result in a reaction.   *(1 mark)*

(d) State one way in which the collision frequency between particles in a gas can be increased without changing the temperature.   *(1 mark)*

(e) Suggest why a small increase in temperature can lead to a large increase in the reaction rate between colliding particles.   *(2 marks)*

(f) Explain in general terms how a catalyst works.   *(2 marks)*

AQA, 2004

9 Equilibria

9.1 The idea of equilibrium

Learning objectives:

■ What is a reversible reaction?

■ What is meant by chemical equilibrium?

■ Do all reactions go to completion?

■ Do reactions stop when equilibrium has been reached?

Specification reference 3.2.3

We usually think of a reaction as starting with the reactants and ending with the products:

$$reactants \longrightarrow products$$

However, some reactions are reversible. For example, when we heat blue hydrated copper sulfate it becomes white anhydrous copper sulfate as the water of crystallisation is driven off. The white copper sulfate returns to blue if we add water.

$$CuSO_4.5H_2O \rightleftharpoons CuSO_4 + 5H_2O$$

blue hydrated   white anhydrous
copper sulfate   copper sulfate

However, something different would happen if we were to do this reaction in a closed container. As soon as the products are formed they react together and form the reactants again, so that instead of reactants *or* products we get a mixture of both. Eventually we get a mixture in which the proportions of all three components remain constant. This mixture is called an **equilibrium mixture**.

⚠ ▦ Setting up an equilibrium

We can understand how an equilibrium mixture is set up by thinking about what happens with a physical process, like the evaporation of water. This is easier to picture than a chemical change.

First imagine a puddle of water out in the open. Some of the water molecules at the surface will move fast enough to escape from the liquid and evaporate. Evaporation will continue until all the water is gone.

But think about putting some water into a *closed* container. At first the water will begin to evaporate as before. The volume of the liquid will get smaller and the number of vapour molecules in the gas phase will go up. But as more molecules enter the vapour, some gas-phase molecules will start to re-enter the liquid, see Figure 1.

After a time, the rate of evaporation and the rate of condensation will become equal. The level of the liquid water will then stay exactly the same. So will the number of molecules in the vapour and in the liquid. The evaporation and condensation are still going on but *at the same rate.* This situation is called a **dynamic equilibrium** and is one of the key ideas of this topic.

In fact, we could have started by filling the empty container with the same mass of water vapour as we originally had liquid water. The vapour would begin to condense and, in time, we would reach exactly the same equilibrium position.

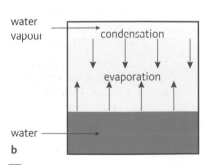

Figure 1 a *Water will evaporate into an empty container. Eventually the rates of evaporation and condensation will be the same.*
b *Equilibrium is set up.*

The conditions for equilibrium

Although the system we have used is very simple, we can pick out four conditions that apply to *all* equilibria:

- Equilibrium can only be reached in a **closed system** (one where the reactants and products can't escape). The system does not have to be sealed. For example, a beaker may be a closed system for a reaction that takes place in a solvent, as long as the reactants, products and solvent do not evaporate.

- Equilibrium can be approached from *either direction* (in the above example, from liquid or from vapour) and the final equilibrium position will be the same (as long as conditions, such as temperature and pressure, stay the same).

- Equilibrium is a dynamic process. It is reached when the *rates* of two opposing processes, which are going on all the time (in this case, evaporation and condensation), *are the same*.

- We know that equilibrium has been reached when the macroscopic properties of the system do not change with time. These are properties like density, concentration, colour and pressure; properties that do not depend on the total quantity of matter.

A reversible reaction which can reach equilibrium is denoted by the symbol $\rightleftharpoons$, for example:

$$\text{liquid water} \rightleftharpoons \text{water vapour}$$

or

$$H_2O(l) \rightleftharpoons H_2O(g)$$

Chemical equilibria

The same principles that we have found for a physical change also apply to chemical equilibria such as:

$$\underset{\text{reactants}}{A + B} \rightleftharpoons \underset{\text{products}}{C + D}$$

- Imagine we start with A and B only. At the start of the reaction the forward rate is fast, because A and B are plentiful. There is no reverse reaction because there is no C and D.

- Then as the concentrations of C and D build up, the reverse reaction speeds up. At the same time the concentrations of A and B decrease so the forward reaction slows down.

- We reach a point where exactly the same number of particles are changing from A + B to C + D as are changing from C + D to A + B. We have reached equilibrium.

One important point to remember is that an equilibrium mixture can have *any* proportions of reactants and products. It is not necessarily half reactants and half products, though it could be. The proportions may be changed depending on the conditions of the reaction, such as temperature, pressure and concentration. But at any given constant conditions the proportions of reactants and products do not change.

Summary questions

1. For each of the following statements about all equilibria, say whether it is true or false.

   a Once equilibrium is reached the concentrations of the reactants and the products do not change.

   b At equilibrium the forward and the backward reactions come to a halt.

   c Equilibrium is only reached in a closed system.

   d An equilibrium mixture always contains half reactants and half products.

2. What can be said about the rates of the forward and the backward reactions when equilibrium is reached?

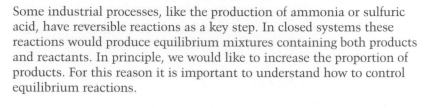

9.2 Changing the conditions of an equilibrium reaction

Learning objectives:

- What is Le Châtelier's principle?

- How is an equilibrium position affected by concentration, temperature, pressure or a catalyst?

Specification reference 3.2.3

Some industrial processes, like the production of ammonia or sulfuric acid, have reversible reactions as a key step. In closed systems these reactions would produce equilibrium mixtures containing both products and reactants. In principle, we would like to increase the proportion of products. For this reason it is important to understand how to control equilibrium reactions.

The equilibrium mixture

It is possible to change the proportion of reactants to products in an equilibrium mixture. In this way we are able to obtain a greater yield of the products. We call this changing the *position* of equilibrium.

- If the proportion of products in the equilibrium mixture is increased, we say that the equilibrium is moved to the right, or in the forward direction.

- If the proportion of reactants in the equilibrium mixture is increased, we say that the equilibrium is moved to the left, or in the backward direction.

We can often move the equilibrium position to the left or right by varying conditions like temperature, the concentration of species involved or the pressure (in the case of reactions involving gases).

Le Châtelier's principle

Le Châtelier's principle is useful because it gives us a rule. It tells us whether the equilibrium moves to the right or to the left when the conditions of an equilibrium mixture are changed.

It states:

If a system at equilibrium is disturbed, the equilibrium moves in the direction that tends to reduce the disturbance.

So in other words, if any factor is changed which affects the equilibrium mixture, the position of equilibrium will shift so as to oppose the change.

Le Châtelier's principle does not tell us *how far* the equilibrium moves so we cannot predict the *quantities* involved.

Changing concentrations

If we **increase** the concentration of one of the reactants, Le Châtelier's principle says that the equilibrium will shift in the direction that tends to **reduce** the concentration of this reactant. Look at the reaction:

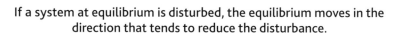

$$A(aq) + B(aq) \rightleftharpoons C(aq) + D(aq)$$

Suppose we add some extra A. This would increase the concentration of A. The only way that this system can reduce the concentration of A, is by some of A reacting with B (thus forming more C and D). So, adding more A uses up more B, produces more C and D, and moves the equilibrium to the right. We end up with a greater proportion of products in the reaction mixture than before we added A. The same thing would happen if we added more B.

Figure 1 *Henri-Louis Le Châtelier was a French chemist who first put forward his 'Loi de stabilité de equilibre chimique' in 1884*

We could also remove C as it was formed. The equilibrium would move to the right to produce more C (and D) using up A and B. The same thing would happen if we removed D as soon as it was formed.

Changing the overall pressure

Pressure changes only affect reactions involving gases. Changing the overall pressure will only change the position of equilibrium of a gaseous reaction if there are a different number of molecules on either side of the equation.

An example of a such a reaction is:

$$N_2O_4(g) \rightleftharpoons 2NO_2(g)$$

dinitrogen tetraoxide   nitrogen dioxide
1 mole   2 moles
colourless   brown

Increasing the pressure of a gas means that there are more molecules of it in a given volume; it is equivalent to increasing the concentration of a solution.

If we increase the pressure on this system, Le Châtelier's principle tells us that the position of equilibrium will move to decrease the pressure. This means that it will move to the left because fewer molecules exert less pressure. In the same way if we decrease the pressure, the equilibrium will move to the right; molecules of N_2O_4 will decompose to form molecules of NO_2, thereby increasing the pressure.

Dinitrogen tetraoxide is a colourless gas and nitrogen dioxide is brown. We can investigate this in the laboratory, by setting up the equilibrium mixture in a syringe. If we decrease the pressure, by pulling out the syringe barrel, we can watch as the equilibrium moves to the right because the colour of the mixture gets browner, see Figure 2.

Note that if there is the same number of moles of gases on both sides of the equation, then pressure has no effect on the equilibrium position. For example:

$$H_2(g) + I_2(g) \rightleftharpoons 2HI(g)$$

2 moles   2 moles

The equilibrium position will not change in this reaction when the pressure is changed so the proportions of the three gases will stay the same.

Changing temperature

Reversible reactions that are exothermic (give out heat) in one direction are endothermic (take in heat) in the other direction, see Topic 7.4. The size of the enthalpy is the same in both directions but the sign changes.

Example 1

Suppose we increase the temperature of an equilibrium mixture that is exothermic in the forward direction. An example is:

$$2SO_2(g) + O_2(g) \rightleftharpoons 2SO_3(g) \quad \Delta H^\ominus = -197\,kJ\,mol^{-1}$$

The negative sign of $\Delta H^\ominus$ means that heat is given out when sulfur dioxide and oxygen react to form sulfur dioxide in the forward direction. This means that heat is absorbed as the reaction goes in the reverse direction, i.e. to the left.

Le Châtelier's principle tells us that if we increase the temperature, the equilibrium moves in the direction that cools the system down. To do

> **Hint**
>
> Increasing the pressure of a mixture of gases increases the concentration of **all** the reactants and products by the same amount, not just one of them.

equilibrium mixture

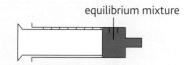

We can decrease the pressure by pulling out the syringe barrel.

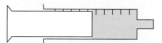

For a moment the mixture becomes paler because we have reduced the concentration of brown NO_2.

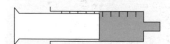

After a few moments the mixture becomes darker brown as the equilibrium moves to the right and more brown NO_2 is formed.

Figure 2 $N_2O_4(g) \rightleftharpoons 2NO_2(g)$
The equilibrium moves to the right as we decrease the pressure

> **Hint**
>
> The **rate** at which equilibrium is reached **will be speeded up** by increasing the pressure, as there will be more collisions in a given time.

this it will move in the direction which absorbs heat (is endothermic) i.e. to the left. The equilibrium mixture will then contain a greater proportion of sulfur dioxide and oxygen than before. In the same way, if we cool the mixture the equilibrium will move to the right and increase the proportion of sulfur trioxide.

Example 2

The effect of temperature on the dinitrogen tetraoxide / nitrogen dioxide equilibrium can also be investigated using the same apparatus as we used for investigating the effect of pressure on this reaction. The reaction is endothermic as it proceeds from dinitrogen tetraoxide to nitrogen dioxide (the forward direction).

$$N_2O_4(g) \rightleftharpoons 2NO_2(g) \quad \Delta H^\ominus = +58\,kJ\,mol^{-1}$$

The gas mixture is contained in a syringe as before. The syringe is then immersed in warm water along with another syringe containing the same volume of air for comparison. The plunger of the syringe containing air will rise as the air expands. The plunger of the syringe containing the N_2O_4 / NO_2 mixture will also rise but by a greater amount. This indicates that more molecules of gas have been formed in this syringe. This is because the equilibrium has moved to the right; each molecule of N_2O_4 that disappears produces two molecules of NO_2. This is consistent with Le Châtelier's principle. When the mixture is warmed up, the equilibrium moves in the endothermic direction, i.e. it absorbs heat which tends to cool the mixture down.

You should be able to predict the colour change that you would see during this experiment and also what would happen if the experiment were repeated in ice water.

Catalysts

Catalysts have no effect on the position of equilibrium so they do not alter the composition of the equilibrium mixture. They work by producing an alternative route for the reaction, which has a lower activation energy of the reaction, see Topic 8.3. This affects the forward and back reactions equally.

Although catalysts have no effect on the position of equilibrium, i.e. the yield of the reaction, they do allow equilibrium to be reached more quickly and are therefore important in industry.

Summary questions

1. In which of the following reactions will the position of equilibrium be affected by changing the pressure? Explain your answers.

   a $2SO_2(g) + O_2(g) \rightleftharpoons 2SO_3(g)$

   b $CH_3CO_2H(aq) \rightleftharpoons CH_3CO_2^-(aq) + H^+(aq)$

   c $H_2(g) + CO_2(g) \rightleftharpoons H_2O(g) + CO(g)$

2. Consider the following equilibrium reaction.

   $N_2(g) + 3H_2(g) \rightleftharpoons 2NH_3(g) \quad \Delta H^\ominus = -92\,kJ\,mol^{-1}$

   a What would be the effect on the equilibrium position of heating the reaction? Choose from 'move to the right', 'move to the left' and 'no change'.

   b What would be the effect on the equilibrium position of adding an iron catalyst? Choose from move to the right', 'move to the left' and 'no change'.

   c What effect would an iron catalyst have on the reaction?

   d To get the maximum yield of ammonia in this reaction would a high or low pressure be best? Explain your answer.

9.3 Equilibrium reactions in industry

Learning objectives

■ Why are compromises made when deciding how to get the best yield in industry?

Specification reference 3.2.3

A number of industrial processes involve reversible reactions. In these cases, the yield of the reaction is important, and Le Châtelier's principle can be used to help find the best conditions for increasing it. However, yield is not the only consideration. Sometimes a low temperature would give the best yield but this would slow the reaction down. The costs of building and running a plant that operates at high temperatures and pressures must also be taken into account. In most cases a compromise set of conditions is used. This topic looks at the industrial production of three important chemicals.

■ Applications and How science works

Ammonia, NH_3

Ammonia is an important chemical in industry. World production is over 140 million tonnes each year. Around 80% is used to make fertilisers like ammonium nitrate, ammonium sulfate and urea. The rest is used to make synthetic fibres (including nylon), dyes, explosives and plastics like polyurethane.

Making ammonia

Nitrogen and hydrogen react together by a reversible reaction which, at equilibrium, forms a mixture of nitrogen, hydrogen and ammonia:

$$N_2(g) + 3H_2(g) \rightleftharpoons 2NH_3(g) \quad \Delta H^\ominus = -92 \, kJ \, mol^{-1}$$

The percentage of ammonia obtained *at equilibrium* depends on temperature and pressure as shown in Figure 1. The graph shows that low temperature and high pressure would give close to 100% conversion whereas low pressure and high temperature would give almost no ammonia.

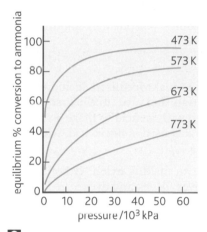

Figure 1 *Equilibrium % conversion of nitrogen and hydrogen to ammonia under different conditions*

1 Explain how Le Châtelier's principle predicts that the highest conversion to ammonia is obtained at a low temperature b high pressure.

The Haber process

Almost all ammonia is made by the Haber process, in which the reaction above is the key step. The process was developed by the German chemist Fritz Haber and the chemical engineer Carl Bosch in the early years of the 20th century. It allowed Germany to make explosives and fertilisers. This prolonged the First World War because, at that time, the source of nitrogen for these products was nitrates from South America. These could be blockaded by the navies of Britain and its allies.

The raw materials

The raw materials for the Haber process are air, which provides the nitrogen, along with water and natural gas (methane, CH_4). These provide the hydrogen by the following reaction:

$$CH_4(g) + H_2O(g) \longrightarrow CO(g) + 3H_2(g)$$

The nitrogen and hydrogen are fed into a converter in the ratio of 1:3 and passed over an iron catalyst.

Most plants run at a pressure of around 20 000 kPa (around 200 atmospheres) and a temperature of about 670 K. This is a lower pressure and a higher temperature than would give the maximum conversion.

2 Use the graph in Figure 1 to find the equilibrium percentage conversion to ammonia at 20 000 kPa and 673 K.

3 Suggest why these compromise conditions are used.

Nitrogen and hydrogen flow continuously over the catalyst so the gases do not spend long enough in contact with the catalyst to reach equilibrium; there is about 15% conversion to ammonia. The ammonia is cooled so that it becomes liquid and is piped off. Any nitrogen and hydrogen that is not converted into ammonia is fed back into the reactor.

The catalyst is iron in pea-sized lumps (to increase the surface area). It lasts about five years before it becomes 'poisoned' by impurities in the gas stream and has to be replaced.

Uses of ammonia

Eighty per cent of ammonia is used to make fertilisers including ammonium sulfate, ammonium nitrate and urea. In the first two cases, ammonia, an alkali, is reacted with an acid to make a salt. In the case of ammonium nitrate, the acid used is nitric acid, which is itself made from ammonia.

The next largest use of ammonia is in making nylon. Other uses include the manufacture of explosives, drugs and dyes.

■ Ethanol, C_2H_5OH

Ethanol is the alcohol in alcoholic drinks and, as such, has been produced by mankind for thousands of years by fermentation from sugars, such as glucose, using the enzymes in yeast as a catalyst:

$$C_6H_{12}O_6(aq) \longrightarrow 2C_2H_5OH(aq) + 2CO_2(g)$$
$$\text{glucose} \qquad\qquad \text{ethanol}$$

Ethanol also has many industrial uses, for example, for making cosmetics, drugs, detergents and inks, and as a motor fuel. UK production is around 330 000 tonnes per year. At present, the main source of ethanol for industrial use is ethene from crude oil. This is obtained by fractional distillation and then cracking.

■ Ethanol is made by the hydration (adding of water) to ethene.

■ The reaction is reversible.

■ It is speeded up by a catalyst of phosphoric acid absorbed on silica.

■ The equation is:

■ $H_2C{=}CH_2(g) + H_2O(g) \rightleftharpoons CH_3CH_2OH(g) \qquad \Delta H^\ominus = -46\,\text{kJ}\,\text{mol}^{-1}$
$\quad\text{ethene} \qquad\qquad\qquad\qquad\qquad \text{ethanol}$

■ The reactants and products are all gaseous at the temperature used.

Applying Le Châtelier's principle to this equilibrium predicts that the maximum yield will be produced with:

■ a high pressure, which will force the equilibrium to move to the right, to the side with fewer molecules

- a low temperature, which will force the equilibrium to move to the right to give out heat
- excess steam, which will force the equilibrium to the right to reduce the steam concentration.

However, there are practical problems:

- Low temperature will reduce the reaction rate and therefore how quickly equilibrium is reached, although this is partially compensated for by the use of a catalyst.
- High pressure tends to cause the ethene to polymerise (to poly(ethene)).
- High pressure increases the costs of building the plant and the energy costs of running it.
- Too much steam dilutes the catalyst.

In practice, conditions of about 570 K and 6500 kPa pressure are used. These give a conversion to ethanol of only about 5% but the unreacted ethene is separated from the reaction mixture and recycled over the catalyst again and again until about 95% conversion is obtained. You will find more details about making ethanol in Topic 16.2.

Methanol, CH_3OH

Methanol is used principally as a **chemical feedstock**, that is, as a starting material for making other chemicals. In particular it is used in the manufacture of methanal (formaldehyde) which in turn is used to make plastics such as Bakelite. Methanol is also used in the manufacture of other plastics such as terylene and perspex. Methanol may also be used (alone or added to petrol) as a motor fuel. It was manufactured for this use in Germany during the Second World War when crude oil supplies were limited by bombing. Indycars in the US run on pure methanol, which has an advantage over petrol because methanol fires can be put out with water. Each year, 33 million tonnes of methanol are made worldwide, mostly from the reversible reaction of hydrogen and carbon monoxide using a copper catalyst:

$$CO(g) + 3H_2(g) \rightleftharpoons CH_3OH(g) \qquad \Delta H^\ominus = -91 \, kJ \, mol^{-1}$$

The starting gas mixture is called synthesis gas and is made by reacting methane or propane with steam.

Le Châtelier's principle tells us that the methanol synthesis reaction will give the highest yield at low temperature and high pressure (as is the case for the ethanol synthesis reaction). But, again, compromise conditions are used. In practice a temperature of around 500 K and a pressure of 10 000 kPa produces around 5–10% yield.

Summary questions

1. The platinum catalyst for the oxidation of ammonia to nitric acid is used in the form of a fine gauze. Suggest why it is used in this form.

2. Explain why ethanol produced by fermentation is a renewable resource while ethanol produced from ethene is not.

3. Is methanol made from synthesis gas a renewable resource? Explain your answer.

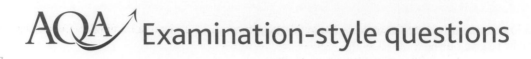
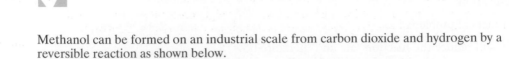
1 Methanol can be formed on an industrial scale from carbon dioxide and hydrogen by a reversible reaction as shown below.

$$CO_2(g) + 3H_2(g) \rightleftharpoons CH_3OH(g) + H_2O(g)$$

The reaction can be carried out in the presence of a chromium-based catalyst at a temperature of 700 K and a pressure of 30 MPa. Under these conditions, equilibrium is reached when 2% of the carbon dioxide has been converted.

(a) How does the rate of the forward reaction compare with that of the backward reaction when 2% of the carbon dioxide has been converted? *(1 mark)*

(b) (i) If the pressure was reduced but the temperature was kept the same, deduce what would happen to the equilibrium yield of methanol. Explain your answer.

　　(ii) Give two reasons why, in general, industry prefers to operate processes at pressures lower than 30 MPa. *(5 marks)*

(c) If the chromium-based catalyst was replaced with a more efficient catalyst but other conditions were kept the same, deduce what would happen to the equilibrium yield of methanol. Explain your answer. *(2 marks)*

(d) In the presence of a very efficient copper-based catalyst, this industrial process can be operated at a lower temperature of 500 K and a pressure of 30 MPa. Under these conditions, at equilibrium, more of the carbon dioxide is converted into methanol.

　　Use this information to deduce the sign of the enthalpy change for the reaction. Explain your deduction. *(3 marks)*

(e) In the processes above, the equilibrium yield of methanol is low. Suggest what is done with the unreacted carbon dioxide and hydrogen. *(1 mark)*

AQA, 2004

2 Methanol can be synthesised from carbon monoxide by the reversible reaction shown below.

$$CO(g) + 2H_2(g) \rightleftharpoons CH_3OH(g) \qquad \Delta H = -91 \text{ kJ mol}^{-1}$$

The process operates at a pressure of 5 MPa and a temperature of 700 K in the presence of a copper-containing catalyst. This reaction can reach dynamic equilibrium.

(a) By reference to rates and concentrations, explain the meaning of the term *dynamic equilibrium*. *(2 marks)*

(b) Explain why a high yield of methanol is favoured by high pressure. *(2 marks)*

(c) Suggest **two** reasons why the operation of this process at a pressure much higher than 5 MPa would be very expensive. *(2 marks)*

(d) State the effect of an increase in temperature on the equilibrium yield of methanol and explain your answer. *(3 marks)*

(e) If a catalyst were not used in this process, the operating temperature would have to be greater than 700 K. Suggest why an increased temperature would be required. *(1 mark)*

AQA, 2003

3 At high temperatures, nitrogen is oxidised by oxygen to form nitrogen monoxide in a reversible reaction as shown in the equation below.

$$N_2(g) + O_2(g) \rightleftharpoons 2NO(g) \qquad \Delta H^\ominus = +180 \text{ kJ mol}^{-1}$$

(a) In terms of electrons, give the meaning of the term *oxidation*. *(1 mark)*

(b) State and explain the effect of an increase in pressure, and the effect of an increase in temperature, on the yield of nitrogen monoxide in the above equilibrium. *(6 marks)*

AQA, 2006

4 Hydrogen is produced on an industrial scale from methane as shown by the equation below.

$$CH_4(g) + H_2O(g) \rightleftharpoons CO(g) + 3H_2(g) \qquad \Delta H^\ominus = +205 \text{ kJ mol}^{-1}$$

(a) State Le Châtelier's principle. *(1 mark)*

(b) The following changes are made to this reaction at equilibrium. In each case, predict what would happen to the yield of hydrogen from a given amount of methane. Use Le Châtelier's principle to explain your answer.

(i) The overall pressure is increased.

(ii) The concentration of steam in the reaction mixture is increased. *(6 marks)*

(c) At equilibrium, a high yield of hydrogen is favoured by high temperature. In a typical industrial process, the operating temperature is usually less than 1200 K. Suggest two reasons why temperatures higher than this are not used. *(2 marks)*

AQA, 2004

5 In the Haber process for the manufacture of ammonia, nitrogen and hydrogen react as shown in the equation.

$$N_2(g) + 3H_2(g) \rightleftharpoons 2NH_3(g) \qquad \Delta H^\ominus = -92 \, kJ \, mol^{-1}$$

The table shows the percentage yield of ammonia, under conditions of pressure and temperature, when the reaction has reached dynamic equilibrium.

Temperature / K	600	800	1000
% yield of ammonia at 10 MPa	50	10	2
% yield of ammonia at 20 MPa	60	16	4
% yield of ammonia at 50 MPa	75	25	7

(a) Explain the meaning of the term *dynamic equilibrium*. *(2 marks)*

(b) Use Le Châtelier's principle to explain why, at a given temperature, the percentage yield of ammonia increases with an increase in overall pressure. *(3 marks)*

(c) Give a reason why a high pressure of 50 MPa is not normally used in the Haber process. *(1 mark)*

(d) Many industrial ammonia plants operate at a compromise temperature of about 800 K.

(i) State and explain, by using Le Châtelier's principle, one advantage, other than cost, of using a temperature lower than 800 K.

(ii) State the major advantage of using a temperature higher than 800 K.

(iii) Hence explain why 800 K is referred to as a *compromise temperature*. *(5 marks)*

AQA, 2006

6 The equation for the formation of ammonia is shown below.

$$N_2(g) + 3H_2(g) \rightleftharpoons 2NH_3(g)$$

Experiment **A** was carried out starting with 1 mol of nitrogen and 3 mol of hydrogen at a constant temperature and a pressure of 20 MPa.

Curve **A** shows how the number of moles of ammonia present changed with time.

Curves **B**, **C** and **D** refer to similar experiments, starting with 1 mol of nitrogen and 3 mol of hydrogen. In each experiment different conditions were used.

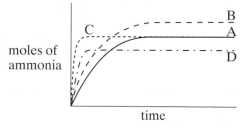

(a) On a copy of curve **A**, mark the point that represents the time at which equilibrium is first reached. Label this point **X**. *(1 mark)*

(b) State Le Châtelier's principle. *(1 mark)*

(c) Use Le Châtelier's principle to identify which one of the curves **B**, **C** or **D** represents an experiment carried out at the same temperature as experiment **A** but at a higher pressure. Explain why this curve is different from curve **A**. *(4 marks)*

(d) Identify which one of the curves **B**, **C** or **D** represents an experiment in which the conditions are the same as in experiment **A** except that a catalyst is added to the reaction mixture. Explain your choice of curve. *(3 marks)*

AQA, 2005

10 Redox reactions

10.1 Oxidation and reduction

Learning objectives:

- What is a redox reaction in terms of oxygen or hydrogen transfer?

- What is a redox reaction in terms of electron transfer?

- What is a half equation?

Specification reference 3.2.4

Redox reactions

The word 'redox' is short for reduction–oxidation. Historically, **oxidation** was used for reactions in which oxygen was added. For example, in the reaction:

$$Cu(s) + \tfrac{1}{2}O_2(g) \longrightarrow CuO(s)$$

copper has been oxidised to copper oxide. Oxygen is called an **oxidising agent**.

The reverse process, **reduction**, described a reaction in which oxygen was removed. For example, in the reaction:

$$CuO(s) + H_2(g) \longrightarrow Cu(s) + H_2O(l)$$

copper oxide has been reduced and hydrogen is the **reducing agent**.

Hydrogen was often used to remove oxygen, so the addition of hydrogen was called reduction. For example, in the reaction:

$$Cl_2(g) + H_2(g) \longrightarrow 2HCl(g)$$

chlorine has been reduced because hydrogen has been added to it.

The reverse, where hydrogen was removed, was called oxidation.

Gaining and losing electrons: redox reactions

If we describe what happens to the **electrons** in the above reactions, we get a much more general picture. When something is oxidised it loses electrons, and when something is reduced it gains electrons. Since **redox reactions** always involve the movement of electrons they are also called electron transfer reactions. We can see the transfer of electrons by separating a redox reaction into two half equations that show the gain and loss of electrons.

Half equations

Example 1

Let us look again at the reaction between copper and oxygen to form copper oxide:

$$Cu + \tfrac{1}{2}O_2 \longrightarrow CuO$$

Copper oxide is an ionic compound so we can write the balanced symbol equation using $(Cu^{2+} + O^{2-})$ (instead of CuO) to show the ions present in copper oxide:

$$Cu + \tfrac{1}{2}O_2 \longrightarrow (Cu^{2+} + O^{2-})$$

Next look at the copper. It has lost two electrons so it has been oxidised.

$$Cu - 2e^- \longrightarrow Cu^{2+} \qquad \text{or} \qquad Cu \longrightarrow Cu^{2+} + 2e^-$$

This is a **half equation**. It is usual to write half equations with plus electrons rather than minus electrons, i.e.

AQA Examiner's tip

Remember to write your half equation with plus electrons rather than minus electrons.

$$Cu \longrightarrow Cu^{2+} + 2e^- \quad \text{rather than}$$

$$Cu - 2e^- \longrightarrow Cu^{2+}$$

Next look at the oxygen. It has gained two electrons so it has been reduced:

$$\tfrac{1}{2}O_2(g) + 2e^- \longrightarrow O^{2-}$$

If we add the two half equations together, we end up with the original equation. Notice that the numbers of electrons cancel out.

$$Cu \longrightarrow Cu^{2+} + 2e^-$$

$$\tfrac{1}{2}O_2(g) + 2e^- \longrightarrow O^{2-}$$

$$Cu(s) + \tfrac{1}{2}O_2(g) \longrightarrow (Cu^{2+} + O^{2-})(s)$$

Example 2

When copper oxide reacts with magnesium, copper and magnesium oxide are produced:

$$CuO(s) + Mg(s) \longrightarrow MgO(s) + Cu(s)$$

We write the equation with copper oxide as $(Cu^{2+} + O^{2-})$ and magnesium oxide as $(Mg^{2+} + O^{2-})$ to show the ions present.

$$(Cu^{2+} + O^{2-}) + Mg \longrightarrow Cu + (Mg^{2+} + O^{2-})$$

Look at the copper. It has gained two electrons so it has been reduced.

$$Cu^{2+} + 2e^- \longrightarrow Cu$$

Look at the magnesium. It has lost electrons so it has been oxidised.

$$Mg \longrightarrow Mg^{2+} + 2e^-$$

Notice that the O^{2-} ion takes no part in the reaction. It is called a **spectator ion**.

If we add these half equations we get:

$$Cu^{2+} + Mg \longrightarrow Cu + Mg^{2+}$$

This is the ionic equation for the redox reaction.

The definition of oxidation and reduction we now use is:

Oxidation Is Loss of electrons.
Reduction Is Gain of electrons.

By this definition, magnesium is oxidised by *anything* that removes electrons from it (not just oxygen) leaving a positive ion. For example, chlorine oxidises magnesium:

$$Mg(s) + Cl_2(g) \longrightarrow (Mg^{2+} + 2Cl^-)(s)$$

Look at the magnesium. It has lost electrons and has therefore been oxidised.

$$Mg \longrightarrow Mg^{2+} + 2e^-$$

Look at the chlorine. It has gained electrons and has therefore been reduced.

$$Cl_2 + 2e \longrightarrow 2Cl^-$$

And adding the two half equations together, the electrons cancel out:

$$Mg(s) + Cl_2(g) \longrightarrow (Mg^{2+} + 2Cl^-)(s)$$

You may find that adding arrows to the equation, which show the transfer of electrons, helps keep track of them, as shown in Figure 1.

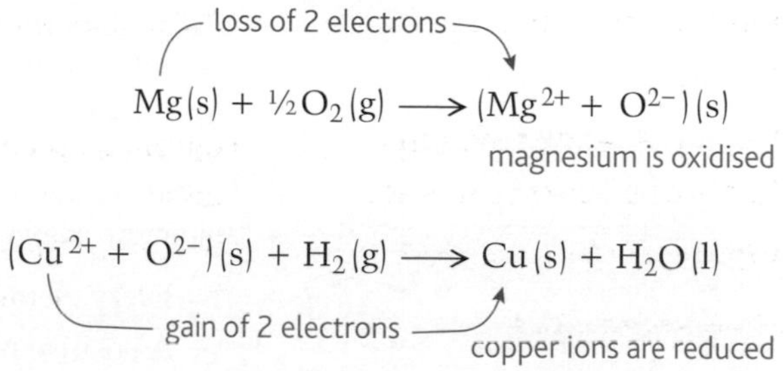

loss of 2 electrons

$$Mg(s) + \tfrac{1}{2}O_2(g) \longrightarrow (Mg^{2+} + O^{2-})(s)$$

magnesium is oxidised

$$(Cu^{2+} + O^{2-})(s) + H_2(g) \longrightarrow Cu(s) + H_2O(l)$$

gain of 2 electrons

copper ions are reduced

Figure 1 *Writing the electrons that are transferred helps to keep track of them*

In a chemical reaction, if one species is oxidised (loses electrons), another **must** be reduced (gains them).

Oxidising and reducing agents

It follows from the above that:

- reducing agents give away electrons – they are electron donors
- oxidising agents accept electrons.

> **Hint**
>
> The phrase OIL RIG makes the definition of oxidation and reduction easy to remember.

Summary questions

1 The following questions are about the reaction:

$$Ca(s) + Br_2(g) \longrightarrow (Ca^{2+} + 2Br^-)(s)$$

a Which element has gained electrons?

b Which element has lost electrons?

c Which element has been oxidised?

d Which element has been reduced?

e Write the half equations for these redox reactions.

f What is the oxidising agent?

g What is the reducing agent?

10.2 Oxidation states

Learning objectives:

- What is an oxidation state?
- How are oxidation states worked out?

Specification reference 3.10.2

Oxidation states

We use the idea of **oxidation states** to see what has been oxidised and what has been reduced in a redox reaction. Oxidation states are also called oxidation numbers.

The idea of oxidation states

Each element in a compound is given an oxidation state. In an ionic compound the oxidation state simply tells us how many electrons it has lost or gained, compared with the element in its uncombined state. In a molecule, the oxidation state tells us about the distribution of electrons between elements of different electronegativity. The more electronegative element is given the negative oxidation state.

- Every element in its uncombined state has an oxidation state of zero.
- A positive number shows that the element has lost electrons, and has therefore been oxidised. For example, Mg^{2+} has an oxidation state of $+2$.
- A negative number shows that the element has gained electrons and has therefore been reduced. For example Cl^- has an oxidation state of -1.
- The more positive the number, the more the element has been oxidised. The more negative the number, the more it has been reduced.
- The numbers always have a $+$ or $-$ sign unless they are zero.

Rules for finding oxidation states

The following rules will allow you to work out oxidation states:

1   Uncombined elements have oxidation state $= 0$.

2   Some elements always have the same oxidation state in all their compounds. Others usually have the same oxidation state. Table 1 gives the oxidation states of these elements.

Table 1 *The usual oxidation states of some elements*

Element	Oxidation state in compound	Example
hydrogen, H	+1 (except in metal hydrides, e.g. NaH, where it is –1)	HCl
Group 1	Always +1	NaCl
Group 2	Always +2	$CaCl_2$
aluminium, Al	Always +3	$AlCl_3$
oxygen, O	–2 (except in peroxides and compounds with F, where it is –1)	Na_2O
fluorine	Always –1	NaF
chlorine	–1 (except in compounds with F and O, where it has positive values)	NaCl

3 The sum of all the oxidation states in a compound = 0, since all compounds are electrically neutral.

4 The sum of the oxidation states of a complex ion, such as NH_4^+ or SO_4^{2-}, equals the charge on the ion.

5 In a compound the most electronegative element always has a negative oxidation state.

🛈 💡 Working out oxidation states of elements in compounds

Start with the correct formula. Look for the elements whose oxidation states you know from the rules. Then deduce the oxidation states of any other element. Some examples are shown below.

Phosphorus pentachloride, PCl₅

We know that chlorine has an oxidation state of –1, so the phosphorus must be +5, to make the sum of the oxidation states zero.

Ammonia, NH₃

We know that hydrogen has an oxidation state of +1, so the nitrogen must be –3, to make the sum of the oxidation states zero. Also, nitrogen is more electronegative than hydrogen, so hydrogen must have a positive oxidation state.

Nitric acid, HNO₃

We know that each oxygen has an oxidation state of –2, making –6 in total.

We know that hydrogen has an oxidation state of +1.

So the nitrogen must be +5, to make the sum of the oxidation states zero.

Notice that nitrogen may have different oxidation states in different compounds. Note here that nitrogen has a positive oxidation state because it is combined with a more electronegative element, oxygen.

Hydrogen sulfide, H₂S

We know that hydrogen has an oxidation state of +1, so the sulfur must be –2, to make the sum of the oxidation states zero.

Sulfate ion, SO₄²⁻

We know that each oxygen has an oxidation state of –2, making –8 in total.

So the sulfur must be +6, to make the sum of the oxidation states equal to the charge on the ion.

Notice that sulfur may have different oxidation states in different compounds.

Black copper oxide, CuO

We know that oxygen has an oxidation state of –2, so the copper must be +2, to make the sum of the oxidation states zero.

Red copper oxide, Cu₂O

We know that oxygen has an oxidation state of –2, so each copper must be +1, to make the sum of the oxidation states zero.

We use oxidation states in Roman numerals to distinguish between similar compounds in which the metal has a different oxidation state. So, black copper oxide is copper(II) oxide and red copper oxide is copper(I) oxide. These compounds are shown in Figure 1.

Figure 1 *The two oxides of copper*

Summary questions

1 Work out the oxidation states of each element in the following compounds:

a $PbCl_2$

b CCl_4

c $NaNO_3$

2 In the reaction:
$CuO + Mg \longrightarrow Cu + MgO$,
what are the oxidation states of oxygen before and after the reaction?

3 In the reaction:
$2Cu + O_2 \longrightarrow 2CuO$, what are the oxidation states of oxygen before and after the reaction?

4 In the reaction:
$FeCl_2 + \frac{1}{2}Cl_2 \longrightarrow FeCl_3$,
what are the oxidation states of iron before and after the reaction?

5 Give the oxidation state of the following:

a P in PO_4^{3-}

b N in NO_3^-

c N in NH_4^+

10.3   Redox equations

Learning objectives:

- How are half equations used to balance an equation?

- How are half equations deduced from a redox equation?

Specification reference 3.2.4

Using oxidation states in redox equations

We saw in Topic 10.1 that we can work out which element has been oxidised and which has been reduced in a redox reaction, by considering electron transfer.

Remember that 'Oxidation is loss of electrons (OIL) and reduction is gain of electrons (RIG)'.

We can also use oxidation states to help us to understand redox reactions.

When an element is reduced, it gains electrons and its oxidation state goes down. In the reaction below, iron is reduced because its oxidation state has gone down from $+3$ to $+2$, while iodide is oxidised:

$$\overset{+3}{Fe^{3+}} + \overset{-1}{I^-} \longrightarrow \overset{+2}{Fe^{2+}} + \overset{0}{\tfrac{1}{2}I_2}$$

Even in complicated reactions, we can see which element has been oxidised and which has been reduced when we put in the oxidation states:

$$\overset{+5\,-2}{2IO_3^-} + \overset{+1\,+4\,-2}{5HSO_3^-} \longrightarrow \overset{0}{I_2} + \overset{+6\,-2}{5SO_4^{2-}} + \overset{+1}{3H^+} + \overset{+1\,-2}{H_2O}$$

Iodine in IO_3^- is reduced ($+5$ to 0) and sulfur in HSO_3^- is oxidised ($+4$ to $+6$). The oxidation states of all the other atoms have not changed.

Balancing redox reactions

We can use the idea of oxidation states to help balance equations for redox reactions.

For an equation to be balanced:

- the numbers of atoms of each element on each side of the equation must be the same
- the total charge on each side of the equation must be the same.

Example 1: the thermit reaction

This is a strongly exothermic reaction in which aluminium reacts with iron(III) oxide to produce molten iron. It was used to weld railway lines.

The unbalanced equation is:

$$Fe_2O_3(s) + Al(s) \longrightarrow Fe(l) + Al_2O_3(s)$$

We write the oxidation states above each element:

$$\overset{+3\,-2}{Fe_2O_3(s)} + \overset{0}{Al(s)} \longrightarrow \overset{0}{Fe(l)} + \overset{+3\,-2}{Al_2O_3(s)}$$

If you look at the equation you can see that that only the iron and aluminium have changed their oxidation state. The oxygen is unchanged.

Each iron atom has been reduced by gaining three electrons so we can write the half equation:

$$Fe^{3+} + 3e^- \longrightarrow Fe$$

Hint

Another way of working is to remember that when an element is reduced it gains electrons and its oxidation state is reduced.

For example, in: $M^{3+} \longrightarrow M^{2+}$ the number of plusses has been reduced so M has been reduced.

It follows that for: $M^{2+} \longrightarrow M^{3+}$ the number of plusses has been increased so M has been oxidised.

Each aluminium atom has been oxidised by losing three electrons:

$$Al \longrightarrow Al^{3+} + 3e^-$$

In the reaction, the number of electrons gained must equal the number of electrons lost. This means that there must be the same number of aluminium atoms as iron atoms. (The oxygen is a spectator ion.) We formed two iron atoms, so we must also have two aluminium atoms. The balanced equation is therefore:

$$Fe_2O_3(s) + 2Al(s) \longrightarrow 2Fe(l) + Al_2O_3(s)$$

Figure 1 *A demonstration of the thermit reaction*

Example 2: aqueous solutions

Sometimes in aqueous solution, species take part in redox reactions but are neither oxidised nor reduced. We must balance them separately. These include water molecules, H^+ ions (in acid solution) and OH^- ions (in alkaline solution). Oxidation states only help us to balance the species that are oxidised or reduced.

Suppose we want to balance the following equation, where dark purple manganate(VII) ions react in acid solution with Fe^{2+} ions to produce pale pink Mn^{2+} ions and Fe^{3+} ions.

The unbalanced equation is:

$$MnO_4^- + Fe^{2+} + H^+ \longrightarrow Mn^{2+} + Fe^{3+} + H_2O$$

1 Write the oxidation state above each element.

$$\overset{+7\ -2}{MnO_4^-} + \overset{+2}{Fe^{2+}} + \overset{+1}{H^+} \longrightarrow \overset{+2}{Mn^{2+}} + \overset{+3}{Fe^{3+}} + \overset{+1\ -2}{H_2O}$$

2 Identify the species that has been oxidised and the species that has been reduced.

$$\overset{+7}{MnO_4^-} \longrightarrow \overset{+2}{Mn^{2+}}$$ Manganese has been reduced from +7 to +2 therefore five electrons must be gained.

$$MnO_4^- + 5e^- \longrightarrow Mn^{2+}$$ (note that this equation is not chemically balanced)

$$\overset{+2}{Fe^{2+}} \longrightarrow \overset{+3}{Fe^{3+}}$$ Fe has been oxidised from +2 to +3 so one electron must be lost.

$$Fe^{2+} \longrightarrow Fe^{3+} + e^-$$

In order to balance the number of electrons that are transferred, this step must be multiplied by 5:

$$5Fe^{2+} \longrightarrow 5Fe^{3+} + 5e^-$$

So, we know that there are $5Fe^{2+}$ ions to every MnO_4^- ion.

3 Include this information in the unbalanced equation, to balance the redox process.

$$MnO_4^- + 5Fe^{2+} + H^+ \longrightarrow Mn^{2+} + 5Fe^{3+} + H_2O$$

(note that this equation is still not chemically balanced)

4 Balance the remaining atoms, those that are neither oxidised nor reduced. In order to 'use up' the four oxygen atoms on the left-hand side, we need $4H_2O$ on the right-hand side, which will in turn require $8H^+$ on the left-hand side.

$$MnO_4^- + 5Fe^{2+} + 8H^+ \longrightarrow Mn^{2+} + 5Fe^{3+} + 4H_2O$$

Notice that this equation is balanced for both atoms and charge.

Half equations from the balanced equation

Example 1

The reaction between copper and *cold dilute* nitric acid produces the gas nitrogen monoxide. The balanced symbol equation is shown:

$$3Cu + 8H^+ + 2NO_3^- \longrightarrow 3Cu^{2+} + 2NO + 4H_2O$$

To work out the half equations, you first need to know which elements have been oxidised and which have been reduced.

1 Put in the numbers and look for a change in the oxidation states:

$$\overset{0}{3Cu} + \overset{+1}{8H^+} + \overset{+5\ -2}{2NO_3^-} \longrightarrow \overset{+2}{3Cu^{2+}} + \overset{+2\ -2}{2NO} + \overset{+1\ -2}{H_2O}$$

Copper has been oxidised and nitrogen has been reduced.

2 Now work out the half equations.

Each of the three copper atoms loses two electrons, a total of 6 electrons:

$$3Cu \longrightarrow 3Cu^{2+} + 6e^-$$

The two nitrogen atoms NO_3^- have each gained three electrons so the half equation must be based on:

$$2NO_3^- + 6e^- \longrightarrow 2NO$$

This half equation is not balanced for atoms or charge. There are six oxygen atoms on the left-hand side and only two on the right-hand side. The total charge on the left is -8 whereas the right-hand side has no charge. Look at the original equation. We need to include the eight H^+ ions on the left-hand side of our half equation (to use up the extra four oxygen atoms that are unaccounted for) and also the four H_2O on the right-hand side. This also accounts for the charge, so the complete half equation is:

$$2NO_3^- + 8H^+ + 6e^- \longrightarrow 2NO + 4H_2O$$

This equation is balanced in both atoms and charge.

Example 2

The reaction between copper and *hot concentrated* nitric acid produces the gas nitrogen dioxide.

1 The balanced symbol equation is shown with the oxidation states included.

$$\overset{0}{Cu} + 4\overset{+1}{H^+} + 2\overset{+5\ -2}{NO_3^-} \longrightarrow \overset{+2}{Cu^{2+}} + 2\overset{+1\ -2}{H_2O} + 2\overset{+4\ -2}{NO_2}$$

Copper has been oxidised and nitrogen has been reduced.

2 Now work out the half equations.

Copper has lost two electrons so the half equation is:

$$Cu \longrightarrow Cu^{2+} + 2e^-$$

Nitrogen in NO_3^- has gained an electron so the half equation must be based on:

$$2NO_3^- + 2e^- \longrightarrow 2NO_2$$

This is not balanced for charge or atoms. There are an extra two oxygens on the left-hand side and a total charge of –4 whereas the right-hand side is neutral. We need to add the four H^+ ions to the left-hand side to use up the extra oxygen. These will also balance the charge. We then need to add two H_2O to the right-hand side.

The half equation is:

$$2NO_3^- + 4H^+ + 2e^- \longrightarrow 2H_2O + 2NO_2$$

Note that if we add the half equations together, the electrons cancel out and we get back to the original balanced equation.

Summary questions

1 The following questions are about the equation:

$$Fe^{2+} + \tfrac{1}{2}Cl_2 \longrightarrow Fe^{3+} + Cl^-$$

a Write the oxidation states above each element.

b Which element has been oxidised? Explain your answer.

c Which element has been reduced? Explain your answer.

d Write the half equations for the reaction.

2 Use oxidation states to balance the following equations:

a $Cl_2 + NaOH \longrightarrow NaClO_3 + NaCl + H_2O$

b $Sn + HNO_3 \longrightarrow SnO_2 + NO_2 + H_2O$

c Write the half equations in **a** and **b**.

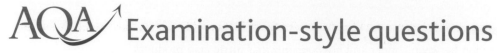

AQA Examination-style questions

1 (a) The following is an equation for a redox reaction.
$$2NO + 12H^+ + 10I^- \longrightarrow 2NH_4^+ + 2H_2O + 5I_2$$
  (i) Define *oxidation* in terms of electrons.
  (ii) Deduce the oxidation state of nitrogen in NO and of nitrogen in NH_4^+
  (iii) Identify the species formed by oxidation in this reaction. *(4 marks)*

 (b) When chlorine gas is bubbled into an aqueous solution of sulfur dioxide, hydrogen ions, sulfate ions and chloride ions are formed.
  (i) Write a half-equation for the formation of chloride ions from chlorine.
  (ii) Write a half-equation for the formation of hydrogen ions and sulfate ions from sulfur dioxide and water.
  (iii) Hence, deduce an overall equation for the reaction which occurs when chlorine is bubbled into aqueous sulfur dioxide. *(3 marks)*

AQA, 2002

2 (a) In terms of electron transfer, what does the reducing agent do in a redox reaction? *(1 mark)*
 (b) What is the oxidation state of an atom in an uncombined element? *(1 mark)*
 (c) Deduce the oxidation state of nitrogen in each of the following compounds.
  (i) NCl_3
  (ii) Mg_3N_2
  (iii) NH_2OH *(3 marks)*

 (d) Lead(IV) oxide, PbO_2, reacts with concentrated hydrochloric acid to produce chlorine, lead(II) ions, Pb^{2+}, and water.
  (i) Write a half-equation for the formation of Pb^{2+} and water from PbO_2 in the presence of H^+ ions.
  (ii) Write a half-equation for the formation of chlorine from chloride ions.
  (iii) Hence deduce an equation for the reaction which occurs when concentrated hydrochloric acid is added to lead(IV) oxide, PbO_2 *(3 marks)*

AQA, 2002

3 (a) In terms of electrons, what happens to an oxidising agent during a redox reaction? *(1 mark)*
 (b) Consider the following redox reaction.
$$SO_2(aq) + 2H_2O(l) + 2Ag^+(aq) \longrightarrow 2Ag(s) + SO_4^{2-}(aq) + 4H^+(aq)$$
  (i) Identify the oxidising agent and the reducing agent in this reaction.
  (ii) Write a half-equation to show how sulfur dioxide is converted into sulfate ions in aqueous solution. *(3 marks)*

 (c) Fe^{2+} ions are oxidised to Fe^{3+} ions by ClO_3^- ions in acidic conditions. The ClO_3^- ions are reduced to Cl^- ions.
  (i) Write a half-equation for the oxidation of Fe^{2+} ions in this reaction.
  (ii) Deduce the oxidation state of chlorine in ClO_3^- ions.
  (iii) Write a half-equation for the reduction of ClO_3^- ions to Cl^- ions in acidic conditions.
  (iv) Hence, write an overall equation for the reaction. *(4 marks)*

 (d) Write an equation to show how sulfur is removed from impure iron obtained from the blast furnace. Identify the oxidising agent in this reaction. *(2 marks)*

AQA, 2003

4 Chlorine and bromine are both oxidising agents.
 (a) Define an *oxidising agent* in terms of electrons. *(1 mark)*
 (b) In aqueous solution, bromine oxidises sulfur dioxide, SO_2, to sulfate ions, SO_4^{2-}
  (i) Deduce the oxidation state of sulfur in SO_2 and in SO_4^{2-}
  (ii) Deduce a half-equation for the reduction of bromine in aqueous solution.

(iii) Deduce a half-equation for the oxidation of SO_2 in aqueous solution forming SO_4^{2-} and H^+ ions.

(iv) Use these two half-equations to construct an overall equation for the reaction between aqueous bromine and sulfur dioxide. *(5 marks)*

AQA, 2004

5 (a) By referring to electrons, explain the meaning of the term *oxidising agent*. *(1 mark)*

(b) For the element **X** in the ionic compound **MX**, explain the meaning of the term *oxidation state*. *(1 mark)*

(c) Complete the table below by deducing the oxidation state of each of the stated elements in the given ion or compound.

	Oxidation state
Carbon in CO_3^{2-}	
Phosphorus in PCl_4^+	
Nitrogen in Mg_3N_2	

(3 marks)

(d) In acidified aqueous solution, nitrate ions, NO_3^- react with copper metal forming nitrogen monoxide, NO, and copper(II) ions.

(i) Write a half-equation for the oxidation of copper to copper(II) ions.

(ii) Write a half-equation for the reduction, in an acidified solution, of nitrate ions to nitrogen monoxide.

(iii) Write an overall equation for this reaction. *(3 marks)*

AQA, 2005

6 (a) Define *reduction* in terms of electrons. *(1 mark)*

(b) The oxide of nitrogen formed when copper reacts with nitric acid depends upon the concentration and the temperature of the acid. The reaction of copper with cold, dilute acid produces NO as indicated by the following equation.

$$3Cu + 8H^+ + 2NO_3^- \longrightarrow 3Cu^{2+} + 4H_2O + 2NO$$

In warm, concentrated acid, NO_2 is formed.

(i) Give the oxidation states of nitrogen in NO_3^-, NO_2 and NO.

(ii) Identify, as oxidation or reduction, the formation of NO_2 from NO_3^- in the presence of H^+ and deduce the half-equation for the reaction.

(iii) Deduce the half-equation for the formation of NO_2 from NO_3^- in the presence of H^+.

(iv) Deduce the overall equation for the reaction of copper with NO_3^- and H^+ to produce Cu^{2+} ions, NO_2 and water. *(8 marks)*

AQA, 2001

7 (a) Explain, with reference to electron transfer, what is meant by the term *oxidising agent*. *(1 mark)*

(b) In the presence of a strong acid, the IO_3^- ion is a powerful oxidising agent. The half-equation (ion–electron equation) for this process is shown below.

$$IO_3^-(aq) + 6H^+(aq) + 5e^- \longrightarrow \text{\textonehalf}I_2(aq) + 3H_2O(l)$$ *(1 mark)*

Under acidic conditions, IO_3^- will oxidise iodide ions to iodine.

(i) Deduce the oxidation numbers of iodine in IO_3^-, I^- and I_2. *(3 marks)*

(ii) Write an ionic equation to show the reaction between aqueous solutions of KIO_3 and KI under acidic conditions. *(2 marks)*

AQA, 2000

8 (a) Nitrogen monoxide, NO, is formed when silver metal reduces nitrate ions, NO_3^- in acid solution. Deduce the oxidation state of nitrogen in NO and in NO_3^-.

(b) Write a half-equation for the reduction of NO_3^- ions in acid solution to form nitrogen monoxide and water.

(c) Write a half-equation for the oxidation of silver metal to $Ag^+(aq)$ ions.

(d) Hence, deduce an overall equation for the reaction between silver metal and nitrate ions in acid solution. *(5 marks)*

AQA, 2006

11 Group 7, the halogens

11.1 The halogens

Learning objectives:

- How and why does atomic radius change in Group 7 of the periodic table?

- How and why does electronegativity change in Group 7 of the periodic table?

Specification reference 3.2.5

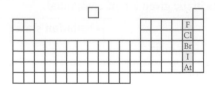

Group 7, on the right-hand side of the periodic table, is made up of non-metals. As elements they exist as diatomic molecules, F_2, Cl_2, Br_2, I_2 and At_2, called the halogens.

Physical properties

The gaseous halogens vary in appearance, as shown in Figure 2. At room temperature, fluorine is a pale yellow gas, chlorine a greenish gas, bromine a red-brown liquid and iodine a black solid – they get darker and denser as we go down the group.

They all have a characteristic 'swimming-bath' smell.

A number of the properties of fluorine are untypical. Many of these untypical properties stem from the fact that the F—F bond is unexpectedly weak, compared with the trend for the rest of the halogens, see Table 1. The small size of the fluorine atom leads to repulsion between non-bonding electrons because they are so close together:

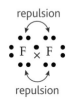

The physical properties of fluorine, chlorine, bromine and iodine are shown in Table 2.

There are some clear trends shown by the red arrows. These can be explained as follows.

Size of atoms

The atoms get bigger as we go down the group because each element has one extra filled main level of electrons compared with the one above it, see Figure 2.

> ### Hint
>
> The word halogen means 'salt former'. The halogens readily react with many metals to form fluoride, chloride, bromide and iodide salts.

Figure 1 *The gaseous halogens: fluorine, chlorine, bromine and iodine*

Table 1 *Bond energies for fluorine, chlorine, bromine and iodine*

Bond	Bond energy / kJ mol^{-1}
F–F	158
Cl–Cl	243
Br–Br	193
I–I	151

Table 2 *The physical properties of Group 7, fluorine to iodine*

Halogen	Atomic number, Z	Electron arrangement	Electronegativity	Atomic (covalent) radius / nm	Melting point T_m / K	Boiling point T_b / K
fluorine	9	[He] $2s^2\ 2p^5$	4.0	0.071	53	85
chlorine	17	[Ne] $3s^2\ 3p^5$	3.0	0.099	172	238
bromine	35	[Ar] $3d^{10}\ 4s^2\ 4p^5$	2.8	0.114	266	332
iodine	53	[Kr] $4d^{10}\ 5s^2\ 5p^5$	2.5	0.133	387	457

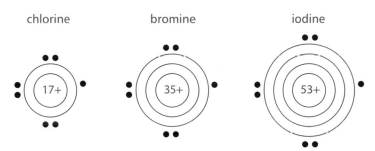

Figure 2 *The outer shell gets further from the nucleus as we go down the group*

Electronegativity

Electronegativity is a measure of the ability of an atom to attract electrons, or electron density, towards itself within a covalent bond (see Topic 3.3).

Electronegativity depends on the attraction between the nucleus and bonding electrons in the outer shell. This, in turn, depends on a balance between the number of protons in the nucleus (nuclear charge) and the distance between the nucleus and the bonding electrons, plus the shielding effect of inner shells of electrons.

Consider the hydrogen halides, HX, for example. The shared electrons in the H—X bond get further away from the nucleus as the atoms get larger going down the group. This makes the shared electrons further from the halogen nucleus and increases the shielding by more inner shells of electrons. These factors are more important than the increasing nuclear charge, so the electronegativity decreases as we go down the group.

Melting and boiling points

These increase as we go down the group. This is because larger atoms have more electrons and this makes the van der Waals forces between the molecules stronger. The lower the boiling point, the more volatile the element. So, chlorine, which is a gas at room temperature, is more volatile than iodine, which is a solid.

Summary questions

1 Predict the properties of astatine compared with the other halogens in terms of:

a physical state at room temperature, including colour

b size of atom

c electronegativity.

2 Explain your answers to question **1**.

3 a Plot a graph of the boiling points of the halogens in Table 2 against atomic number. Use the graph to estimate the boiling point of astatine.

b Why would you expect the boiling point of astatine to be the largest?

The chemical reactions of the halogens

Learning objectives:

- What is the trend in oxidising ability of the halogens?

- What experimental evidence confirms this trend?

Specification reference 3.2.5

Hint

Remember OIL RIG: **O**xidation **I**s **L**oss of electrons. **R**eduction **I**s **G**ain of electrons.

Trends in oxidising ability

Halogens usually react by gaining electrons to become negative ions, with a charge of –1. So these reactions are redox reactions; halogens are oxidising agents and are themselves reduced. For example:

$$Cl_2 + 2e^- \xrightarrow{\text{gain of electrons}} 2Cl^-$$

The oxidising ability of the halogens increases as we go up the group.

Fluorine is one of the most powerful oxidising agents known.

Displacement reactions

Halogens will react with metal halides in solution in such a way that the halide in the compound will be displaced by a more reactive halogen (but not by a less reactive one). This is called a **displacement reaction**.

So for example, chlorine will displace bromide ions, but iodine will not.

$$\overset{0}{Cl_2}(aq) + 2\overset{-1}{Na}Br(aq) \longrightarrow \overset{0}{Br_2}(aq) + 2\overset{-1}{Na}Cl(aq)$$

ionically:

$$Cl_2(aq) + \cancel{2Na^+(aq)} + 2Br^-(aq) \longrightarrow Br_2(aq) + \cancel{2Na^+(aq)} + 2Cl^-(aq)$$

The sodium ions are spectator ions.

The two colourless starting materials react to produce the red-brown colour of bromine.

In this redox reaction the chlorine is acting as an oxidising agent, by removing electrons from Br^- and so oxidising $2Br^-$ to Br_2 (the oxidation number of the bromine increases from –1 to 0). In general, a halogen will always displace the ion of a halogen below it in the periodic table, see Table 1.

Table 1 *The oxidation of a halide by a halogen*

	F⁻	Cl⁻	Br⁻	I⁻
F_2	–	yes	yes	yes
Cl_2	no	–	yes	yes
Br_2	no	no	–	yes
I_2	no	no	no	–

We cannot investigate fluorine in an aqueous solution because it reacts with water.

fluorine   chlorine   bromine   iodine

⟵ increasing oxidising power ⟶

The extraction of bromine from sea water

The oxidation of a halide by a halogen is the basis of a method for extracting bromine from sea water. Sea water contains small amounts of bromide ions which can be oxidised by chlorine to produce bromine, as in the reaction discussed above and shown again here:

$$Cl_2(aq) + 2Br^-(aq) \longrightarrow Br_2(aq) + 2Cl^-(aq)$$

There is a plant which does this in Anglesey, North Wales, see Figure 1.

Figure 1 *Plant for extracting bromine from seawater*

Extraction of iodine from kelp

Iodine was discovered in 1811. It was extracted from kelp, which is obtained by burning seaweed. Some iodine is still produced in this way. Salts such as sodium chloride, potassium chloride and potassium sulfate are removed from the kelp by washing with water. The residue is then heated with manganese dioxide and concentrated sulfuric acid, and iodine is liberated.

$$2I^- + MnO_2 + 4H^+ \longrightarrow Mn^{2+} + 2H_2O + I_2$$

1   Is the reaction an oxidation or a reduction of the iodide ion? Explain your answer.

2   Find out why our table salt often has potassium iodide added to it.

Summary questions

1   a Which of the following mixtures would react?

   i $Br_2(aq) + 2NaCl(aq)$

   ii $Cl_2(aq) + 2NaI(aq)$

   b Explain why you chose your answers.

   c Complete the equation for the mixture that reacts.

11.3 Reactions of halide ions

Learning objectives:

■ What is the trend in reducing ability of halide ions?

■ How is this trend linked to ionic radius?

■ How are halide ions identified using silver nitrate?

Specification reference 3.2.5

■ Halide ions as reducing agents

Halide ions can act as reducing agents. In these reactions the halide ions lose (give away) electrons and become halogen molecules. There is a definite trend in their reducing ability. This is linked to the size of the ions. The larger the ion, the more easily it loses an electron. This is because the electron is lost from the outer shell which is further from the nucleus as the ion gets larger.

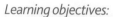

— increasing reducing power ——→

	F^-	Cl^-	Br^-	I^-
Ionic radius	0.133 nm	0.180 nm	0.195 nm	0.215 nm

This trend can be seen in the reactions of solid sodium halides with concentrated sulfuric acid.

The reactions of sodium halides with concentrated sulfuric acid

Solid sodium halides all react with concentrated sulfuric acid. The products are different and reflect the reducing powers of the halide ions shown above.

Sodium chloride (solid)

In this reaction, drops of concentrated sulfuric acid are added to solid sodium chloride. Steamy fumes of hydrogen chloride are seen. The solid product is sodium hydrogensulfate.

The reaction is:

$$NaCl(s) + H_2SO_4(l) \longrightarrow NaHSO_4(s) + HCl(g)$$

This is not a redox reaction because no oxidation state has changed. The chloride ion is too weak a reducing agent to reduce the sulfur (oxidation state = +6) in sulfuric acid. It is an acid–base reaction.

$$\overset{+1\ -1}{Na\,Cl}(s) + \overset{+1\ +6\ -2}{H_2\,S\,O_4}(l) \longrightarrow \overset{+1\ +1\ +6\ -2}{Na\,H\,S\,O_4}(s) + \overset{+1\ -1}{H\,Cl}(g)$$

This reaction can be used to prepare hydrogen chloride gas which, because of this reaction, was once called salt gas.

A similar reaction occurs with sodium fluoride to produce hydrogen fluoride, an extremely dangerous gas that will etch glass. The fluoride ion is an even weaker reducing agent than the chloride ion.

Sodium bromide (solid)

In this case we see steamy fumes of hydrogen bromide *and* brown fumes of bromine. Colourless sulfur dioxide is also formed.

Two reactions occur.

First sodium hydrogensulfate and hydrogen bromide are produced (in a similar acid–base reaction to sodium chloride).

$$NaBr(s) + H_2SO_4(l) \longrightarrow NaHSO_4(s) + HBr(g)$$

However, bromide ions are strong enough reducing agents to reduce the sulfuric acid to sulfur dioxide. The oxidation state of the sulfur is reduced from +6 to +4 and that of the bromine increases from –1 to 0.

$$\overset{-1}{2H^+ + 2Br^-} + \overset{+6}{H_2SO_4(l)} \longrightarrow \overset{+4}{SO_2(g)} + 2H_2O(l) + \overset{0}{Br_2(l)}$$

This is a redox reaction. The reactions are exothermic and some of the bromine vaporises.

Sodium iodide (solid)

In this case we see steamy fumes of hydrogen iodide and the black solid of iodine, plus the bad egg smell of hydrogen sulfide gas is present. Yellow solid sulfur may also be seen. Colourless sulfur dioxide is also evolved.

Several reactions occur. Hydrogen iodide is produced in an acid–base reaction as before.

$$NaI(s) + H_2SO_4(l) \longrightarrow NaHSO_4(s) + HI(g)$$

Iodide ions are better reducing agents than bromide ions so they reduce the sulfur in sulfuric acid even further (from +6 to zero and –2) so that sulfur dioxide, sulfur and hydrogen sulfide gas are produced. For example,

$$\overset{-1}{2H^+ + 2I^-} + \overset{+6}{H_2SO_4(l)} \longrightarrow \overset{-2}{H_2S(g)} + 4H_2O(l) + \overset{0}{I_2(s)}$$

During the reduction from +6 to –2, the sulfur passes through oxidation state 0 and some yellow, solid sulfur may be seen.

AQA Examiner's tip

Remember that the reactions take place between **solid** halide salts and **concentrated** sulfuric acid.

■ **Hint**

Try to work out the balanced equations for the formation of S and SO_2 using the oxidation number techniques..

⚗ Identifying metal halides with silver ions

All metal halides (except fluorides) react with silver ions in aqueous solution, for example in silver nitrate, to form a precipitate of the insoluble silver halide. For example:

$$Cl^-(aq) + Ag^+(aq) \longrightarrow AgCl(s)$$

Silver fluoride does not form a precipitate because it is soluble in water.

1 Dilute nitric acid HNO_3 or ($H^+(aq) + NO_3^-(aq)$) is first added to the halide solution to get rid of any soluble carbonate, $CO_3^{2-}(aq)$, or hydroxide, $OH^-(aq)$ impurities:

$$CO_3^{2-}(aq) + 2H^+(aq) + 2NO_3^-(aq) \longrightarrow CO_2(g) + H_2O(l) + 2NO_3^-(aq)$$

$$OH^-(aq) + H^+(aq) + NO_3^-(aq) \longrightarrow H_2O(l) + NO_3^-(aq)$$

These would interfere with the test by forming insoluble silver carbonate:

$$2Ag^+(aq) + CO_3^{2-}(aq) \longrightarrow Ag_2CO_3(s)$$

or insoluble silver hydroxide

$$Ag^+(aq) + OH^-(aq) \longrightarrow AgOH(s)$$

2 Then a few drops of silver nitrate solution are added and the halide precipitate forms.

The reaction can be used as a test for halides because we can tell from the colour of the precipitate which halide has formed, see Table 1. The colours of silver bromide and silver iodide are similar but if we add a few drops of concentrated ammonia solution, silver bromide dissolves but silver iodide does not.

Table 1 *Tests for halides*

Halide	silver fluoride	silver chloride	silver bromide	silver iodide
Colour	no precipitate	white ppt	cream ppt	pale yellow ppt
Further test		dissolves in dilute ammonia	dissolves in concentrated ammonia	insoluble in concentrated ammonia

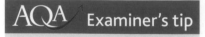

Examiner's tip

You need to learn the colours of the silver halides, especially AgBr and AgI.

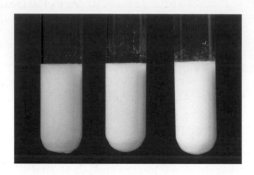

Figure 1 *The colours of the silver halides: (from left to right) AgCl, AgBr, AgI*

Summary questions

1 The reaction between concentrated sulfuric acid and solid sodium fluoride is not usually carried out in the laboratory.

a How does the reducing power of the fluoride ion compare with the other halide ions?

b Explain why you would predict this.

c Write a balanced symbol equation for the reaction between concentrated sulfuric acid and sodium fluoride.

d Is this a redox reaction? Explain your answer.

2 A few drops of silver nitrate were added to an acidified solution, to show the presence of sodium bromide.

a What would you see?

b Write the equation for the reaction.

c What would happen if you now added a few drops of concentrated ammonia solution?

d Why is an acid added to sodium bromide solution initially?

e Neither hydrochloric nor sulfuric acid may be used to acidify the solution. Explain why this is so.

f Why can't this test be used to find out if fluoride ions are present?

11.4 Uses of chlorine

11.4 Uses of chlorine

Learning objectives:

- How does chlorine react with water?

- How does chlorine react with alkali?

Specification reference 3.2.5

ℹ️ How science works

Water fit to drink

The supply of germ-free drinking water is one of the major achievements of science in public health. Before chlorination of water, at around the beginning of the twentieth century, epidemics of cholera and typhoid were common. The concentration of chlorine in drinking water is about $0.7\,mg\,dm^{-3}$. In swimming pools the concentration is higher and monitored carefully because it is important to make sure the concentration is sufficient to kill the germs, without being toxic.

Summary questions

1. Write the equations for bromine reacting with:

   a water

   b alkali.

2. Why is chlorine added to the domestic water supply?

3. a What products are obtained when an aqueous solution of chlorine is left in the sunlight?

   b Write the equation for the reaction, giving the oxidation states of every atom before and after reaction.

   c What has been oxidised?

   d What has been reduced?

   e What is the oxidising agent?

   f What is the reducing agent?

Chlorine is a poisonous gas and was notoriously used as such in the First World War. However, it is soluble in water and in this form has become an essential part of our life in the treatment of water both for drinking and in swimming pools.

🔬 Reaction with water

Chlorine reacts with water in a reversible reaction to form chloric(I) acid (HClO), and hydrochloric acid (HCl):

$$\overset{0}{Cl_2}(g) + H_2O(l) \rightleftharpoons \overset{+1}{HClO}(aq) + \overset{-1}{HCl}(aq)$$

In this reaction, the oxidation number of one of the chlorine atoms increases from 0 to +1 and that of the other decreases from 0 to −1. This type of redox reaction, where the oxidation state of some atoms of the same element increase and others decrease, is called **disproportionation**.

This reaction takes place when chlorine is used to purify water for drinking and in swimming baths, to prevent life-threatening diseases. Chloric(I) acid is an oxidising agent and kills bacteria by oxidation. It is also a bleach.

The other halogens react similarly, but much more slowly as we go down the group.

In sunlight a different reaction occurs:

$$2Cl_2(g) + 2H_2O(l) \longrightarrow 4HCl(aq) + O_2(g)$$

pale green   colourless

Chlorine is rapidly lost from pool water in sunlight so that shallow pools need frequent addition of chlorine.

An alternative to the direct chlorination of swimming pools is to add solid sodium (or calcium) chlorate(I). This dissolves in water to form chloric(I) acid, $HClO(aq,)$ in a reversible reaction:

$$NaClO(s) + H_2O \rightleftharpoons Na^+(aq) + OH^-(aq) + HClO(aq)$$

In alkaline solution, this equilibrium moves to the left and the HClO is removed as ClO^- ions. To prevent this happening, swimming pools need to be kept slightly acidic. However, this is carefully monitored and the 'water' never gets acidic enough to corrode metal components and affect swimmers.

◼ Reaction with alkali

Chlorine reacts with cold, dilute sodium hydroxide to form sodium chlorate(I), NaClO. This is an oxidising agent and the active ingredient in household bleach. This is also a disproportionation reaction; see the oxidation numbers above the relevant species.

$$\overset{0}{Cl_2}(g) + 2NaOH(aq) \longrightarrow \overset{+1}{Na}ClO(aq) + \overset{-1}{Na}Cl(aq) + H_2O(l)$$

The other halogens behave similarly.

1   (a)   State the trend in electronegativity of the elements down Group 7. Explain this
          trend.   *(3 marks)*
    (b)   (i)   State the trend in reducing ability of the halide ions down Group 7.
          (ii) Give an example of a reagent which could be used to show that the reducing
                ability of bromide ions is different from that of chloride ions.   *(2 marks)*
    (c)   The addition of silver nitrate solution followed by dilute aqueous ammonia can
          be used as a test to distinguish between chloride and bromide ions. For each ion,
          state what you would observe if an aqueous solution containing the ion was tested
          in this way.   *(4 marks)*
    (d)   Write an equation for the reaction between chlorine and cold, dilute aqueous
          sodium hydroxide. Give two uses of the resulting solution.   *(3 marks)*
                                                                                            AQA, 2006

2   (a)   Explain, by referring to electrons, the meaning of the terms *reduction* and
          reducing agent.   *(2 marks)*
    (b)   Iodide ions can reduce sulfuric acid to three different products.
          (i)   Name the **three** reduction products and give the oxidation state of sulfur in
                each of these products.
          (ii) Describe how observations of the reaction between solid potassium iodide
                and concentrated sulfuric acid can be used to indicate the presence of any
                two of these reduction products.
          (iii) Write half-equations to show how two of these products are formed by
                reduction of sulfuric acid.   *(10 marks)*
    (c)   Write an equation for the reaction that occurs when chlorine is added to cold
          water. State whether or not the water is oxidised and explain your answer.   *(3 marks)*
                                                                                            AQA, 2006

3   (a)   State the trend in the boiling points of the halogens from fluorine to iodine and
          explain this trend.   *(4 marks)*
    (b)   Each of the following reactions may be used to identify bromide ions. For each
          reaction, state what you would observe and, where indicated, write an appropriate equation.
          (i)   The reaction of aqueous bromide ions with chlorine gas
          (ii) The reaction of aqueous bromide ions with aqueous silver nitrate followed by
                the addition of concentrated aqueous ammonia
          (iii) The reaction of solid potassium bromide with concentrated sulfuric acid   *(7 marks)*
    (c)   Write an equation for the redox reaction that occurs when potassium bromide
          reacts with concentrated sulfuric acid.   *(2 marks)*
                                                                                            AQA, 2005

4   (a)   State and explain the trend in electronegativity down Group 7 from fluorine to
          iodine.   *(3 marks)*
    (b)   State what you would observe when chlorine gas is bubbled into an aqueous
          solution of potassium iodide. Write an equation for the reaction that occurs.   *(2 marks)*
    (c)   Identify **two** sulfur-containing reduction products formed when concentrated
          sulfuric acid oxidises iodide ions. For each reduction product, write a half-
          equation to illustrate its formation from sulfuric acid.   *(4 marks)*
    (d)   Write an equation for the reaction between chlorine gas and dilute aqueous
          sodium hydroxide. Name the **two** chlorine-containing products of this reaction
          and give the oxidation state of chlorine in each of these products.   *(5 marks)*
                                                                                            AQA, 2005

5 (a) Identify the halogen that is the strongest oxidising agent. *(1 mark)*

   (b) Give the formula of the halide ion that is the strongest reducing agent. *(1 mark)*

   (c) Describe what you would observe in each case when aqueous silver nitrate is added separately to dilute aqueous sodium fluoride and to dilute aqueous sodium iodide. Write an equation, including state symbols, for the reaction between aqueous sodium iodide and aqueous silver nitrate. *(3 marks)*

   (d) Describe what you would observe when concentrated sulfuric acid is added to solid sodium chloride. Write an equation for the reaction that occurs. *(2 marks)*

   (e) Describe two observations that you would make when concentrated sulfuric acid is added to solid sodium iodide. Write an equation for a reaction that occurs in which iodide ions are oxidised by the sulfuric acid. *(4 marks)*

   AQA, 2005

6 (a) Describe and explain the trend in the boiling points of the elements down Group 7 from fluorine to iodine. *(4 marks)*

   (b) Describe what you would observe when aqueous silver nitrate, followed by dilute aqueous ammonia, is added to separate aqueous solutions of sodium chloride and sodium bromide. *(4 marks)*

   (c) State the trend in the oxidising abilities of the elements down Group 7 from chlorine to iodine.

   Explain how this trend can be shown by displacement reactions between halogens and halide ions in aqueous solutions.

   Illustrate your answer with appropriate observations and equations. *(7 marks)*

   AQA, 2003

7 (a) State why chlorine is added to drinking water. *(1 mark)*

   (b) Write an equation for the reaction which occurs when chlorine is bubbled into water.

   Identify the substance which causes the resulting solution to be pale green. *(2 marks)*

8 (a) State and explain the trend in electronegativity down Group 7 from fluorine to iodine.

   (b) (i) Describe what you would observe when an aqueous solution of bromine is added to an aqueous solution containing iodide ions. Write an equation for the reaction occurring.

      (ii) Explain why bromine does not react with aqueous chloride ions. *(3 marks)*

   (c) Describe what you would observe when aqueous silver nitrate is added to separate aqueous solutions of potassium fluoride and potassium bromide. *(2 marks)*

   (d) Write an equation to show how solid potassium fluoride reacts with concentrated sulfuric acid. *(1 mark)*

   (e) Write an equation for the redox reaction of sodium bromide with concentrated sulfuric acid. *(2 marks)*

   AQA, 2003

9 (a) Concentrated sulfuric acid can be reduced by some solid sodium halides to H_2S.

      (i) Give the oxidation state of sulfur in H_2S

      (ii) Give **one** solid sodium halide which will reduce concentrated sulfuric acid, forming H_2S

      (iii) State **one** way in which the presence of H_2S could be recognised.

      (iv) Write a half-equation for the formation of H_2S from sulfuric acid. *(4 marks)*

   (b) A different solid sodium halide reacts with concentrated sulfuric acid without reduction forming a halogen-containing product **X**.

      (i) Suggest an identity for **X**.

      (ii) Identify the solid sodium halide which produces **X**.

      (iii) State the role of sulfuric acid in the formation of **X**.

      (iv) Write an equation for the reaction with concentrated sulfuric acid in which **X** is formed. *(4 marks)*

   AQA, 2002

12 Group 2, the alkaline earth metals

12.1 The physical and chemical properties of Group 2

Learning objectives:

■ How and why does the atomic radius of the Group 2 elements change from Mg to Ba?

■ How and why does the first ionisation energy of the Group 2 elements change from Mg to Ba?

■ How and why does the melting point of the Group 2 elements change from Mg to Ba?

■ What is the trend in reactivity of the group?

■ What is the trend in solubilities of a) the hydroxides b) the sulfates?

Specification reference 3.2.6

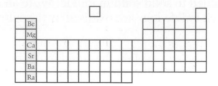

The elements in Group 2 are sometimes called the **alkaline earth metals**. This is because their oxides and hydroxides are alkaline. Like Group 1, they are s-block elements. They are similar in many ways to Group 1 but they are less reactive. Beryllium is not typical of the group and is not considered here.

The physical properties of the Group 2 elements, Mg to Ba

A summary of some of the physical properties of the elements from magnesium to barium is given in Table 1. Trends in properties are shown by the arrows, which show the direction of increase.

Electron arrangement

The elements all have two electrons in an outer s-orbital. This s-orbital becomes further away from the nucleus as we go down the group.

The sizes of the atoms

The atoms get bigger as we go down the group. The atomic (metallic) radii increase because each element has an extra filled main level of electrons compared with the one above it.

Melting points

Group 2 elements are metals with high melting points, typical of a giant metallic structure, see Topic 3.4. As we go down the group, the electrons in the 'sea' of delocalised electrons are further away from the positive nuclei. As a result, the strength of the metallic bonds decreases as we go down the group. For this reason the melting points of Group 2 elements decrease slightly as we go down the group, starting with calcium.

Magnesium, with the lowest melting point, does not fit this trend. This is because the lattice arrangement of atoms is different from that of the elements below, which makes them slightly easier to separate.

Ionisation energies

In *all* their reactions, atoms of elements in Group 2 lose their two outer electrons to form ions with two positive charges.

$$M \longrightarrow M^{2+} + 2e^-$$

Table 1 *The physical properties of Group 2, magnesium to barium*

	Atomic number Z	Electron arrangement	Metallic radius / nm	First + second IEs / kJ mol^{-1}	T_m / K	T_b / K	Density ρ / g cm^{-3}
Mg magnesium	12	[Ne]3s^2	0.160	738 + 1451 = 2189	922	1380	1.74
Ca calcium	20	[Ar]4s^2	0.197	590 + 1145 = 1735	1112	1757	1.54
Sr strontium	38	[Kr]5s^2	0.215	550 + 1064 = 1614	1042	1657	2.60
Ba barium	56	[Xe]6s^2	0.224	503 + 965 = 1468	998	1913	3.51

So, an amount of energy equal to the sum of the first and the second ionisation energies is needed for complete ionisation.

$$M \longrightarrow M^{1+} + e^- \quad \text{plus} \quad M^{1+} \longrightarrow M^{2+} + e^-$$

Both the first ionisation energy and the second ionisation energy decrease as we go down the group; it takes less energy to remove the electrons as they become further and further away from the positive nucleus. The nucleus is more effectively shielded by more inner shells of electrons.

In all their reactions, the metals get more reactive as we go down the group.

⚗ The chemical reactions of the Group 2 elements, Mg to Ba

Oxidation is loss of electrons so in all their reactions the Group 2 metals are oxidised. The metals go from oxidation state 0 to oxidation state +2. These are redox reactions.

Reaction with water

With water we see the same trend in reactivity; the metals get more reactive as we go down the group. These are also redox reactions. The basic reaction is as follows, where M is any Group 2 metal:

$$\overset{0}{M}(s) + 2\overset{+1}{H_2}O(l) \longrightarrow \overset{+2}{M}(OH)_2(aq) + \overset{0}{H_2}(g)$$

Magnesium hydroxide is 'milk of magnesia' and is used in indigestion remedies to neutralise excess stomach acid.

Magnesium reacts very slowly with cold water but rapidly with steam to form an alkaline oxide and hydrogen.

$$Mg(s) + H_2O(g) \longrightarrow MgO(s) + H_2(g)$$

Calcium reacts in the same way but more vigorously, even with cold water. Strontium and barium react more vigorously still. Calcium hydroxide is sometimes called 'slaked lime' and is used to treat acidic soil. Most plants have an optimum level of acidity or alkalinity in which they thrive. For example, grass prefers a pH of around 6 so if the soil has a pH much below this, then it will not grow as well as it could. Crops such as wheat, corn, oats and barley prefer soil that is nearly neutral.

> **Hint**
>
> Remember **lower** pH means **more** acidic.

The solubilities of the hydroxides and sulfates

Hydroxides

There is a clear trend in the solubilities of the hydroxides, as we go down the group: they become more soluble. The hydroxides are all white solids.

■ **Hint**

The symbol **aq** is used to represent an unspecified amount of water.

■ **How science works**

Epsom salts

Magnesium sulfate also has medicinal uses. The hydrated salt $MgSO_4.7H_2O$ is called Epsom salts and is used as a mild laxative. It is soluble in water and is also found in bath salts.

Figure 1 *Two applications of Group 2 hydroxides: a medicine and lime being spread on a field*

i Magnesium hydroxide, $Mg(OH)_2$ (milk of magnesia), is almost insoluble. It is sold as a suspension in water, rather than a solution.

■ Calcium hydroxide, $Ca(OH)_2$, is sparingly soluble and a solution is used as lime water.

■ Strontium hydroxide, $Sr(OH)_2$, is more soluble.

■ Barium hydroxide, $Ba(OH)_2$, dissolves to produce a strongly alkaline solution:

$$Ba(OH)_2(s) + aq \longrightarrow Ba^{2+}(aq) + 2(OH)^-(aq)$$

Sulfates

The solubility trend in the sulfates is exactly the opposite; they become less soluble as we go down the group. So, barium sulfate is virtually insoluble. This means that it can be taken by mouth as a 'barium meal' to outline the gut in medical X-rays. (The heavy barium atom is very good at absorbing X-rays.) This test is safe, despite the fact that barium compounds are highly toxic, because barium sulfate is so insoluble.

The insolubility of barium sulfate is also used in a simple test for sulfate ions in solution. The solution is first acidified with nitric or hydrochloric acid. Then barium chloride solution is added to the solution under test and if a sulfate is present a white precipitate of barium sulfate is formed.

$$Ba^{2+}(aq) + SO_4^{2-}(aq) \longrightarrow BaSO_4(s)$$

The addition of acid removes carbonate ions as carbon dioxide. (Barium carbonate is also a white insoluble solid, which would be indistinguishable from barium sulfate).

■ **Summary questions**

1 **a** What is the oxidation number of all Group 2 elements in their compounds?

   b Explain your answer.

2 Why does it become easier to form 2+ ions as we go down Group 2?

3 Explain why the reaction
$Ca + Cl_2 \longrightarrow CaCl_2$,
is a redox reaction.

4 Write the equation for the reaction of calcium with water.

5 How would you expect the reaction of strontium with water to compare with those of the following? Explain your answers.

   a calcium

   b barium

6 Radium is below strontium in Group 2. How would you predict the solubilities of the following compounds would compare with the other members of the group? Explain your answers.

   a radium hydroxide

   b radium sulfate

1   State and explain the trend in melting point of the Group 2 elements Ca to Ba. *(3 marks)*

AQA, 2006

2   State the trends in solubility of the hydroxides and of the sulfates of the Group 2 elements Mg to Ba.

Describe a chemical test you could perform to distinguish between separate aqueous solutions of sodium sulfate and sodium nitrate. State the observation you would make with each solution. Write an equation for any reaction which occurs. *(6 marks)*

AQA, 2006

3   (a) A small sample of barium metal was added to water in a flask. When the reaction had ceased, the contents of the flask were treated with a small amount of dilute aqueous sodium sulfate.

Describe all that you would observe and write equations, with state symbols, for the reactions that occur. *(8 marks)*

(b) Dilute sodium hydroxide solution was added dropwise until in excess to separate dilute aqueous solutions of magnesium chloride and barium chloride.

Describe what you would observe in each case and account for your observations. *(5 marks)*

AQA, 2002

4   (a) For the elements Mg to Ba, state how the solubilities of the hydroxides and the solubilities of the sulfates change down Group 2.

(b) Describe a test to show the presence of sulfate ions in an aqueous solution. Give the results of this test when performed on separate aqueous solutions of magnesium chloride and magnesium sulfate. Write equations for any reactions occurring.

(c) State the trend in the reactivity of the Group 2 elements Mg to Ba with water.

Write an equation for the reaction of barium with water. *(9 marks)*

AQA, 2005

5   There is a trend in the reactivity of the Group 2 metals, Mg to Ba, with water. State this trend and give the conditions under which magnesium reacts rapidly with water.

Write an equation to represent this reaction. *(3 marks)*

AQA, 2004

6   State and explain the trend in first ionisation energy of the elements Mg to Ba *(3 marks)*

7   The presence of sulfate ions in an aqueous solution can be shown by means of a simple chemical test.

(a) Identify a reagent you would use in this chemical test.

(b) State what you would observe if the test were positive.

(c) Write an ionic equation for the reaction occurring when the test is positive. *(3 marks)*

AQA, 2004

8   (a) State the trend in atomic radius down Group 2 from Mg to Ba and give a reason for this trend. *(2 marks)*

(b) State and explain the trend in melting points of the elements down Group 2I from Mg to Ba. *(3 marks)*

(c) State the trend in reactivity with water of the elements down Group 2 from Mg to Ba.

Write an equation for the reaction of magnesium with steam and an equation for the reaction of strontium with water. *(3 marks)*

(d) Sulfates of the Group 2 elements from Mg to Ba have different solubilities. Give the formula of the least soluble of these sulfates and state **one** use that depends upon the insolubility of this sulfate. *(2 marks)*

AQA, 2002

13 The extraction of metals

13.1 The principles of metal extraction

Learning objectives:

- With which two elements are metals most commonly combined?

- How are sulfide ores converted into oxides?

- What are the environmental problems created in this process?

- How does the blast furnace produce iron?

Specification reference 3.2.7

Because of their properties such as strength, thermal and electrical conductivity and ease of working, metals are among the most useful materials known to mankind.

However, with a few exceptions such as gold, metals are not found in nature uncombined. They are usually found in ores containing minerals, in which the metals are combined with oxygen or sulfur. So, in order to obtain the metal, the oxygen or sulfur has to be removed.

This is a reduction reaction; in oxides and sulfides the metals have positive oxidation states. As elements, metals have oxidation states of 0, see Topic 10.2.

For example:

In iron oxide, $\overset{+3\ -2}{Fe_2O_3}$ the oxidation state of iron is $+3$ so $Fe^{3+} \longrightarrow Fe$ is a reduction.

In copper sulfide, $\overset{+2\ -2}{CuS}$, the oxidation state of copper is $+2$ so $Cu^{2+} \longrightarrow Cu$ is a reduction.

The chemist must select a suitable reducing agent. Ideally this should be cheap and readily available. Any by-products should be non-polluting and easy to dispose of.

As well as the metal-containing compound, ores contain unwanted materials such as clay and rock that have to be removed. These materials are called gangue. An ore must contain enough metal for it to be economic to mine and extract the metal. If the metal is a valuable one, the ore could be worth mining even if it contains relatively little of the metal.

Converting sulfide ores to oxides

Before reduction, sulfide ores are usually converted to oxides by heating them in air, a process usually called **roasting**.

For example, zinc sulfide is converted into zinc oxide:

$$ZnS(s) + 1\tfrac{1}{2}O_2(g) \longrightarrow ZnO(s) + SO_2(g)$$

zinc sulfide   oxygen   zinc oxide   sulfur dioxide

The problem here is that the by-product, sulfur dioxide, is an acidic gas which, if it is allowed to escape, is converted into sulfuric acid by reaction with water and oxygen in the atmosphere. This is a contributor to acid rain.

Fortunately, this sulfur dioxide may be collected and converted to sulfuric acid in controlled conditions. It can then be sold for a variety of purposes, which makes the industrial process more economical.

$$SO_2(g) + H_2O(g) + \tfrac{1}{2}O_2(g) \longrightarrow H_2SO_4(l)$$

sulfur dioxide   water   oxygen   sulfuric acid

Choosing a reducing agent

■ Coke (an impure form of carbon) is often chosen as a reducing agent for the extraction of metals. It is cheaply obtained by heating coal in the absence of air. However, for some metals the temperature required for reaction with carbon is so high that the process is uneconomic. Also, at high temperatures, reactive metals react with carbon to form carbides

■ Another possible reducing agent is hydrogen (made from methane, CH_4, and water, H_2O); this method is used to extract tungsten.

■ Metals higher up the reactivity series, such as sodium and aluminium, may be reduced by electrolysis.

■ Another possibility is to use a more reactive metal as a reducing agent.

■ Some examples of metal extraction

Iron (and its alloy, steel) is by far the most commonly used metal; over half a billion tonnes are produced each year worldwide.

The iron itself is usually found as the ores magnetite, Fe_3O_4, and haematite, Fe_2O_3. The major impurity is silica, SiO_2 (sand).

🝢 Iron – reduction by carbon in the blast furnace

Extraction of iron from its oxide ores is done using coke in tall brick towers, called blast furnaces, that are up to 70 m high. A typical blast furnace can produce up to 10 000 tonnes of iron per day.

These run continuously for years at a time. The hopper is charged with a mixture of iron ore, coke and limestone (calcium carbonate).

Inside the blast furnace

At the base of the furnace the coke burns in a blast of hot air. Heat is generated by this exothermic process so that the temperature is around 2000 K. (The melting point of iron is 1808 K.) Carbon dioxide is formed which then reacts with more carbon to form carbon monoxide.

$$C(s) + O_2(g) \longrightarrow CO_2(g)$$

then

$$CO_2(g) + C(s) \longrightarrow 2CO(g)$$

The carbon monoxide is the reducing agent. It reacts with the iron oxide to produce molten iron.

$$Fe_2O_3(s) + 3CO(g) \longrightarrow 2Fe(l) + 3CO_2(g)$$

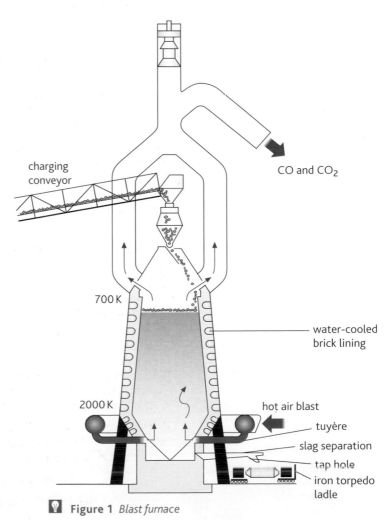

charging conveyor

CO and CO_2

700 K

water-cooled brick lining

2000 K

hot air blast

tuyère

slag separation

tap hole

iron torpedo ladle

🝢 **Figure 1** *Blast furnace*

Stainless steel

Most of the mined iron is used to make steels. These are alloys – mixtures of iron and other elements which alter the properties of iron. Carbon is the most cost-effective alloying element.

Harry Brearley invented stainless steel around 1913. He was one of nine children. At the age of twelve years, Harry left school and eventually joined the steel works, where his father worked, as a bottle washer in the laboratory. From here he studied metallurgy and learned so quickly that he became the leader of the research team.

He was given the task of finding an alloy which would prolong the life of gun barrels, which were affected by the high temperatures that developed inside the barrels when the guns were fired. Chromium was known to raise the melting point of steel so he made several alloys – with mixtures containing from 6 per cent to 15 per cent chromium with varying amounts of carbon. He found that a mixture containing 12.8 per cent chromium and 0.24 per cent carbon was extremely resistant to *chemical* attack. He called his alloy 'rustless steel', but it was decided that 'stainless steel' was a better name.

After Brearley left the firm, his successor, W. H. Hatfield continued the research and made a stainless steel that we use today. If you look on stainless steel saucepans the numbers 18/8 stand for 18 per cent chromium and 8 per cent nickel.

Figure 2 *Stainless steel saucepan*

Summary questions

1 What is the reducing agent in the blast furnace for the extraction of iron?

2 What are the advantages of this reducing agent?

3 Why is this reducing agent not economic for all metals?

4 Write the equation for the reduction of manganese dioxide, MnO_2, by carbon. Include the changes in oxidation state.

5 Zinc can be extracted from zinc sulfide by roasting, followed by reduction with carbon.

   a Name two gases given off in these processes that may be harmful to the environment.

   b Explain what atmospheric problems these gases may cause.

Other metals

Other relatively unreactive metals can also be extracted from their ores by high temperature reduction with carbon and/or carbon monoxide. Manganese, Mn, is produced by reduction of its oxide with carbon. Copper is another example, although the method is not used much nowadays. The original ore was converted to copper oxide. In the case of malachite, which contains copper carbonate, this can be done by heating it.

$$CuCO_3 \longrightarrow CuO + CO_2$$

The oxide was then heated with coke.

$$2CuO(s) + C(s) \longrightarrow 2Cu(l) + CO_2(g)$$

Nowadays, some copper ores are converted into solutions containing Cu^{2+} ions. This can be done by spraying copper mining waste with dilute acid in the presence of a bacterium, *Thiobacillus ferrooxidans*. This is particularly efficient because the bacteria will work on low grade ores that contain little copper, including copper mining waste. The copper is extracted from the solution by reduction with scrap iron:

$$Cu^{2+}(aq) + Fe(s) \longrightarrow Cu(s) + Fe^{2+}(aq)$$

This reaction makes economic sense because the price of copper is much greater than that of iron, and at present scrap iron is relatively cheap and readily available. It is also environmentally sound because no carbon dioxide is produced in this extraction process and it also uses much less energy than the reduction of a copper ore with carbon. It must be remembered though that the iron itself has had to be extracted from its own ore, using carbon originally, which required energy.

13.2 Extracting other metals

Specification reference 3.2.7

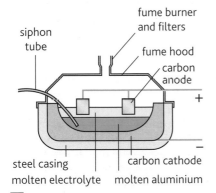

Figure 1 *Electrolysis cell for aluminium extraction*

Aluminium – reduction by electrolysis

Aluminium is extracted from purified bauxite ore, which is largely aluminium oxide. This is found in Brazil, Jamaica, Australia and Guinea as well as Les Baux in France, which is where its name comes from. The process by which aluminium is extracted is called the Hall–Héroult process after its inventors. It was developed almost simultaneously in 1886 by the American chemist Charles Martin Hall and the Frenchman Paul Héroult who worked entirely independently and on different sides of the Atlantic. However, this is not the only remarkable coincidence that links the two men; both were born in the same year (1863) and died in the same year (1914).

The oxide is dissolved in molten cryolite, Na_3AlF_6, to form a solution, which melts at around 1240 K, compared with the melting temperature of pure aluminium oxide of 2345 K. This solution is electrolysed in rows of cells using currents of up to 300 000 A, see Figure 1.

Aluminium is produced at the negative electrode (the steel casing of the cell):

$$2Al^{3+} + 6e^- \longrightarrow 2Al$$

and oxygen at the positive electrode (made of carbon):

$$3O^{2-} \longrightarrow 1\tfrac{1}{2}O_2 + 6e^-$$

The overall process is the decomposition of aluminium oxide. The equation for this can be obtained by adding the two half equations. Note that the electrons cancel out.

$$Al_2O_3 \longrightarrow 2Al + 1\tfrac{1}{2}O_2$$

The process runs continuously and the solution is kept molten by the heat generated by the passage of the current. The aluminium is formed as a liquid and is siphoned off, while the oxygen burns the carbon electrodes away to carbon dioxide. Because of this the carbon electrodes have to be regularly replaced.

The main cost of the process is the electricity so it makes economic sense in countries where cheap hydroelectricity is available e.g. Canada.

Titanium – reduction by a more reactive metal

Titanium is an excellent constructional metal; it is strong, of low density and resistant to corrosion. Its ores are also relatively abundant. Titanium oxide cannot be reduced with carbon because the formation of titanium carbide makes the metal brittle. It is therefore produced by reduction with a more reactive metal, sodium or magnesium. This is a very expensive process, involving two different processes.

Conversion of titanium oxide to titanium chloride

The ore, called rutile is largely titanium(IV) oxide. Rutile is converted to titanium(IV) chloride by reacting it with coke and chlorine at 1173 K

$$TiO_2(s) + 2C(s) + 2Cl_2(g) \longrightarrow TiCl_4(l) + 2CO(g)$$

The liquid titanium chloride is purified by distillation.

Reduction of titanium chloride

Titanium chloride is reduced with molten sodium under an inert argon atmosphere at 1300 K. The argon is needed to prevent the metals from reacting with nitrogen and oxygen in the air.

$$TiCl_4(l) + 4Na(l) \longrightarrow Ti(l) + 4NaCl(l)$$

Magnesium is another reactive metal that can be used as an alternative to sodium.

Unlike the blast furnace and the Hall–Héroult process, which run continuously, this is a batch process. These are generally less efficient than continuous ones. In batch processes the reaction vessels have to be heated back up to operating temperatures after each batch is removed.

ℹ Tungsten – reduction with hydrogen

Tungsten is a moderately rare element with an abundance in the Earth's crust estimated at about 1.5 parts per million. It is a useful metal, used in light bulb filaments because of its high melting point. Like titanium, tungsten ore cannot be reduced by carbon because a carbide is formed. It is extracted from its oxide, WO_3, by reduction with hydrogen at a high temperature:

$$WO_3 + 3H_2 \longrightarrow W + 3H_2O$$

Clearly the practical difficulties of using a flammable gas mean that using hydrogen as a reducing agent is a last resort.

■ Recycling and the environment

Iron

Metals are relatively straightforward to recycle because they can be melted down again and reformed into new articles.

- This reduces the scrap iron that the industrial world discards in landfill sites, for example.
- Scrap iron has already been extracted from its ore. It is also easily seperated from other material because it is magnetic.
- Thinking in terms of greenhouse gases, melting scrap iron does not in itself produce carbon dioxide whereas extracting iron from its ore does. However, the energy needed to melt the scrap iron usually does involve the production of carbon dioxide.

Note that the electric arc steelmaking process uses only scrap steel that is melted electrically.

Aluminium

Aluminium is also recycled by melting, the recycling of drinks cans being a prime example.

- Recycled aluminium uses only about 5% of the enormous amount of energy used to extract aluminium from its ore.
- Recycling avoids the production of large amounts of carbon dioxide.

Increasing amounts of recycling domestic metal waste is taking place. However, this does give rise to the financial and energy costs involved in sorting and transporting the recycled material.

■ How science works

Metal extraction and technological advance

The history of mankind can be viewed through the lens of the discovery and extraction of metals. Gold and silver have been known and used from prehistoric times because they are unreactive enough to be found uncombined and therefore need no extraction. The discovery and use of bronze (an alloy of copper and tin) delineated the Bronze Age; copper and tin are relatively easy to extract, perhaps by reaction of the ore with charcoal in a camp fire. The extraction of iron in the Iron Age marked an enormous thrust forward in terms of tool shaping and weapon making. Iron requires a higher temperature to be reduced by carbon from its ores. As mankind became more and more skilled at wresting the metals from their ores – by the invention of electrolysis for example, metals such as aluminium were isolated. Before the development of electrolysis, this now commonplace metal was so rare that Louis Napoleon, the French emperor in the mid 1800s, had a state dinner service made from it. This was considered more precious than gold.

Summary questions

1. Why do the carbon anodes in the electrolysis of aluminium have to be replaced periodically?

2. The melting temperature of aluminium oxide is 2345 K. Why is the aluminium oxide dissolved in cryolite before electrolysis?

3. The extraction of titanium is a costly process. Suggest four reasons for this.

4. Write an equation for the reduction of titanium chloride by magnesium.

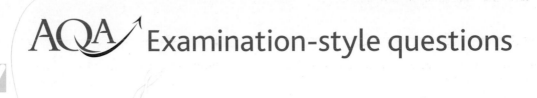

AQA Examination-style questions

1   Reducing agents are used in the extraction of metals.
   (a) In terms of electrons, state the function of a reducing agent.   *(1 mark)*
   (b) Identify a reducing agent used in the extraction of iron. Write an equation for the
        redox reaction in which iron is formed from iron(III) oxide using this reducing agent.   *(2 marks)*
   (c) Identify a reducing agent used to obtain titanium metal from titanium(IV) chloride.
        In addition to a high temperature, state a condition that is used for this reaction and
        explain why this condition is necessary.   *(3 marks)*
   (d) (i)   State **two** essential conditions used for the electrolytic extraction of aluminium
             from aluminium oxide.
        (ii) Write an equation to illustrate how aluminium is formed from aluminium ions in
             this process.   *(3 marks)*

AQA, 2005

2   (a) When iron(III) oxide is reduced in the blast furnace, both carbon and carbon
        monoxide act as reducing agents.
        (i)   Write an equation to illustrate how carbon monoxide is formed in the blast furnace.
        (ii) Write an equation to illustrate how carbon monoxide reduces iron(III) oxide.
        (iii) Suggest in terms of collisions why, in the blast furnace, carbon monoxide reacts
             more rapidly with iron(III) oxide than does carbon.   *(4 marks)*
   (b) State why carbon is not used to reduce the oxide of titanium to the metal.   *(1 mark)*
   (c) Explain **two** major benefits of using some scrap iron in this converter.   *(7 marks)*

AQA, 2005

3   Iron is extracted from iron(III) oxide in a continuous process, whereas titanium is extracted
   from titanium(IV) oxide in a batch process.
   (a) Suggest why a high-temperature batch process is less energy-efficient than a high-
        temperature continuous process.   *(2 marks)*
   (b) Write an overall equation for the reduction of iron(III) oxide in the blast furnace.   *(2 marks)*
   (c) Write two equations to show how titanium is extracted from titanium(IV) oxide in a
        two-stage process.   *(4 marks)*
   (d) Give a reason why titanium cannot be extracted in a similar way to iron.   *(1 mark)*
   (e) Give the major reason why aluminium is more expensive to extract than iron.   *(1 mark)*

AQA, 2006

4   In this question, where appropriate, illustrate your answer with equations.
   Explain how iron is produced in the blast furnace from an iron ore that does not contain
   sulfur impurities. In your answer, state the source of the energy for this process and
   mention any environmental problems that may arise from the operation of the blast furnace.   *(10 marks)*

AQA, 2006

5   State the major economic benefit arising from the recycling of aluminium. What is the
   major problem associated with this recycling process?   *(3 marks)*

6   Tungsten can be extracted from tungsten oxide using a gaseous reducing agent.
   State the name of this reducing agent and a risk that is possible when using it.   *(2 marks)*
   Write an equation for the reaction of tungsten with this reducing agent.   *(1 mark)*
   State why tungsten cannot be extracted by reduction using carbon.   *(1 mark)*

7   Copper can be extracted by reacting copper(II) oxide with carbon. Write an equation for
   this reaction and state why the process is expensive.   *(2 marks)*
   Copper can also be obtained by reacting copper sulfate solution with iron. Give one
   environmental advantage why this process is often carried out using scrap iron.   *(1 mark)*

14.1 Haloalkanes – introduction

Specification reference 3.2.8

Learning objectives

- Why are haloalkanes more reactive than alkanes?

- Why are carbon–halogen bonds polar?

- What are the trends in bond enthalpy and bond polarity of the carbon–halogen bond?

Not many haloalkanes occur naturally but they are the basis of many synthetic compounds. Some examples of these are PVC, used to make drainpipes, Teflon, the non-stick coating on pans, and a number of anaesthetics and solvents. Haloalkanes have an alkane skeleton with one or more halogen (fluorine, chlorine, bromine or iodine) atoms in place of hydrogen atoms.

The general formula

The general formula of a haloalkane with a single halogen atom is $C_nH_{2n+1}X$ where X is the halogen. This is often shortened to R—X.

How to name haloalkanes

- The prefixes fluoro-, chloro-, bromo- and iodo- tell us which halogen is present.

- Numbers are used, if needed, to show on which carbon the halogen is bonded:

Figure 1 Applications of haloalkanes

1-chloropropane

1-iodopropane

2-bromo-2-methylpropane

- We use the prefixes di-, tri-, tetra-, etc. to show *how many* atoms of each halogen are present.

- When a compound contains different halogens they are listed in alphabetical order, *not* in order of the number of the carbon atom to which they are bonded. For example:

is 3-chloro-2-iodopentane not 2-iodo-3-chloropentane. (C is before I in the alphabet.)

Bond polarity

Haloalkanes have a C—X bond. This bond is polar, $C^{\delta+}$—$X^{\delta-}$, because halogens are more electronegative than carbon. The electronegativities of carbon and the halogens are shown in Table 1. Notice that as we go down the group, the bonds get less polar.

Table 1 Electronegativities of carbon and the halogens

Element	Electronegativity
carbon	2.5
fluorine	4.0
chlorine	3.5
bromine	2.8
iodine	2.6

Physical properties of haloalkanes

Solubility

- The polar $C^{\delta+}$—$X^{\delta-}$ bonds are not polar enough to make the haloalkanes soluble in water.
- The main intermolecular forces of attraction are dipole–dipole attractions and van der Waal forces.
- Haloalkanes mix with hydrocarbons so they can be used as dry-cleaning fluids and to remove oily stains. (Oil is a mixture of hydrocarbons.)

Boiling point

The boiling point depends on the number of carbon atoms and halogen atoms.

- Boiling point increases with increased chain length.
- Boiling point increases as we go down the halogen group.

Both these effects are caused by increased van der Waals forces because the larger the molecules, the greater the number of electrons (and therefore the larger the van der Waals forces).

As in other homologous series, increased branching of the carbon chain will tend to lower the melting point.

Haloalkanes have higher boiling points than alkanes of similar chain lengths because a) they have higher relative molecular masses and b) they are more polar.

How the haloalkanes react – the reactivity of the C—X bond

When haloalkanes react it is almost always the C—X bond that breaks. There are two factors that determine how readily the C—X bond reacts. These are:

- the $C^{\delta+}$—$X^{\delta-}$ bond polarity
- the C—X bond enthalpy.

Bond polarity

The halogens are more electronegative than carbon so the bond polarity will be $C^{\delta+}$—$X^{\delta-}$. This means that the carbon bonded to the halogen has a partial positive charge; it is electron deficient. This means that it can be attacked by reagents that are electron rich or have electron-rich areas. These are called **nucleophiles**. A nucleophile is an electron pair donor, see Topic 14.2.

The polarity of the C—X bond would predict that the C—F bond would be the most reactive. It is the most polar, so the $C^{\delta+}$ has the most positive charge and is therefore most easily attacked by a nucleophile. This

argument would make the C—I bond least reactive because it is the least polar.

Bond enthalpies

C—X bond enthalpies are listed in Table 2. The bonds get weaker as we go down the group. Fluorine is the smallest atom of the halogens and the shared electrons in the C—F bond are strongly attracted to the fluorine nucleus. This makes for a strong bond. As we go down the group, the shared electrons in the C—X bond get further and further away from the halogen nucleus, so the bond becomes weaker.

The bond enthalpies would predict that iodo-compounds, with the weakest bonds, are the most reactive, and fluoro-compounds, with the strongest bonds, are the least reactive.

In fact, experiments show us that reactivity increases as we go down the group. This means that bond enthalpy is a more important factor than bond polarity.

Table 2 *Carbon–halogen bond enthalpies*

Bond	BE / kJ mol^{-1}	
C—F	467	
[C—H	413]	
C—Cl	346	stronger ↑
C—Br	290	
C—I	228	

Summary questions

1 These questions are about the following haloalkanes:

    i $CH_3CH_2CH_2CH_2I$

    ii $CH_3CHBrCH_3$

    iii $CH_2ClCH_2CH_2CH_3$

    iv $CH_3CH_2CHBrCH_3$

  a Draw the displayed formula for each haloalkane and mark the polarity of the C—X bond.

  b Name each haloalkane.

  c Predict which of them would have the highest boiling point and explain your answer.

2 Why do the haloalkanes get less reactive as we go up the halogen group?

14.2 Nucleophilic substitution in haloalkanes

Learning objectives

■ What is a nucleophile?

■ What is nucleophilic substitution?

■ Why do ⁻OH, ⁻CN and NH_3 behave as nucleophiles?

■ What is the mechanism of nucleophilic substitution?

Specification reference 3.2.8

Most reactions of organic compounds take place via a series of steps. We can often predict these steps by thinking about how electrons are likely to move. This can help you understand why reactions take place as they do, and this can save a great deal of rote learning.

💡 Nucleophiles

Nucleophiles are reagents that attack and form bonds with positively charged carbon atoms.

■ A nucleophile is either a negatively charged ion or has an atom with a δ– charge.

■ A nucleophile has a lone (unshared) pair of electrons which it can use to form a covalent bond.

■ The lone pair is situated on an electronegative atom.

So, in organic chemistry a nucleophile is a species that has a lone pair of electrons with which it can form a bond by donating its electrons to an electron deficient carbon atom. Some common nucleophiles are:

■ the hydroxide ion, ⁻:OH

■ ammonia, :NH_3

■ the cyanide ion, ⁻:CN

They will each replace the halogen in a haloalkane. These reactions are called **nucleophilic substitutions** and they all follow essentially the same reaction mechanism.

A reaction mechanism describes a route from reactants to products via a series of theoretical steps. These may involve short-lived intermediates.

⚠ Nucleophilic substitution

The general equation for nucleophilic substitution, using :Nu⁻ to represent any negatively charged nucleophile and X to represent a halogen atom is:

$$
\begin{array}{c}
\text{H} \\
| \\
\text{R}-\text{C}-\text{X} \\
| \\
\text{H}
\end{array}
+ \ :\text{Nu}^- \longrightarrow
\begin{array}{c}
\text{H} \\
| \\
\text{R}-\text{C}-\text{Nu} \\
| \\
\text{H}
\end{array}
+ \ :\text{X}^-
$$

Reaction mechanisms and 'curly arrows'

We use curly arrows to show how electron pairs move in organic reactions. So, we can write the reaction above as:

$$
\begin{array}{c}
\quad \quad :\text{Nu}^- \\
\text{H} \\
| \ ^{\delta+} \quad ^{\delta-} \\
\text{R}-\text{C}-\text{X} \\
| \\
\text{H}
\end{array}
\longrightarrow
\begin{array}{c}
\text{H} \\
| \\
\text{R}-\text{C}-\text{Nu} \\
| \\
\text{H}
\end{array}
+ \ :\text{X}^-
$$

The lone pair of electrons of a nucleophile is attracted towards a partially positively charged carbon atom. A curly arrow starts at a lone pair of electrons and moves towards $C^{\delta+}$.

The lower curly arrow shows the electron pair in the C—X bond moving to the halogen atom, X and making it a halide ion. The halide ion is called the **leaving group**.

The rate of substitution depends on the halogen. Fluoro-compounds are unreactive due to the strength of the C—F bond. Then, as we go down the group, the rate of reaction increases as the C—X bond strength decreases, see Topic 14.1.

Examples of nucleophilic substitution reactions

All these reactions are similar. Remember the basic pattern, shown above. Then work out the product with a particular nucleophile. This is easier than trying to remember the separate reactions.

Haloalkanes with aqueous sodium (or potassium) hydroxide

The nucleophile is the hydroxide ion, $^-$:OH

This reaction can take place at room temperature. Haloalkanes do not mix with water, so ethanol is used as a solvent in which the haloalkane and the aqueous sodium (or potassium) hydroxide both mix. This is called a hydrolysis reaction.

The overall reaction is:

$$R–X + OH^- \longrightarrow ROH + X^-$$

so an alcohol, ROH, is formed.

For example:

$$C_2H_5Br + OH^- \longrightarrow C_2H_5OH + Br^-$$
bromoethane · ethanol

This is the mechanism:

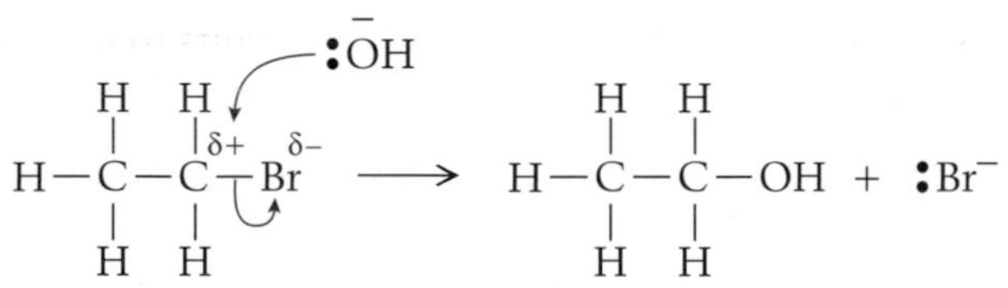

Haloalkanes with cyanide ions

The nucleophile is the cyanide ion $^-$:CN

The reaction is:

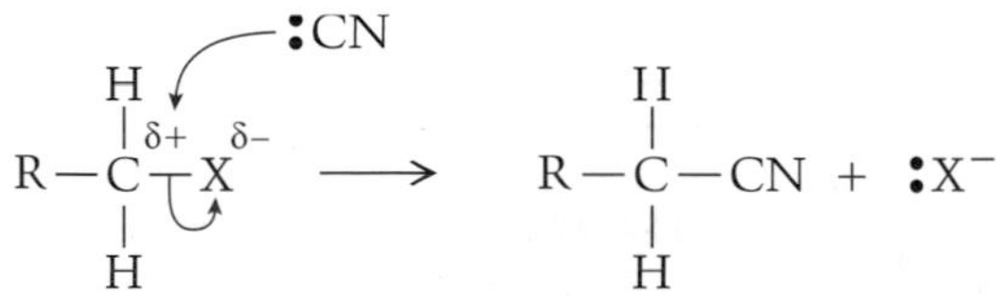

The product is called a nitrile. It has one extra carbon in the chain than the starting haloalkane. This is often useful if we want to make a product that has one carbon more than the starting material.

Hint

Nitriles have the functional group —C≡N. They are named using the suffix nitrile. The carbon of the —CN group is counted as part of the root, so CH_3CH_2CN is propanenitrile, not ethanenitrile.

Hint

Primary amines have the functional group —NH$_2$, and are named with the suffix amine attached to the appropriate side chain stem, rather than the usual root name, so C$_2$H$_5$NH$_2$ is ethylamine not ethanamine.

AQA Examiner's tip

Each step of a reaction mechanism must balance for atoms and charges. The sum of the steps equals the balanced equation.

Haloalkanes with ammonia

The nucleophile is ammonia, :NH$_3$

The reaction of haloalkanes with an excess concentrated solution of ammonia in ethanol is carried out under pressure. The reaction produces a primary amine, RNH$_2$.

$$R\text{–}X + 2NH_3 \longrightarrow RNH_2 + NH_4X$$

This is the mechanism:

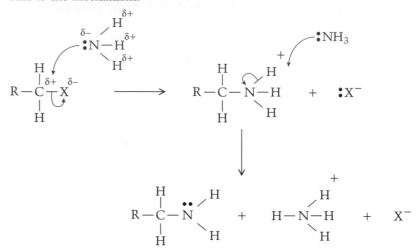

Ammonia is a nucleophile because it has a lone pair of electrons that it can donate (although it has no negative charge) and the nitrogen atom has a δ– charge. Because ammonia is a neutral nucleophile, a proton, H$^+$, must be lost to form the neutral product, called a primary amine. The H$^+$ ion reacts with a second ammonia molecule to form an NH$_4^+$ ion.

■ The uses of nucleophilic substitution

Nucleophilic substitution reactions are useful because they are a way of introducing new functional groups into organic compounds. Haloalkanes can be converted into alcohols, amines and nitriles. These in turn can be converted to other functional groups.

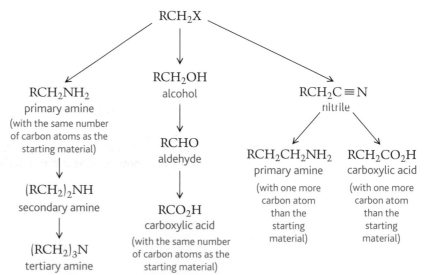

Figure 1 *Uses of nucleophilic reactions*

Summary questions

1 This equation represents the hydrolysis of a haloalkane by sodium hydroxide solution:

$$R\text{–}X + OH^- \longrightarrow ROH + X^-$$

  a Why is the reaction carried out in ethanol?

  b What is the nucleophile?

  c Why is this a substitution?

  d Which is the leaving group?

  e Which would have the fastest reaction R—F, R—Cl, R—Br or R—I?

2 a Starting with bromoethane, what nucleophile will produce a product with three carbon atoms?

  b Give the equation for this, using curly arrows to show the mechanism of the reaction.

  c Name the product.

14.3 Elimination reactions in haloalkanes

Learning objectives

- What is an elimination reaction?

- What is the mechanism for elimination reactions in haloalkanes?

- What conditions favour elimination rather than substitution?

- When and how are isomeric alkenes formed?

Specification reference 3.2.8

Haloalkanes typically react by nucleophilic substitution. But, under different conditions they react by **elimination**. A hydrogen halide is eliminated from the molecule, leaving a double bond in its place so that an alkene is formed.

■ OH⁻ ion acting as a base

We saw in Topic 14.2 that the OH^- ion, from aqueous sodium or potassium hydroxide, is a nucleophile and its lone pair will attack a haloalkane at $C^{\delta+}$ to form an alcohol.

Under different conditions, the OH^- ion can act as a **base**, removing an H^+ ion from the haloalkane. In this case we have an elimination reaction rather than a substitution. In the example below, bromoethane reacts with potassium hydroxide to form ethene. A molecule of hydrogen bromide, HBr, is eliminated in the process.

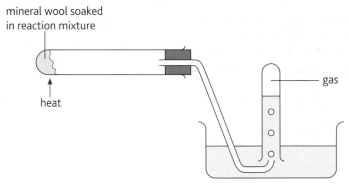

The conditions of reaction

The sodium (or potassium) hydroxide is dissolved in ethanol and mixed with the haloalkane. *There is no water present*. The mixture is heated. The experiment can be carried out using the apparatus shown in Figure 1.

mineral wool soaked in reaction mixture

heat

gas

Figure 1 *Apparatus for elimination of hydrogen bromide from bromoethane*

The product is ethene. Ethene burns and also decolourises bromine solution, showing that it has a carbon–carbon double bond.

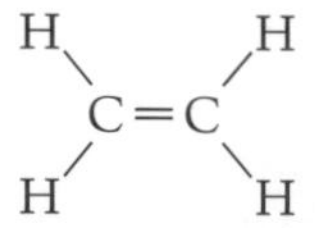

Figure 2 *A better representation of the shape of ethene*

■ The mechanism of elimination

Hydrogen bromide is eliminated as follows. The curly arrows show the movement of electron pairs:

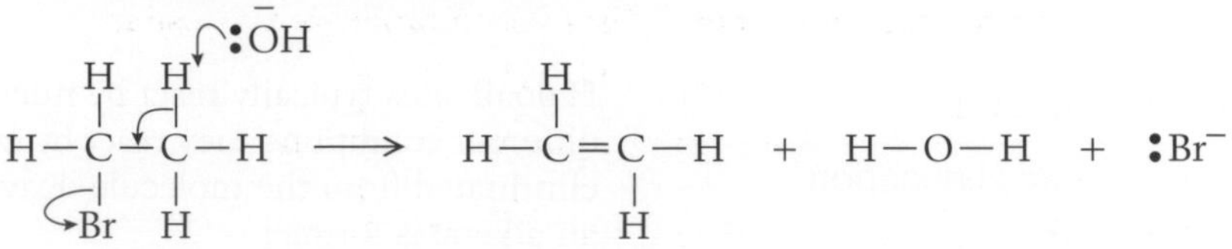

$$H-C-C-H \longrightarrow H-C=C-H \ + \ H-O-H \ + \ :Br^-$$

- ■ The OH⁻ ion uses its lone pair to form a bond with one of the hydrogen atoms on the carbon next to the C—Br bond. These hydrogen atoms are very slightly δ+.
- ■ The electron pair from the C—H bond now becomes part of a carbon–carbon double bond.
- ■ The bromine takes the a pair of electrons in the C—Br bond and leaves as a bromide ion (the leaving group).

This reaction is a useful way of making molecules with carbon–carbon double bonds.

💡 Substitution or elimination?

Since the hydroxide ion will react with haloalkanes as a nucleophile *or* as a base, there is competition between substitution and elimination. In general we produce a mixture of an alcohol and an alkene. For example:

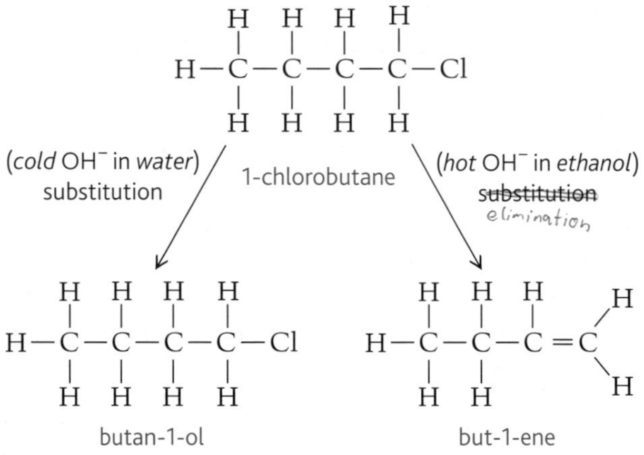

1-chlorobutane

(*cold* OH⁻ in *water*) substitution

(*hot* OH⁻ in *ethanol*) ~~substitution~~ elimination

butan-1-ol   but-1-ene

The reaction that predominates depends on two factors: the reaction conditions (aqueous or ethanolic solution) and the type of haloalkane (primary, secondary or tertiary).

The conditions of the reaction

- ■ Hydroxide ions at room temperature, dissolved in water (aqueous), favour substitution.
- ■ Hydroxide ions at high temperature, dissolved in ethanol, favour elimination.

The type of haloalkane

Primary haloalkanes tend to react by substitution and tertiary ones by elimination. Secondary will do both.

primary   secondary   tertiary

◄——————— elimination ———————

——————— substitution ———————►

In some cases a mixture of isomeric elimination products is possible.

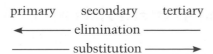

H H Cl H
| | | |
H—C—C—C—C—H
| | | |
H H H H

2-chlorobutane

– HCl (left)   – HCl (right)

H   H
\\   /
C=C
/   \\
CH₃   CH₃
Z-but-2-ene

and

H   CH₃
\\   /
C=C
/   \\
CH₃   H
E-but-2-ene

H   H
\\   /
C=C
/   \\
CH₂   H
|
CH₃   but-1-ene

Link

The prefixes *Z* and *E* are explained in Topic 15.1.

Haloalkanes and the environment

Chlorofluorocarbons

Chlorofluorocarbons are haloalkanes containing both chlorine and fluorine atoms but no hydrogen for example, CCl_3F, trichlorofluoromethane.

- They are also called CFCs.
- They are very unreactive under normal conditions.
- The short-chain ones are gases and were used, for example, as aerosol propellants, refrigerants and blowing agents for foams like expanded polystyrene.
- Longer-chain ones are used as dry cleaning and de-greasing solvents.

CFC gases eventually end up in the atmosphere, and there they decompose to give chlorine atoms. Chlorine atoms decompose ozone, O_3, in the stratosphere, see Topic 14.4, which has caused a hole in the Earth's ozone layer. Upper atmosphere research together with laboratory research showed how O_3 is broken down. Politicians were influenced by scientists and, under international agreement, CFCs are being phased out and replaced by other, safer, compounds including hydrochlorofluorocarbons (HCFCs) such as CF_3CHCl_2. However, a vast reservoir of CFCs remains in the atmosphere and it will be many years before the ozone layer recovers.

Link

Haloalkanes are classified as primary, secondary and tertiary according to whether the halogen atom is at the end of the hydrocarbon chain (primary), in the body of the chain (secondary) or at a branch in the chain (tertiary). The same system is used for alcohols, see Topic 16.1.

Summary questions

1. In elimination reactions of haloalkanes, the OH⁻ group is acting as which of the following?

   a A base   b An acid

   c A nucleophile   d An electrophile

2. Which of the following molecules is a CFC?

   a CH_3CH_2Cl b $CF_2{=}CF_2$ c CF_3CH_2Cl d CCl_2F_2

3. a Name the two possible products when 2-bromopropane reacts with hydroxide ions.

   b How could you show that one of the products is an alkene?

   c Give the mechanism (using curly arrows) of the reaction that is an elimination.

14.4 The formation of haloalkanes

When we put a mixture of an alkane and a halogen into bright sunlight, or shine a photoflood lamp onto the mixture, the alkane and the halogen will react to form a haloalkane. The ultraviolet component of the light starts the reaction. Alkanes do not react with halogens in the dark at room temperature.

For example, if you put a mixture of hexane and a little liquid bromine into a test tube and leave it in the dark it stays red-brown (the colour of bromine). However, if you shine ultraviolet light onto it, the mixture becomes colourless and misty fumes of hydrogen bromide appear.

A substitution reaction has taken place. One of the hydrogen atoms in the alkane has been replaced by a bromine atom and hydrogen bromide is given off as a gas. The main reaction is:

$$C_6H_{14}(g) + Br_2(l) \longrightarrow C_6H_{13}Br(l) + HBr(g)$$
$$\text{hexane} \qquad \text{bromine} \qquad \text{bromohexane} \quad \text{hydrogen bromide}$$

Bromohexane is a haloalkane.

Chain reactions

The reaction above is called a free-radical substitution. It starts off a **chain reaction** which takes place in three stages: **initiation**, **propagation** and **termination**.

The reaction between any alkane and a halogen goes by the same mechanism.

For example, methane and chlorine:

$$CH_4(g) + Cl_2(g) \longrightarrow CH_3Cl(g) + HCl(g)$$

Initiation

■ The first, or initiation, step of the reaction is the breaking of the Cl—Cl bond to form two chlorine atoms.

■ The chlorine molecule absorbs the energy of a single quantum of ultraviolet (UV) light. The energy of one quantum of UV light is greater than the Cl—Cl bond energy, so the bond will break.

■ Since both atoms are the same, the Cl—Cl bond breaks homolytically, i.e. one electron going to each chlorine atom.

■ This results in two separate chlorine atoms, written Cl•. They are called **free radicals**. The dot is used to show the unpaired electron.

$$Cl—Cl \xrightarrow{\text{UV light}} 2Cl•$$

■ Free radicals are highly reactive.

■ The C—H bond in the alkane needs more energy to break than is available in a quantum of ultraviolet radiation, so this bond does not break.

Figure 1 *'Slip-Slop-Slap' is the name for the health campaign in Australia exhorting people to 'slip on a shirt, slop on sunscreen, and slap on a hat'*

Propagation

This takes place in two stages:

1 The chlorine free radical takes a hydrogen atom from methane to form hydrogen chloride, a stable compound. This leaves a methyl free radical, $\bullet CH_3$.

$$Cl\bullet + CH_4 \longrightarrow HCl + \bullet CH_3$$

2 The methyl free radical is also very reactive and reacts with a chlorine molecule. This produces another chlorine free radical and a molecule of chloromethane – a stable compound.

$$\bullet CH_3 + Cl_2 \longrightarrow CH_3Cl + Cl\bullet$$

The effect of these two steps is to produce hydrogen chloride, chloromethane and a new $Cl\bullet$ free radical. This is ready to react with more methane and repeat the two steps. This is the chain part of the chain reaction. These steps may take place thousands of times before the radicals are destroyed in the termination step.

Termination

Termination is the step in which the free radicals are removed. This can happen in any of the following three ways:

$$Cl\bullet + Cl\bullet \longrightarrow Cl_2$$

Two chlorine free radicals react together to give chlorine.

$$\bullet CH_3 + \bullet CH_3 \longrightarrow C_2H_6$$

Two methyl free radicals react together to give ethane.

$$Cl\bullet + \bullet CH_3 \longrightarrow CH_3Cl$$

A chlorine free radical and a methyl free radical react together to give chloromethane.

Notice that in every case, two free radicals react to form a stable compound with no unpaired electrons.

Other products of the chain reaction

Other products are formed as well as the main ones, chloromethane and hydrogen chloride.

- Some ethane is produced at the termination stage, as shown above.
- Dichloromethane may be made at the propagation stage, if a chlorine radical reacts with some chloromethane that has already formed.

$$CH_3Cl + Cl\bullet \longrightarrow \bullet CH_2Cl + HCl$$

followed by $\bullet CH_2Cl + Cl_2 \longrightarrow CH_2Cl_2 + Cl\bullet$

- With longer-chain alkanes there will be many isomers formed because the $Cl\bullet$ can replace *any* of the hydrogen atoms.
- Chain reactions are not very useful because they produce such a mixture of products. They will also occur without light at high temperatures.

🔦 🖊 🔬 Why are chain reactions important?

We saw in Topic 14.3 that CFCs in the stratosphere are destroying the ozone layer.

Ozone is a molecule made from three oxygen atoms, O_3. It decomposes to oxygen. Too much ozone at ground level causes lung irritation and degradation of paints and plastics, but high in the atmosphere it has a vital role.

The ozone layer is important because it protects the Earth from the harmful exposure to too many ultraviolet (UV) rays. Without this protective layer, life on Earth would be very different. For example, plankton in the sea, which are at the very bottom of the food chain of the oceans, need protection from too much UV radiation. Also, too much UV radiation causes skin cancer in people by damaging DNA.

Chlorine free radicals are formed from CFCs because the C–Cl breaks homolytically in the presence of UV radiation to produce chlorine free radicals $Cl\bullet$. Ozone molecules are attacked by these chlorine free radicals, $Cl\bullet$.

$$Cl\bullet + O_3 \longrightarrow ClO\bullet + O_2$$
$$\text{free radical}$$

The resulting free radicals also attack ozone and regenerate $Cl\bullet$:

$$ClO\bullet + O_3 \longrightarrow 2O_2 + Cl\bullet$$

Adding the two equations, you can see that the chlorine free radical is not destroyed in this process. It acts as a catalyst in the breakdown of ozone to oxygen.

$$2O_3 \longrightarrow 3O_2$$

Summary questions

1 What stage of a free-radical reaction of bromine with methane is represented by the following?

a $Br\bullet + Br\bullet \longrightarrow Br_2$

b $CH_4 + Br\bullet \longrightarrow CH_3\bullet + HBr$

c $\bullet CH_3 + Br_2 \longrightarrow CH_3Br + Br\bullet$

d $Br_2 \longrightarrow 2Br\bullet$

2 Look at the equations for the destruction of ozone in the last section of this topic.

a Which two are propagation steps?

b Suggest three possible termination steps.

1 (a) State the benefit to humans of the presence of the ozone layer. *(1 mark)*

(b) Chlorofluoro compounds damage the ozone layer by chlorine radicals reacting with ozone. Copy and complete the following equations to show how this reaction proceeds.

$$Cl\bullet + O_3 \longrightarrow \underline{\quad} + \underline{\quad}$$ *(1 mark)*

$$\underline{\quad} + O_3 \longrightarrow Cl\bullet + \underline{\quad}$$ *(1 mark)*

(c) Give one use of chlorofluorocarbons. *(1 mark)*

2 The table below gives some of the names and structures of isomers having the molecular formula C_4H_9Br

Structure	Name
$CH_3CH_2CH_2CH_2Br$	
$H_3C-\overset{\displaystyle CH_3}{\underset{\displaystyle Br}{\overset{\displaystyle \mid}{\underset{\displaystyle \mid}{C}}}}-CH_3$	2-bromo-2-methylpropane
	1-bromo-2-methylpropane
$CH_3CH_2-\overset{}{\underset{\displaystyle Br}{\overset{}{\underset{\displaystyle \mid}{C}}}}-CH_3$	2-bromobutane

(a) Copy and complete the table. *(2 marks)*

(b) Name and outline a mechanism for the reaction of 2-bromo-2-methylpropane with ethanolic potassium hydroxide to form the alkene 2-methylpropene, $(CH_3)_2C{=}CH_2$ *(4 marks)*

(d) When 2-bromo-2-methylpropane reacts with aqueous potassium hydroxide, 2-methylpropan-2-ol is formed as shown by the following equation.

$$H_3C-\overset{\displaystyle CH_3}{\underset{\displaystyle Br}{\overset{\displaystyle \mid}{\underset{\displaystyle \mid}{C}}}}-CH_3 \; + \; KOH \; \longrightarrow \; H_3C-\overset{\displaystyle CH_3}{\underset{\displaystyle OH}{\overset{\displaystyle \mid}{\underset{\displaystyle \mid}{C}}}}-CH_3 \; + \; KBr$$

State the role of the hydroxide ions in this reaction. *(1 mark)*

(e) Write an equation for the reaction that occurs when $CH_3CH_2CH_2CH_2Br$ reacts with an excess of ammonia. Name the organic product of this reaction. *(3 marks)*

AQA, 2006

3 The reaction of bromine with ethane is similar to that of chlorine with ethane. Three steps in the bromination of ethane are shown below.

Step **1** $\quad\quad\quad\quad Br_2 \longrightarrow 2Br\bullet$

Step **2** $\quad\quad Br\bullet + CH_3CH_3 \longrightarrow CH_3CH_2\bullet + HBr$

Step **3** $\quad\quad CH_3CH_2\bullet + Br_2 \longrightarrow CH_3CH_2Br + Br\bullet$

(a) (i) Name this type of mechanism.

(ii) Suggest an essential condition for this reaction.

(iii) Steps **2** and **3** are of the same type. Name this type of step.

(iv) In this mechanism, another type of step occurs in which free radicals combine. Name this type of step. Write an equation to illustrate this step. *(5 marks)*

(b) Further substitution in the reaction of bromine with ethane produces a mixture of liquid organic compounds.

(i) Name a technique which could be used to separate the different compounds in this mixture.

(ii) Write an equation for the reaction between bromine and ethane which produces hexabromoethane, C_2Br_6, by this substitution reaction. *(2 marks)*

(c) The compound 1,2-dibromo-1,1,2,2-tetrafluoroethane is used in some fire extinguishers. Draw the structure of this compound. *(1 mark)*

(d) Halothane is used as an anaesthetic and has the following structure.

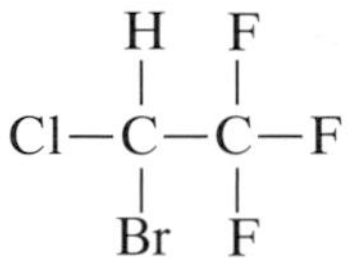

$$\begin{array}{ccc} & H & F \\ & | & | \\ Cl-&C-&C-F \\ & | & | \\ & Br & F \end{array}$$

(i) Give the systematic name of halothane.

(ii) Calculate the M_r of halothane.

(iii) Calculate the percentage by mass of fluorine in halothane. *(3 marks)*

AQA, 2006

4 (a) The equation below shows the reaction of 2-bromopropane with an excess of ammonia.

$$CH_3CHBrCH_3 + 2NH_3 \longrightarrow CH_3CH(NH_2)CH_3 + NH_4Br$$

Name and outline the mechanism involved. *(5 marks)*

(b) When 2-bromopropane is heated with ethanolic potassium hydroxide, an elimination reaction occurs. State the role of potassium hydroxide and outline a mechanism for this reaction. *(5 marks)*

AQA, 2002

5 (a) Dichloromethane, CH_2Cl_2, is one of the products formed when chloromethane, CH_3Cl, reacts with chlorine.

(i) Name the type of mechanism involved in this reaction and write an equation for each of the steps named below.

Name of type of mechanism

Initiation step

First propagation step

Second propagation step

(ii) Write an overall equation for the formation of dichloromethane from chloromethane. *(5 marks)*

(b) A compound contains 10.1% carbon and 89.9% chlorine by mass. Calculate the molecular formula of this compound, given that its relative molecular mass (M_r) is 237.0 *(3 marks)*

(c) Suggest the formulae of two bromine-containing organic compounds formed when dibromomethane, CH_2Br_2, reacts with bromine. *(2 marks)*

AQA, 2006

6 (a) Chloromethane can be made by the reaction of chlorine with methane.

(i) Give **one** essential condition for this reaction.

(ii) Name the mechanism for this reaction.

(iii) Further substitution can occur during this reaction. Identify the main organic product when a large excess of chlorine is used in this reaction. *(3 marks)*

(b) Ethanenitrile can be made by reacting chloromethane with potassium cyanide.

(i) Write an equation for this reaction.

(ii) Name the mechanism for this reaction.

(iii) Explain, in terms of bond enthalpies, why bromomethane reacts faster than chloromethane with potassium cyanide. *(3 marks)*

AQA, 2004

15 Alkenes

15.1 Alkenes

Learning objectives

- What are alkenes?

- What kind of isomerism do alkenes display?

- Why are they reactive?

Specification reference 3.2.9

Alkenes are **unsaturated** hydrocarbons. They are made of carbon and hydrogen only and have one or more carbon–carbon double bonds. This means that alkenes have fewer than the maximum possible number of hydrogen atoms. The double bond makes them more reactive than alkanes. Ethene, the simplest alkene, is the starting material for a large range of products, including polymers such as polythene, PVC, polystyrene and terylene fabric, as well as products like antifreeze and paints. Alkenes are produced in large quantities when crude oil is thermally cracked.

The general formula

The homologous series of alkenes with one double bond has the general formula C_nH_{2n}.

How to name alkenes

We cannot have a carbon–carbon double bond if there is only one carbon. So, the simplest alkene is ethene, $CH_2 = CH_2$ followed by propene, $CH_3CH = CH_2$.

💡 Structure

The shape of alkenes

Ethene is a planar (flat) molecule. This makes the angles between each bond roughly 120°.

Unlike the C—C bonds in alkanes, there is no rotation about the double bond. This is because of the make up of a double bond. Any molecules in which a hydrogen atom in ethene is replaced with another atom or group will have the same flat shape around the carbon–carbon double bond.

Applications and How science works

Why a double bond cannot rotate

As well as a normal C—C single bond, there is a p-orbital (that contains a single electron) on each carbon. These two orbitals overlap to form one single orbital with a cloud of electron density above and below the single bond, see Figure 1 and Figure 2. This is called a π orbital (pronounced pi) and its presence means the bond cannot rotate. This is sometimes called restricted rotation.

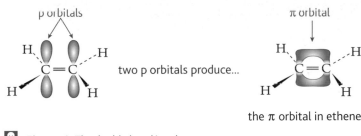

Figure 1 *The double bond in ethene*

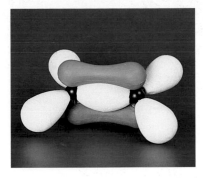

Figure 2 *Model of ethene showing orbitals*

Isomers

Alkenes with more than three carbons can form different types of isomers and we name them according to the IUPAC system, see Topic 5.2, using the suffix -ene to indicate a double bond.

As well as chain isomers like those found in alkanes, alkenes can form two types of isomers that involve the double bond:

■ Position isomers
■ Geometrical isomers

Position isomers

These are isomers with the double bond in different positions, i.e. between a pair of adjacent carbon atoms in different positions in the carbon chain.

but-2-ene   but-1-ene

The longer the carbon chain, the more possibilities there will be and therefore the greater the number of isomers.

Geometrical isomers

Geometrical isomerism is a form of stereoisomerism. The two stereoisomers have the same structural formula but the bonds are arranged differently in space. It occurs only around C=C double bonds. For example, but-2-ene, above, can exist as shown below.

Z-but-2-ene   E-but-2-ene

The isomer in which both –CH$_3$ groups are on the same side of the double bond is called Z-but-2-ene and the one in which they are on opposite sides is called E-but-2-ene. This type of isomerism is often called E-Z isomerism.

Applications and How science works

Nomenclature

The number of known organic compounds is huge, and increasing all the time. Finding information about these in databases, books and journals would be almost impossible if chemists did not agree on how they should be named. That is why the Interntional Union of Pure and Applied Chemistry (IUPAC) lays down the rules for nomenclature. The *E-Z* notation is one example.

E-Z isomerism, until fairly recently, used to be known as *cis-trans* isomerism, and the prefixes *cis-* and *trans-* were used instead of *Z-* and *E-*, respectively. So, for example, *Z*-but-2-ene was named *cis*-but-2-ene and *E*-but-2-ene was *trans*-but-2-ene. This notation is still often found in older books. However, a disadvantage of the older notation was that it did not work when there were more than two *different* substituents around a double bond. For example:

To give these two isomers different and unambiguous names we use the *E-Z* notation.

Simply, the *E-Z* notation is based on atomic numbers. We look at the atoms attached to each of the carbon atoms in the double bond. When the two atoms (of each pair) of higher atomic number are on the same side of the C=C, the isomer is described as *Z*, from the German word for together, *zusammen*.

So this is *Z*-1-bromo-2-chloro-1-fluoroethene.

The other isomer has the positions of the H and Cl atoms reversed.

So this is *E*-1-bromo-2-chloro-1-fluoroethene. See how this fits the IUPAC naming system.

The simplest interpretation of this naming system is that if the two atoms with the greatest atomic number are on the *same* side of the double bond it is *Z*. If not, it is *E*, from the German word for opposite, *entgegen*. However, the *cis-trans* notation is still commonly used when there is no possibility of confusion.

Physical properties of alkenes

The double bond does not really affect properties such as boiling and melting points. van der Waals forces are the only intermolecular forces that act between the alkene molecules. This means that the physical properties of alkenes are very similar to those of the alkanes. The melting and boiling points increase with the number of carbon atoms present. Alkenes are not soluble in water because they are non-polar.

How alkenes react

The double bond makes a big difference to the reactivity of alkenes as compared with alkanes. The bond enthalpy for $C-C$ is $347\,kJ\,mol^{-1}$ and that for $C=C$ is $612\,kJ\,mol^{-1}$ so we might predict that alkenes would be less reactive than alkanes. In fact alkenes are *more* reactive than alkanes.

The $C=C$ forms an electron-rich area in the molecule, which can easily be attacked by positively charged reagents. These reagents are called **electrophiles** (electron liking). They are electron pair acceptors. An example of a good electrophile is the H^+ ion. As alkenes are unsaturated they can undergo addition reactions.

In conclusion, most of the reactions of alkenes are **electrophilic additions**.

AQA Examiner's tip

Learn the definition: an electrophile is an electron pair acceptor.

Summary questions

1 What is the name of $CH_3CH=CHCH_2CH_2CH_3$?

2 Draw the structural formula for hex-1-ene.

3 There are six isomeric pentenes. Draw their displayed formulae.

4 Which of these attacks the double bond in an alkene? Choose from a, b, c and d.

   a Electrophiles

   b Nucleophiles

   c Alkanes

5 The double bond in an alkene can best be described by which of the following? Choose from a, b, c and d.

   a Electron-rich

   b Electron-deficient

   c Positively charged

   d Acidic

15.2 Reactions of alkenes

Learning objectives

■ What are electrophilic addition reactions?

■ What is the mechanism for these?

Specification reference 3.2.9

■ Combustion

Alkenes will burn in air:

$$\underset{\text{ethene}}{\overset{\displaystyle H\diagdown \quad \diagup H}{\underset{\displaystyle H\diagup \quad \diagdown H}{C=C}}} \text{(g)} + 3O_2\text{(g)} \longrightarrow \underset{\text{carbon dioxide}}{2CO_2\text{(g)}} + \underset{\text{water}}{2H_2O\text{(l)}}$$

oxygen

However, they are not used as fuels. This is because their reactivity makes them very useful for other purposes.

⚠ Electrophilic addition reactions

The reactions of alkenes are typically electrophilic additions, see Topic 15.1. The four electrons in the carbon–carbon double bond make it a centre of high electron density. Electrophiles are attracted to it and can form a bond by using two of the four electrons in the $C=C$ double bond (of the four electrons, the two that are in a π-bond, see Topic 15.1).

The mechanism is always essentially the same:

■ The electrophile is attracted to the double bond.

■ Electrophiles are positively charged and accept a pair of electrons from the double bond. The electrophile may be a positively charged ion or have a positively charged area.

■ A positive ion (a **carbocation**) is formed.

■ A negatively charged ion forms a bond with the carbocation.

See how the examples below fit this general mechanism.

Reaction with hydrogen halides

Hydrogen halides, HCl, HBr and HI, add across the double bond to form a haloalkane. For example:

$$\underset{\text{ethene}}{\overset{\displaystyle H\diagdown \quad \diagup H}{\underset{\displaystyle H\diagup \quad \diagdown H}{C=C}}} + \underset{\substack{\text{hydrogen}\\ \text{bromide}}}{HBr} \longrightarrow \underset{\text{bromoethane}}{H-\overset{\displaystyle H}{\underset{\displaystyle H}{C}}-\overset{\displaystyle H}{\underset{\displaystyle H}{C}}-Br}$$

■ Bromine is more electronegative than hydrogen, so the hydrogen bromide molecule is polar, $H^{\delta+}-Br^{\delta-}$.

■ The electrophile is the $H^{\delta+}$ of the $H^{\delta+}-Br^{\delta-}$.

■ The $H^{\delta+}$ of HBr is attracted to the $C=C$ double bond because of the double bond's high electron density.

■ One of the pairs of electrons from the $C=C$ forms a bond with the $H^{\delta+}$ to form a positive ion (called a carbocation), while at the same time the electrons in the $H^{\delta+}-Br^{\delta-}$ bond are drawn towards the $Br^{\delta-}$.

- The bond in hydrogen bromide breaks heterolytically. Both electrons from the shared pair in the bond goes to the Br atom because it is more electronegative than H, to leave a Br⁻ ion.
- The Br⁻ ion attaches to the positively charged carbon of the carbocation forming a bond with one of its electron pairs.

Asymmetrical alkenes

When hydrogen bromide adds to ethene, bromoethane is the only possible product.

However, when the double bond is not in the exact middle of the chain, there are two possible products: the bromine of the hydrogen bromide could bond to either of the carbon atoms of the double bond.

For example, propene could produce:

2-bromopropane

propene + HBr

1-bromopropane

In fact the product is almost entirely 2-bromopropane.

To explain this, we need to know that alkyl groups, for example CH_3— or C_2H_5—, have a tendency to release electrons. This is known as a **positive inductive effect** and is sometimes represented by an arrow along their bonds to show the direction of the release.

This electron-releasing effect tends to stabilise the positive charge of the intermediate carbocation. The more alkyl groups there are attached to the positively-charged carbon atom, the more stable is the carbocation. So, a positively-charged carbon atom which has three alkyl groups (called a tertiary carbocation) is more stable than one with two alkyl groups (a secondary carbocation) which is more stable than one with just one (a primary carbocation), see Figure 1.

The product will tend to come from the more stable carbocation.

Hint
There is simple way to work out the product. When hydrogen halides add on to alkenes, the hydrogen adds on to the carbon atom which already has the most hydrogens.

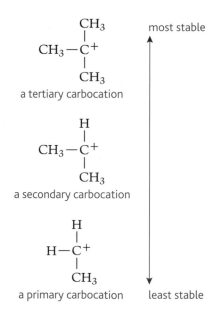

Figure 1 *Stability of primary, secondary and tertiary carbocations*

So, the two possible carbocations when propene reacts with HBr are:

$$\underset{\substack{\text{a secondary carbocation}\\ \text{(more stable, product}\\ \text{formed from this)}}}{\text{H}-\overset{\displaystyle\overset{\text{H}}{|}}{\text{C}}-\overset{\displaystyle\overset{\text{CH}_3}{|}}{\underset{+}{\text{C}}}-\text{H}} \qquad \underset{\substack{\text{a primary carbocation}\\ \text{(less stable)}}}{\text{H}-\overset{\displaystyle\overset{\text{H}}{|}}{\underset{+}{\text{C}}}\leftarrow\overset{\displaystyle\overset{\text{CH}_3}{|}}{\underset{\displaystyle\underset{\text{H}}{|}}{\text{C}}}-\text{H}}$$

$$\downarrow \text{Br}^-$$

$$\underset{\text{2-bromopropane}}{\text{H}-\overset{\displaystyle\overset{\text{H}}{|}}{\underset{\displaystyle\underset{\text{H}}{|}}{\text{C}}}-\overset{\displaystyle\overset{\text{CH}_3}{|}}{\underset{\displaystyle\underset{\text{Br}}{|}}{\text{C}}}-\text{H}}$$

The secondary carbocation is more stable because it has two methyl groups releasing electrons towards the positive carbon. The majority of the product is formed from this.

Reaction of alkenes with halogens

Alkenes react rapidly with chlorine gas, or with solutions of bromine and iodine in an organic solvent, to give dihaloalkanes.

$$\underset{\text{H}}{\overset{\text{H}}{\diagdown}}\text{C}=\text{C}\underset{\text{H}}{\overset{\text{H}}{\diagup}} \;+\; X_2 \longrightarrow \text{H}-\overset{\displaystyle\overset{X}{|}}{\underset{\displaystyle\underset{\text{H}}{|}}{\text{C}}}-\overset{\displaystyle\overset{X}{|}}{\underset{\displaystyle\underset{\text{H}}{|}}{\text{C}}}-\text{H}$$

The halogen atoms *add* across the double bond.

In this case the halogen molecules act as electrophiles:

■ At any instant, a bromine (or any other halogen) molecule is likely to have an instantaneous dipole: $Br^{\delta+}$—$Br^{\delta-}$. (An instant later, the dipole could be reversed $Br^{\delta-}$—$Br^{\delta+}$.) The $\delta+$ end of this dipole is attracted to the electron-rich double bond in the alkene; the bromine molecule has become an electrophile.

■ The electrons in the double bond are attracted to the $Br^{\delta+}$. They repel the electrons in the Br—Br bond and this strengthens the dipole of the bromine molecule.

$$\underset{\text{H}}{\overset{\text{H}}{\diagdown}}\text{C}=\text{C}\underset{\text{H}}{\overset{\text{H}}{\diagup}}$$
$$\text{Br}^{\delta+}$$
$$\text{Br}^{\delta-}$$

■ Two of the electrons from the double bond form a bond with the $Br^{\delta+}$ and the other bromine atom becomes a Br$^-$ ion. This leaves a carbocation, in which the carbon atom that is *not* bonded to the bromine has the positive charge.

■ The Br$^-$ ion now forms a bond with the carbocation.

$$\text{H}-\overset{\displaystyle\overset{\text{H}}{|}}{\underset{\displaystyle\underset{\text{Br}}{|}}{\text{C}}}-\overset{+}{\text{C}}\underset{\text{H}}{\overset{\text{H}}{\diagup}} \;+\; \text{Br}^- \longrightarrow \text{H}-\overset{\displaystyle\overset{\text{H}}{|}}{\underset{\displaystyle\underset{\text{Br}}{|}}{\text{C}}}-\overset{\displaystyle\overset{\text{H}}{|}}{\underset{\displaystyle\underset{\text{Br}}{|}}{\text{C}}}-\text{H}$$

■ **Hint**

This dipole is also induced when a bromine molecule collides with the electron-rich double bond.

■ **Hint**

The carbocation will react with any nucleophile ion that is present. In aqueous solution, such as bromine water, water reacts with the carbocation, forming some CH_2BrCH_2OH, 2-bromoethanol.

So the addition takes place in two steps:

1 Formation of the carbocation by electrophilic addition
2 Rapid reaction with a negative ion

The test for a double bond

This addition reaction is used to test for a carbon–carbon double bond. When a few drops of bromine solution, sometimes called bromine water (which is reddish-brown) are added to an alkene, the solution is decolourised because the products are colourless.

Reaction with concentrated sulfuric acid

Concentrated sulfuric acid also adds across the double bond. The reaction occurs at room temperature and is exothermic.

ethene → ethyl hydrogensulfate

The electrophile is a partially positively charged hydrogen atom in the sulfuric acid molecule. This can be shown as $H^{\delta+}$—$O^{\delta-}$—SO_3H

The carbocation which forms then reacts rapidly with the negatively charged hydrogensulfate ion.

When water is added to the product an alcohol is formed and sulfuric acid reforms.

ethyl hydrogensulfate · ethanol

The overall affect is to add water H—OH across the double bond and the sulfuric acid is a catalyst for the process.

Asymmetrical alkenes

With an asymmetrical alkene, such as propene, the carbocation is exactly the same as that found in the reaction with hydrogen bromide. This means that we can predict the products by looking at the relative stability of the possible carbocations that could form.

Reaction with water

Water also adds on across the double bond in alkenes. The reaction is used industrially to make alcohols and is carried out with steam, at a suitable temperature and pressure, using an acid catalyst such as phosphoric acid, H_3PO_4. This is discussed in Topic 9.3.

Summary questions

1 Write the equation for the complete combustion of propene.

2 Which of the following are typical reactions of alkenes?
   a Electrophilic additions
   b Electrophilic substitutions
   c Nucleophilic substitutions

3 a What are the two possible products of the reaction between propene and hydrogen bromide?
   b Which is the main product?
   c Explain why this product is the more likely.

4 What is the product of the reaction between ethene and hydrogen chloride?

5 Which of the following is the test for a carbon–carbon double bond?
   a Forms a white precipitate with silver nitrate
   b Turns limewater milky
   c Decolourises bromine solution

15.3 Polymerisation of alkenes

Learning objectives

- What type of polymer is formed from alkenes?

- What is the repeating unit of a polymer?

- What are the environmental problems associated with poly(alkenes)?

- How are these problems being tackled?

Specification reference 3.2.9

Polymers are long chain molecules made up from joining together small molecules, called **monomers** which are linked together.

Addition polymerisation

Alkenes can polymerise, joining together to form long chains with very high relative molecular masses (as much as 1 000 000).

For example, ethene, C_2H_4, polymerises to form poly(ethene):

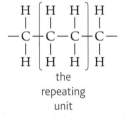

ethene

poly(ethene)

Ethene is the monomer.

This reaction is **addition polymerisation**. The polymer is named poly(ethene) from the monomer but is usually called polythene. Despite the ending -ene the polymer is actually an alkane and is therefore unreactive. The chains may be straight or have some degree of branching.

The repeating unit

The repeating unit of a polymer is the smallest group of atoms that produce the polymer when repeated over and over, see Figure 1. In polythene the repeating unit is CH_2CH_2 (shown in brackets).

Different forms of poly(ethene) can be made depending on the conditions of temperature, pressure and catalyst. These differ in chain length and also in the amount of branching.

the repeating unit

Figure 1 *The repeating unit of polythene*

Figure 2 *Bottles made from HD and LD polythene*

How science works

High and low density polythene

Low density poly(ethene) (polythene) is made by polymerising ethene at high pressure and high temperature via a free-radical mechanism. This produces a polymer with a certain amount of chain branching. This is a consequence of the rather random nature of free-radical reactions. The branched chains do not pack together particularly well and the product is quite flexible, stretches well and has a fairly low density. These properties make it suitable for packaging (plastic bags), sheeting and insulation for electrical cables.

High density polythene is made at temperatures and pressures little greater than room conditions and uses a Ziegler–Natta catalyst, named after its developers. This results in a polymer with much less chain branching (around one branch for every 200 carbons on the main chain). The chains can pack together well. This makes the density of the plastic greater and its melting temperature higher. Typical uses are milk crates, buckets and bottles for which low density polythene would be insufficiently rigid.

Another similar polymer is poly(propene). This is formed from the monomer propene, $CH_3CH=CH_2$:

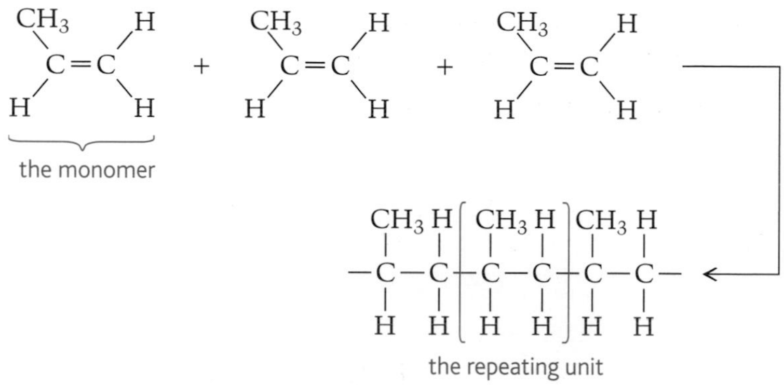

the monomer

the repeating unit

poly(propene)

💡 The repeating unit is shown in brackets.

Table 1 gives a summary of some polymers using monomers based on the ethene molecule in which one of the hydrogen atoms has been replaced by another group. The repeating unit is bracketed.

💡 **Table 1** *Some polymers in everyday use. The repeating units for the polymers are shown in brackets.*

Monomer	Polymer	Systemic chemical name	Common name or trade name (in capitals)	Typical uses
$CH_2=CH_2$	$+CH_2-CH_2+_n$	poly(ethene)	polythene or polyethylene ALKATHENE	washing-up bowls, plastic bags
CH_3 | $CH=CH_2$	$+CH-CH_2+_n$ | CH_3	poly(propene)	polypropylene	rope
Cl | $CH=CH_2$	$+CH-CH_2+_n$ | Cl	poly(chlorethene)	polyvinylchloride PVC	vinyl records
CN | $CH=CH_2$	$+CH-CH_2+_n$ | CN	poly(propenenitrile)	polyacrylonitrile acrylic fibre COURTELLE	clothing
$CF_2=CF_2$	$+CF_2-CF_2+_n$	poly(1,1,2,2-tetrafluoroethene)	TEFLON	coating cookware

How science works

Plastics, where would we be without them?

Plastics are very beneficial to us in many ways, e.g. Teflon sprays on house base boards prevent insects entering the house because they slip off. This removes the need to use insecticides.

Hint

One could argue that the repeating unit in poly(ethene) is just —CH_2— rather than —CH_2—CH_2— but it is usual to quote the repeating unit based on the monomer.

■ Problems with plastics

Plastics are very versatile materials and their many applications have become essential in today's world. However, their use is not without problems.

Most plastics are not broken down by microbes quickly, and many not at all. They are not **biodegradable**. This is a problem that has become more obvious with time as more and more plastic litter has been produced. Buried plastics in landfill sites may take hundreds of years to decompose.

Plastic litter is also a problem for animals that ingest it because it blocks their intestinal tracts.

Figure 4 *Plastic litter gets washed up on beaches*

■ The solutions

We need to reduce the amount of plastic we use or to recycle it.

Mechanical recycling

The simplest form of recycling is called mechanical recycling. The first step is to separate the different types of plastics. (Plastic containers are now collected in recycling facilities for this purpose.) The plastics are then washed and once they are sorted they may be ground up into small pellets. These can be melted and remoulded. For example, recycled soft drinks bottles made from PET (polyethylene terephthalate) are used to make fleece clothes.

Feedstock recycling

Here, the plastics are heated to a temperature that will break the polymer bonds and produce monomers. These can then be used to make new plastics.

There are problems with recycling. Poly(propene), for example, is a thermoplastic polymer. This means that it will soften when heated so it can be melted and re-used. However, this can only be done a limited number of times because at each heating some of the chains break and become shorter thus degrading the plastic's properties.

Summary questions

1 Poly(ethene) is which of the following?

a An alcohol

b An alkane

c An alkene

2 A sample of poly(ethene) has an average relative molecular mass of 28 000. How many monomers are linked together to form the chain?

3 Identify **a** the monomer and **b** the repeating unit in each of the following:

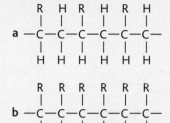

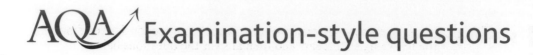

1   The table below gives the names and structures of three isomeric alkenes.

Name	Structure
but-1-ene	$CH_3CH_2CH{=}CH_2$
but-2-ene	$CH_3CH{=}CHCH_3$
methylpropene	CH_3 $\mid$ $H_3C{-}C{=}CH_2$

(a) Give the molecular formula and the empirical formula of but-2-ene.   *(2 marks)*

(b) Methylpropene reacts with hydrogen bromide to produce 2-bromo-2-methylpropane as the major product.

  (i) Name and outline the mechanism for this reaction.

  (ii) Draw the structure of another product of this reaction and explain why it is formed in smaller amounts.   *(8 marks)*

(c) Draw the structures and give the names of the two stereoisomers of but-2-ene.   *(2 marks)*

AQA, 2004

2   (a) Copy and complete the mechanism below by drawing appropriate curly arrows.

$H\bar{O}{:}$

$$
\begin{array}{c}
\quad\ \ H\ \ H\ \ H \\
\quad\ \ \mid\ \ \ \mid\ \ \ \mid \\
H_3C{-}C{-}C{-}C{-}CH_3 \qquad\qquad CH_3CH_2CH{=}CHCH_3\ \ +\ \ H_2O\ \ +\ \ Br^- \\
\quad\ \ \mid\ \ \ \mid\ \ \ \mid \\
\quad\ \ H\ \ H\ \ Br
\end{array}
$$

   2-bromopentane   pent-2-ene   *(3 marks)*

(b) Pent-1-ene reacts with hydrogen bromide to produce 2-bromopentane as the major product.

  (i) Outline the mechanism for this reaction.

  (ii) Explain why 2-bromopentane is the major product of this reaction.   *(6 marks)*

AQA, 2005

3   (a) Propene reacts with hydrogen bromide by an electrophilic addition mechanism forming 2-bromopropane as the major product.

   The equation for this reaction is shown below.

$$
\begin{array}{ccc}
H_3C\diagdown & H & \qquad\qquad\qquad\qquad Br\ \ H \\
\qquad C{=}C & \qquad +\ \ HBr\ \longrightarrow & \qquad\ \ \mid\ \ \ \mid \\
H\diagup & \diagdown H & \qquad\qquad\ \ H_3C{-}C{-}C{-}H \\
& & \qquad\qquad\qquad\quad \mid\ \ \ \mid \\
& & \qquad\qquad\qquad\quad H\ \ H
\end{array}
$$

  (i) Outline the mechanism for this reaction, showing the structure of the intermediate carbocation formed.

  (ii) Give the structure of the alternative carbocation which could be formed in the reaction between propene and hydrogen bromide.   *(5 marks)*

AQA, 2003

4 This question concerns the chemistry of ethene and compounds derived from it.
Consider the following statements and then answer the questions below.

- Ethene may be polymerised to form poly(ethene).
- Treatment of ethene with bromine gives a compound **C**.

(a) (i) Explain what is meant by the term *polymerisation*. *(2 marks)*

(ii) Write an equation to represent the polymerisation of ethene. *(1 mark)*

(b) Give the name of compound **C**. *(1 mark)*

(c) Give the name of the mechanism of the reaction between ethene and bromine.
Draw the mechanism for this reaction. *(4 marks)*

AQA, 2001

5 The reaction scheme below shows the conversion of compound **A**, 2-methylbut-1-ene, into compound **B** and then into compound **C**.

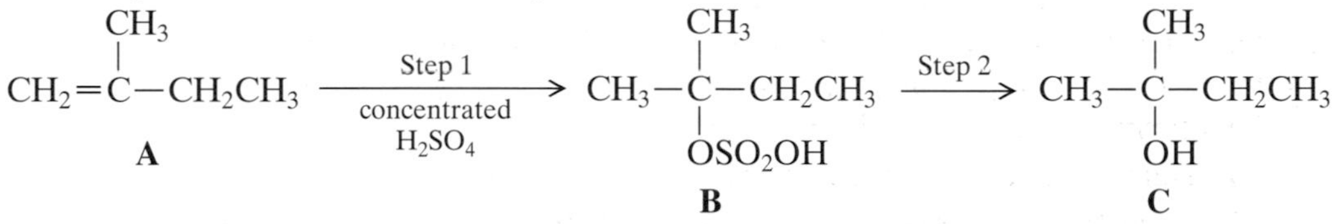

$$CH_2{=}\underset{\underset{\textbf{A}}{}}{\overset{\overset{CH_3}{|}}{C}}{-}CH_2CH_3 \xrightarrow[\text{concentrated } H_2SO_4]{\text{Step 1}} CH_3{-}\underset{\underset{\textbf{B}}{OSO_2OH}}{\overset{\overset{CH_3}{|}}{C}}{-}CH_2CH_3 \xrightarrow{\text{Step 2}} CH_3{-}\underset{\underset{\textbf{C}}{OH}}{\overset{\overset{CH_3}{|}}{C}}{-}CH_2CH_3$$

(a) The structure of **A** is shown below. Circle those carbon atoms which must lie in the same plane. *(1 mark)*

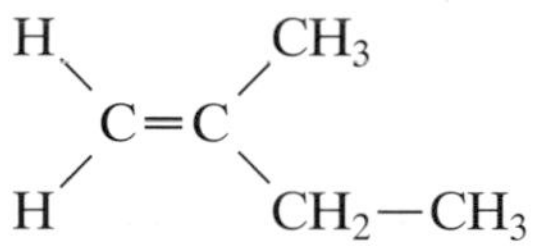

$$\underset{H}{\overset{H}{\diagdown}}C{=}C\underset{CH_2{-}CH_3}{\overset{CH_3}{\diagup}}$$

(b) Outline a mechanism for the reaction in Step 1. *(4 marks)*

(c) State the reagent used in Step 2. *(1 mark)*

AQA, 2002

6 Propene reacts with bromine by a mechanism known as electrophilic addition.

(a) Explain what is meant by the term *electrophile* and by the term *addition*. *(2 marks)*

(b) Outline the mechanism for the electrophilic addition of bromine to propene. Give the name of the product formed. *(5 marks)*

(c) The polymerisation of propene to form poly(propene) is an important industrial process.
Name the type of polymerisation involved. *(1 mark)*

AQA, 2002

7 (a) (i) Name the alkene $CH_3CH_2CH{=}CH_2$

(ii) Explain why $CH_3CH_2CH{=}CH_2$ does not show stereoisomerism.

(iii) Draw an isomer of $CH_3CH_2CH{=}CH_2$ which does show *E–Z* isomerism.

(iv) Draw another isomer of $CH_3CH_2CH{=}CH_2$ which does not show *E–Z* isomerism. *(4 marks)*

(b) (i) Name the type of mechanism for the reaction shown by alkenes with concentrated sulfuric acid.

(ii) Write a mechanism showing the formation of the major product in the reaction of concentrated sulfuric acid with $CH_3CH_2CH{=}CH_2$.

(iii) Explain why this compound is the major product. *(6 marks)*

16 Alcohols

16.1 Alcohols – introduction

Figure 1 *Some alcoholic drinks and their percentage alcohol content*

Ethanol is possibly our oldest social drug as it is derived from the fermentation of sugars in fruits etc. It is the alcohol in alcoholic drinks. It may, in moderation, promote a feeling of well-being and reduce normal inhibitions. It is in fact a nervous system depressant (i.e. it interferes with the transmission of nerve impulses). In larger amounts it leads to loss of balance, poor hand–eye co-ordination, impaired vision and inability to judge speed. Large amounts can be fatal. Excessive long-term use can lead to addiction – alcoholism.

The ethanol in alcoholic drinks is absorbed through the walls of the stomach and small intestine into the bloodstream. Some is eliminated unchanged in urine and in the breath. The rest is broken down by the liver. The combined effect of these processes is that an average person can eliminate about $10\,cm^3$ of ethanol per hour. This is approximately the amount of ethanol in half a pint of beer, a small glass of wine (125 ml) or a 'short' (25 ml of spirits). So some simple arithmetic should enable you to work out how long it would take to sober up.

The general formula

Alcohols have the functional group —OH attached to a hydrocarbon chain. They are relatively reactive. The alcohol most commonly encountered in everyday life is ethanol.

The general formula of an alcohol is $C_nH_{2n+1}OH$. This is often shortened to ROH.

How to name alcohols

The name of the functional group (the —OH group) is normally given by the suffix '-ol'. (The prefix hydroxy- is used if some other functional groups are present.)

$$
\begin{array}{c}
\quad\ \ H\ \ \ H\ \ \ H\ \ \ H \\
\quad\ \ |\ \ \ \ |\ \ \ \ |\ \ \ \ | \\
H-C-C-C-C-O-H \qquad \text{is butanol} \\
\quad\ \ |\ \ \ \ |\ \ \ \ |\ \ \ \ | \\
\quad\ \ H\ \ \ H\ \ \ H\ \ \ H
\end{array}
$$

With chains longer than ethanol, we need a number to show where the —OH group is.

$$
\begin{array}{c}
H\ \ \ H\ \ \ H \\
|\ \ \ \ |\ \ \ \ | \\
H-C-C-C-O-H \qquad \text{is propan-1-ol, and}
\\
|\ \ \ \ |\ \ \ \ | \\
H\ \ \ H\ \ \ H
\end{array}
\qquad
\begin{array}{c}
\qquad\quad H \\
\qquad\quad | \\
H\ \ \ O\ \ \ H \\
|\ \ \ \ |\ \ \ \ | \\
H-C-C-C-H \qquad \text{is propan-2-ol} \\
|\ \ \ \ |\ \ \ \ | \\
H\ \ \ H\ \ \ H
\end{array}
$$

If there is more than one —OH group we use di-, tri-, tetra-, etc. to say *how many* —OH groups there are and numbers to say *where* they are.

So $HO-\overset{\displaystyle H}{\underset{\displaystyle H}{\overset{|}{\underset{|}{C}}}}-\overset{\displaystyle H}{\underset{\displaystyle H}{\overset{|}{\underset{|}{C}}}}-\overset{\displaystyle H}{\underset{\displaystyle H}{\overset{|}{\underset{|}{C}}}}-\overset{\displaystyle H}{\underset{\displaystyle H}{\overset{|}{\underset{|}{C}}}}-OH$ is butane-1,4-diol

and $\begin{array}{l}CH_2OH \\ | \\ CHOH \\ | \\ CH_2OH\end{array}$ is propane-1,2,3-triol

This is also known as glycerol, which may be obtained from the fats and oils found in living organisms.

Shape

In alcohols, the oxygen atom has two bonding pairs of electrons and two lone pairs. The C—O—H angle is about 105° because the 109.5° angle of a perfect tetrahedron is 'squeezed down' by the presence of the lone pairs. These two lone pairs will repel each other more than the pairs of electrons in a covalent bond, see Topic 3.9.

■ Classification of alcohols

Alcohols are classified as **primary** (1°), **secondary** (2°) or **tertiary** (3°) according to how many other groups (R) are bonded to the carbon that has the —OH group.

Primary alcohols

In a primary alcohol, this carbon has one R group (and therefore two hydrogen atoms).

propan-1-ol is a primary alcohol

methanol, where the carbon has no R groups is counted as a primary alcohol

A primary alcohol has the —OH group at the end of a chain.

Secondary alcohols

In a secondary alcohol, the —OH group is attached to a carbon with two R groups (and therefore one hydrogen atom).

propan-2-ol is a secondary alcohol

A secondary alcohol has the —OH group in the body of the chain.

Tertiary alcohols

Tertiary alcohols have three R groups attached to the carbon that is bonded to the —OH (so this carbon has no hydrogen atoms).

2-methylpropan-2-ol is a tertiary alcohol

A tertiary alcohol has the —OH group at a branch in the chain.

■ Physical properties

The —OH group in alcohols means that hydrogen bonding occurs between the molecules. This is the reason that alcohols have higher melting and boiling points than alkanes of similar relative molecular mass.

Hydrogen bonding also makes the shorter chain alcohols soluble in water because hydrogen bonds can form between the —OH groups and water molecules.

■ Summary questions

1. Draw the displayed formula and name the alcohol $C_2H_5CHOHCH_3$.

2. Sort these alcohols into primary, secondary and tertiary:

   butan-2-ol

   2-methylpentan-2-ol

   methanol

3. Why is the C—O—H angle in alcohols less than 109.5°?

16.2 Ethanol production

Industrial chemistry of alcohols

Alcohols are very important in industrial chemistry because they are used as intermediates. They are easily made and easily converted into other compounds. Methanol is made from methane (natural gas) and is increasingly being used as a starting material for making other organic chemicals.

Ethanol

Ethanol, C_2H_5OH, is by far the most important alcohol. It is used as an intermediate in the manufacture of other organic chemicals. In everyday life it is often the solvent in cosmetics, such as aftershave and perfumes. It is also used in the manufacture of drugs, detergents, inks and coatings.

It is made industrially by reacting ethene (made from the cracking of crude oil) with steam, using a catalyst of phosphoric acid. It is also made from sugars by fermentation, as in the production of alcoholic drinks.

Beers have about 5% ethanol and wines about 12%. Spirits, such as gin and whisky, contain about 40% ethanol; these have been concentrated by distillation.

Making ethanol from crude oil

Ethene is produced when crude oil fractions are cracked, see Topic 6.3. The main source is from ethane (from natural gas) but some comes from the naphtha fraction.

Ethene is hydrated, which means that water is added across the double bond.

$$CH_2 \!=\! CH_2 + H_2O \xrightarrow[\text{catalyst}]{\text{phosphoric acid}} C_2H_5OH$$

This reaction is covered in detail in Topic 9.3.

Making ethanol by fermentation

During fermentation, carbohydrates from plants are broken down into sugars, and then converted into ethanol by the action of enzymes from yeast. The carbohydrates come from crops such as sugar cane and sugar beet.

The key step is the break down of sugar in a process called **anaerobic respiration**:

enzymes from yeast

$$C_6H_{12}O_6(aq) \longrightarrow 2C_2H_5OH(aq) + 2CO_2(g)$$

glucose (a sugar)   ethanol   carbon dioxide

- The rate of this chemical reaction is affected by temperature. It is slow at low temperatures but the enzymes are made ineffective if the temperature is too high. A compromise temperature of about 35 °C, a little below our body temperature, is used.

- Air is kept out of the fermentation vessels to prevent oxidation of ethanol to ethanoic acid (the acid in vinegar).

- Once the fermenting solution contains about 15% ethanol the enzymes are unable to function and fermentation stops.

Table 1 *Different methods of producing ethanol*

	Starting material	
	Crude oil non-renewable	Carbohydrates (sugars) renewable
Method	cracking and dehydration	fermentation and distillation
Rate of reaction	fast	slow
Type of process	continuous	batch
Purity	essentially pure	aqueous solution of ethanol is produced

Ethanol is useful as a motor fuel; it is mixed in with petrol. Ethanol made by fermentation is produced from renewable crops so it is an example of a biofuel, see Topic 9.3. When this ethanol is burned as a fuel, exactly the same amount of carbon dioxide is returned to the atmosphere as was originally locked up in the crop. So in this sense the ethanol is carbon neutral. Of course, there are other carbon 'costs' in its production and distribution (as there are with other fuels). However, the essential point is that ethanol made by fermentation is a renewable source, whereas ethanol made from ethene produced from crude oil is not. The table compares the two methods.

Carbon neutrality

Many conventional petrol engines will run on ethanol, or mixtures of petrol and ethanol, with little modification, and much of the petrol sold in the UK at present has 5–10% ethanol added.

Ethanol made from ethene is not a renewable fuel because it comes originally from crude oil. However, ethanol made by fermentation *is* renewable because the sugars come from plants such as sugar cane and beet, which can be grown annually.

Current fuels are almost all carbon-based. One concern is that they release carbon dioxide into the atmosphere. Rising carbon dioxide levels are associated with global warming and climate change. Ethanol made by fermentation is sometimes termed a **carbon-neutral** fuel. This means that the carbon dioxide released when it is burnt is balanced by the carbon dioxide absorbed by the plant from which it was originally obtained, during photosynthesis. This can be seen from Table 2. This argument concentrates on the chemistry of fuel production and use. There are inevitably other carbon costs associated with the energy needed to transport crops and the fuel, and to process the crops.

Table 2 *The carbon dioxide balance sheet for ethanol made by fermentation*

Carbon dioxide absorbed	Carbon dioxide released
Photosynthesis in the growing plant $6H_2O(l) + 6CO_2(g)$ $\downarrow$ $C_6H_{12}O_6(aq) + 6O_2(g)$ 6 molecules of CO_2 absorbed	Fermentation $C_6H_{12}O_6(aq) \longrightarrow 2C_2H_5OH(aq) + 2CO_2(g)$ 2 molecules of CO_2 released
	Combustion $2C_2H_5OH(aq) + 6O_2(g) \longrightarrow 4CO_2(g) + 6H_2O(l)$ 4 molecules of CO_2 released
6 molecules of CO_2 absorbed	**6 molecules of CO_2 released**

A renewable source of ethene

Ethene is a vital industrial chemical; it is the starting material for poly(ethene) and many other important chemicals. We could produce ethene by dehydrating ethanol made from sugar and this would give us a renewable source of ethene.

At present ethene is made from crude oil and then converted into ethanol. In the future it may become more economical to make ethene from ethanol made by fermentation, see Figure 1.

Hint

A **biofuel** is a fuel derived or produced from renewable biological sources.

How science works

Bioethanol

Find out online whether bioethanol is the fuel of the future or not?

Summary questions

1 Suggest how ethanol, produced by fermentation, can be separated from its aqueous solution.

2 What are the advantages and disadvantages of producing ethanol from fermentation compared with its production from crude oil?

3 Why is ethanol made by fermentation a carbon-neutral fuel?

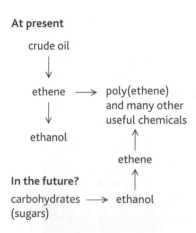

Figure 1 *Ethene and ethanol production*

16.3 The reactions of alcohols

Learning objectives

- What are the products when primary, secondary and tertiary alcohols are oxidised?

- How is the oxidation of a primary alcohol controlled?

- What are aldehydes and ketones?

- How can a mild oxidising agent be used to distinguish between an aldehyde and a ketone?

- What are elimination reactions?

- How are alcohols dehydrated to form alkenes?

Specification reference 3.2.10

Figure 1 *Alcohol burning stove*

Combustion

Alcohols burn completely to carbon dioxide and water if there is enough oxygen available. (Otherwise we can have incomplete combustion and carbon monoxide or even carbon is produced.) This is the equation for the complete combustion of ethanol:

$$C_2H_5OH(l) + 3O_2(g) \longrightarrow 2CO_2(g) + 3H_2O(l)$$

Ethanol is often used as a fuel, for example, in picnic stoves that burn methylated spirits. Methylated spirits is ethanol with a small percentage of poisonous methanol added to make it unfit to drink. In this way it can be sold without the tax which is levied on alcoholic drinks. A purple dye is also added to show that it should not be drunk.

Oxidation

Combustion is usually complete oxidation. Alcohols can also be oxidised gently and in stages. Primary alcohols are oxidised to **aldehydes**, RCHO. Aldehydes can be further oxidised to carboxylic acids, RCOOH. For example:

ethanol —[O] oxidation (alcohol in excess – no reflux)→ ethanal (an aldehyde) $+H_2O$ —[O] oxidation (oxidising agent in excess – reflux)→ ethanoic acid (a carboxylic acid)

Secondary alcohols are oxidised to **ketones**, R_2CO. Ketones are not oxidised further.

propan-2-ol —[O]→ propanone (a ketone) + H_2O

Tertiary alcohols are not easily oxidised. This is because oxidation would need a C—C bond to break, rather than a C—H bond (which is what happens when an aldehyde is oxidised). Ketones do not oxidise further for the same reason.

Many aldehydes and ketones have pleasant smells.

The experimental details

A solution of potassium dichromate, acidified with dilute sulfuric acid, is often used to oxidise alcohols to aldehydes and ketones. It is the oxidising agent. In the reaction, the orange dichromate(VI) ions are reduced to green chromium(III) ions.

To oxidise ethanol to ethanal – an aldehyde

We use dilute acid and less potassium dichromate(VI) than is needed for complete oxidation to carboxylic acid. We heat the mixture gently in apparatus like that shown in Figure 3, but with the receiver cooled in ice to reduce evaporation of the product. Ethanal (boiling temperature 294 K, 21 °C) vaporises as soon as it is formed and distils off. This stops it from being oxidised further to ethanoic acid. Unreacted ethanol remains in the flask.

We often use [O] to represent oxygen from the oxidising agent. The reaction is given by the equation:

$$CH_2CH_3OH(l) + [O] \longrightarrow CH_3CHO(g) + H_2O(l)$$
ethanol   ethanal

To oxidise ethanol to ethanoic acid – a carboxylic acid

We use concentrated sulfuric acid and more than enough potassium dichromate(VI) for complete reaction (the dichromate(VI) is in excess). We reflux the mixture in the apparatus shown in Figure 2. 'Reflux' means that vapour condenses and drips back into the reaction flask.

While the reaction mixture is refluxing, any ethanol or ethanal vapour will condense and drip back into the flask until, eventually, it is all oxidised to the acid. After refluxing for around 20 minutes, we can distil off the ethanoic acid, boiling temperature 391 K (118 °C) (along with any water) by rearranging the apparatus to that shown in Figure 3.

Using [O] to represent oxygen from the oxidising agent, the equation is:

$$CH_3CH_2OH(l) + 2[O] \longrightarrow CH_3COOH(g) + H_2O(l)$$
ethanol   ethanoic acid

Notice that twice as much oxidising agent is used in this reaction compared with the oxidation to ethanal.

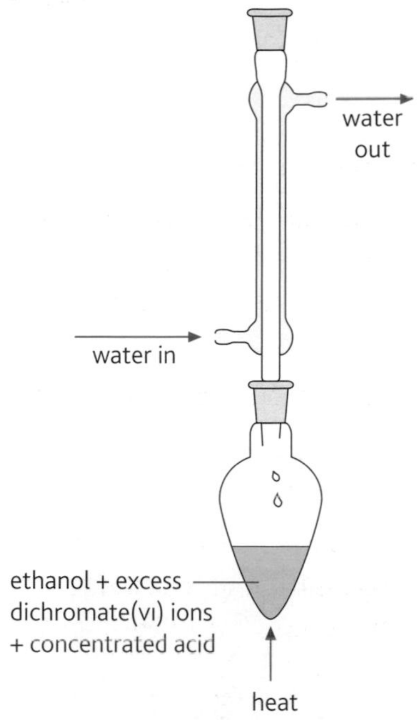

water out

water in

ethanol + excess dichromate(VI) ions + concentrated acid

heat

Figure 2 *Reflux apparatus for oxidation of ethanol to ethanoic acid*

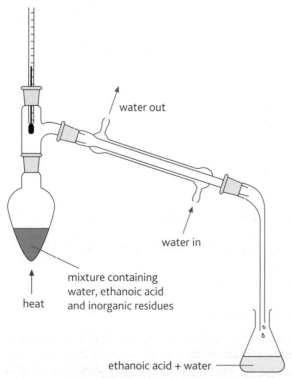

water out

water in

heat

mixture containing water, ethanoic acid and inorganic residues

ethanoic acid + water

Figure 3 *Apparatus for distilling ethanoic acid from the reaction mixture*

Oxidising a secondary alcohol to a ketone

Secondary alcohols are oxidised to ketones by acidified dichromate. We do not have to worry about further oxidation of the ketone.

> **Hint**
>
> Notice that even if we use the notation [O] for oxidation, the equation must still balance.

$$H-\underset{\underset{H}{|}}{\overset{\overset{H}{|}}{C}}-\underset{\underset{H}{|}}{\overset{\overset{O}{|}}{C}}-\underset{\underset{H}{|}}{\overset{\overset{H}{|}}{C}}-H \;+\; [O] \longrightarrow H-\underset{\underset{H}{|}}{\overset{\overset{H}{|}}{C}}-\underset{}{\overset{\overset{O}{\parallel}}{C}}-\underset{\underset{H}{|}}{\overset{\overset{H}{|}}{C}}-H \;+\; H_2O$$

⚗ Aldehydes and ketones

Aldehydes and ketones both have the C=O group. This is called the carbonyl group.

In aldehydes it is at the end of the hydrocarbon chain:

$$\underset{H}{\overset{R}{\diagdown}}C=O$$

or RCHO

In ketones it is in the body of the hydrocarbon chain:

$$\underset{R'}{\overset{R}{\diagdown}}C=O$$

or RCOR′

Aldehydes are usually named using the suffix –al and ketones with the suffix –one.

So CH_3CHO is ethan**al** (two carbons) and CH_3COCH_3 is propan**one** (three carbons).

Tests for aldehydes and ketones

Aldehydes and ketones have similar physical properties but there are two tests that can tell them apart. Both these tests involve gentle oxidation.

- ■ Aldehydes are oxidised to carboxylic acids:

    RCHO + [O] ⟶ RCOOH

    (This is the second stage of the oxidation of a primary alcohol.)
- ■ Ketones are not changed by gentle oxidation.

Figure 4 *The silver mirror test*

The Tollens' (silver mirror) test

Tollens' reagent is a gentle oxidising agent. It is a solution of silver nitrate in aqueous ammonia. It oxidises aldehydes but has no affect on ketones. It contains colourless silver(I) complex ions which are reduced to metallic silver, as the aldehyde is oxidised.

On warming an aldehyde with Tollens' reagent, a deposit of metallic silver is formed on the inside of the test tube – the silver mirror, see Figure 4. This reaction was once used commercially for making mirrors.

The Fehling's/Benedict's tests

Both Fehling's reagent and Benedict's reagent are gentle oxidising agents. Both contain blue copper(II) complex ions which will oxidise aldehydes

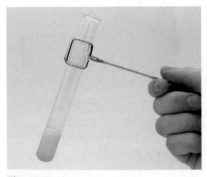

Figure 5 *The Benedict's test*

but not ketones. During the oxidation with either reagent, the blue solution gradually changes to a brick red precipitate of copper(I) oxide, $(Cu^{2+} + e^- \longrightarrow Cu^+)$.

On warming an aldehyde with blue Fehling's or Benedict's solution a brick red precipitate gradually forms.

Elimination reactions

Elimination reactions are ones in which a small molecule leaves the parent molecule. In the case of alcohols, this molecule is always water. The water is made from the —OH group and a hydrogen atom from the carbon next to the —OH group. So, the elimination reactions of alcohols are always dehydrations.

Dehydration

Alcohols can be dehydrated with excess hot concentrated sulphuric acid or by passing their vapours over heated aluminium oxide. An alkene is formed. For example, propan-1-ol is dehydrated to propene:

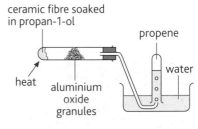

The apparatus used in the laboratory is shown in Figure 6.

Phosphoric(V) acid is an alternative dehydrating agent.

💡 Isomeric alkenes

Dehydration of longer chain or branched alcohols may produce a mixture of alkenes, including ones with Z and E isomers.

For example, with butan-2-ol there are three possible products: but-1-ene, Z-but-2-ene and E-but-2-ene.

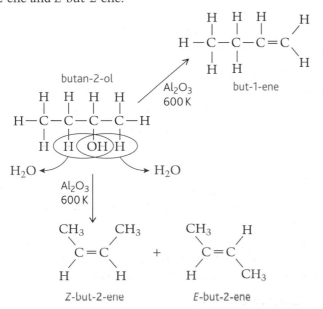

> ### Hint
> In order to be dehydrated an alcohol must have a hydrogen atom on a carbon next to the —OH group.

ceramic fibre soaked in propan-1-ol

propene

water

heat   aluminium oxide granules

Figure 6 *Dehydration of an alcohol*

Summary questions

1 State what happens in each case when the following alcohols are oxidised as much as possible, by acidified potassium dichromate.

  a A primary alcohol

  b A secondary alcohol

2 Why is a tertiary alcohol not oxidised by the method outlined in question **1**?

3 What is the difference between distilling and refluxing?

4 Suggest how you would distinguish between a primary alcohol and a secondary alcohol, using Tollens' reagent or Fehling's solution.

5 Write the equation for the elimination of water from ethanol and name the product.

6 What are the possible products of dehydrating pentan-2-ol?

1 (a) Ethanol, C_2H_5OH, can be made from glucose, $C_6H_{12}O_6$
    (i) Write an equation to represent this reaction.
    (ii) Give the name of this process for making ethanol. *(2 marks)*
  (b) Ethanol can be used as a fuel in the internal combustion engine of a motor car.
    (i) Write an equation for the complete combustion of ethanol.
    (ii) Identify a pollutant produced when ethanol is burned in a limited supply of air. *(2 marks)*

AQA, 2004

2 (a) Give a suitable reagent and state the necessary conditions for the conversion of propan-2-ol into propanone. Name the type of reaction.
  (b) Propanal is an isomer of propanone.
    (i) Draw the structure of propanal.
    (ii) A chemical test can be used to distinguish between separate samples of propanone and propanal. Give a suitable reagent for the test and describe what you would observe with propanone and with propanal. *(4 marks)*

AQA, 2004

3 Glucose, $C_6H_{12}O_6$, can be converted into ethanol. Ethanol can be used as a fuel or can be converted into ethene by acid-catalysed dehydration. Most of the ethene used by industry is formed by the thermal cracking of alkanes.
  (a) State **four** essential conditions for the conversion of glucose into ethanol. Name the process and give an equation for the reaction which takes place. Write an equation for the complete combustion of ethanol. *(7 marks)*
  (b) Explain what is meant by the term *dehydration*. Identify a catalyst which could be used in the acid-catalysed dehydration of ethanol. Write an equation for the reaction which takes place. *(3 marks)*

AQA, 2006

4 Consider the following pairs of structural isomers.

Molecular formula	Structure	Structure
$C_4H_{10}O$	Isomer **A** 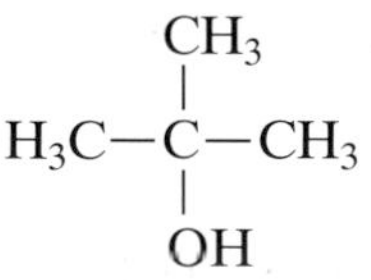 $\begin{array}{c} CH_3 \\ | \\ H_3C-C-CH_3 \\ | \\ OH \end{array}$	Isomer **B** $CH_3CH_2CH_2CH_2OH$
	Isomer **C** 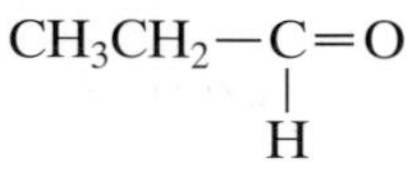 $\begin{array}{c} CH_3CH_2-C=O \\ | \\ H \end{array}$	Isomer **D** $\begin{array}{c} H_3C-C-CH_3 \\ || \\ O \end{array}$
C_6H_{12}	Isomer **E** 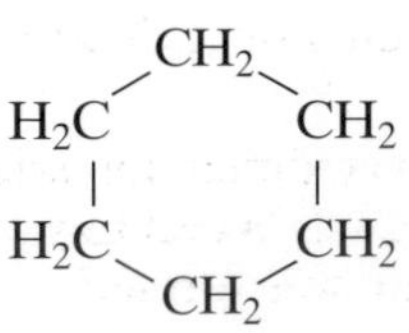 $\begin{array}{c} CH_2 \\ H_2C \quad CH_2 \\ H_2C \quad CH_2 \\ CH_2 \end{array}$	Isomer **F** $CH_3CH_2CH=CHCH_2CH_3$

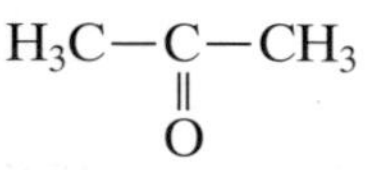

(a) (i) Explain what is meant by the term *structural isomers*.

    (ii) Complete the table to show the molecular formula of isomers **C** and **D**.

    (iii) Give the empirical formula of isomers **E** and **F**. *(4 marks)*

(b) A simple chemical test can be used to distinguish between separate samples of isomer **A** and isomer **B**. Suggest a suitable test reagent and state what you would observe in each case. *(3 marks)*

(c) A simple chemical test can be used to distinguish between separate samples of isomer **C** and isomer **D**. Suggest a suitable test reagent and state what you would observe in each case. *(3 marks)*

(d) A simple chemical test can be used to distinguish between separate samples of isomer **E** and isomer **F**. Suggest a suitable test reagent and state what you would observe in each case. *(3 marks)*

AQA, 2006

5 (a) (i) Pentan-1-ol, $CH_3CH_2CH_2CH_2CH_2OH$, was oxidised by adding it dropwise to acidified potassium dichromate(VI) and distilling off the organic product immediately. Write an equation for this reaction showing clearly the structural formula of the organic product. You may use [O] to represent the oxidising agent.

    (ii) Pentan-2-ol, $CH_3CH_2CH_2CH(OH)CH_3$, was oxidised by heating it under reflux with acidified potassium dichromate(VI). Write an equation for this reaction showing clearly the structural formula of the organic product. You may use [O] to represent the oxidising agent. *(4 marks)*

(b) By stating the reagents, conditions and observations, show how you would distinguish between the two oxidation products formed in parts (a)(i) and (a)(ii). *(4 marks)*

AQA, 2001

6 (a) Pentanal, $CH_3CH_2CH_2CH_2CHO$, can be oxidised to a carboxylic acid.

    (i) Write an equation for this reaction. Use [O] to represent the oxidising agent.

    (ii) Name the carboxylic acid formed in this reaction. *(2 marks)*

(b) Pentanal can be formed by the oxidation of an alcohol.

    (i) Identify this alcohol.

    (ii) State the class to which this alcohol belongs. *(2 marks)*

AQA, 2006

7 (a) An alcohol containing carbon, hydrogen and oxygen only has 64.9% carbon and 13.5% hydrogen by mass. Using these data, show that the empirical formula of the alcohol is $C_4H_{10}O$ *(3 marks)*

(b) The structural formulae of two of the four possible alcohols of molecular formula $C_4H_{10}O$ are shown below.

$$CH_3-\underset{\underset{CH_3}{|}}{\overset{\overset{OH}{|}}{C}}-CH_3 \qquad\qquad CH_3CH_2CH_2CH_2OH$$

    isomer 1   *isomer 2*

    (i) What type of alcohol is isomer 1? Suggest a reason why this type of alcohol is not easily oxidised.

    (ii) Draw the structural formulae of the two remaining alcohols of molecular formula $C_4H_{10}O$. *(4 marks)*

(c) Isomer 2 was oxidised by adding it dropwise to acidified potassium dichromate(VI) solution and immediately distilling off the product. When this product was treated with Fehling's solution, a red precipitate was formed.

(i)   State the type of product distilled off during the oxidation by acidified potassium dichromate(VI) solution.

(ii) Write an equation for the oxidation by potassium dichromate(VI), showing clearly the structure of the organic product. Use [O] to represent the oxidising agent.

(iii) Name and draw a structure for the organic product formed by the reaction with Fehling's solution.   *(5 marks)*

(d) State **one** advantage and **one** disadvantage of the production of ethanol by the hydration of ethene compared to the fermentation of glucose.   *(2 marks)*

AQA, 2002

8 Some alcohols can be oxidised to form aldehydes, which can then be oxidised further to form carboxylic acids.

Some alcohols can be oxidised to form ketones, which resist further oxidation. Other alcohols are resistant to oxidation.

(a) Draw the structures of the **two** straight-chain isomeric alcohols with molecular formula, $C_4H_{10}O$ *(2 marks)*

(b) Draw the structures of the oxidation products obtained when the two alcohols from part (a) are oxidised separately by acidified potassium dichromate(VI). Write equations for any reactions which occur, using [O] to represent the oxidising agent.   *(6 marks)*

(c) Draw the structure and give the name of the alcohol with molecular formula $C_4H_{10}O$ which is resistant to oxidation by acidified potassium dichromate(VI).   *(2 marks)*

AQA, 2005

9 Consider the following reaction schemes involving two alcohols, **A** and **B**, which are position isomers of each other.

$$CH_3CH_2CH_2CH_2OH \longrightarrow CH_3CH_2CH_2CHO \longrightarrow CH_3CH_2CH_2COOH$$
$$\textbf{A} \qquad\qquad\qquad\qquad \text{butanal} \qquad\qquad\qquad \text{butanoic acid}$$

$$CH_3CH_2CH(OH)CH_3 \longrightarrow CH_3CH_2COCH_3$$
$$\textbf{B} \qquad\qquad\qquad\qquad \textbf{C}$$

(a) State what is meant by the term *position isomers*.   *(2 marks)*

(b) Name compound **A** and name the class of compounds to which **C** belongs.   *(2 marks)*

(c) Each of the reactions shown in the schemes above is of the same type and uses the same combination of reagents.

(i)   State the type of reaction.

(ii) Identify a suitable combination of reagents.

(iii) State how you would ensure that compound **A** is converted into butanoic acid rather than into butanal.

(iv) Draw the structure of an isomer of compound **A** which does not react with this combination of reagents.

(v)   Draw the structure of the carboxylic acid formed by the reaction of methanol with this combination of reagents.   *(6 marks)*

(d) (i)   State a reagent which could be used to distinguish between butanal and compound **C**.

(ii) Draw the structure of another aldehyde which is an isomer of butanal.   *(2 marks)*

AQA, 2005

10 (a) Four isomers with the formula C_4H_9OH are given below.

Isomer	Name
$CH_3CH_2CH_2CH_2OH$	butan-1-ol
$\begin{array}{c} CH_3 \\ | \\ CH_3-C-CH_3 \\ | \\ OH \end{array}$	2-methylpropan-2-ol
$\begin{array}{c} CH_3-C-CH_2OH \\ | \\ CH_3 \end{array}$	
$\begin{array}{c} CH_3CH_2-CH-CH_3 \\ | \\ OH \end{array}$	

     (i) Complete the naming of the isomers in the table above. *(2 marks)*

 (b) One of the isomers in part (a) is resistant to oxidation by acidified potassium dichromate(VI).

     (i) Identify this isomer.

     (ii) This isomer can be dehydrated. Give a suitable dehydrating agent and write an equation for this dehydration reaction. *(3 marks)*

 (c) (i) Identify the isomer in part (a) which can be oxidised to a ketone. Give the structure of the ketone formed.

     (ii) Identify **one** of the isomers in part (a) which can be oxidised to an aldehyde. Give the structure of the aldehyde formed.

     (iii) Give a reagent that can be used in a test to distinguish between a ketone and an aldehyde. State what you would observe in the test. *(7 marks)*

 (d) Butan-1-ol can be oxidised to form a carboxylic acid. Using [O] to represent the oxidising agent, write an equation for this reaction and name the product. *(2 marks)*

AQA, 2003

11 Glucose can be used as a source of ethanol. Ethanol can be burned as a fuel or can be converted into ethene.

$$C_6H_{12}O_6 \longrightarrow CH_3CH_2OH \longrightarrow H_2C=CH_2$$
$$\text{glucose} \qquad \text{ethanol} \qquad \text{ethene}$$

 (a) Name the types of reaction illustrated by the two reactions above. *(2 marks)*

 (b) (i) State what must be added to an aqueous solution of glucose so that ethanol is formed.

     (ii) Identify a suitable catalyst for the conversion of ethanol into ethene. *(2 marks)*

 (c) (i) State the class of alcohols to which ethanol belongs.

     (ii) Give **one** advantage of using ethanol as a fuel compared with using a petroleum fraction. *(2 marks)*

 (d) Most of the ethene used by industry is produced when ethane is heated to 900 °C in the absence of air. Write an equation for this reaction. *(1 mark)*

AQA, 2005

12 Explain the meaning of the term *biofuel*. *(1 mark)*

Suggest two reasons why ethanol produced by fermentation is considered to be a carbon neutral fuel. *(2 marks)*

Suggest why production of ethanol by fermentation is considered to be environmentally friendly. *(2 marks)*

17.1 Mass spectrometry

Learning objectives

- What is meant by the term molecular ion?

- What does the mass of a molecular ion tell us?

- Why are there so many peaks in the mass spectrum of a compound?

- What can a high resolution mass spectrum tell us?

Specification reference 3.2.11

How science works

Mass spectrometry and sport

One of the many applications of mass spectrometry is testing athletes for the presence of drugs in urine samples. It is also used in forensic work.

Hint

- In any spectrum of an organic compound there will be a tiny peak one mass unit to the right of the molecular ion. This is caused by ions containing the ^{13}C isotope.

- Don't confuse the peak for the molecular ion with the tallest peak in the spectrum. This is often called the base peak.

We saw in Topic 1.4 how mass spectrometry is used to measure the relative **atomic** masses of atoms. It is also the main method for finding the relative **molecular** mass of organic compounds. The compound enters the mass spectrometer as a gas or a vapour. It is ionised by an electron gun and the positive ions are accelerated through the instrument as a beam of ionised molecules. These are then deflected by a magnetic field.

The strength of the magnetic field required to deflect the ion into the detector depends on the mass and charge of the ion.

The output is then presented as a graph of relative abundance (vertical axis) against mass/charge ratio (horizontal axis). However, since the charge on the ions is normally $1+$, the horizontal axis is effectively relative mass. This graph is called a mass spectrum.

The mass spectrum of ethanol is shown in Figure 1. Notice that it contains many lines and not just one as we might expect.

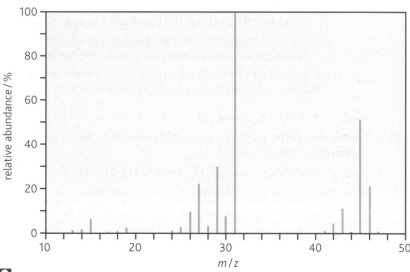

Figure 1 *The mass spectrum of ethanol*

Why are there so many peaks in a mass spectrum of a compound?

When ethanol is ionised it forms the ion $C_2H_5OH^+$ ($CH_3CH_2OH^+$). This is called the **molecular ion**. Many of these ions will then break up; some of their bonds break as they are ionised, so we have other ions of smaller molecular mass. This process is called fragmentation. Each of these produces a line in the mass spectrum. These can provide information that will help to deduce the structure of the compound. They also act as a 'fingerprint' to help identify it.

However, there are normally a few ionised molecules remaining intact to give a peak corresponding to the relative molecular mass, M_r, of the compound.

The main peak furthest to the right of the mass spectrum, corresponds to the molecular ion (it has the highest mass). The molecular ion peak for ethanol is at mass 46; this tells us the relative molecular mass of ethanol.

Mass spectrometry is the most important technique for measuring the relative molecular mass of organic compounds.

High resolution mass spectrometry

The mass spectrum in Figure 1 shows masses to the nearest whole number only. However, many mass spectrometers can measure masses to three or even four decimal places. This method allows us to work out the molecular formula of the parent ion. It makes use of the fact that isotopes of atoms do not have exactly whole number atomic masses (except for carbon-12 which is exactly twelve by definition), for example, $^{16}O = 15.99491$ and $^{1}H = 1.007829$.

A parent ion of mass 200, to the nearest whole number, could have the following molecular formulae:

$$C_{10}H_{16}O_4, \ C_{11}H_4O_4, \ C_{11}H_{20}O_3$$

Adding up the accurate atomic masses gives the following M_rs:

$$C_{10}H_{16}O_4 = 200.1049$$
$$C_{11}H_4O_4 = 200.0110$$
$$C_{11}H_{20}O_3 = 200.1413$$

These can easily be distinguished by high resolution mass spectrometry.

How science works

Water sampling

Water boards sample the water from the rivers in their areas to monitor pollutants. The pollutants are separated by chromatography and fed into a mass spectrometer. Each pollutant can be identified from its spectrum; a computer matches its spectrum with known compounds in a library of spectra.

Summary questions

1 Look at the mass spectrum of the organic compound below.

a What is the mass/charge ratio of the molecular ion?

b What is the relative molecular mass of the compound?

c What assumption are you making about the charge on the ion in your answer to part **b**?

2 a How are ions formed from molecules in a mass spectrometer?

b What sign of charge do the ions have as a result of this?

3 A compound was found to have a molecular ion with a mass to charge ration of 136.125. Which of the following molecular formulae could it have? $C_9H_{12}O$ or $C_{10}H_{16}$

You will need to work out the accurate M_r of each of these molecules.

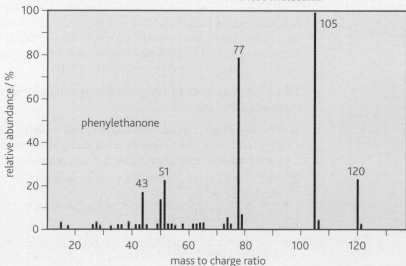

17.2 Infra-red spectroscopy

Learning objectives

- How can the absorption of infra-red radiation be used to indicate the presence of certain functional groups in an organic molecule?

- What is the fingerprint region and where is it found?

- How can infra-red spectroscopy be used to confirm the identity of a compound?

- How can an infra-red spectrum be used to show the presence of impurities?

Specification reference 3.2.11

Infra-red (IR) spectroscopy is often used by organic chemists to help them identify compounds.

💡 How infra-red spectroscopy works

A pair of atoms joined by a chemical bond is always vibrating. The system behaves rather like two balls (the atoms) joined by a spring (the bond). Stronger bonds vibrate faster (at higher frequency) and heavier atoms make the bond vibrate more slowly (at lower frequency). Every bond has its own unique natural frequency that is in the infra-red region of the electromagnetic spectrum.

When we shine a beam of infra-red radiation (heat energy) through a sample, the bonds in the sample can absorb energy from the radiation and vibrate more. However, any particular bond can only absorb radiation that has the same frequency as the natural frequency of the bond. Therefore, the radiation that emerges from the sample will be missing the frequencies that correspond to the bonds in the sample, see Figure 1.

The infra-red spectrometer

This is what happens in an infra-red spectrometer:

- A beam of infra-red radiation containing a spread of frequencies is passed through a sample.
- The radiation that emerges is missing the frequencies that correspond to the types of bonds found in the sample.
- The instrument plots a graph of the intensity of the radiation emerging from the sample, called the transmittance, against the frequency of radiation.
- The frequency is expressed as a wavenumber, measured in cm^{-1}.

The infra-red spectrum

A typical graph, called an infra-red spectrum is shown in Figure 2. The dips in the graph (confusingly, they are usually called peaks) represent particular bonds. Figure 3 and Table 1 show the wavenumbers for some bonds commonly found in organic chemistry.

These can help us to identify the functional groups present in a compound. For example:

- The O—H bond produces a broad peak at about between 3230 and 3550 cm^{-1} and this is found in alcohols, ROH; and a very broad O—H peak between 2500 and 3000 cm^{-1} in carboxylic acids, RCOOH.
- The C=O bond produces a peak between 1680 and 1750 cm^{-1}. This bond is found in:
  aldehydes, RCHO
  ketones, R_2CO
  carboxylic acids, RCOOH.

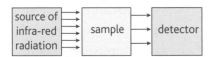

Figure 1 *Schematic diagram of an infra-red spectrometer*

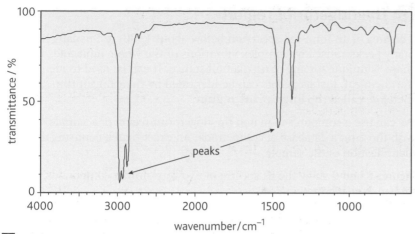

Figure 2 *A typical infra-red spectrum. Note that wavenumber gets smaller as we go from left to right.*

Table 1 *Characteristic infra-red absorptions in organic molecules*

Bond	Location	Wavenumber / cm^{-1}
C—O	alcohols, esters	1000–1300
C=O	aldehydes, ketones, carboxylic acids, esters	1680–1750
O—H	hydrogen bonded in carboxylic acids	2500–3000 (broad)
N—H	primary amines	3100–3500
O—H	hydrogen bonded in alcohols, phenols	3230–3550

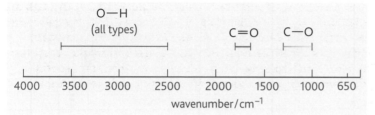

Figure 3 *The ranges of wavenumbers at which some bonds absorb infra-red radiation*

Data about the frequencies that correspond to different bonds can be found on the AQA data sheet at the back of the book.

Figures 4, 5 and 6 show the infra-red spectra of ethanal, ethanol and ethanoic acid with the key peaks marked.

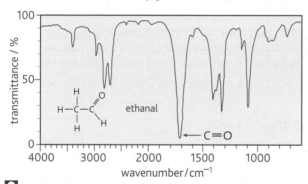

Figure 4 *Infra-red spectrum of ethanal*

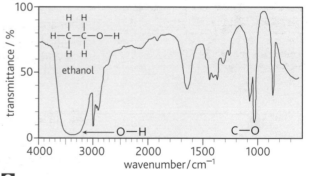

Figure 5 *Infra-red spectrum of ethanol*

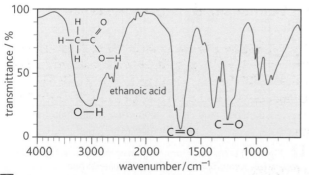

Figure 6 *Infra-red spectrum of ethanoic acid*

⚗ The fingerprint region

The area of an infra-red spectrum below about $1500\,cm^{-1}$ usually has many peaks caused by complex vibrations of the whole molecule. This shape is unique for any particular substance. It can be used to identify the chemical, just as people can be identified by their fingerprints. It is therefore called the **fingerprint region**.

We can use a computer to match the fingerprint region of a sample with those on a database of compounds. An exact match confirms the identification of the sample.

Figures 8 and 9 show the IR spectra of two very similar compounds, propan-1-ol and propan-2-ol.

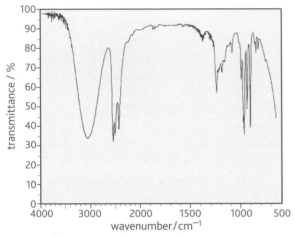

Figure 8 *Infra-red spectrum of propan-1-ol*

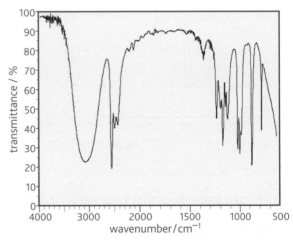

Figure 9 *Infra-red spectrum of propan-2-ol*

They are as expected, very similar overall. However, superimposing the spectra, Figure 10, shows that their fingerprint regions are quite distinct. This is shown more clearly in Figure 11, where the fingerprint region has been enlarged.

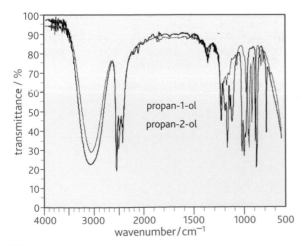

Figure 10 *Infra-red spectra of propan-1-ol superimposed on propan-2-ol*

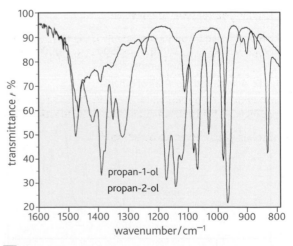

Figure 11 *The fingerprint region of the infra-red spectra of propan-1-ol superimposed on propan-2-ol enlarged*

Identifying impurities

Infra-red spectra can also be used to show up the presence of impurities. These may be revealed by peaks that should not be there in the pure compound. Figures 12 and 13 show the spectrum of a sample of pure caffeine and that of caffeine extracted from tea. The broad peak at around 3000 cm⁻¹ in the impure sample (Figure 13) is an O—H stretch caused by water in the sample that has not been completely dried. Notice that there are no O—H bonds in caffeine (Figure 14).

In practice, analytical chemists will often use a combination of spectroscopic techniques to identify unknown compounds.

Figure 12 *The infra-red spectra of pure caffeine*

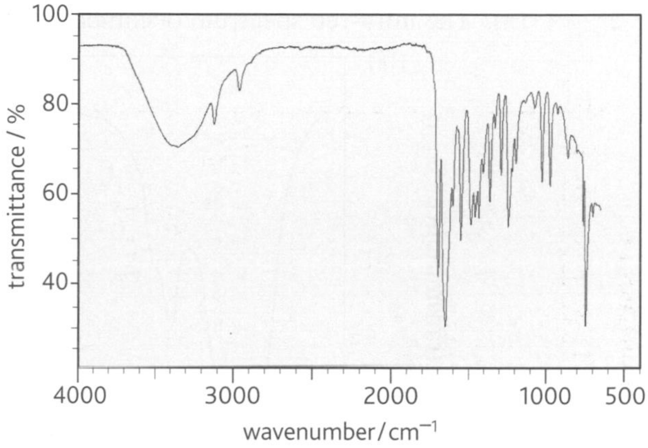

Figure 13 *The infra-red spectra of impure caffeine*

Summary questions

1 An organic compound has a peak in the IR spectrum at about 1725 cm⁻¹. Which of the following compounds could it be?

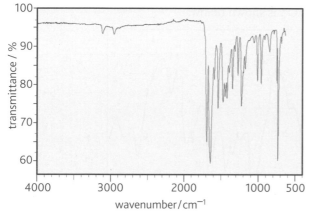

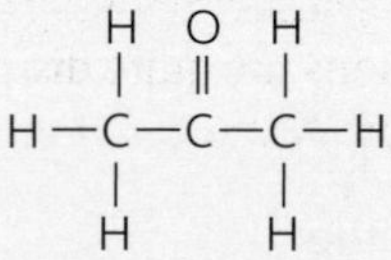

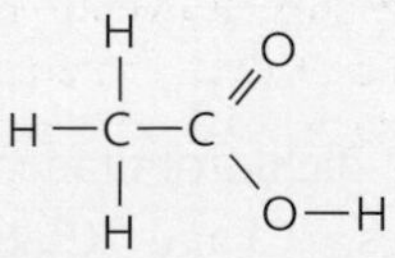

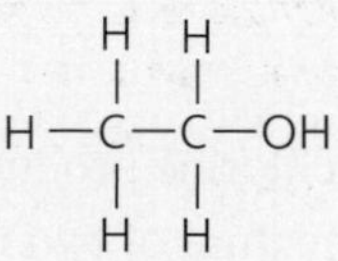

2 Explain your answer to question **1**.

3 An organic compound has a peak in the IR spectrum at about 3300 cm⁻¹. Which of the compounds in question **1** could it be?

4 Explain your answer to question **3**.

5 An organic compound has a peak in the IR spectrum at 1725 and 3300 cm⁻¹. Which of the compounds in question **1** could it be?

6 Explain your answer to question **5**.

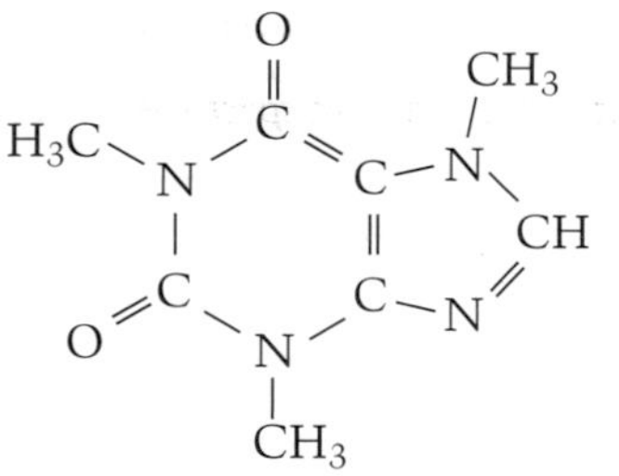

Figure 14 *The structural formula of caffeine. It has no O—H bonds.*

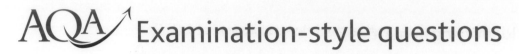
1   The mass spectrum of CH_3Br contains two molecular ion peaks of equal abundance with m/z values of 94 and 96. Deduce the number of molecular ion peaks in the spectrum of the compound CH_2Br_2. Give their relative abundances and the m/z value of the molecular ion with the greatest mass.   *(4 marks)*

AQA, 2001

2   (a) The infra-red spectrum of compound **A**, $C_3H_6O_2$, is shown below.

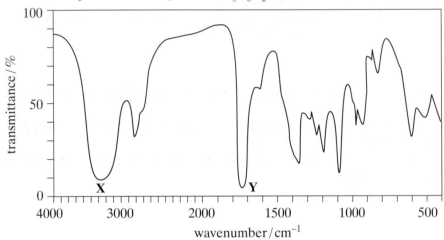

Identify the functional groups which cause the absorptions labelled **X** and **Y**.
Using this information draw the structures of the three possible structural isomers for **A**.   *(5 marks)*

AQA, 2006

3   The reaction of but-1-ene with chlorine produces 1,2-dichlorobutane, $C_4H_8Cl_2$
Given that chlorine exists as a mixture of two isotopes, ^{35}Cl and ^{37}Cl, predict the number of molecular ion peaks and their m/z values in the mass spectrum of $C_4H_8Cl_2$

AQA, 2006

4   Compound **U** is shown below.

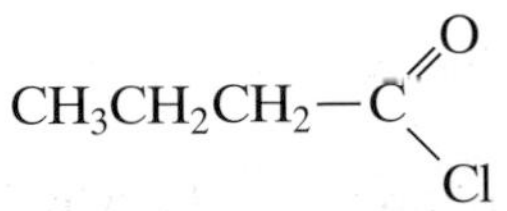

$$CH_3CH_2CH_2-C\overset{\displaystyle O}{\underset{\displaystyle Cl}{\big<}}$$

(a) State why the mass spectrum of **U** contains two molecular ion peaks.
(b) Give the m/z values of these two peaks.   *(2 marks)*

AQA, 2005

5   Compounds **C** and **D**, shown below, are isomers of $C_5H_{10}O$

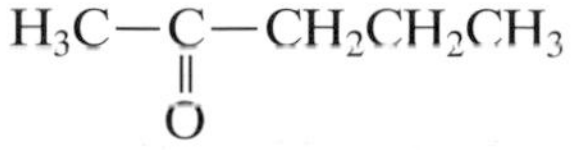

$$H_3C-\underset{\underset{O}{\|}}{C}-CH_2CH_2CH_3$$

C 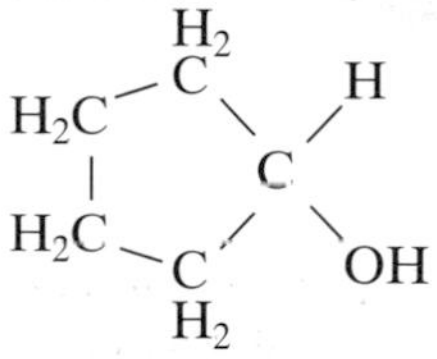   **D**

(a) Name compound **C**.   *(1 mark)*

(b) Use the data page at the back of the book to help you to answer this question.

(i) Suggest the wavenumber of an absorption which is present in the infra-red spectrum of **C** but not in that of **D**.

(ii) Suggest the wavenumber of an absorption which is present in the infra-red spectrum of **D** but not in that of **C**.   *(2 marks)*

AQA, 2005

6   Compound **Q** has the molecular formula C_4H_7ClO and does not produce misty fumes when added to water.

(a) The infra-red spectrum of **Q** contains a major absorption at $1724\,cm^{-1}$. Identify the bond responsible for this absorption.   *(1 mark)*

(b) The mass spectrum of **Q** contains two molecular ion peaks at $m/z = 106$ and $m/z = 108$.

It also has a major peak at $m/z = 43$.

Suggest why there are two molecular ion peaks.   *(1 mark)*

AQA, 2004

7   Use the data page at the back of the book to help you answer this question.

Compounds **F** and **G** have the structural formulae shown below

$$F \qquad CH_3-CH_2-O-CH_2-CH_2-\underset{\overset{\|}{O}}{C}-CH_3$$

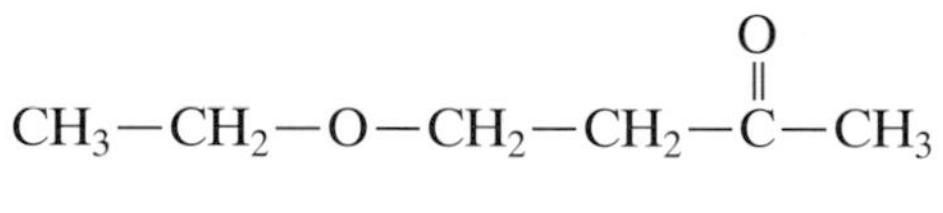

$$G \qquad H_3C-\underset{\underset{O}{\|}}{C}-CH_2CH_2CH_3$$

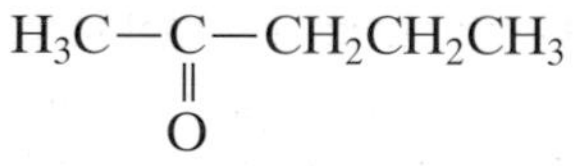

Suggest the wavenumber of the infra-red absorption caused by the functional group found in **F** and **G**   *(1 mark)*

AQA, 2004

8   Predict the wavenumber of a peak which will be present in both compounds and explain your prediction.

Suggest how the infra-red spectrum of propan1-ol might differ from that of propan-2-ol.

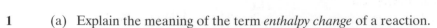

1   (a)   Explain the meaning of the term *enthalpy change* of a reaction.   *(2 marks)*

       (b)   Write the equation for the reaction for which the enthalpy change is the standard enthalpy of formation of the gas nitrous oxide, N_2O *(1 mark)*

       (c)   The equation for the formation of nitrogen trifluoride is given below.

$$\tfrac{1}{2}N_2(g) + 1\tfrac{1}{2}F_2(g) + \longrightarrow NF_3(g)$$

          (i)   Using the mean bond enthalpy values given in the table, calculate a value for the enthalpy of formation of nitrogen trifluoride.

Bond	N—F	N≡N	F—F
Mean bond enthalpy / $kJ\,mol^{-1}$	278	945	159

         (ii)   A data book value for the enthalpy of formation of nitrogen trifluoride is $-114\,kJ\,mol^{-1}$. Give one reason why the answer you have calculated in part (c)(i) is different from this data book value.   *(4 marks)*

       (d)   Some standard enthalpies of formation are given in the table below.

Substance	$NH_3(g)$	$F_2(g)$	$NF_3(g)$	$NH_4F(s)$
$\Delta H_f^{\ominus}$ / $kJ\,mol^{-1}$	−46	0	−114	−467

         (i)   State why the enthalpy of formation of fluorine is zero.

         (ii)   Use these data to calculate the enthalpy change for the following reaction.

$$4NH_3(g) + 3F_2(g) \longrightarrow NF_3(g) + 3NH_4F(s)$$
    (4 marks)

AQA, 2007

2   When nitrogen monoxide reacts with oxygen, a dynamic equilibrium is established.

$$2NO(g) + O_2(g) \rightleftharpoons 2NO_2(g) \qquad \Delta H^{\ominus} = -115\,kJ\,mol^{-1}$$

       (a)   State what is meant by *dynamic equilibrium*.   *(2 marks)*

       (b)   State and explain how the total pressure in this equilibrium reaction should be changed to give a higher equilibrium yield of NO_2 *(3 marks)*

       (c)   State and explain the effect of an increase in temperature on the yield of NO_2 in this equilibrium reaction.   *(3 marks)*

       (d)   Deduce the oxidation state of nitrogen in NO_3^- and in NO_2^+ *(2 marks)*

AQA, 2007

3   (a)   (i)   State the trend in oxidising ability of the halogens from fluorine to iodine.

         (ii)   Write an equation to show how chlorine reacts with aqueous potassium bromide.

         (iii)   Explain why students must take care when using chlorine in this reaction.   *(3 marks)*

       (b)   Use the following information to identify the species **J, K, L, M, N** and **Q.**

         When silver nitrate solution is added to a solution of sodium halide **J,** a colourless solution remains and no precipitate is formed.

         When silver nitrate solution is added to a solution of a sodium halide **K,** a yellow solid is formed.

         When concentrated sulfuric acid is added to solid sodium halide **L,** a brown gas **M** and two colourless gases **N** and **Q** are formed. Gases **N** and **Q** both dissolve in water to form acidic solutions.   *(6 marks)*

AQA, 2007

4 (a) Give the formula of the least soluble hydroxide of the Group 2 elements Mg to Ba. *(1 mark)*

   (b) An aqueous solution of sodium chloride may be distinguished from an aqueous solution of sodium sulfate using a simple chemical test.

      (i) Identify a reagent for this test.

      (ii) State the observations you would expect to make if the reagent identified in part (b)(i) is added to a separate sample of each solution. Write an equation for any reaction which occurs. *(4 marks)*

   AQA, 2007

5 (a) The extraction of iron involves the reduction of iron(III) oxide, Fe_2O_3, in the blast furnace by a reducing agent.

      (i) In terms of electrons, state what is meant by *reduction* and *reducing agent*.

      (ii) Identify a reducing agent that can reduce Fe_2O_3 to iron in the blast furnace. Write an equation for the reaction between Fe_2O_3 and the reducing agent you have stated.

      (iii) Give one essential condition needed for this reduction. *(5 marks)*

   (b) Molten iron obtained from the blast furnace contains carbon as an impurity. This is removed by blowing oxygen into the iron to make carbon dioxide. It has been suggested that since the carbon dioxide gas is acidic it could be absorbed by an alkaline solution rather than releasing it into the atmosphere. Suggest 2 reasons why this may not be a good idea. *(2 marks)*

   (c) (i) Titanium is extracted from titanium(IV) oxide, TiO_2, in a two-stage process. Write equations for the reaction occurring in stage 1 and stage 2 of this extraction.

      (ii) Give one essential condition, other than temperature, for the second stage, and state why it is necessary. *(4 marks)*

   (d) Give two reasons why titanium is expensive to extract. *(2 marks)*

   AQA, 2007

6 Consider the following sequence of reactions.

$$C_6H_{12}C_6 \xrightarrow[\text{yeast}]{\text{Reaction 1}} CH_3CH_2OH \xrightarrow{\text{Reaction 2}} H_2C{=}CH_2$$

glucose

$$\text{Reaction 3} \downarrow Br_2$$

$$\text{compound W} \xleftarrow[\text{KCN}]{\text{Reaction 4}} \begin{array}{c} CH_2Br \\ | \\ CH_2Br \end{array}$$

   (a) (i) Name the process in Reaction **1**.

      (ii) Write an equation for Reaction **1**. *(2 marks)*

   (b) Name the type of mechanism in Reaction **2**. *(1 mark)*

   (c) Outline a mechanism for Reaction **3**. *(4 marks)*

   (d) Compound **W** is formed in Reaction **4**.

      (i) Name the type of mechanism in Reaction **4**.

      (ii) Draw the structural formula of compound **W**, ($M_r = 80.0$), showing all of the bonds in the molecule. *(2 marks)*

   AQA, 2007

   (e) Explain how infra red spectroscopy can be used to distinguish between CH_3CH_2OH and $CH_2{=}CH_2$

7 The table below gives the structures of the four isomeric alkenes with molecular formula C_4H_8

Isomer **1**	Isomer **2**
CH_3CH_2 $\diagdown$ C=C $\diagup$ H $\diagup$ H $\diagdown$ H	H_3C $\diagdown$ C=C $\diagup$ H H_3C $\diagup$ $\diagdown$ H
Isomer **3**	Isomer **4**
H $\diagdown$ C=C $\diagup$ CH_3 H_3C $\diagup$ $\diagdown$ H	H $\diagdown$ C=C $\diagup$ H H_3C $\diagup$ $\diagdown$ CH_3

(a) Name Isomer **1** and Isomer **2**. *(2 marks)*

(b) (i) State what is meant by the term *stereoisomers*.

    (ii) From the table, identify two isomers which are stereoisomers. *(3 marks)*

(c) Isomer **2** reacts with concentrated sulfuric acid to form compound **W** as shown in the equation below. Name and outline a mechanism for this reaction.

$$H_3C-\underset{\underset{CH_3}{|}}{C}=CH_2 \; + \; H_2SO_4 \longrightarrow H_3C-\underset{\underset{CH_3}{|}}{\overset{\overset{OSO_2OH}{|}}{C}}-CH_3$$

Isomer **2**   **W**

(5 marks)

Suggest what safety precautions should be taken when this reaction is carried out on a large scale. *(1 mark)*

AQA, 2007

(d) Isomer **1** can be polymerised to form polymer **X**.

    (i) Draw the structure of polymer **X** and state the type of polymerisation which occurs. *(2 marks)*

    (ii) Explain why polymers like **X** are difficult to recycle. *(1 mark)*

8 (a) Draw a graph to show a Maxwell–Boltzmann distribution of molecular energies for a gas. Label the axes. On the same axes draw a second curve to show the distribution for the gas at a higher temperature. Label this second curve **W**. *(6 marks)*

(b) A reaction of nitrogen monoxide is shown below.

$$2NO(g) + O_2(g) \longrightarrow 2NO_2(g)$$

The rate of reaction can be found by measuring the concentration of NO_2 at different times.

Define the term *rate of reaction*. Draw a graph to show how the concentration of NO_2 changes with time. Indicate how the initial rate of reaction could be obtained from your graph. *(4 marks)*

(c) In the manufacture of sulfur trioxide from sulfur dioxide, nitrogen monoxide can be used in a two-stage process to increase the rate of production.

$$2NO(g) + O_2(g) \longrightarrow 2NO_2(g)$$
$$NO_2(g) + SO_2(g) \longrightarrow NO(g) + SO_3(g)$$

Construct an overall equation for the production of SO_3 from SO_2

State and explain fully the role of NO in this process.

(d) These reactions are in the gaseous phase. State a precaution a company should take before carrying this out on a large scale. *(6 marks)*

AQA, 2007

9 Consider the following sequence of reactions.

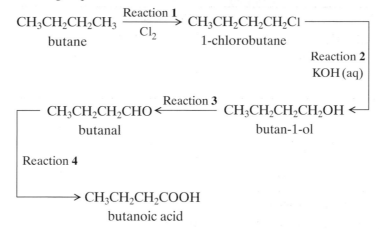

(a) The type of mechanism for Reaction **1** is the same as that for the chlorination of methane. Identify the type of reactive intermediate and state the conditions for this reaction.

Give the name of each step in this type of mechanism.

Write an overall equation for the reaction that occurs when C_4H_{10} reacts with a large excess of chlorine to form C_4Cl_{10} *(6 marks)*

(b) In Reaction **2**, a nucleophile reacts with 1-chlorobutane to form butan-1-ol as the main organic product. State what is meant by the term *nucleophile*.

Identify the nucleophile in Reaction **2** and the feature of the 1-chlorobutane molecule which makes it susceptible to nucleophilic attack.

Give **one** change to the reaction conditions for Reaction **2** so that the main organic product is but-1-ene rather than butan-1-ol. *(4 marks)*

(c) Reactions **3** and **4** are of the same type. For these two reactions, state the type of reaction involved, identify a suitable reagent or combination of reagents and state how a high yield of butanoic acid can be obtained.

Outline a simple chemical test to detect the presence of any unreacted butanal in the final reaction mixture. *(5 marks)*

AQA, 2007

10 Isomers are compounds with the same molecular formula.
(a) Compound **X** is the alcohol, $CH_3CH(OH)CH_3$
  (i) Name compound **X**.
  (ii) Draw the structure of the position isomer of compound **X**. *(2 marks)*
(b) Compound **Y** is the alkene, $(CH_3)_2C{=}C(CH_3)_2$
  (i) Name compound **Y**.
  (ii) Draw the structure of a straight-chain isomer of compound **Y**. *(2 marks)*

AQA, 2007

Data

Gas constant $R = 8.31\,\text{J}\,\text{K}^{-1}\,\text{mol}^{-1}$

Infra-red absorption data

Bond	Wavenumber / cm^{-1}
C—H	2850–3300
C—C	750–1100
C=C	1620–1680
C=O	1680–1750
C—O	1000–1300
O—H (alcohols)	3230–3550
O—H (acids)	2500–3000
N—H	3300–3500

The Periodic Table of the Elements

Key

relative atomic mass
atomic symbol
name
atomic (proton) number

1.0 **H** hydrogen 1

(1)	(2)		(3)	(4)	(5)	(6)	(7)	(8)	(9)	(10)	(11)	(12)	(13)	(14)	(15)	(16)	(17)	0 (18)
																		4.0 **He** helium 2
6.9 **Li** lithium 3	9.0 **Be** beryllium 4												10.8 **B** boron 5	12.0 **C** carbon 6	14.0 **N** nitrogen 7	16.0 **O** oxygen 8	19.0 **F** fluorine 9	20.2 **Ne** neon 10
23.0 **Na** sodium 11	24.3 **Mg** magnesium 12												27.0 **Al** aluminium 13	28.1 **Si** silicon 14	31.0 **P** phosphorus 15	32.1 **S** sulfur 16	35.5 **Cl** chlorine 17	39.9 **Ar** argon 18
39.1 **K** potassium 19	40.1 **Ca** calcium 20		45.0 **Sc** scandium 21	47.9 **Ti** titanium 22	50.9 **V** vanadium 23	52.0 **Cr** chromium 24	54.9 **Mn** manganese 25	55.8 **Fe** iron 26	58.9 **Co** cobalt 27	58.7 **Ni** nickel 28	63.5 **Cu** copper 29	65.4 **Zn** zinc 30	69.7 **Ga** gallium 31	72.6 **Ge** germanium 32	74.9 **As** arsenic 33	79.0 **Se** selenium 34	79.9 **Br** bromine 35	83.8 **Kr** krypton 36
85.5 **Rb** rubidium 37	87.6 **Sr** strontium 38		88.9 **Y** yttrium 39	91.2 **Zr** zirconium 40	92.9 **Nb** niobium 41	95.9 **Mo** molybdenum 42	[98] **Tc** technetium 43	101.1 **Ru** ruthenium 44	102.9 **Rh** rhodium 45	106.4 **Pd** palladium 46	107.9 **Ag** silver 47	112.4 **Cd** cadmium 48	114.8 **In** indium 49	118.7 **Sn** tin 50	121.8 **Sb** antimony 51	127.6 **Te** tellurium 52	126.9 **I** iodine 53	131.3 **Xe** xenon 54
132.9 **Cs** caesium 55	137.3 **Ba** barium 56		138.9 **La*** lanthanum 57	178.5 **Hf** hafnium 72	180.9 **Ta** tantalum 73	183.8 **W** tungsten 74	186.2 **Re** rhenium 75	190.2 **Os** osmium 76	192.2 **Ir** iridium 77	195.1 **Pt** platinum 78	197.0 **Au** gold 79	200.6 **Hg** mercury 80	204.4 **Tl** thallium 81	207.2 **Pb** lead 82	209.0 **Bi** bismuth 83	[209] **Po** polonium 84	[210] **At** astatine 85	[222] **Rn** radon 86
[223] **Fr** francium 87	[226] **Ra** radium 88		[227] **Ac†** actinium 89	[261] **Rf** rutherfordium 104	[262] **Db** dubnium 105	[266] **Sg** seaborgium 106	[264] **Bh** bohrium 107	[277] **Hs** hassium 108	[268] **Mt** meitnerium 109	[271] **Ds** darmstadtium 110	[272] **Rg** roentgenium 111							

Elements with atomic numbers 112-116 have been reported but not fully authenticated

* 58 – 71 Lanthanides

140.1 **Ce** cerium 58	140.9 **Pr** praseodymium 59	144.2 **Nd** neodymium 60	144.9 **Pm** promethium 61	150.4 **Sm** samarium 62	152.0 **Eu** europium 63	157.3 **Gd** gadolinium 64	158.9 **Tb** terbium 65	162.5 **Dy** dysprosium 66	164.9 **Ho** holmium 67	167.3 **Er** erbium 68	168.9 **Tm** thulium 69	173.0 **Yb** ytterbium 70	175.0 **Lu** lutetium 71

† 90 – 103 Actinides

232.0 **Th** thorium 90	231.0 **Pa** protactinium 91	238.0 **U** uranium 92	237.0 **Np** neptunium 93	239.1 **Pu** plutonium 94	243.1 **Am** americium 95	247.1 **Cm** curium 96	247.1 **Bk** berkelium 97	252.1 **Cf** californium 98	[252] **Es** einsteinium 99	[257] **Fm** fermium 100	[258] **Md** mendelevium 101	[259] **No** nobelium 102	[260] **Lr** lawrencium 103

Glossary

A

Activation energy The minimum energy that a particle needs in order to react; the energy (enthalpy) difference between the reactants and the transition state.

Aldehyde An organic compound with the general formula RCHO in which there is a $C = O$ double bond.

Alkaline earth metals The metals in Group 2 of the periodic table.

Alkane A hydrocarbon with C—C and C—H single bonds only, with the general formula C_nH_{2n+2}.

Allotropes Pure elements which can exist in different physical forms in which their atoms are arranged differently. For example, diamond, graphite and buckminsterfullerene are allotropes of carbon.

Anaerobic respiration The process by which energy is released and new compounds formed in living things in the absence of oxygen.

Atom economy This describes the efficiency of a chemical reaction by comparing the total number of atoms in the product with the total number of atoms in the starting materials. It is defined by:

$$\% \text{ Atom economy} = \frac{\text{mass of desired product}}{\text{total mass of reactants}} \times 100$$

Atomic orbital A region of space around an atomic nucleus where there is a high probability of finding an electron.

Avogadro constant The total number of particles in a mole of substance. Also called the **Avogadro number**. It is numerically equal to 6.022×10^{23}.

C

Calorimeter An instrument for measuring the heat changes that accompany chemical reactions.

Catalyst A substance that alters the rate of a chemical reaction but is not used up in the reaction.

Catalytic cracking The breaking, with the aid of a catalyst, of long-chain alkane molecules (obtained from crude oil) into shorter chain hydrocarbons some of which are alkenes.

Carbocation An organic ion in which one of the carbon atoms has a positive charge.

Carbon-neutral A process, or series of processes, in which as much carbon dioxide is absorbed from the air as is given out.

Chemical feedstock The starting materials in an industrial chemical process.

Co-ordinate bonding Covalent bonding in which both the electrons in the bond come from one of the atoms in the bond. (Also called dative covalent bonding.)

Covalent bonding Describes a chemical bond in which electrons are shared between two atoms.

Cracking The breaking of long-chain alkane molecules (obtained from crude oil) into shorter chain hydrocarbons, some of which are alkenes.

D

Dative covalent bonding Covalent bonding in which both the electrons in the bond come from one of the atoms in the bond. (Also called co-ordinate bonding.)

Delocalised Describes electrons that are spread over several atoms and help to bond them together.

Dipole–dipole force An intermolecular force that results from the attraction between molecules with permanent dipoles.

Displacement reaction A chemical reaction in which one atom or group of atoms replaces another in a compound, for example, $Zn + CuO \rightarrow ZnO + Cu$.

Displayed formula The formula of a compound drawn out so that each atom and each bond is shown.

Disproportionation Describes a redox reaction in which the oxidation number of some atoms of a particular element increases and that of other atoms of the same element decreases.

Dynamic equilibrium A situation in which the composition of a reaction mixture does not change because both forward and backward reactions are proceeding at the same rate.

E

Electron density The probability of an electron being found in a particular volume of space.

Electron pair repulsion theory A theory which explains the shapes of simple molecules by assuming that pairs of electrons around a central atom repel each other and thus take up positions as far away as possible from each other in space.

Electronegativity The power of an atom to attract the electrons in a covalent bond.

Electrophile An electron-deficient atom, ion or molecule that takes part in an organic reaction by attacking areas of high electron density in another reactant.

Electrophilic addition A reaction in which a carbon–carbon double bond is saturated and in which the initial reaction is an attack by an electrophile.

Electrostatic forces The forces of attraction and repulsion between electrically charged particles.

Elimination A reaction in which an atom or group of atoms is removed from a reactant.

Empirical formula The simplest whole number ratio in which the atoms in a compound combine together.

Endothermic Describes a reaction in which heat is taken in as the reactants change to products; the temperature thus drops.

Enthalpy change A measure of heat energy given out or taken in when a chemical or physical change occurs at constant pressure.

Enthalpy diagrams Diagrams in which the enthalpies (energies) of the reactants and products of a chemical reaction are plotted on a vertical scale to show their relative levels.

Equilibrium mixture The mixture of reactants and products formed when a reversible reaction is allowed to proceed in a closed container until no further change occurs. The forward and backward reactions are still proceeding but at the same rate.

Exothermic Describes a reaction in which heat is given out as the reactants change to products; the temperature thus rises.

F

Fingerprint region The area of an infra-red spectrum below about $1500 \, cm^{-1}$. It is caused by complex vibrations of the whole molecule and is characteristic of a particular molecule.

Fraction A mixture of hydrocarbons collected over a particular range of boiling points during the fractional distillation of crude oil.

Free radical A chemical species with an unpaired electron – usually highly reactive.

Functional group An atom or group of atoms in an organic molecule which is responsible for the characteristic reactions of that molecule.

G

Group A vertical column of elements in the periodic table. The elements have similar properties because they have the same outer electron arrangement.

H

Half equation An equation for a redox reaction which considers just one of the species involved and shows explicitly the electrons transferred to or from it.

Heterogeneous catalyst A catalyst which is in a different phase from the reactants. For example, iron (solid) in the Haber process conversion of nitrogen

and hydrogen (both gases) to ammonia.

Homogeneous catalyst A catalyst which is in the same phase as the reactants.

Homologous series A set of organic compounds with the same functional group. The compounds differ in the length of their hydrocarbon chains.

Hydrogen bonding A type of intermolecular force in which a hydrogen atom covalently bonded to an electronegative atom interacts with another electronegative atom.

I

Incomplete combustion A combustion reaction in which there is insufficient oxygen for all the carbon in the fuel to burn to carbon dioxide. Carbon monoxide and/or carbon (soot) are formed.

Ionic bonding Describes a chemical bond in which an electron or electrons are transferred from one atom to another, resulting in the formation of oppositely charged ions with electrostatic forces of attraction between them.

Ionisation energy The energy required to remove a mole of electrons from a mole of isolated gaseous atoms or ions.

Isomer One of two (or more) compounds with the same molecular formula but different structural formula, i.e. the same atoms are arranged differently in space.

K

Ketone An organic compound with the general formula R_2CO in which there is a $C = O$ double bond.

L

Lattice A regular three-dimensional arrangement of atoms, ions or molecules.

Leaving group In an organic substitution reaction, the leaving group is an atom or group of atoms that is ejected from the starting material, normally taking with it an electron pair and forming a negative ion.

Lone pair A pair of electrons in the outer shell of an atom that is not involved in bonding. Also called an unshared pair.

M

Maxwell–Boltzmann distribution The distribution of energies (and therefore speeds) of the molecules in a gas or liquid.

Mean bond enthalpy The energy (enthalpy) that must be put in to break a particular bond, e.g. O—H. It is the average for the bond in question taken over a range of compounds containing that bond.

Metallic bonding Describes a chemical bond in which outer electrons are spread over a lattice of metal ions in a delocalised system.

Mole A quantity of a substance that contains the Avogadro number (6.022×10^{23}) of particles (e.g. atoms, molecules or ions).

Molecular formula A formula that tells us the numbers of atoms of each different element that make up a molecule of a compound.

Molecular ion In mass spectrometry this is a molecule of the sample which has been ionised but which has not broken up during its flight through the instrument.

Monomer A small molecule that combines with many other monomers to form a polymer.

N

Nucleons Protons and neutrons – the sub-atomic particles found in the nuclei of atoms.

Nucleophile An ion or group of atoms with a negative charge or a partially negatively-charged area that takes part in an organic reaction by attacking an electron-deficient area in another reactant.

Nucleophilic substitution An organic reaction in which a molecule with a partially positively charged carbon atom is attacked by a reagent with a negative charge or partially negatively charged area (a nucleophile). It results in the replacement of one of the groups or atoms on the original molecule by the nucleophile.

Nucleus The tiny, positively charged centre of at atom composed of protons and neutrons.

O

Oxidation A reaction in which an atom or group of atoms loses electrons.

Oxidation state The number of electrons lost or gained by an atom in a compound compared to the uncombined atom. It forms the basis of a way of keeping track of redox (electron transfer) reactions. Also called oxidation number.

Oxidising agent A reagent that oxidises (removes electrons from) another species.

P

Percentage yield In a chemical reaction this is the actual amount of product produced divided by the theoretical amount (predicted from the chemical equation) expressed as a percentage.

Period A horizontal row of elements in the periodic table. There are trends in the properties of the elements as we cross a period.

Periodicity The regular recurrence of the properties of elements when they are arranged in atomic number order as in the periodic table.

Polar Describes a molecule in which the charge is not symmetrically distributed so that one area is slightly positively charged and another slightly negatively charged.

Positive inductive effect Describes the tendency of some atoms or groups of atoms to release electrons via a covalent bond.

Proton number The number of protons in the nucleus of an atom; the same as the atomic number.

R

Redox reaction Short for reduction–oxidation reaction, it describes reactions in which electrons are transferred from one species to another.

Reducing agent A reagent that reduces (adds electrons to) another species.

Reduction A reaction in which an atom or group of atoms gain electrons.

Relative atomic mass, A_r

$$A_r = \frac{\text{average mass of an atom}}{\frac{1}{12}\text{th mass of 1 atom of } ^{12}\text{C}}$$

Relative formula mass, M_r

$$M_r = \frac{\text{average mass of an entity}}{\frac{1}{12}\text{th mass of 1 atom of } ^{12}\text{C}}$$

Relative molecular mass, M_r

$$M_r = \frac{\text{average mass of a molecule}}{\frac{1}{12}\text{th mass of 1 atom of } ^{12}\text{C}}$$

S

Saturated hydrocarbon A compound containing only hydrogen and carbon with only C–C and C–H single bonds, i.e. one to which no more hydrogen can be added.

Specific heat capacity, c The amount of heat needed to raise the temperature of 1 g of substance by 1 K.

Spectator ions Ions that are unchanged during a chemical reaction, i.e. they take no part in the reaction.

Standard molar enthalpy change of combustion, $\Delta H_c^\ominus$ The amount of heat energy given out when 1 mole of a substance is completely burned in oxygen with all reactants and products in their standard states (298 K and 100 kPa).

Standard molar enthalpy change of formation, $\Delta H_f^\ominus$ The heat change when 1 mole of substance is formed from its elements with all reactants and products in their standard states (298 K and 100 kPa).

Stoichiometry Describes the simple whole number ratios in which chemical species react.

Strong nuclear force The force that holds protons and neutrons together within the nucleus of the atom.

Structural formula A way of writing the formula of an organic compound in which bonds are not shown but each carbon atom is written separately with the atoms or groups of atoms attached to it, e.g. butan-2-ol is written $CH_3CH_2CH(OH)CH_3$

T

Thermochemical cycle A sequence of chemical reactions (with their enthalpy changes) that convert a reactant into a product. The total enthalpy change of the sequence of reactions will be the same as that for the conversion of the reactant to the product directly (or by any other route).

V

van der Waals force A type of intermolecular force of attraction that is caused by instantaneous dipoles and acts between all atoms and molecules.

Answers to summary questions

1.1

1   **a**   proton, neutron   **b**   proton, neutron

     c   proton, electron   **d**   neutron   **e**   electron

2   **a**   Because they have opposite charges of the same size and the atom is neutral.

     b   In J J Thomson's model, the electrons are embedded in a sphere of positive charge. In Rutherford's model, the mass and positive charge of the atom is concentrated in a tiny central nucleus with the electrons outside this and a considerable distance away from it.

3   Rutherford's team fired alpha particles (He^{2+} ions) at a thin sheet of gold. Most passed straight through, indicating that most of the atom was empty space. A small number were deflected through large angles, suggesting that there was a concentration of mass and positive charge inside the atom.

1.2

1

     a   **b**   **c**

2   **a**   2,2   **b**   2,8,3   **c**   2,8,8

3 A^{2+}, C^-, E^+

1.3

Carbon dating

1   17 190 years (three half-lives)

2   Not necessarily – it tells us when the tree from which the wood of bowl was made died. The bowl may have been made later than this and would therefore not be so old.

1   **a**   1 proton, 1 neutron, 1 electron

     b   1 proton, 2 neutrons, 1 electron

2   X and Z

3

Element	W	X	Y	Z
a Number of protons	15	7	8	7
b Mass number	31	14	16	15
c Number of neutrons	16	7	8	8

1.4

1   Because they have lost one (or more) electrons (which have a negative charge)

2   They are attracted by a positively charged plate.

3   The ions pass through a series of holes or slits.

4   A magnetic field at right angles to their direction of motion.

5   72.63

6   63.6

1.5

1   **a** $1s^2\ 2s^2\ 2p^6\ 3s^2\ 3p^3$ **b** $[Ne]\ 3s^2\ 3p^3$

2   **a**   **i** $1s^2\ 2s^2\ 2p^6\ 3s^2\ 3p^6$ **ii** $1s^2\ 2s^2\ 2p^6$ **b**   [Ar], [Ne]

1.6

1   The second electron is being removed from a positively charged ion while the first is being removed from a neutral atom. This means more energy is needed to overcome the additional attractive force and so the second ionisation energy is higher.

2

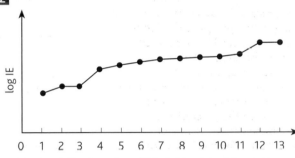

     y-axis: log IE   *x-axis:* Total number of electrons removed

3   **a**   Group 4

     b   The large jump in ionisation energy comes after the removal of the fourth electron showing that there are four electrons in the outer shell.

2.1

1   **a**   16.0   **b**   106.0   **c**   58.3   **d**   132.1

2   Many answers possible such that the relative atomic masses add up to 16.0, e.g. 16 hydrogen atoms; or one carbon atom and 4 hydrogen atoms.

3   **a**   selenium   **b**   beryllium   **c**   scandium

4   **a**   2   **b**   0.05   **c**   0.1

5 $4g\ O_2$

6 $11g\ CO_2$

2.2

1   **a**   Approximately 8 500 000   **b**   The same as part **a**

2   50 360 cm^3 **b**   113 000 Pa

3   1.94

4   The same as in question **3**. The same number of moles of any gas has the same volume under the same conditions of temperature and pressure.

2.3

1 **a** H_2SO_4 sulfuric acid

 b $Ca(OH)_2$ calcium hydroxide

 c $MgCl_2$ magnesium chloride

2 **a** 0.16 mol Mg, 0.16 mol O **b** MgO

3 **a** CH_2 **b** CHCl **c** CH

4 $C_2H_6O_2$

5 C_3H_6O

6 **a** CH **b** C_6H_6

2.4

1 **a** 1 mol dm^{-3} **b** 0.125 mol dm^{-3} **c** 10 mol dm^{-3}

2 **a** 0.002 **b** 0.025 **c** 0.05

3 **a** 58.5 **b** 0.004 **c** 0.016

2.5

1 **a** **i** $2Mg + O_2 \longrightarrow 2MgO$

 ii $Ca(OH)_2 + 2HCl \longrightarrow CaCl_2 + 2H_2O$

 iii $Na_2O + 2HNO_3 \longrightarrow 2NaNO_3 + H_2O$

 b **i** $2Mg + O_2 \longrightarrow 2MgO$
      2   1   2

 ii $Ca(OH)_2 + 2HCl \longrightarrow CaCl_2 + 2H_2O$
       1   2   1   2

 iii $Na_2O + 2HNO_3 \longrightarrow 2NaNO_3 + H_2O$
        1   2   2   1

2 0.25 mol dm^{-3}

3 **a** Yes, there are 0.108 mol Mg. This would be enough to react with 0.0.217 mol HCl, but there is only 0.100 mol HCl

 b 2480 cm^3

4 **a** **i** $H_2SO_4(aq) + 2NaOH(aq) \longrightarrow Na_2SO_4(aq) + 2H_2O(l)$

 ii $2H^+ + SO_4^{2-} + 2Na^+ + 2OH^- \longrightarrow 2Na^+ + SO_4^{2-} + 2H_2O$

 b Na^+ and SO_4^{2-}

 c $2H^+ + 2OH^- \longrightarrow 2H_2O$

2.6

The synthesis of ibuprofen old and new

1 41.2 kg

2 16.5 kg

1 $CaCOOO \longrightarrow CaO + COO$ 56.0%

2 79.8%

3 100% All the reactants are incorporated into the desired product.

4 **a** 1 mol **b** 5.6 g **c** 64.3%

3.1

1 **b** and **c**, they are both metal / non-metal compounds

2 Because they have strong electrostatic attraction between the ions that extends through the whole structure

3 When they are molten or in aqueous solution

4 **a**

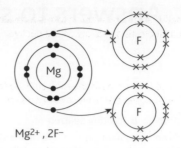

Mg^{2+}, 2F$^-$

 b

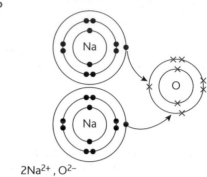

2Na^{2+}, O^{2-}

5 MgF$_2$ Na$_2$O

6 Neon

3.2

1 A pair of electrons shared between two non-metal atoms (usually) that holds the atoms together.

2 **b** and **d**, they are both non-metal / non-metal compounds

3 Because covalent bonds are localised between the two atoms that they bond and there is little attraction between the individual molecules

4

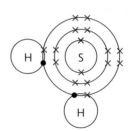

5

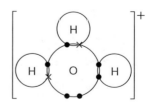

3.3

1 Fluorine is a smaller atom and when it forms a covalent bond, the shared electrons are closer to the nucleus.

2 $H^{\delta+}\!-Cl^{\delta-}$

3 **a** **i** and **ii**

b In both case, the two atoms in the molecule are the same and therefore the electrons in the bond are equally shared.

4 **a** H—N < H—O < H—F

b The order of the polarity is the same as the order of electronegativity of the second atom.

3.4

1 For example: metals conduct heat and electricity well, non-metals do not; metals are shiny, malleable and ductile, non-metals are not.

2 $1s^2\ 2s^2\ 2p^6\ 3s^2\ 3p^6\ 4s^2$

3 2

4 2

5 **a** Sodium would have a lower melting temperature because there are fewer electrons in the delocalised system and the charge on the ions is smaller.

b Magnesium would be stronger as there are more electrons in the delocalised system and the charge on the ions is greater.

3.5

1 He, Ne, Ar, Kr. The van der Waals forces increase as the number of electrons in the atom increases.

2 H_2. It cannot have a permanent dipole because both atoms are the same.

3 Hexane (C_6H_{12}) is a larger molecule than butane (C_4H_{10}) and so has more electrons. This means that there are larger van der Waals forces between the molecules.

4
$$\begin{matrix} \delta+ & \delta- & & \delta+ & \delta- \\ H & —Br & \longleftarrow\text{-----}\longrightarrow & H & —Br \end{matrix}$$

attraction

3.6

1 HBr

2 **a** There is no sufficiently electronegative atom.

b There is no hydrogen atom.

3

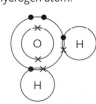

a 2 **b** 2

c A hydrogen bond requires both a lone pair of electrons on an atom of N, O or F and a hydrogen atom. In water there are two lone pairs and two hydrogen atoms, allowing the formation of two hydrogen bonds. In ammonia, although there are three hydrogen atoms, there is only one lone pair of electrons on the N. This means that only one hydrogen bond can form.

3.7

1 **a** In a molecular crystal, there is strong covalent bonding between the atoms within the molecules but weaker intermolecular forces between the molecules. In a macromolecular crystal, all the atoms within the crystal are covalently bonded.

b Macromolecular crystals have higher melting and boiling temperatures.

2 Both elements consist of molecular crystals. The van der Waals forces between the S_8 molecules are greater than those between P_4 because the sulfur molecules have more electrons.

3 The layers of carbon atoms are held together by weak van der Waals forces which allow the layers to slide over one another. They may also allow other molecules such as oxygen to penetrate between the layers.

4 Electricity is conducted via the delocalised electrons that spread along the layers of carbon atoms. Graphite conducts well along the layers but poorly at right angles to them. Metals conduct well in all directions.

5 Both have giant structures in which covalent bonding occurs between many atoms.

3.8

1 A, C, D

2 B

3 A

4 B, D

5 C

6 D

3.9

1

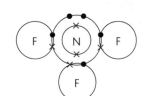

8 electrons gives 4 pairs of electrons. This is a distorted tetrahedron or triangular pyramid.

2

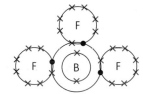

BF_3 has three electron pairs in its outer shell and is therefore trigonal planar. NF_3 has four electron pairs in its outer shell and its shape is therefore based on that of a tetrahedron (the bond angle is 'squeezed down' by a couple of degrees because one of the electron pairs is a lone pair).

3

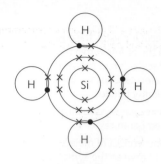

The shape is perfectly tetrahedral.

4 109.5°

5 Angular. It is similar to a water molecule.

4.1

1 a i Any two from Br, K, Fe   ii Br and Cl or K and Cs
   iii Br, Cl

2 b i Fe   ii K or Cs

3 a Xe   b Ge   c Sr   d Ge   e W

4.2

1 a left   b right

2 a 0   b 4

4.3

1 decrease

2 increase

3 increase

4 Because they have the highest nuclear charge

4.4

1 a $1s^2\,2s^2$ b $1s^2\,2s^2\,2p^1$

2 a 2s   b 2p

3 Level 2p is of higher energy than 2s.

4 a Group 5

   b The jump in IEs occurs after the fifth IE.

5.1

1 a 0.4 mol b 1.0 mol   c C_2H_5 d C_4H_{10}

   e $CH_3CH_2CH_2CH_3$

   f

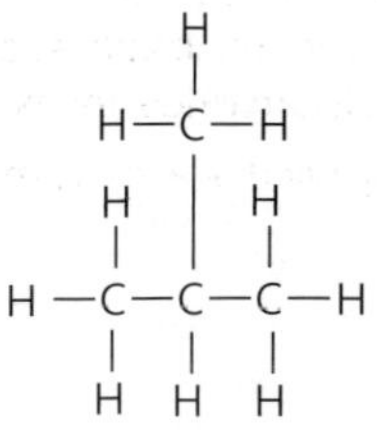

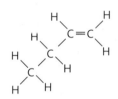

5.2

1 a 1-chloropropane   b pentane
   c pent-2-ene   d 2-methylpentane

2 a

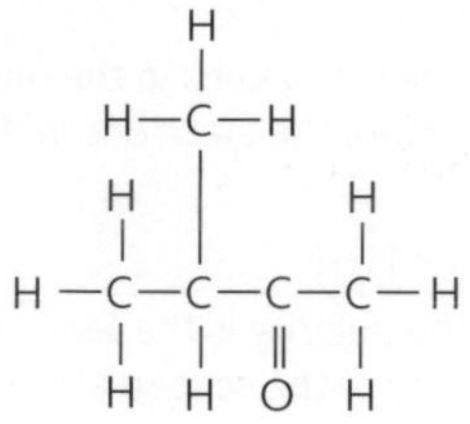

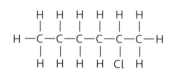

   b

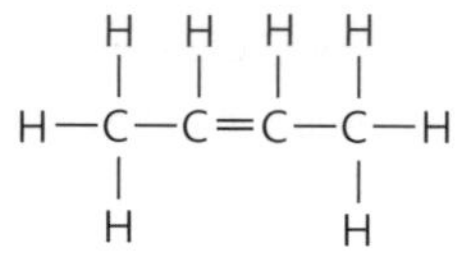

   c

   d

5.3

1 a B   b A   c C

2 a

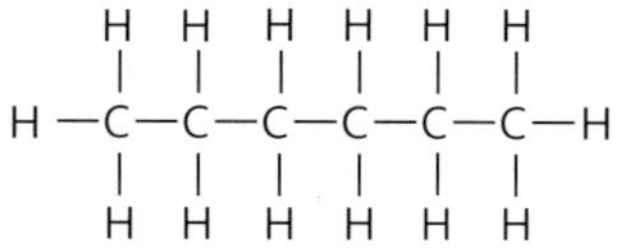

$CH_3CH_2CH_2CH_2CH_2CH_3$

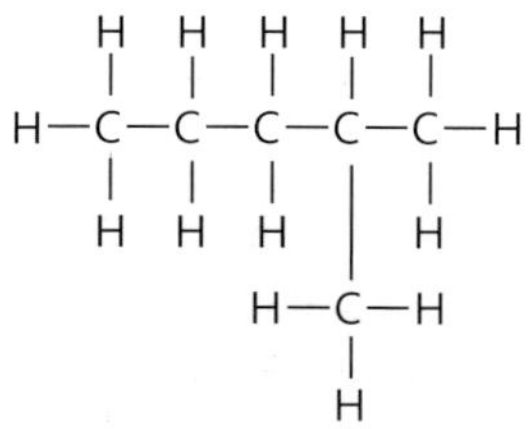

$CH_3CH_2CH_2CH(CH_3)CH_3$

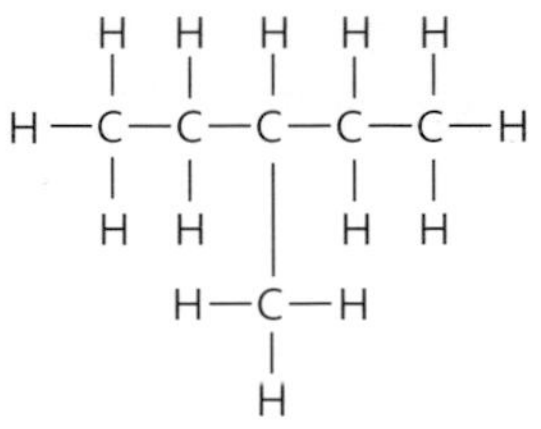

$CH_3CH_2CH(CH_3)CH_2CH_3$

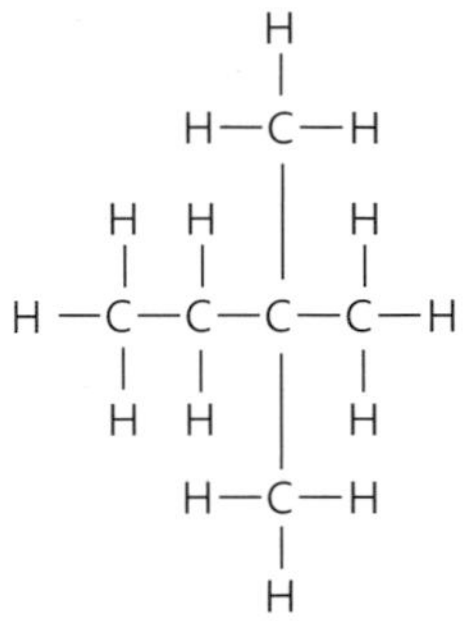

$CH_3CH_2C(CH_3)_2CH_3$

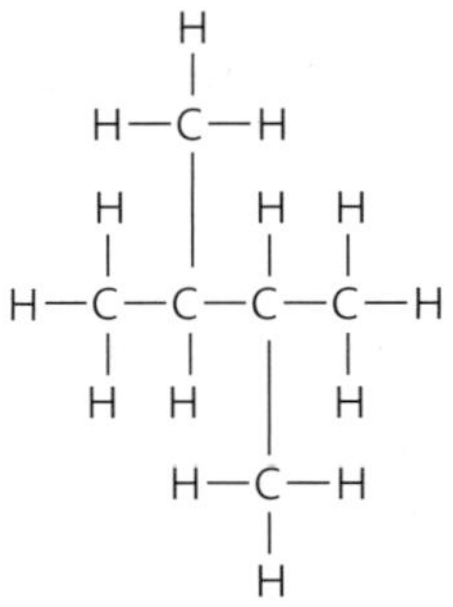

$CH_3CH(CH_3)CH(CH_3)CH_3$

b hexane   2-methylpentane   3-methylpentane
2,2-dimethylbutane   2,3-dimethylbutane

6.1

1 Methylbutane

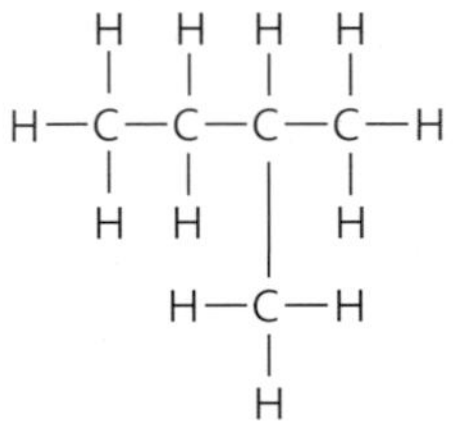

2

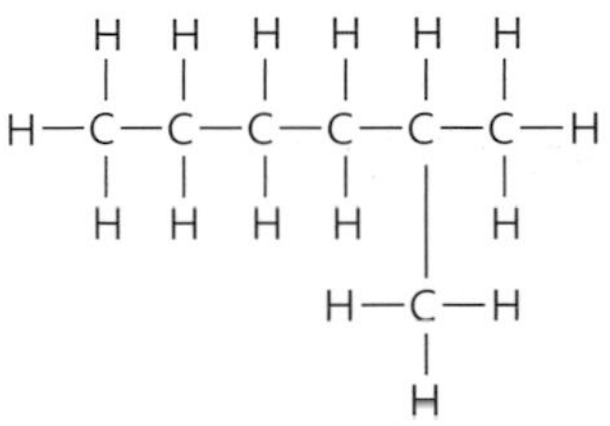

$CH_3CH_2CH_2CH_2CH(CH_3)CH_3$

3 Heptane

4 Heptane will have a higher boiling temperature because its straight chains will pack together more closely.

6.2

1

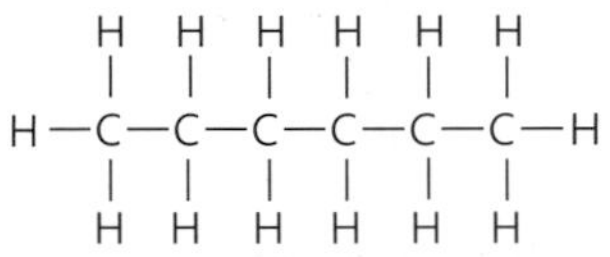

$CH_3CH_2CH_2CH_2CH_2CH_3$

2 Petrol

3 Fractional distillation separates a mixture into several components with different ranges of boiling temperatures whereas distillation simply separates all the volatile components of a mixture from the non-volatile ones.

6.3

1 decane $\longrightarrow$ octane + ethene

2 Many of the products are gases rather than liquids.

3 Octane itself has a short enough chain length to be in demand.

4 By using a catalyst

5 Short chain products are in greater demand than long chain ones. Alkenes are more useful than alkanes as starting materials for further chemical reactions.

6.4

1 **a** propane + oxygen $\longrightarrow$ carbon dioxide + water
$C_3H_8(g) + 5O_2(g) \longrightarrow 3CO_2(g) + 4H_2O(l)$

 b butane + oxygen $\longrightarrow$ carbon monoxide + water
$C_4H_{10}(g) + 4\frac{1}{2}O_2 \longrightarrow 4CO(g) + 5H_2O(l)$

2 **a** They produce carbon dioxide (a greenhouse gas) when they burn. They may produce poisonous carbon monoxide when burnt in a restricted supply of oxygen. They are in general non-renewable resources. They may produce nitrogen oxides and sulfur oxides when burnt. Cancer-causing carbon particulates may be produced and unburnt hydrocarbons (which contribute to photochemical smog) may be released into the atmosphere.

 b Burn as little fuel as possible and/or offset the CO_2 produced by planting trees, for example. Ensure that burners are serviced and adjusted to burn the fuel completely. Remove sulfur from the fuel before burning or remove SO_2 from the combustion products (by reacting with calcium oxide, for example).

3 Possibilities include wind power, wave power and nuclear power.

7.1

The energy values of fuels

1 $2H_2 + O_2 \longrightarrow 2H_2O$

1 There is no carbon dioxide formed.

3 Carbon dioxide is a greenhouse gas.

1 445 kJ

2 Endothermic

3 It is the reverse of the reaction in question **1**.

4 1.6 g

7.2

1 **a** A change   **b** Enthalpy (heat energy)

   c That the enthalpy change is measured at 298 K

   d That heat is given out   **e** Exothermic

   f

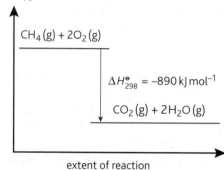

7.3

Application – Working out the enthalpy change – an example

1 There may be draughts that take heat away from the calorimeter.

Heat is lost from the top and sides of the calorimeter.

The beaker and the rest of the apparatus itself get heated rather than just the water.

Not all the methanol burns completely to carbon dioxide. This is incomplete combustion. If there is not enough oxygen available, then we get some carbon monoxide and carbon formed. There will be soot (carbon) on the bottom of the beaker if this has happened.

2 The lid and insulation reduce heat loss from the beaker.

The screen reduces draughts.

3 Copper is a very good conductor of heat and will conduct the heat carried by the gaseous products directly to the water.

There is no heat loss from draughts.

To make sure we have complete combustion.

1 $-672\,kJ\,mol^{-1}$

2 **a** $-46.2\,kJ\,mol^{-1}$

   b It will be smaller (less negative).

   c This is caused by heat loss.

3 **a** The enthalpy change

   b The mass of water (or other substance in which the heat is collected)

   c The specific heat capacity of the water (or other substance)

   d The temperature change

4 $-1008\,kJ\,mol^{-1}$

7.4

1 **a** $-70\,kJ\,mol^{-1}$ **b** $-217\,kJ\,mol^{-1}$ **c** $-97\,kJ\,mol^{-1}$

   d $-191\,kJ\,mol^{-1}$ **e** $+301\,kJ\,mol^{-1}$

7.5

1 **a** via $\Delta H_f^{\ominus}$ $-85\,kJ\,mol^{-1}$

   b via $\Delta H_c^{\ominus}$ $-86\,kJ\,mol^{-1}$

   (The difference is due to rounding errors in the data.)

7.6

1 **a** $-70\,kJ\,mol^{-1}$ **b** $217\,kJ\,mol^{-1}$ **c** $-97\,kJ\,mol^{-1}$

   d $-191\,kJ\,mol^{-1}$ **e** $\pm301\,kJ\,mol^{-1}$

7.7

1 **a**

$$H-\underset{\underset{H}{|}}{\overset{\overset{H}{|}}{C}}-\underset{\underset{H}{|}}{\overset{\overset{H}{|}}{C}}-H + Br-Br \longrightarrow H-\underset{\underset{H}{|}}{\overset{\overset{H}{|}}{C}}-\underset{\underset{H}{|}}{\overset{\overset{H}{|}}{C}}-Br + H-Br$$

2 **a** $1 \times$ C—C, $6 \times$ C—H, $1 \times$ Br—Br   **b** $3018\,kJ\,mol^{-1}$

3 **a** $1 \times$ C—C, $5 \times$ C—H, $1 \times$ C—Br, $1 \times$ H—Br

   b $3063\,kJ\,mol^{-1}$

4 $45\,kJ\,mol^{-1}$

5 **a** $-45\,kJ\,mol^{-1}$ **b** Exothermic

8.1

1 Temperature, concentration of reactants, surface area of solid reactants, pressure of gaseous reactants, catalyst

2 **a** Reactants   **b** Products

   c Transition state or activated complex

   d Activation energy

3 **a** Exothermic

   b The products have less energy (enthalpy) than the reactants.

8.2

1 **a** Fraction of particles with energy E

   b Energy E

   c The number of particles with enough energy to react

   d Moves to the right   **e** No change

8.3

1 a A = enthalpy, B = extent of reaction, C = transition state with catalyst, D = transition state without catalyst, R = reactants, P = products

b The activation energies without and with catalyst respectively

c Exothermic

9.1

1 a true　　b false　　c true　　　d false

2 They are the same.

9.2

1 a Yes. This is a gas phase reaction with different numbers of particles on each side of the arrow.

b No. This is not a gas phase reaction.

c No. This is a gas phase reaction with the same number of particles on each side of the arrow.

2 a move to the left　　　　　b no change

c Equilibrium would be set up more quickly but the final position would be unchanged.

d High pressure. It would force the equilibrium in the direction of fewest particles.

9.3

Ammonia, NH_3

Making ammonia

1 a The reaction is exothermic, so low temperature would move the equilibrium to the right so that heat is given out.

b High pressure forces the equilibrium to the side with fewer molecules, i.e. the ammonia side.

The Haber process

2 Approximately 40%

3 A lower temperature would reduce the reaction rate unacceptably. A higher temperature would require more expensive plant both in construction to withstand the higher pressure and in the costs of running compressors etc.

1 For increased surface area

2 The raw material for fermentation is sugar which is a crop which can be grown regularly. Ethene is made from crude oil which is non-renewable.

3 No, because synthesis gas is made from methane or propane which are derived from crude oil and/or natural gas.

10.1

1 a Bromine　b Calcium　c Calcium　d Bromine

e $Ca \longrightarrow Ca^{2+} + 2e^-$　$Br_2 + 2e^- \longrightarrow 2Br^-$

f Bromine　g Calcium

10.2

1 a Pb +2, Cl –1　　b C +4, Cl –1　　c Na +1, N +5, O –2

2 –2 before and after

3 Before 0, after –2

4 Before +2, after +3

5 a +5　　　　　b +5　　　　　c –3

10.3

1 a +2　　　0　　　+3　　–1
$$Fe^{2+} + ½Cl_2 \longrightarrow Fe^{3+} + Cl^-$$

b Iron, because its oxidation number has increased

c Chlorine, because its oxidation number has decreased

d $Fe^{2+} \longrightarrow Fe^{3+} + e^-$　　　　$½Cl_2 + e^- \longrightarrow Cl^-$

2 a $3Cl_2 + 6NaOH \longrightarrow NaClO_3 + 5NaCl + 3H_2O$

b $Sn + 4HNO_3 \longrightarrow SnO_2 + 4NO_2 + 2H_2O$

c a $2½Cl_2 + 5e^- \longrightarrow 5Cl^-$
$½Cl_2 + 6OH^- \rightarrow ClO_3^- + 5e^- + 3H_2O$

b $Sn + 2H_2O \longrightarrow SnO_2 + 4H^+ + 4e^-$
$4HNO_3 + 4H^+ + 4e^- \longrightarrow 4NO_2 + 4H_2O$

11.1

1 a Solid, very dark colour　　　b The largest atom

c The least electronegative

2 These properties can be predicted by extrapolating the trends observed with the halogens from F to I.

3 a Approximately 600 K

b It has the most electrons and therefore the strongest van der Waals forces.

11.2

Extraction of iodine from kelp

1 It is an oxidation – the oxidation state of the iodine atom goes from –1 to 0.

2 It is added to prevent thyroid problems which can be caused by lack of iodine in the diet.

1 a Mixture ii only

b Chlorine is a better oxidising agent than iodine and bromine. Therefore it can displace iodine from iodide salt, but bromine cannot displace chlorine from chloride salts.

c $Cl_2(aq) + 2NaI(aq) \longrightarrow I_2(s) + 2NaCl(aq)$

11.3

1 **a** It has the least reducing power.

b The F$^-$ ion is the smallest halide ion which means that it is hardest for it to lose an electron (which comes from an outer shell close to the nucleus).

c $2NaF(s) + H_2SO_4(l) \longrightarrow Na_2SO_4(s) + 2HF(g)$

d No, the oxidation state of the fluorine remains as –1.

2 **a** Formation of a cream precipitate

b $AgNO_3(aq) + NaBr(aq) \longrightarrow NaNO_3(aq) + AgBr(s)$

c The precipitate would dissolve.

d To remove ions such as carbonate and hydroxide which would also produce a precipitate

e Chloride ions (from HCl) and sulfate ions (from H_2SO_4) would also form precipitates with silver ions.

f Silver fluoride is soluble in water and does not form a precipitate.

11.4

1 **a** $Br_2(g) + H_2O(l) \longrightarrow HBrO(aq) + HBr(aq)$

b $Br_2(g) + 2NaOH(aq) \longrightarrow NaBrO\ (aq) + NaBr(aq)$
$+ H_2O(l)$

2 To kill micro-organisms and make the water safe to drink

3 **a** Hydrochloric acid and oxygen

b $\quad 0 \qquad\quad +1\ -2 \qquad\quad +1\ -1 \qquad 0$
$2Cl_2(g) + 2H_2O(l) \longrightarrow 4HCl(aq) + O_2(g)$

c Oxygen has been oxidised.

d Chlorine has been reduced.   **e** Chlorine   **f** Oxygen

12.1

1 **a** +2   **b** They all lose their two outer electrons when they form compounds.

2 The outer electrons become further from the nucleus and are thus more easily lost.

3 Electrons are transferred from calcium to chlorine.

4 $Ca(s) + 2H_2O(l) \longrightarrow Ca(OH)_2(aq) + H_2(g)$

5 **a** More vigorous

b Less vigorous. The Group 2 metals become more reactive as we descend the group due, in part, to the fact that the outer electrons become further from the nucleus and are thus more easily lost.

6 **a** Most soluble   **b** Least soluble. These are the trends found in the rest of the group.

13.1

1 Carbon monoxide (or carbon)

2 It is relatively cheap.

3 A very high temperature is required for some metals.

4 $+4\ -2 \qquad 0 \qquad\quad 0 \qquad +4\ -2$
$MnO_2(s) + C(s) \longrightarrow Mn(s) + CO_2(g)$

5 Sulfur dioxide and carbon dioxide (or carbon monoxide). Sulfur dioxide causes acid rain and carbon dioxide is a greenhouse gas. Carbon monoxide is poisonous.

13.2

1 They burn away in the oxygen that is formed from the electrolysis.

2 To lower the melting temperature of the electrolyte

3 It is a three step process. An expensive reducing agent (sodium) has to be used. A high temperature is required. It is a batch (rather than a continuous) process.

4 $TiCl_4 + 2Mg \longrightarrow Ti + 2MgCl_2$

14.1

1 **a**

A

B

C

D

The bond polarity is always $C^{\delta+}-X^{\delta-}$

b A 1-iodobutane   B 2-bromopropane
C 1-chlorobutane   D 2-bromobutane

c A, because it has the highest M_r and therefore most electrons and highest van der Waals forces.

2 Because the C—X bond becomes stronger

14.2

1 **a** Because haloalkanes do not dissolve in aqueous solutions

b OH$^-$

c Because the OH group replaces the halogen atom

d X$^-$ **e** R–I

2 **a** CN$^-$

b

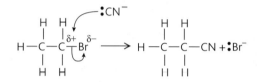

c Propanenitrile

14.3

1 a A base

2 d CCl_2F_2

3 a Propan-2-ol, propene

b Show that it decolourises a solution of bromine

c

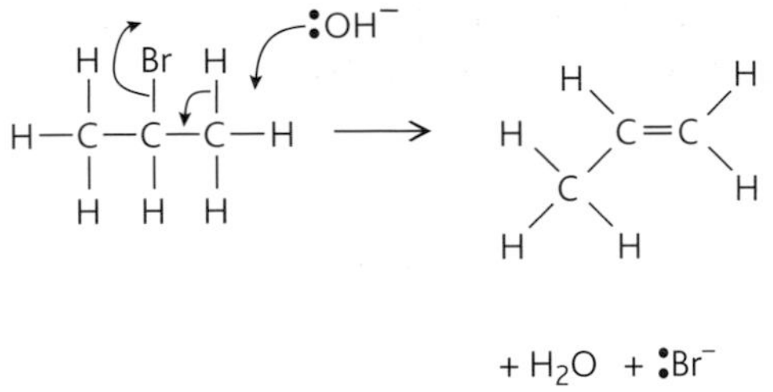

$$+ H_2O + :Br^-$$

14.4

1 a Termination   b Propagation

c Propagation   d Initiation

2 a $Cl\bullet + O_3 \longrightarrow ClO\bullet + O_2$ and $ClO\bullet + O_3 \longrightarrow 2O_2 + Cl\bullet$

b $Cl\bullet + Cl\bullet$ $ClO\bullet + ClO\bullet$ $Cl\bullet + ClO\bullet$

15.1

1 Hex-2-ene

2 $CH_3CH_2CH_2CH_2CH=CH_2$

3

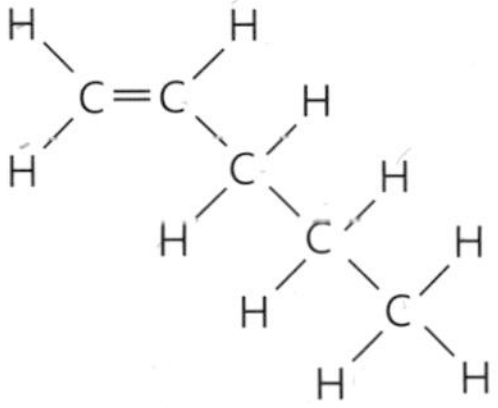

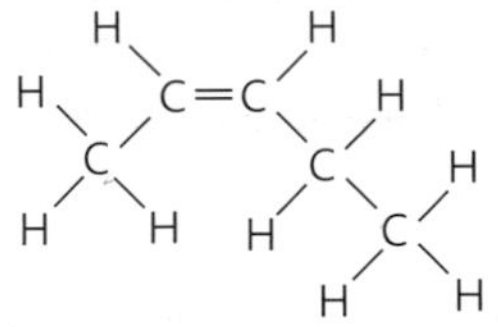

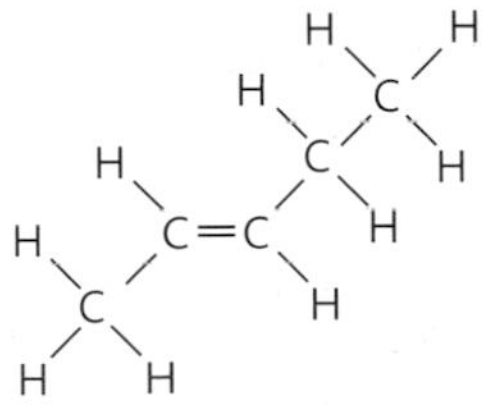

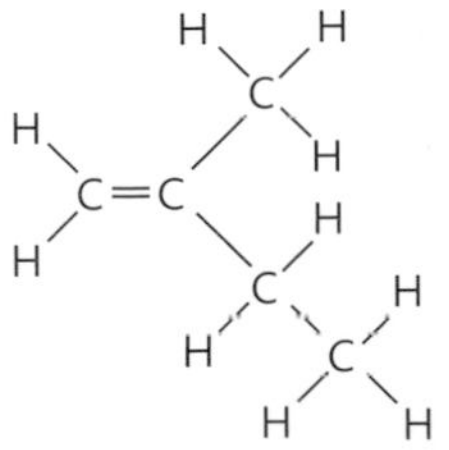

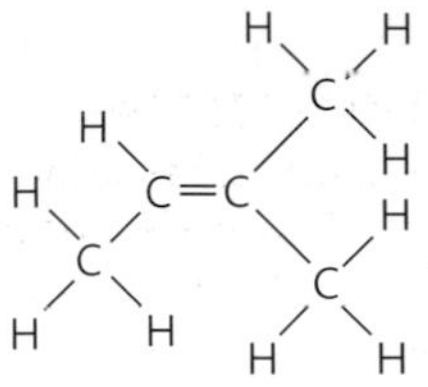

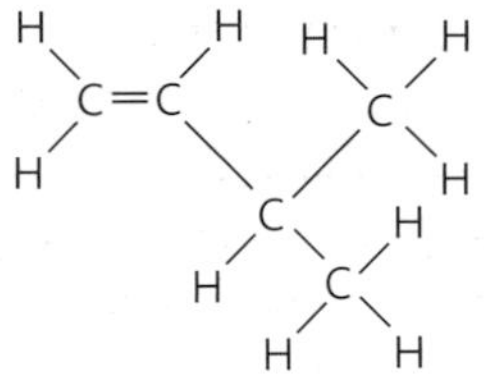

4 a Electrophiles

5 a Electron-rich

15.2

1 $CH_2CHCH_3 + 4\frac{1}{2}O_2 \longrightarrow 3CO_2 + 3H_2O$

2 a Electrophilic additions

3 a 1-bromopropane and 2-bromopropane

b 2-bromopropane

c It is formed from the more stable of the two intermediate carbocations.

4 Chloroethane

5 c Bromine solution is discoloured.

15.3

1 b An alkane

2 1000

3 a i monomer is $CHR=CH_2$ ii repeating unit is $CHRCH_2$

b i monomer is $CHR=CHR$ ii repeating unit is $CHRCHR$

16.1

Antifreeze

1

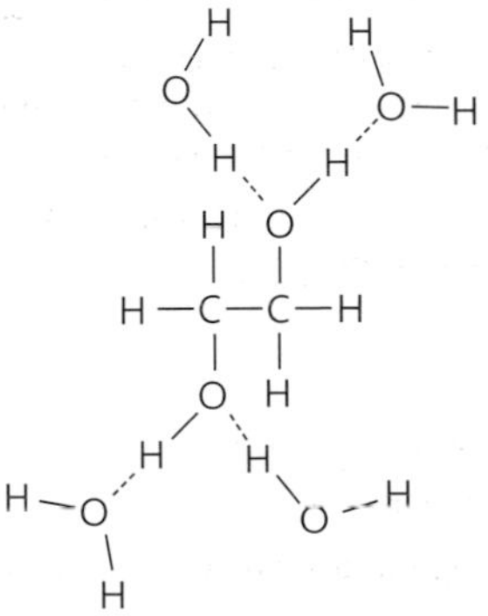

2 The ethane-1,2-diol molecules can form hydrogen bonds with water but cannot fit into the regular three-dimensional structure of ice, see Topic 3.6. So these solutions remain liquid at lower temperatures than pure water.

1

$$H-\overset{\overset{\displaystyle H}{|}}{\underset{\underset{\displaystyle H}{|}}{C}}-\overset{\overset{\displaystyle H}{|}}{\underset{\underset{\displaystyle H}{|}}{C}}-\overset{\overset{\displaystyle H}{|}}{\underset{\underset{\displaystyle O}{|}}{C}}-\overset{\overset{\displaystyle H}{|}}{\underset{\underset{\displaystyle H}{|}}{C}}-H$$

Butan-2-ol   H

2 Primary: methanol   Secondary: butan-2-ol
Tertiary: 2-methylpentan-2-ol

3 Because the oxygen atom has two lone pairs which repel more than bonding pairs

16.2

1 By distillation. The ethanol has a lower boiling temperature than water and would distil off first.

2 Advantages: It is renewable. The process takes place at a low temperature.
Disadvantages: The process is slow. It is a batch process rather than a continuous one. An aqueous solution of ethanol is produced rather than pure ethanol.

3 Growing the raw material (sugar) absorbs as much carbon dioxide as is given out when the ethanol is burned. (Although this ignores the carbon 'costs' involved in the manufacturing process.)

16.3

1 **a** A carboxylic acid is formed.   **b** A ketone is formed.

2 This would require a C—C bond to break.

3 In distillation, the vapour is removed from the original flask and condensed in a different one. In refluxing, the vapour is condensed and returned to the original flask.

4 Gently oxidise the alcohols. In the case of the primary alcohol, an aldehyde will be formed that will give a positive silver mirror or Benedict's test. In the case of the secondary alcohol, a ketone will be formed that will not give a positive silver mirror or Benedict's test.

5 $CH_3CH_2OH \longrightarrow CH_2{=}CH_2 + H_2O$ ethene

6 Pent-1-ene and pent-2-ene (E- and Z-isomers)

17.1

1 **a** 120   **b** 120   **c** That it has a single charge

2 **a** Electrons are ejected from the molecule during bombardment by a stream of high speed electrons.

b Positive

3 $C_{10}H_{16}$

17.2

1 **a** or **b**

2 This IR peak is caused by C=O which is present in both **a** and **b** but not **c**.

3 **b** or **c**

4 This IR peak is caused by O—H which is present in **b** and **c** but not **a**.

5 **b**

6 This compound has both C=O and O—H.

Index

Acknowledgements

The authors and publisher are grateful to the following for permission to reproduce photographs and other copyright material in this book.

Photograph acknowledgements

Alamy/Leslie Garland Picture Library: p 10; **Alamy/Martin Shields:** p 218 (bottom); **Alamy/Science Photos:** p 166; **Corbis/Hulton-Deutsch Collection:** p 25; **Corbis/Sunset Boulevard/Sygma:** p 216 (bottom); **Corel 205:** p 224; **Fotolia:** p 98; **Getty Images:** p viii; **Great Lakes UK:** p 169; **GreenGate Publishing:** p 99, p 178 (top); **IBM:** p 4; **iStock:** p 102, p 182; **Martyn Chillmaid:** p 3, p 23, p 29, p 96 (both), p 112, p 120, p 186, p 199, p 212, p 216 (top), p 251; **Science Photo Library:** p 72, p 148; **Science Photo Library/Alfred Pasieka:** p 111, p 142 (top); **Science Photo Library/Andrew Lambert Photography:** p 172, p 206, p 218 (top); **Science Photo Library/CC Studio:** p 142 (bottom); **Science Photo Library/Charles D. Winters:** p 161; **Science Photo Library/Colin Cuthbert Newcastle University:** p 225 **Science Photo Library/David Munns:** p 58; **Science Photo Library/Detlev van Ravenswaay:** p 13; **Science Photo Library/E. R. Degginger:** p 101; **Science Photo Library/Martyn Chillmaid:** p 159; **Science Photo Library/Russ Munn/Agstockusa:** p 178 (bottom); **Science Photo Library/Sheila Terry:** p 102 (bottom); **Science Photo Library/Simon Fraser:** p 208.

Artwork acknowledgements

Figure 1 on p 224 and Figures 2 and 4–13 on pp 227–9 courtesy of SpectraSchool (www.spectraschool.org).

Every effort has been made to trace and contact all copyright holders and we apologise if any have been overlooked. The publisher will be pleased to make the necessary arrangements at the first opportunity.